A Dictionary of Japanese Counting Words

日本語数詞
英和辞典

A Dictionary of Japanese Counting Words

日本語数詞
英和辞典

Jason・Monti
ジェイソン・マンティ

Jason・Monti
Orlando, Florida
United States of America

ISBN-10: 1460911342
ISBN-13: 978-1460911341
Copyright © 2010 and 2011 Jason Monti

All rights reserved. No part of this book may be reproduced or transmitted in any form or by any means, electronic or mechanical, including, but not limited to, photocopying, recording, or by any information storage and retrieval system, without permission from the author, except for the inclusion of brief quotations in a review.

Cover design, book design, and page layout by Jason Monti © 2010 and 2011

Disclaimer:
The author makes no guarantee that the material contained herein is accurate or complete, although every effort was made to do so. Discrepancies abounded in the source materials. Many counting words appeared in multiple sources but others appeared in only one source. Consultation was made with several native Japanese-speakers to resolve differences. The author specifically disclaims any responsibility for any liabilities, loss, or risk, personal or otherwise, which is incurred as a consequence, directly or indirectly, of the use and application of any of the contents of this book.

Published in the United States of America
Jason Monti
Orlando, Florida

Acknowledgements

I would like to thank, first and foremost, my mother and father, without whose patience, generosity, and support I could never have finished this book. I would also like to thank my mother for inspiring and encouraging me to begin this project in the first place, and for all her help in the technical aspects of putting together a publishable book (I did not even know what "front matter" was until I began this arduous process).

Next, I would like to thank Janet Akaike-Toste and Susan Kubota, the two professors under whom I learned the majority of my Japanese before graduating. They both made learning Japanese fun and interesting.

I would like to also thank Hisae Senko for her work editing this volume, as well as Masayuki Tsuda, and Takahiro Kobayashi.

Finally, I would like to thank a few friends of mine from across the world whose real names I may never learn, but with whom I chat on a regular basis over the internet. Your vexaciously frequent "Hey! When's that book gonna be ready so I can buy it?" helped prod me along and eventually finish this project even when I did not really feel like working on it for at least another month.

Thank you all.

Jason Monti
2011

Introduction

The Japanese counting system can prove daunting for the new learner. On top of having not one but *two* counting systems from which to choose, one must use counter words (or just *counters*) with them. One does not simply say *five plates* or *three dogs*. Instead, one must choose the proper counter and combine it with the proper counting system, *and* combine them properly—many of the counters begin with a consonant that changes when that counter combines with certain numbers.

Romanization

Each chart will have four columns: *Numeral*, *Kanji*, *Hiragana*, and *Roomaji*. For *Roomaji*, I essentially use the Hepburn system (though rather than vowels with a macron over them, I use a one-to-one transcription of each *kana* in the word):

1. Rather than *ā*, I use *aa* for あぁ (the long A).
2. Rather than *ī*, I use *ii* for いい (the long I).
3. Rather than *ū*, I use *uu* for うう (the long U).
4. Rather than *ē*, I use *ei* for えい (the long E). However, in the case of foreign words, or where the long E actually is ええ, I use *ee*. For example, the word 映画 is *eiga*, but the word お姉さん would be *o-nee-san* and the word ページ would be *peeji*.
5. Rather than *ō*, I use *ou* for おう (the long O) and *oo* for おお (the other long O). For example, 到着 would be *touchaku*, whilst 通り would be *toori*.
6. If the syllable-final N falls before a P, B, M, or W, I will render it as *m* rather than *n*.
7. I render し as *shi*, ち as *chi*, つ as *tsu*, じ as *ji*, ぢ as *ji*, and づ as *zu*.
8. I render the *little-tsu* as *-t-* where nothing qualifies it, but change it to the appropriate consonant when something does qualify it as in *rop-pon* rather than *rot-pon*.

Finally, I break from convention when writing the numbers by inserting hyphens in between each of the number components. Thus, I write *juu-kyuu-nichi* rather than *juukyuunichi*.

Measurements and Large Numbers

There are a few places throughout this book where I give equivalent measurements or extremely large numbers. For measurements, I give the United States customary measures followed by their metric (*Système Internationale d'Unités*—S. I.) equivalent.

1. I give lengths in inches (in) and meters (m). If the length in inches exceeds one foot, I will give the number in feet (ft) or miles (mi) in parentheses.
2. I give areas in square inches (in²) and square meters (m²). If the area in inches exceeds one square foot, I will give the number in square feet (ft²) in parentheses.
3. I give volumes in fluid ounces (fl oz) and liters (L). If the volume in cubic inches exceeds one gallon, I will give the number in gallons (gal) in parentheses.
4. I give weights/masses in ounces (oz) and grams (g). If the weight in ounces exceeds one pound, I will give the number in pounds (lbs) in parentheses.
5. I give all conversions to five decimal places, or ten decimal where necessary.

For extremely large numbers, I use the Short Scale, which means that each number name goes up three powers of ten (for example, one million is 10^6, one billion is 10^9, and one trillion is 10^{12}).

Irregularity Patterns

Because the first consonant in many of the counters causes the preceding number's pronunciation to change, a series of "irregularity patterns" have developed. There are two systems of counting in Japanese: a native system (和) and a Sino-Japanese system derived from Chinese (漢). There are seven Sino-Japanese patterns. Most of them center on the numbers one, six, eight, and ten, but a couple of them also include three, and one hundred, one thousand, and ten thousand.

1. 漢 **K** means that . . .
    a. 1 か: いち + か becomes いっか (*ik-ka*)
    b. 6 か: ろく + か becomes ろっか (*rok-ka*)
    c. 8 か: はち + か becomes はっか (*hak-ka*) or はちか (*hachi-ka*)
    d. 10 か: じゅう + か becomes じゅっか (*juk-ka*) or じっか (*jik-ka*)
    e. 100 か: ひゃく + か becomes ひゃっか (*hyakka*)
    f. This also applies to き (*ki*), く (*ku*), け (*ke*), こ (*ko*), きゃ (*kya*), きゅ (*kyu*), and きょ (*kyo*)
2. 漢 **S** means that . . .
    a. 1 さ: いち + さ becomes いっさ (*is-sa*)
    b. 8 さ: はち + さ becomes はっさ (*has-sa*) or はちさ (*hachi-sa*)
    c. 10 さ: じゅう + さ becomes じゅっさ (*jus-sa*) or じっさ (*jis-sa*)
    d. This also applies to し (*shi*), す (*su*), せ (*se*), そ (*so*), しゃ (*sha*), しゅ (*shu*), and しょ (*sho*)

3. 漢 **T** means that . . .
   a. 1 た: いち ＋ た becomes いった (*it-ta*)
   b. 8 た: はち ＋ た becomes はった (*hat-ta*) or はちた (*hachi-ta*)
   c. 10 た: じゅう ＋ た becomes じゅった (*jut-ta*) or じった (*jit-ta*)
   d. This also applies to ち (*chi*), つ (*tsu*), て (*te*), と (*to*), ちゃ (*cha*), ちゅ (*chu*), and ちょ (*cho*).
4. 漢 **P** means that . . .
   a. 1 ぱ: いち ＋ ぱ becomes いっぱ (*ip-pa*)
   b. 6 ぱ: ろく ＋ ぱ becomes ろっぱ (*rop-pa*)
   c. 8 ぱ: はち ＋ ぱ becomes はっぱ (*hap-pa*)
   d. 10 ぱ: じゅう ＋ ぱ becomes じゅっぱ (*jup-pa*) or じっぱ (*jip-pa*)
   e. 100 ぱ: ひゃく ＋ ぱ becomes ひゃっぱ (*hyap-pa*)
   f. This also applies to ぴ (*pi*), ぷ (*pu*), ぺ (*pe*), ぽ (*po*), ぴゃ (*pya*), ぴゅ (*pyu*), and ぴょ (*pyo*).
5. 漢 **H** means that . . .
   a. 1 は: いち ＋ は becomes いっぱ (*ip-pa*)
   b. 3 は: さん ＋ は becomes さんば (*sam-ba*) or さんぱ (*sam-pa*)
   c. 4 は: よん ＋ は *can* become よんぱ (*yom-pa*)
   d. 6 は: ろく ＋ は becomes ろっぱ (*rop-pa*)
   e. 8 は: はち ＋ は becomes はっぱ (*hap-pa*)
   f. 10 は: じゅう ＋ は becomes じゅっぱ (*jup-pa*) or じっぱ (*jip-pa*)
   g. 100 は: ひゃく ＋ は becomes ひゃっぱ (*hyap-pa*)
   h. 1,000 は: せん ＋ は becomes せんば (*sem-ba*) or せんぱ (*sem-pa*)
   i. 10,000 は: まん ＋ は becomes まんば (*mam-ba*) or まんぱ (*mam-pa*)
   j. 何は: なん ＋ は becomes なんば (*nam-ba*) or なんぱ (*nam-pa*)
   k. This also applies to ひ (*hi*), へ (*he*), ほ (*ho*), ひゃ (*hya*), ひゅ (*hyu*), and ひょ (*hyo*), **BUT NOT** ふ (*fu*).
6. 漢 **Fu** means that . . .
   a. 1 ふ: いち ＋ ふ becomes いっぷ (*ip-pu*)
   b. 3 ふ: さん ＋ ふ becomes さんぶ (*sam-pu*)
   c. 4 は: よん ＋ ふ *can* become よんぶ (*yom-pu*)
   d. 6 ふ: ろく ＋ ふ becomes ろっぷ (*rop-pu*)
   e. 8 ふ: ふち ＋ ふ becomes はっぷ (*hap-pu*)
   f. 10 ふ: じゅう ＋ ふ becomes じゅっぷ (*jup-pu*) or じっぷ (*jip-pu*)
   g. 100 ふ: ひゃく ＋ ふ becomes ひゃっぷ (*hyap-pu*)
   h. 1,000 ふ: せん ＋ ふ becomes せんぷ (*sem-pu*)
   i. 10,000 ふ: まん ＋ ふ becomes まんぷ (*mam-pu*)
   j. 何は: なん ＋ ふ becomes なんぶ (*nam-pu*)

7. 漢 **Wa** means that...
   a. 3 わ: さん + わ becomes さんば (*sam-ba*)
   b. 4 は: よん + わ *can* become よんば (*yom-ba*)
   c. 6 わ: ろく + わ becomes ろっぱ (*rop-pa*)
   d. 8 は: はち + わ *can* become はっぱ (*hap-pa*)
   e. 10 わ: じゅう + わ becomes じっぱ (*jip-pa*)
   f. 100 は: ひゃく + わ *can* become ひゃっぱ (*hyap-pa*)

There are four 和 patterns: 和 I, 和 II, 和 III, and 和 IV.

1. 和 **I** means that the first two in the series are native Japanese, and the rest are in the Sino-Japanese system: *hito-*, *futa-*, *san-*, *yon-*, *go-*, *roku-*, *nana-*, *hachi-*, *kyuu-*, *juu-*, *juu-ichi-* . . .

2. 和 **II** means that the first three in the series are native Japanese, and the rest are in the Sino-Japanese system: *hito-*, *futa-*, *mi-*, *yon-*, *go-*, *roku-*, *nana-*, *hachi-*, *kyuu-*, *juu-*, *juu-ichi-* . . .

3. 和 **III** means that the first four in the series are native Japanese, and the rest are in the Sino-Japanese system: *hito-*, *futa-*, *mi-*, *yo-*, *go-*, *roku-*, *nana-*, *hachi-*, *kyuu-*, *juu-*, *juu-ichi-* . . .

4. 和 **IV** means that the first ten in the series are native Japanese, and the rest are in the Sino-Japanese system: *hito-*, *futa-*, *mi-*, *yo-*, *itsu-*, *mu-*, *nana-*, *ya-*, *kokono-*, *too-*, *juu-ichi-* . . .

和 I through 和 III each turn into the Sino-Japanese irregularity patterns after the second, third, or fourth number. Thus, a counter whose first three are native Japanese (和 II) that starts with a K would be 和 II-K instead of just 和 II. However, 和 IV does not follow any of the Sino-Japanese irregularity patterns after ten. For example, 筆 (*fude*) follows the 和 IV pattern, but 十一筆 is *juu-ichi-fude*, NOT *juu-ip-pude*, which one might have expected. Finally, whereas typically 何 is pronounced *nan*, with 和 IV, it is pronounced *nani*.

Wherever irregularities occur, I underline them. Typically, this will only be in columns three and four, but sometimes, irregular *kanji* are used and underlined as well.

Some of the counters have multiple patterns. In these cases, the pattern listed first is the most common, whist the succeeding patterns are less common, but no less acceptable. Any time there are multiple readings, the same principle applies. In some places, I use the symbol ○. This is akin to our use of *x* to mean a wild card or variable. In most places it means *insert appropriate number here*, and in one case it means *insert appropriate measurement here*.

Table of Contents

Romanization *vii*
Measurements and Large Numbers *vii*
Irregularity Patterns *viii*
あ—*A* 1
a—アール—*aaru* 1
埃—あい—*ai* 2
アイテム—*aitemu* 3
握—あく—*aku* 4
阿僧祇—あそうぎ—*asougi* 5
咫—あた—*ata* 6
雨—あめ—*ame* 7
案—あん—*an* 8
A—アンペア—*ampea* 9
い—*I* 10
位—い—*i* 10
圏・イーチャン—いいちゃん—*iichan* 11
イニング—*iningu* 12
色—いろ—*iro* 13
員—いん—*in* 14
院—いん—*in* 15
吋・インチ—いんち—*inchi* 16
う—*U* 17
宇—う—*u* 17
臼—うす—*usu* 18
え—*E* 19
柄—え—*e* 19
重—え—*e* 20
エーカー—*eekaa* 21
駅—えき—*eki* 22
枝—えだ—*eda* 23
円—えん—*en* 24
園—えん—*en* 25
お—*O* 26
泓—おう—*ou* 26
扇—おうぎ—*ougi* 27
往復—おうふく—*oufuku* 28
Ω・オーム—おおむ—*oomu* 29
億—おく—*oku* 30

オクターブ—*okutaabu* 31
桶—おけ—*oke* 32
折り—おり—*ori* 33
音—おん—*on* 34
oz—オンス—*onsu* 35
か・が—*Ka/Ga* 36
価—か—*ka* 36
日—か—*ka* 37
第○日—だい○かにち—*dai-○-nichi* 39
日間—かかん—*ka-kan* 40
架—か—*ka* 41
箇—か—*ka* 42
荷—か—*ka* 43
菓—か—*ka* 44
課—か—*ka* 45
顆・果—か—*ka* 46
河—が—*ga* 47
カートン—*kaaton* 48
回—かい—*kai* 49
貝—かい—*kai* 50
海—かい—*kai* 51
蓋—かい—*kai* 52
階—かい—*kai* 53
垓—がい—*gai* 54
蓋—がい—*gai* 55
回忌—かいき—*kaiki* 56
階級—かいきゅう—*kaikyuu* 57
回線—かいせん—*kaisen* 58
海里・浬—かいり—*kairi* 59
角—かく—*kaku* 60
画—かく—*kaku* 61
郭—かく—*kaku* 62
岳—がく—*gaku* 63
楽節—がくせつ—*gakusetsu* 64
学年—がくねん—*gakunen* 65
片・片ら—かけ（ら）—*kake* 66
掛け—かけ—*kake* 67

掛け—かけ—*kake* 68
懸け—かけ—*kake* 69
籠・篭—かご—*kago* 70
ヶ国—かこく—*ka-koku* 71
ヶ国語—かこくご—*ka-kokugo* 72
襲—かさね—*kasane* 73
重ね—かさね—*kasane* 74
ヶ所—かしょ—*ka-sho* 75
ヶ条—かじょう—*ka-jou* 76
頭—かしら—*kashira* 77
綛・桛—かせ—*kase* 78
河川—かせん—*kasen* 79
画素—がそ—*gaso* 80
家族—かぞく—*kazoku* 81
方—かた—*kata* 82
肩—かた—*kata* 83
型—かた・がた—*kata* 84
片食—かたけ—*katake* 85
担げ—かたげ—*katage* 86
片付—かたづけ—*katazuke* 87
塊—かたまり—*katamari* 88
括—かつ—*katsu* 89
月—がつ—*gatsu* 90
ヶ月・箇月—かげつ—*ka-getsu* 92
学期—がっき—*gakki* 93
学級—がっきゅう—*gakkyuu* 94
角形—かっけい—*kakkei* 95
カット—*katto* 96
cup—カップ—*kappu* 97
ヶ年—かねん—*ka-nen* 98
株—かぶ—*kabu* 99
花弁—かべん—*kaben* 100
釜—かま—*kama* 101
叺—かます—*kamasu* 102
瓶・甕—かめ—*kame* 103
日目—かめ—*kame* 104
柄・幹—から—*kara* 105

xi

カラー—karaa 106
CD/kt— カラット—karatto 107
cal— カロリー—karorii 108
gal—ガロン—garon 109
航—かわら—kawara 110
缶・罐—かん—kan 111
冠—かん—kan 112
巻—かん—kan 113
竿—かん—kan 114
款—かん—kan 115
管—かん—kan 116
艦—かん—kan 117
館—かん—kan 118
貫—かん—kan 119
貫目—かんめ—kamme 120
澗—かん—kan 121
き・ぎ—Ki/Gi 122
寸—き—ki 122
匹・疋—き・ぎ—ki/gi 123
季—き—ki 124
紀—き—ki 125
基—き—ki 126
期—き—ki 127
機—き—ki 128
騎—き—ki 129
簣—き—ki 130
饋—き—ki 131
儀—ぎ—gi 132
気圧—きあつ—kiatsu 133
掬—きく—kiku 134
機種—きしゅ—kishu 135
段・常—きだ—kida 136
規定—きてい—kitei 137
気筒—きとう—kitou 138
客—きゃく—kyaku 139
脚—きゃく—kyaku 140
弓—きゅう—kyuu 141
丘—きゅう—kyuu 142
級—きゅう—kyuu 143
球—きゅう—kyuu 144
京—きょう—kyou 145
橋—きょう—kyou 146

行—ぎょう—gyou 147
曲—きょく—kyoku 148
局—きょく—kyoku 149
切り・限—きり—kiri 150
切れ—きれ—kire 151
瓩・キログラム—きろぐらむ—kiro-guramu 152
粁・キロメートル—きろめえとる—kiro-meetoru 153
竏・キロリットル—きろりっとる—kiro-rittoru 154
斤—きん—kin 155
金—きん—kin 156
く・ぐ—Ku/Gu 157
区—く—ku 157
口—く—ku 158
句—く—ku 159
躯・軀—く—ku 160
駒—く—ku 161
具—ぐ—gu 162
クール—kuuru 163
区画—くかく—kukaku 164
区間—くかん—kukan 165
茎—くき—kuki 166
括り—くくり—kukuri 167
鎖—くさり—kusari 168
串—くし—kushi 169
癖—くせ—kuse 170
行—くだり—kudari 171
領・襲—くだり—kudari 172
口—くち—kuchi 173
組—くみ—kumi 174
位—くらい—kurai 176
クラス—kurasu 177
瓦・グラム—ぐらむ—guramu 178
グループ—guruupu 179
車分—くるまふん—kuruma-fun 180
クローネ—kuroone 181

グロス—gurosu 182
軍—ぐん—gun 183
群—ぐん—gun 184
け・げ—Ke/Ge 185
茎—けい—kei 185
景—けい—kei 186
京—けい—kei 187
圭—けい—kei 188
芸—げい—gei 189
系統—けいとう—keitou 190
ゲーム—geemu 191
桁—けた—keta 192
穴—けつ—ketsu 193
月—げつ—getsu 194
犬—けん—ken 195
件—けん—ken 196
間—けん—ken 197
軒—けん—ken 198
鍵—けん—ken 199
剣—けん—ken 200
元—げん—gen 201
弦—げん—gen 202
言—げん—gen 203
限—げん—gen 204
原子—げんし—genshi 205
こ・ご—Ko/Go 206
戸—こ—ko 206
個・箇・个・ヶ—こ—ko 207
絇—こ—ko 208
湖—こ—ko 209
壺—こ—ko 210
語—ご—go 211
口—こう—kou 212
行—こう—kou 213
更—こう—kou 214
岬—こう—kou 215
校—こう—kou 216
項—こう—kou 217
稿—こう—kou 218
講—こう—kou 219
溝—こう—kou 220
号—ごう—gou 221
合—ごう—gou 222
盒—ごう—gou 223

xii

航海―こうかい―*koukai* 224
恒河沙―ごうがしゃ―*gougasha* 225
号車―ごうしゃ―*gousha* 226
工程―こうてい―*koutei* 227
光年―こうねん―*kounen* 228
項目―こうもく―*koumoku* 229
声―こえ―*koe* 230
ゴール―*gooru* 231
石―こく―*koku* 232
国―こく―*koku* 233
極―ごく―*goku* 234
腰―こし―*koshi* 235
個体―こたい―*kotai* 236
忽―こつ―*kotsu* 237
言―こと―*koto* 238
コペック―*kopekku* 239
小間―*koma* 240
コマ・駒・齣―こま―*koma* 241
梱―こり―*kori* 242
両・塊―ころ―*koro* 243
喉―こん―*kon* 244
献―こん―*kon* 245
言―ごん―*gon* 246
さ・ざ―*Sa/Za* 247
座―ざ―*za* 247
才―さい―*sai* 248
菜―さい―*sai* 249
彩―さい―*sai* 250
歳・才―さい―*sai* 251
十路―そじ―*soji* 252
載―さい―*sai* 253
剤―ざい―*zai* 254
c―サイクル―*saikuru* 255
竿・棹―さお―*sao* 256
尺―さか―*saka* 257
さく―*saku* 258
作―さく―*saku* 259
作品―さくひん―*sakuhin* 260
下げ―さげ―*sage* 261

提げ―さげ―*sage* 262
差し―さし―*sashi* 263
点し―さし―*sashi* 264
匙―さじ―*saji* 265
冊―さつ―*satsu* 266
札―さつ―*satsu* 267
刷―さつ―*satsu* 268
撮―さつ―*satsu* 269
莢―さや―*saya* 270
皿・盤―さら―*sara* 271
盞―さん―*san* 272
山―ざん―*zan* 273
し・じ―*Shi/Ji* 274
市―し―*shi* 274
子―し―*shi* 275
枝―し―*shi* 276
指―し―*shi* 277
紙―し―*shi* 278
誌―し―*shi* 279
歯―し―*shi* 280
翅―し―*shi* 281
詩―し―*shi* 282
秭・秭―し―*shi* 283
糸―し―*shi* 284
児―じ―*ji* 285
宇―じ―*ji* 286
寺―じ―*ji* 287
時―じ―*ji* 288
時間―じかん―*ji-kan* 290
次―じ―*ji* 291
耳―じ―*ji* 292
試合―しあい―*shiai* 293
cc―シーシー―*shiishii* 294
シーズン―*shiizun* 295
シート―*shiito* 296
入―しお―*shio* 297
塩―しお―*shio* 298
式―しき―*shiki* 299
軸―じく―*jiku* 300
時限―じげん―*jigen* 301
次元―じげん―*jigen* 302
雫・滴―しずく―*shizuku* 303
室―しつ―*shitsu* 304
品―しな―*shina* 305
締め―しめ―*shime* 306

社―しゃ―*sha* 307
車―しゃ―*sha* 308
者―しゃ―*sha* 309
沙―しゃ―*sha* 310
勺―しゃく―*shaku* 311
尺―しゃく―*shaku* 312
隻―しゃく―*shaku* 313
車線―しゃせん―*shasen* 314
炷―しゅ―*shu* 315
首―しゅ―*shu* 316
朱―しゅ―*shu* 317
株―しゅ―*shu* 318
種―しゅ―*shu* 319
樹―じゅ―*ju* 320
舟―しゅう―*shuu* 321
周―しゅう―*shuu* 322
第〇週―だい〇しゅう―*dai-○-shuu* 323
週間―しゅうかん―*shuukan* 324
十―じゅう―*juu* 325
什―じゅう―*juu* 326
汁―じゅう―*juu* 327
重―じゅう―*juu* 328
銃―じゅう―*juu* 329
周忌―しゅうき―*shuuki* 330
周年―しゅうねん―*shuunen* 331
宿―しゅく―*shuku* 332
種目―しゅもく―*shumoku* 333
種類―しゅるい―*shurui* 334
巡―じゅん―*jun* 335
旬―じゅん―*jun* 336
女―じょ―*jo* 337
秭・秭―じょ―*jo* 338
勝―しょう―*shou* 339
升―しょう―*shou* 340
床―しょう―*shou* 341
章―しょう―*shou* 342
抄―しょう―*shou* 343
丈―じょう―*jou* 344
条―じょう―*jou* 345
帖―じょう―*jou* 346

乗・乘—じょう—*jou* 347
城—じょう—*jou* 348
畳—じょう—*jou* 349
錠—じょう—*jou* 351
穣—じょう—*jou* 352
勝負—しょうぶ—*shoubu* 353
色—しょく—*shoku* 354
食—しょく—*shoku* 355
尻—しり—*shiri* 356
シリング—*shiringu* 357
針—しん—*shin* 358
審—しん—*shin* 359
陣—じん—*jin* 360
尋・仞・忍—じん—*jin* 361
塵—じん—*jin* 362
進数—しんすう—*shinsuu* 363
親等—しんとう—*shintou* 364
進法—しんほう—*shinhou* 365
す・ず—*Su/Zu* 366
図—ず—*zu* 366
頭—ず—*zu* 367
錘—すい—*sui* 368
据え—すえ—*sue* 369
掬い—すくい—*sukui* 370
筋—すじ—*suji* 371
ステージ—*suteeji* 372
刷り—すり—*suri* 373
据わり—すわり—*suwari* 374
寸—すん—*sun* 375
せ・ぜ—*Se/Ze* 376
背—せ—*se* 376
畝—せ—*se* 377
世—せい—*sei* 378
正—せい—*sei* 379
声—せい—*sei* 380
星—せい—*sei* 381
世紀—せいき—*seiki* 382
世紀間—せいきかん—*seiki-kan* 383
石—せき—*seki* 384
席—せき—*seki* 385

隻—せき—*seki* 386
関—せき—*seki* 387
齣—せき—*seki* 388
世帯—せたい—*setai* 389
世代—せだい—*sedai* 390
節—せつ—*setsu* 391
説—せつ—*setsu* 392
絶—ぜつ—*zetsu* 393
セット—*setto* 394
千—せん—*sen* 395
川—せん—*sen* 396
泉—せん—*sen* 397
扇—せん—*sen* 398
戦—せん—*sen* 399
煎—せん—*sen* 400
銭—せん—*sen* 401
選—せん—*sen* 402
繊—せん—*sen* 403
前—ぜん—*zen* 404
膳—ぜん—*zen* 405
船団—せんだん—*sendan* 406
センチメートル・糎—せんちめえとる—*senchi-meetoru* 407
センチグラム・瓱—せんちぐらむ—*senchi-guramu* 408
センチリットル・竰—せんちりっとる—*senchi-rittoru* 409
セント・仙—せんと—*sento* 410
そ・ぞ—*So/Zo* 411
雙・双—そう—*sou* 411
層—そう—*sou* 412
槍—そう—*sou* 413
槽—そう—*sou* 414
艘—そう—*sou* 415
叢—そう—*sou* 416
束—そく—*soku* 417
足—そく—*soku* 418
則—そく—*soku* 419
息—そく—*soku* 420
速—そく—*soku* 421
粟—ぞく—*zoku* 422
具—そなえ—*sonae* 423

揃い—そろい—*soroi* 424
村—そん—*son* 425
尊—そん—*son* 426
た・だ—*Ta/Da* 427
打—だ—*da* 427
朶—だ—*da* 428
駄—だ—*da* 429
ダース・打—だあす—*daasu* 430
体—たい—*tai* 431
袋—たい—*tai* 432
隊—たい—*tai* 433
代—だい—*dai* 434
台—だい—*dai* 435
弟—だい—*dai* 436
第—だい—*dai* 437
題—だい—*dai* 438
代目—だいめ—*dai-me* 439
卓—たく—*taku* 440
打席—だせき—*daseki* 441
立—たて—*tate* 442
立て—だて—*date* 443
束—たば—*taba* 444
度—たび—*tabi* 445
玉—たま—*tama* 446
珠—たま—*tama* 447
樽—たる—*taru* 448
垂れ—たれ—*tare* 449
反・段—たん—*tan* 450
担—たん—*tan* 451
端—たん—*tan* 452
団—だん—*dan* 453
段—だん—*dan* 454
弾—だん—*dan* 455
単位—たんい—*tan'i* 456
段階—だんかい—*dankai* 457
反歩・段歩—たんぶ—*tambu* 458
段落—だんらく—*danraku* 459
ち・ぢ—*Chi/Ji* 460
地区—ちく—*chiku* 460
帙—ちつ—*chitsu* 461
地点—ちてん—*chiten* 462
着—ちゃく—*chaku* 463

丁—ちょう—*chou* 464
町—ちょう—*chou* 465
丁目・町目—ちょうめ—*chou-me* 466
兆—ちょう—*chou* 467
挺・丁—ちょう—*chou* 468
張—ちょう—*chou* 469
貼—ちょう—*chou* 470
提—ちょう—*chou* 471
調—ちょう—*chou* 472
町歩—ちょうぶ—*choubu* 473
つ・づ—*Tsu/Zu* 474
つ—*tsu* 474
対—つい—*tsui* 475
通—つう—*tsuu* 476
通話—つうわ—*tsuuwa* 477
束—つか—*tsuka* 478
番—つがい—*tsugai* 479
月—つき—*tsuki* 480
次—つぎ—*tsugi* 481
筒—つつ—*tsutsu* 483
続き—つづき—*tsuzuki* 484
包み—つつみ—*tsutsumi* 485
綴り—つづり—*tsuzuri* 486
粒—つぶ—*tsubu* 487
坪—つぼ—*tsubo* 488
壺—つぼ—*tsubo* 489
摘み・撮み—つまみ—*tsumami* 490
て・で—*Te/De* 491
dK—ディーケー—*diikee* 491
手—て—*te* 492
邸—てい—*tei* 493
挺—てい—*tei* 494
幀—てい—*tei* 495
艇—てい—*tei* 496
蹄—てい—*tei* 497
訂—てい—*tei* 498
daa/dka—デカール—*deka-aru* 499

デカグラム・瓱—でかぐらむ—*deka-guramu* 500
デカメートル・籵—でかめえとる—*deka-meetoru* 501
デカリットル・竍—デカリットル—*deka-rittoru* 502
滴—てき—*teki* 503
デシグラム・瓰—でしぐらむ—*deshi-guramu* 504
デシメートル・粉—でしめえとる—*deshi-meetoru* 505
デシリットル・竕—でしりっとる—*deshi-rittoru* 506
鉄—てつ—*tetsu* 507
店—てん—*ten* 508
点—てん—*ten* 509
店舗—てんぽ—*tempo* 510
と・ど—*To/Do* 511
斗—と—*to* 511
度—ど—*do* 512
灯・燈—とう—*tou* 513
投—とう—*tou* 514
套—とう—*tou* 515
刀—とう—*tou* 516
島—とう—*tou* 517
盗—とう—*tou* 518
塔—とう—*tou* 519
棟—とう—*tou* 520
湯—とう—*tou* 521
等—とう—*tou* 522
筒—とう—*tou* 523
統—とう—*tou* 524
頭—とう—*tou* 525
党—とう—*tou* 526
洞—どう—*dou* 527
堂—どう—*dou* 528
道—どう—*dou* 529
銅—どう—*dou* 530
等分—とうぶん—*toubun* 531
通し—とおし—*tooshi* 532
通り—とおり—*toori* 533
時—とき—*toki* 534

床—とこ—*toko* 535
所・処—ところ—*tokoro* 536
度数—どすう—*dosuu* 537
年・歳—とせ—*tose* 538
戸前—とまえ—*tomae* 539
度目—どめ—*do-me* 540
撮り—どり—*dori* 541
ドル・弗—どる—*doru* 542
トン・瓲・噸・噸—とん—*ton* 543
な—*Na* 544
流れ—ながれ—*nagare* 544
七日—なぬか・なのか—*nanuka/nanoka* 545
鍋—なべ—*nabe* 546
男—なん—*nan* 547
に—*Ni* 548
握り—にぎり—*nigiri* 548
人—にん・たり・り—*nin/tari/ri* 549
人組—にんぐみ—*nin-gumi* 550
人工—にんく—*ninku* 551
人時—にんじ—*ninji* 552
人月—にんげつ—*ningetsu* 553
人前—にんまえ—*ninmae* 554
ぬ—*Nu* 555
貫き—ぬき—*nuki* 555
ね—*Ne* 556
ネット—*netto* 556
年—ねん—*nen* 557
Japanese Years *vs.* the Gregorian Calendar 558
年間—ねんかん—*nen-kan* 559
年生—ねんせい—*nensei* 560
年代—ねんだい—*nendai* 561
の—*No* 562
幅・布—の—*no* 562
能—のう—*nou* 563
kn—ノット—*notto* 564

は・ば・ぱ—Ha/Ba/Pa 565
波—は—ha 565
派—は—ha 566
場—ば—ba 567
%—パーセント—paasento 568
ᴃ—バーツ—baatsu 569
杯・盃—はい—hai 570
敗—はい—hai 571
貝—ばい—bai 572
倍—ばい—bai 573
バイト—baito 574
拍—はく—haku 575
泊—はく—haku 576
刷毛—はけ—hake 577
箱—はこ—hako 578
箸—はし—hashi 579
場所—ばしょ—basho 580
柱—はしら—hashira 581
馬身—ばしん—bashin 582
鉢—はち—hachi 583
発—はつ—hatsu 584
パック—pakku 585
羽—はね—hane 586
腹・肚—はら—hara 587
針—はり—hari 588
張り—はり—hari 589
bbl—バレル—bareru 590
furlongs—ハロン—haron 591
犯—はん—han 592
判—はん—han 593
版—はん—han 594
斑—はん—han 595
飯—はん—han 596
晩—ばん—ban 597
番—ばん—ban 598
第○番—だい○ばん—dai-○-ban 599
番線—ばんせん—bansen 600
番地—ばんち—banchi 601
番手—ばんて—bante 602
番目—ばんめ—bam-me 603

ひ・び・ぴ—Hi/Bi/Pi 604
ヒ—ひ—hi 604
日—ひ—hi 605
尾—び—bi 606
微—び—bi 607
ピース—piisu 608
ppm—ピーピーエム—piipiiemu 609
匹—ひき—hiki 610
疋—ひき—hiki 611
ピクセル—pikuseru 612
ピクル・担—びくる—pikuru 613
筆—ひつ—hitsu 614
bits—ビット—bitto 615
百—ひゃく—hyaku 616
百目—ひゃくめ—hyakume 617
俵—ひょう—hyou 618
票—ひょう—hyou 619
瓢—ひょう—hyou 620
秒—びょう—byou 621
拍子—ひょうし—hyoushi 622
片—ひら—hira 623
尋—ひろ—hiro 624
品—ひん—hin 625
便—びん—bin 626
瓶—びん—bin 627
品目—ひんもく—hinmoku 628

ふ・ぶ・ぷ—Fu/Bu/Pu 629
節・編—ふ—fu 629
分—ぶ—bu 630
歩—ぶ—bu 631
部—ぶ—bu 632
フィート・呎—ふぃいと—fuiito 633
封—ふう—fuu 634
服—ふく—fuku 635
幅—ふく—fuku 636
袋—ふくろ—fukuro 637
房—ふさ—fusa 638
節—ふし—fushi 639

伏せ—ぶせ—buse 640
仏—ぶつ—butsu 641
筆—ふで—fude 642
舟—ふね—fune 643
F—フラン—furan 644
振り—ふり—furi 645
降り—ふり—furi 646
ロ—ふり—furi 647
ブロック—burokku 648
分(間)—ふん(かん)—fun(kan) 649
分—ぶん—bun 650
文—ぶん—bun 651
文節—ぶんせつ—bunsetsu 652

へ・べ・ぺ—He/Be/Pe 653
瓶—へい—hei 653
平方○—へいほう○—heihou○ 654
ページ・頁—ぺえじ—peeji 655
ベース—beesu 656
ha—ヘクタール—hekutaaru 657
ヘクトグラム・瓱—へくとぐらむ—hekutoguramu 658
ヘクトメートル・粨—へくとめえとる—hekutomeetoru 659
ヘクトリットル—竡—へくとりっとる—hekutorittoru 660
ペセタ—peseta 661
ペソ—ぺそ—peso 662
部屋—へや—heya 663
Hz—ヘルツ—herutsu 664
片—へん—hen 665
遍・辺—へん—hen 666
編・篇—へん—hen 667
弁—べん—ben 668

ほ・ぼ・ぽ—Ho/Bo/Po 669
歩—ほ—ho 669
畝—ほ—ho 670

舗・鋪―ほ―*ho* 671
幅―ほ―*ho* 672
ポイント―*pointo* 673
包―ほう―*hou* 674
報―ほう―*hou* 675
峰―ほう―*hou* 676
法―ほう―*hou* 677
木―ほく―*boku* 678
V―ぼると―*boruto* 679
本―ほん―*hon* 680
ポンド・听―ぽんど―*pondo* 681
ポンド・封・磅―ぽんど―*pondo* 682
ま―*Ma* 683
間―ま―*ma* 683
枚―まい―*mai* 684
マイル・哩―まいる―*mairu* 685
巻き―まき―*maki* 686
幕―まく―*maku* 687
第〇幕―だい〇まく―*dai-〇-maku* 688
幕目―まくめ―*maku-me* 689
升―ます―*masu* 690
曲げ―まげ―*mage* 691
マルク―まるく―*maruku* 692
回り・廻り・周り―まわり―*mawari* 693
万・萬―まん―*man* 694
み―*Mi* 695
味―み―*mi* 695
ミリグラム・瓱―ミリグラム―*miri-guramu* 696
ミリバール―みりばある―*miri-baaru* 697
ミリメートル・粍―みりめえとる―*miri-meetoru* 698
ミリリットル・竓―みりりっとる―*miri-rittoru* 699
む―*Mu* 700
棟―むね―*mune* 700

匹・疋―むら―*mura* 701
群・叢・簇―むら―*mura* 702
群れ―むれ―*mure* 703
め―*Me* 704
目―め―*me* 704
名―めい―*mei* 705
メートル・米―めえとる―*meetoru* 706
面―めん―*men* 707
も―*Mo* 708
毛・毫―もう―*mou* 708
目―もく―*moku* 709
文字―もじ―*moji* 710
本・連―もと―*moto* 711
盛―もり―*mori* 712
文―もん―*mon* 713
門―もん―*mon* 714
問―もん―*mon* 715
匁―もんめ―*monme* 716
や―*Ya* 717
夜―や―*ya* 717
ヤード・碼―やあど―*yaado* 718
役―やく―*yaku* 719
社―やしろ―*yashiro* 720
山―やま―*yama* 721
ゆ―*Yu* 722
湯―ゆ―*yu* 722
ユアン・元―ゆあん―*yuan* 723
結い―ゆい―*yui* 724
裄―ゆき―*yuki* 725
ユニット―ゆにっと―*yunitto* 726
よ―*Yo* 727
夜―よ―*yo* 727
余―よ―*yo* 728
葉―よう―*you* 729
腰―よう―*you* 730
翼―よく―*yoku* 731
装い―よそい―*yosoi* 732
度―より―*yori* 733
具―よろい―*yoroi* 734
ら―*Ra* 735

ラウンド―*raundo* 735
り―*Ri* 736
里―り―*ri* 736
リットル・立―りっとる―*rittoru* 737
立方〇―りっぽう〇―*rippou-〇* 738
旒・流―りゅう―*ryuu* 739
笠―りゅう―*ryuu* 740
粒―りゅう―*ryuu* 741
両―りょう―*ryou* 742
嶺―りょう―*ryou* 743
輌―りょう―*ryou* 744
領―りょう―*ryou* 745
リラ―りら―*rira* 746
厘―りん―*rin* 747
輪―りん―*rin* 748
鱗―りん―*rin* 749
る―*Ru* 750
塁―るい―*rui* 750
類―るい―*rui* 751
ルーブル・pуб―るうぶる―*ruuburu* 752
ルクス・lx―ルクス―*rukusu* 753
ルピー・Rs―るぴい―*rupii* 754
れ―*Re* 755
礼―れい―*rei* 755
嶺―れい―*rei* 756
レース―*reesu* 757
レーン―*reen* 758
列―れつ―*retsu* 759
列車―れっしゃ―*ressha* 760
聯・聨―れん―*ren* 761
連―れん―*ren* 762
ろ―*Ro* 763
浪―ろう―*rou* 763
ロール―*rooru* 764
路線―ろせん―*rosen* 765
わ―*Wa* 766
把―わ―*wa* 766
羽―わ―*wa* 767
話―わ―*wa* 768

ワード—わあど—*waado* 769
盃・沸—わかし—*wakashi* 770
枠—わく—*waku* 771
ワット・W—わっと—*watto* 772
割—わり—*wari* 773
碗・椀—わん—*wan* 774

Index of English Meanings 775
Bibliography 790

あ—A
a—アール—aaru

Japanese: アール
Romanized: *aaru*
Pattern: 漢 Ø
Used with, or Means: ares (S. I. symbol: a), a unit of area, 100 m²/1,076.39104 ft²

1 a	1アール	いちあある	*ichi-aaru*
2 a	2アール	にあある	*ni-aaru*
3 a	3アール	さんあある	*san-aaru*
4 a	4アール	よんあある	*yon-aaru*
5 a	5アール	ごあある	*go-aaru*
6 a	6アール	ろくあある	*roku-aaru*
7 a	7アール	ななあある	*nana-aaru*
8 a	8アール	はちあある	*hachi-aaru*
9 a	9アール	きゅうあある	*kyuu-aaru*
10 a	10アール	じゅうあある	*juu-aaru*

Irregularities or Special beyond Ten: none
Notes: We typically only use its derived form, the hectare (ha, 100 ares, 10,000 m²).

埃——あい——ai

Japanese: あい
Romanized: *ai*
Pattern: 漢 Ø
Used with, or Means: 1/10,000,000,000th, 10^{-10}

10^{-10}	一埃	いちあい	*ichi-ai*
2×10^{-10}	二埃	にあい	*ni-ai*
3×10^{-10}	三埃	さんあい	*san-ai*
4×10^{-10}	四埃	よんあい	*yon-ai*
5×10^{-10}	五埃	ごあい	*go-ai*
6×10^{-10}	六埃	ろくあい	*roku-ai*
7×10^{-10}	七埃	ななあい	*nana-ai*
8×10^{-10}	八埃	はちあい	*hachi-ai*
9×10^{-10}	九埃	きゅうあい	*kyuu-ai*
10^{-9}	十埃	じゅうあい	*juu-ai*

Irregularities or Special beyond Ten:

10^{-8}	百埃	ひゃくあい	*hyaku-ai*
10^{-7}	千埃	せんあい	*sen-ai*

Notes: none

アイテム—*aitemu*

Japanese: あいてむ
Romanized: *aitemu*
Pattern: 漢 ∅
Used with, or Means: items, see also 品 (*hin*), see also 点 (*ten*)

1 item	1アイテム	いちあいてむ	*ichi-aitemu*
2 items	2アイテム	にあいてむ	*ni-aitemu*
3 items	3アイテム	さんあいてむ	*san-aitemu*
4 items	4アイテム	よんあいてむ	*yon-aitemu*
5 items	5アイテム	ごあいてむ	*go-aitemu*
6 items	6アイテム	ろくあいてむ	*roku-aitemu*
7 items	7アイテム	ななあいてむ	*nana-aitemu*
8 items	8アイテム	はちあいてむ	*hachi-aitemu*
9 items	9アイテム	きゅうあいてむ	*kyuu-aitemu*
10 items	10アイテム	じゅうあいてむ	*juu-aitemu*

Irregularities or Special beyond Ten: none
Notes: none

握 — あく — *aku*

Japanese: あく
Romanized: *aku*
Pattern: 漢 ∅
Used with, or Means: handfuls (of sand, for example), see also 握り (*nigiri*), see also 掴み (*tsukami*); the length of a samurai's four-finger grip (on their sword hilt)

1 handful	一握	いちあく	*ichi-aku*
2 handfuls	二握	にあく	*ni-aku*

Irregularities or Special beyond Ten: none
Notes: none

阿僧祇—あそうぎ—*asougi*

Japanese: あそうぎ
Romanized: *asougi*
Pattern: 漢 ∅
Used with, or Means: 10,000 恒河沙 (*gougasha*), 100 septendecillion, 10^{56}

10^{56}	一阿僧祇	いちあそうぎ	*ichi-asougi*
2×10^{56}	二阿僧祇	にあそうぎ	*ni-asougi*
3×10^{56}	三阿僧祇	さんあそうぎ	*san-asougi*
4×10^{56}	四阿僧祇	よんあそうぎ	*yon-asougi*
5×10^{56}	五阿僧祇	ごあそうぎ	*go-asougi*
6×10^{56}	六阿僧祇	ろくあそうぎ	*roku-asougi*
7×10^{56}	七阿僧祇	ななあそうぎ	*nana-asougi*
8×10^{56}	八阿僧祇	はちあそうぎ	*hachi-asougi*
9×10^{56}	九阿僧祇	きゅうあそうぎ	*kyuu-asougi*
10^{57}	十阿僧祇	じゅうあそうぎ	*juu-asougi*

Irregularities or Special beyond Ten:

10^{58}	百阿僧祇	ひゃくあそうぎ	*hyaku-asougi*
10^{59}	千阿僧祇	せんあそうぎ	*sen-asougi*

Notes: 10^{56} is 100 000 000 000 000 000 000 000 000 000 000 000 000 000 000 000 000 000 000

咫 — あた — *ata*

Japanese: あた
Romanized: *ata*
Pattern: 和 IV
Used with, or Means: *ata*, an ancient unit of length from the bottom of the palm to the tip of the middle finger

1 *ata*	一咫	ひとあた	*hito-ata*
2 *ata*	二咫	ふたあた	*futa-ata*
3 *ata*	三咫	みあた	*mi-ata*
4 *ata*	四咫	よあた	*yo-ata*
5 *ata*	五咫	いつあた	*itsu-ata*
6 *ata*	六咫	むあた	*mu-ata*
7 *ata*	七咫	ななあた	*nana-ata*
8 *ata*	八咫	やあた / やた	*ya-ata* / *ya-ta*
9 *ata*	九咫	ここのあた	*kokono-ata*
10 *ata*	十咫	とおあた	*too-ata*

Irregularities or Special beyond Ten:

100 *ata*	百咫	ももあた	*momo-ata*
1,000 *ata*	千咫	ちあた	*chi-ata*
10,000 *ata*	一万咫	よろずあた	*yorozu-ata*
how many *ata*?	何咫	なんあた	*nan-ata*

Notes: One can also read 八咫 as やた (*yata*), as in one of the three items of the imperial regalia: 八咫の鏡 (*yata no kagami*) the *eight-hand mirror*.

雨 — あめ — *ame*

Japanese: あめ
Romanized: *ame*
Pattern: 和 IV
Used with, or Means: rainfall, a shower

        a shower   一雨   ひとあめ   *hito-ame*

Irregularities or Special beyond Ten: none
Notes: none

案—あん—*an*

Japanese: あん
Romanized: *an*
Pattern: 漢 ∅
Used with, or Means: Shinto offering tables

1 offering table	一案	いちあん	*ichi-an*
2 offering tables	二案	にあん	*ni-an*
3 offering tables	三案	さんあん	*san-an*
4 offering tables	四案	よんあん	*yon-an*
5 offering tables	五案	ごあん	*go-an*
6 offering tables	六案	ろくあん	*roku-an*
7 offering tables	七案	ななあん	*nana-an*
8 offering tables	八案	はちあん	*hachi-an*
9 offering tables	九案	きゅうあん	*kyuu-an*
10 offering tables	十案	じゅうあん	*juu-an*

Irregularities or Special beyond Ten: none
Notes: none

A—アンペア—*ampea*

Japanese: アンペア
Romanized: *ampea*
Pattern: 漢 Ø
Used with, or Means: amperes, amps (S. I. symbol: A), a measure of the amount of electric charge passing a point per unit time, 1 ampere is 1 coulomb per second

1 A	1アンペア	いちあんぺあ	*ichi-ampea*
2 A	2アンペア	にあんぺあ	*ni-ampea*
3 A	3アンペア	さんあんぺあ	*san-ampea*
4 A	4アンペア	よんあんぺあ	*yon-ampea*
5 A	5アンペア	ごあんぺあ	*go-ampea*
6 A	6アンペア	ろくあんぺあ	*roku-ampea*
7 A	7アンペア	ななあんぺあ	*nana-ampea*
8 A	8アンペア	はちあんぺあ	*hachi-ampea*
9 A	9アンペア	きゅうあんぺあ	*kyuu-ampea*
10 A	10アンペア	じゅうあんぺあ	*juu-ampea*

Irregularities or Special beyond Ten: none
Notes: none

い—I
位—い—i

Japanese: い
Romanized: *i*
Pattern: 漢 Ø
Used with, or Means: ranking, place, standard (順位 *jun'i*); spirits of the dead

1 spirit	一位	いちい	*ichi-i*
2 spirits	二位	にい	*ni-i*
3 spirits	三位	さんい	*san-i*
4 spirits	四位	よんい	*yon-i*
5 spirits	五位	ごい	*go-i*
6 spirits	六位	ろくい	*roku-i*
7 spirits	七位	なない	*nana-i*
8 spirits	八位	はちい	*hachi-i*
9 spirits	九位	きゅうい	*kyuu-i*
10 spirits	十位	じゅうい	*juu-i*

Irregularities or Special beyond Ten: none
Notes: none

圏・イーチャン—いいちゃん—iichan

Japanese: いいちゃん
Romanized: *iichan*
Pattern: 漢 ∅
Used with, or Means: games of mahjonng

1 game	一圏・イーチャン	いちいいちゃん	*ichi-iichan*
2 games	二圏・イーチャン	にいいちゃん	*ni-iichan*
3 games	三圏・イーチャン	さんいいちゃん	*san-iichan*
4 games	四圏・イーチャン	よんいいちゃん	*yon-iichan*
5 games	五圏・イーチャン	ごいいちゃん	*go-iichan*
6 games	六圏・イーチャン	ろくいいちゃん	*roku-iichan*
7 games	七圏・イーチャン	なないいちゃん	*nana-iichan*
8 games	八圏・イーチャン	はちいいちゃん	*hachi-iichan*
9 games	九圏・イーチャン	きゅういいちゃん	*kyuu-iichan*
10 games	十圏・イーチャン	じゅういいちゃん	*juu-iichan*

Irregularities or Special beyond Ten: none
Notes: none

イニング—*iningu*

Japanese: いにんぐ
Romanized: *iningu*
Pattern: 漢 ∅
Used with, or Means: innings, see also 回 (*kai*)

1 inning	1 イニング	いちいにんぐ	*ichi-iningu*
2 innings	2 イニング	にいにんぐ	*ni-iningu*
3 innings	3 イニング	さんいにんぐ	*san-iningu*
4 innings	4 イニング	よんいにんぐ	*yon-iningu*
5 innings	5 イニング	ごいにんぐ	*go-iningu*
6 innings	6 イニング	ろくいにんぐ	*roku-iningu*
7 innings	7 イニング	なないにんぐ	*nana-iningu*
8 innings	8 イニング	はちいにんぐ	*hachi-iningu*
9 innings	9 イニング	きゅういにんぐ	*kyuu-iningu*
10 innings	10 イニング	じゅういにんぐ	*juu-iningu*

Irregularities or Special beyond Ten: none
Notes: none

色—いろ—iro

Japanese: いろ
Romanized: *iro*
Pattern: 和 II
Used with, or Means: colors; kinds, see also カラー (*karaa*), see also 色 (*shoku*)

1 color	一色	ひといろ	*hito-iro*
2 colors	二色	ふたいろ	*futa-iro*
3 colors	三色	みいろ	*mi-iro*
4 colors	四色	よんいろ	*yon-iro*
5 colors	五色	ごいろ	*go-iro*
6 colors	六色	ろくいろ	*roku-iro*
7 colors	七色	なないろ	*nana-iro*
8 colors	八色	はちいろ	*hachi-iro*
9 colors	九色	きゅういろ	*kyuu-iro*
10 colors	十色	じゅういろ	*juu-iro*

Irregularities or Special beyond Ten: none
Notes: none

員 — いん — in

Japanese: いん
Romanized: *in*
Pattern: 漢 ∅
Used with, or Means: members, employees

1 member	一員	いちいん	*ichi-in*
2 members	二員	にいん	*ni-in*
3 members	三員	さんいん	*san-in*
4 members	四員	よんいん	*yon-in*
5 members	五員	ごいん	*go-in*
6 members	六員	ろくいん	*roku-in*
7 members	七員	なないん	*nana-in*
8 members	八員	はちいん	*hachi-in*
9 members	九員	きゅういん	*kyuu-in*
10 members	十員	じゅういん	*juu-in*

Irregularities or Special beyond Ten: none
Notes: none

院 — いん — *in*

Japanese: いん
Romanized: *in*
Pattern: 漢 Ø
Used with, or Means: (literary language) hospitals

1 hospital	一院	いちいん	*ichi-in*
2 hospitals	二院	にいん	*ni-in*
3 hospitals	三院	さんいん	*san-in*
4 hospitals	四院	よんいん	*yon-in*
5 hospitals	五院	ごいん	*go-in*
6 hospitals	六院	ろくいん	*roku-in*
7 hospitals	七院	なないん	*nana-in*
8 hospitals	八院	はちいん	*hachi-in*
9 hospitals	九院	きゅういん	*kyuu-in*
10 hospitals	十院	じゅういん	*juu-in*

Irregularities or Special beyond Ten: none
Notes: none

吋・インチ—いんち—*inchi*

Japanese: インチ
Romanized: *inchi*
Pattern: 漢 Ø
Used with, or Means: inches (symbol: in), a unit of length, 0.0254 m

1 in	一吋・インチ	いちいんち	*ichi-inchi*
2 in	二吋・インチ	にいんち	*ni-inchi*
3 in	三吋・インチ	さんいんち	*san-inchi*
4 in	四吋・インチ	よんいんち	*yon-inchi*
5 in	五吋・インチ	ごいんち	*go-inchi*
6 in	六吋・インチ	ろくいんち	*roku-inchi*
7 in	七吋・インチ	なないんち	*nana-inchi*
8 in	八吋・インチ	はちいんち	*hachi-inchi*
9 in	九吋・インチ	きゅういんち	*kyuu-inchi*
10 in	十吋・インチ	じゅういんち	*juu-inchi*

Irregularities or Special beyond Ten: none
Notes: none

う—U
宇—う—u

Japanese: う
Romanized: u
Pattern: 漢 ∅
Used with, or Means: temple buildings (お堂 *odou*); Buddhist household alters (仏壇 *butsudan*); Shinto shrines; mausoleums; Tibetan Buddhist monasteries; buildings with roofs

1 temple building	一宇	いちう	*ichi-u*
2 temple buildings	二宇	にう	*ni-u*
3 temple buildings	三宇	さんう	*san-u*
4 temple buildings	四宇	よんう	*yon-u*
5 temple buildings	五宇	ごう	*go-u*
6 temple buildings	六宇	ろくう	*roku-u*
7 temple buildings	七宇	ななう / しちう	*nana-u* / *shichi-u*
8 temple buildings	八宇	はちう	*hachi-u*
9 temple buildings	九宇	きゅうう	*kyuu-u*
10 temple buildings	十宇	じゅうう	*juu-u*

Irregularities or Special beyond Ten: none
Notes: none

臼—うす—*usu*

Japanese: うす
Romanized: *usu*
Pattern: 和 II
Used with, or Means: dollops of mortar

1 dollop of mortar	一臼	ひとうす	*hito-usu*
2 dollops of mortar	二臼	ふたうす	*futa-usu*
3 dollops of mortar	三臼	みうす	*mi-usu*
4 dollops of mortar	四臼	よんうす	*yon-usu*
5 dollops of mortar	五臼	ごうす	*go-usu*
6 dollops of mortar	六臼	ろくうす	*roku-usu*
7 dollops of mortar	七臼	ななうす / しちうす	*nana-usu* / *shichi-usu*
8 dollops of mortar	八臼	はちうす	*hachi-usu*
9 dollops of mortar	九臼	きゅううす	*kyuu-usu*
10 dollops of mortar	十臼	じゅううす	*juu-usu*

Irregularities or Special beyond Ten: none
Notes: none

え — E
柄 — え — *e*

Japanese: え
Romanized: *e*
Pattern: 和 I
Used with, or Means: halberds (薙刀 *naginata*), kitchen knives, cleavers, see also 柄 (*kara*), see also 柄 (*hei*)

1 knife	一柄	ひとえ	*hito-e*
2 knives	二柄	ふたえ	*futa-e*
3 knives	三柄	さんえ	*san-e*
4 knives	四柄	よんえ	*yon-e*
5 knives	五柄	ごえ	*go-e*
6 knives	六柄	ろくえ	*roku-e*
7 knives	七柄	ななえ / しちえ	*nana-e* / *shichi-e*
8 knives	八柄	はちえ	*hachi-e*
9 knives	九柄	きゅうえ	*kyuu-e*
10 knives	十柄	じゅうえ	*juu-e*

Irregularities or Special beyond Ten: none
Notes: none

重 — え — *e*

Japanese: え
Romanized: *e*
Pattern: 和 II
Used with, or Means: fold, ply (of garments, cloth), see also 重 (*juu*), see also 襲 (*kasane*), see also 重ね (*kasane*)

1 fold	一重	ひとえ	*hito-e*
2 folds	二重	ふたえ	*futa-e*
3 folds	三重	みえ	*mi-e*
4 folds	四重	よんえ	*yon-e*
5 folds	五重	ごえ	*go-e*
6 folds	六重	ろくえ	*roku-e*
7 folds	七重	ななえ	*nana-e*
8 folds	八重	やちえ	*ya-e*
9 folds	九重	きゅうえ	*kyuu-e*
10 folds	十重	じゅうえ	*juu-e*

Irregularities or Special beyond Ten: none
Notes: none

エーカー—*eekaa*

Japanese: えєかあ
Romanized: *eekaa*
Pattern: 漢 ∅
Used with, or Means: acres, a unit of area, 43,560 ft^2/4,046.85642 m^2

1 acre	1エーカー	いちええかあ	*ichi-eekaa*
2 acres	2エーカー	にええかあ	*ni-eekaa*
3 acres	3エーカー	さんええかあ	*san-eekaa*
4 acres	4エーカー	よんええかあ	*yon-eekaa*
5 acres	5エーカー	ごええかあ	*go-eekaa*
6 acres	6エーカー	ろくええかあ	*roku-eekaa*
7 acres	7エーカー	ななええかあ	*nana-eekaa*
8 acres	8エーカー	はちええかあ	*hachi-eekaa*
9 acres	9エーカー	きゅうええかあ	*kyuu-eekaa*
10 acres	10エーカー	じゅうええかあ	*juu-eekaa*

Irregularities or Special beyond Ten: none
Notes: none

駅—えき—eki

Japanese: えき
Romanized: *eki*
Pattern: 和 I
Used with, or Means: train stations, bus stops (バス停 *basu-tei*)

1 station	一駅	ひとえき	*hito-eki*
2 stations	二駅	ふたえき	*futa-eki*
3 stations	三駅	さんえき	*san-eki*
4 stations	四駅	よんえき	*yon-eki*
5 stations	五駅	ごえき	*go-eki*
6 stations	六駅	ろくえき	*roku-eki*
7 stations	七駅	ななえき / しちえき	*nana-eki* / *shichi-eki*
8 stations	八駅	はちえき	*hachi-eki*
9 stations	九駅	きゅうえき	*kyuu-eki*
10 stations	十駅	じゅうえき	*juu-eki*

Irregularities or Special beyond Ten: none
Notes: none

枝—えだ—eda

Japanese: えだ
Romanized: *eda*
Pattern: 和 I
Used with, or Means: flowers, branches, stems, see also 枝 (*shi*)

1 stem	一枝	ひとえだ	*hito-eda*
2 stems	二枝	ふたえだ	*futa-eda*
3 stems	三枝	さんえだ	*san-eda*
4 stems	四枝	よんえだ	*yon-eda*
5 stems	五枝	ごえだ	*go-eda*
6 stems	六枝	ろくえだ	*roku-eda*
7 stems	七枝	ななえだ / しちえだ	*nana-eda* / *shichi-eda*
8 stems	八枝	はちえだ	*hachi-eda*
9 stems	九枝	きゅうえだ	*kyuu-eda*
10 stems	十枝	じゅうえだ	*juu-eda*

Irregularities or Special beyond Ten: none
Notes: none

円—えん—*en*

Japanese: えん
Romanized: *en*
Pattern: 漢 ∅
Used with, or Means: yen, ¥, 100 銭 (*sen*)

1 ¥	一円	いちえん ひとえん	*ichi-en* <u>*hito-en*</u>
2 ¥	二円	にえん ふたえん	*ni-en* <u>*futa-en*</u>
3 ¥	三円	さんえん	*san-en*
4 ¥	四円	よんえん	*yon-en*
5 ¥	五円	ごえん	*go-en*
6 ¥	六円	ろくえん	*roku-en*
7 ¥	七円	ななえん しちえん	*nana-en* *shichi-en*
8 ¥	八円	はちえん	*hachi-en*
9 ¥	九円	きゅうえん	*kyuu-en*
10 ¥	十円	じゅうえん とおえん	*juu-en* <u>*too-en*</u>

Irregularities or Special beyond Ten: none
Notes: In business and economics, one uses *hito-en*, *futa-en*, and *too-en*, rather than *ichi-en*, *ni-en*, and *juu-en*.

園 — えん — en

Japanese: えん
Romanized: *en*
Pattern: 漢 ∅
Used with, or Means: kindergartens, parks

1 kindergarten	一園	いちえん	*ichi-en*
2 kindergartens	二園	にえん	*ni-en*
3 kindergartens	三園	さんえん	*san-en*
4 kindergartens	四園	よんえん	*yon-en*
5 kindergartens	五園	ごえん	*go-en*
6 kindergartens	六園	ろくえん	*roku-en*
7 kindergartens	七園	ななえん / しちえん	*nana-en* / *shichi-en*
8 kindergartens	八園	はちえん	*hachi-en*
9 kindergartens	九園	きゅうえん	*kyuu-en*
10 kindergartens	十園	じゅうえん	*juu-en*

Irregularities or Special beyond Ten: none
Notes: none

お—O
泓—おう—*ou*

Japanese: おう
Romanized: *ou*
Pattern: 漢 ∅
Used with, or Means: (literary language) lakes

1 lake	一泓	いちおう	*ichi-ou*
2 lakes	二泓	におう	*ni-ou*
3 lakes	三泓	さんおう	*san-ou*
4 lakes	四泓	よんおう	*yon-ou*
5 lakes	五泓	ごおう	*go-ou*
6 lakes	六泓	ろくおう	*roku-ou*
7 lakes	七泓	ななおう / しちおう	*nana-ou* / *shichi-ou*
8 lakes	八泓	はちおう	*hachi-ou*
9 lakes	九泓	きゅうおう	*kyuu-ou*
10 lakes	十泓	じゅうおう	*juu-ou*

Irregularities or Special beyond Ten: none
Notes: none

扇—おうぎ—*ougi*

Japanese: おうぎ
Romanized: *ougi*
Pattern: 和 III
Used with, or Means: (literary language) folding fans, see also 扇 (*sen*)

1 folding fan	一扇	ひとおうぎ	*hito-ougi*
2 folding fans	二扇	ふたおうぎ	*futa-ougi*
3 folding fans	三扇	みおうぎ	*mi-ougi*
4 folding fans	四扇	よおうぎ	*yo-ougi*
5 folding fans	五扇	ごおうぎ	*go-ougi*
6 folding fans	六扇	ろくおうぎ	*roku-ougi*
7 folding fans	七扇	ななおうぎ しちおうぎ	*nana-ougi* *shichi-ougi*
8 folding fans	八扇	はちおうぎ	*hachi-ougi*
9 folding fans	九扇	きゅうおうぎ	*kyuu-ougi*
10 folding fans	十扇	じゅうおうぎ	*juu-ougi*

Irregularities or Special beyond Ten: none
Notes: none

往復—おうふく—*oufuku*

Japanese: おうふく
Romanized: *oufuku*
Pattern: 漢 ∅
Used with, or Means: round trips

1 round trip	一往復	いちおうふく	*ichi-oufuku*
2 round trips	二往復	におうふく	*ni-oufuku*
3 round trips	三往復	さんおうふく	*san-oufuku*
4 round trips	四往復	よんおうふく	*yon-oufuku*
5 round trips	五往復	ごおうふく	*go-oufuku*
6 round trips	六往復	ろくおうふく	*roku-oufuku*
7 round trips	七往復	ななおうふく / しちおうふく	*nana-oufuku* / *shichi-oufuku*
8 round trips	八往復	はちおうふく	*hachi-oufuku*
9 round trips	九往復	きゅうおうふく	*kyuu-oufuku*
10 round trips	十往復	じゅうおうふく	*juu-oufuku*

Irregularities or Special beyond Ten: none
Notes: none

Ω・オーム—おおむ—*oomu*

Japanese: オーム
Romanized: *oomu*
Pattern: 漢 ∅
Used with, or Means: ohms (S. I. symbol: Ω); 1 ohm = 1 m^2·kg·s^{-3}·A^{-2}

1 Ω	1 Ω・オーム	いちおおむ	*ichi-oomu*
2 Ω	2 Ω・オーム	におおむ	*ni-oomu*
3 Ω	3 Ω・オーム	さんおおむ	*san-oomu*
4 Ω	4 Ω・オーム	よんおおむ	*yon-oomu*
5 Ω	5 Ω・オーム	ごおおむ	*go-oomu*
6 Ω	6 Ω・オーム	ろくおおむ	*roku-oomu*
7 Ω	7 Ω・オーム	ななおおむ	*nana-oomu*
8 Ω	8 Ω・オーム	はちおおむ	*hachi-oomu*
9 Ω	9 Ω・オーム	きゅうおおむ	*kyuu-oomu*
10 Ω	10 Ω・オーム	じゅうおおむ	*juu-oomu*

Irregularities or Special beyond Ten: none
Notes: none

億—おく—*oku*

Japanese: おく
Romanized: *oku*
Pattern: 漢 ∅
Used with, or Means: 10,000 万 (*man*), 100 million, 10⁸

10⁸	一億	いちおく	*ichi-oku*
2×10⁸	二億	におく	*ni-oku*
3×10⁸	三億	さんおく	*san-oku*
4×10⁸	四億	よんおく	*yon-oku*
5×10⁸	五億	ごおく	*go-oku*
6×10⁸	六億	ろくおく	*roku-oku*
7×10⁸	七億	ななおく / しちおく	*nana-oku* / *shichi-oku*
8×10⁸	八億	はちおく	*hachi-oku*
9×10⁸	九億	きゅうおく	*kyuu-oku*
10⁹	十億	じゅうおく	*juu-oku*

Irregularities or Special beyond Ten:

10¹⁰	百億	ひゃくおく	*hyaku-oku*
10¹¹	千億	せんおく	*sen-oku*

Notes: 10⁸ is 100 000 000

オクターブ—*okutaabu*

Japanese: おくたあぶ
Romanized: *okutaabu*
Pattern: 漢 ∅
Used with, or Means: octaves

1 octave	1 オクターブ	いちおくたあぶ	*ichi-okutaabu*
2 octaves	2 オクターブ	におくたあぶ	*ni-okutaabu*
3 octaves	3 オクターブ	さんおくたあぶ	*san-okutaabu*
4 octaves	4 オクターブ	よんおくたあぶ	*yon-okutaabu*
5 octaves	5 オクターブ	ごおくたあぶ	*go-okutaabu*
6 octaves	6 オクターブ	ろくおくたあぶ	*roku-okutaabu*
7 octaves	7 オクターブ	ななおくたあぶ しちおくたあぶ	*nana-okutaabu* *shichi-okutaabu*
8 octaves	8 オクターブ	はちおくたあぶ	*hachi-okutaabu*
9 octaves	9 オクターブ	きゅうおくたあぶ	*kyuu-okutaabu*
10 octaves	10 オクターブ	じゅうおくたあぶ	*juu-okutaabu*

Irregularities or Special beyond Ten: none
Notes: none

桶—おけ—*oke*

Japanese: おけ
Romanized: *oke*
Pattern: 和 I
Used with, or Means: buckets, pails, bathtubs (浴槽 *yokusou*)

1 bucket	一桶	ひとおけ	*hito-oke*
2 buckets	二桶	ふたおけ	*futa-oke*
3 buckets	三桶	さんおけ	*san-oke*
4 buckets	四桶	よんおけ	*yon-oke*
5 buckets	五桶	ごおけ	*go-oke*
6 buckets	六桶	ろくおけ	*roku-oke*
7 buckets	七桶	ななおけ / しちおけ	*nana-oke* / *shichi-oke*
8 buckets	八桶	はちおけ	*hachi-oke*
9 buckets	九桶	きゅうおけ	*kyuu-oke*
10 buckets	十桶	じゅうおけ	*juu-oke*

Irregularities or Special beyond Ten: none
Notes: none

折り—おり—*ori*

Japanese: おり
Romanized: *ori*
Pattern: 和 I
Used with, or Means: small boxes of food (折り詰め *orizume*), catered boxed lunches (仕出し弁当 *shidashi bentou*); number of foldings, see also 箱 (*hako*)

1 boxed lunch	一折り	ひとおり	*hito-ori*
2 boxed lunches	二折り	ふたおり	*futa-ori*
3 boxed lunches	三折り	さんおり	*san-ori*
4 boxed lunches	四折り	よんおり	*yon-ori*
5 boxed lunches	五折り	ごおり	*go-ori*
6 boxed lunches	六折り	ろくおり	*roku-ori*
7 boxed lunches	七折り	ななおり / しちおり	*nana-ori* / *shichi-ori*
8 boxed lunches	八折り	はちおり	*hachi-ori*
9 boxed lunches	九折り	きゅうおり	*kyuu-ori*
10 boxed lunches	十折り	じゅうおり	*juu-ori*

Irregularities or Special beyond Ten: none
Notes: none

音—おん—*on*

Japanese: おん
Romanized: *on*
Pattern: 漢 ∅
Used with, or Means: sounds

1 sound	一音	いちおん	*ichi-on*
2 sounds	二音	におん	*ni-on*
3 sounds	三音	さんおん	*san-on*
4 sounds	四音	よんおん	*yon-on*
5 sounds	五音	ごおん	*go-on*
6 sounds	六音	ろくおん	*roku-on*
7 sounds	七音	ななおん / しちおん	*nana-on* / *shichi-on*
8 sounds	八音	はちおん	*hachi-on*
9 sounds	九音	きゅうおん	*kyuu-on*
10 sounds	十音	じゅうおん	*juu-on*

Irregularities or Special beyond Ten: none
Notes: none

oz—オンス—onsu

Japanese: オンス
Romanized: onsu
Pattern: 漢 ∅
Used with, or Means: ounces (symbol: oz), a unit of weight, about 28.34952 g

1 oz	1オンス	いちおんす	ichi-onsu
2 oz	2オンス	におんす	ni-onsu
3 oz	3オンス	さんおんす	san-onsu
4 oz	4オンス	よんおんす	yon-onsu
5 oz	5オンス	ごおんす	go-onsu
6 oz	6オンス	ろくおんす	roku-onsu
7 oz	7オンス	ななおんす	nana-onsu
8 oz	8オンス	はちおんす	hachi-onsu
9 oz	9オンス	きゅうおんす	kyuu-onsu
10 oz	10オンス	じゅうおんす	juu-onsu

Irregularities or Special beyond Ten: none
Notes: none

か・が—*Ka/Ga*
価—か—*ka*

Japanese: か
Romanized: *ka*
Pattern: 漢 K
Used with, or Means: valence (Physics)

1 valence	一価	いっか	*ik-ka*
2 valences	二価	にか	*ni-ka*
3 valences	三価	さんか	*san-ka*
4 valences	四価	よんか	*yon-ka*
5 valences	五価	ごか	*go-ka*
6 valences	六価	ろっか	*rok-ka*
7 valences	七価	ななか	*nana-ka*
8 valences	八価	はっか	*hak-ka*
9 valences	九価	きゅうか	*kyuu-ka*
10 valences	十価	じゅっか / じっか	*juk-ka* / *jik-ka*

Irregularities or Special beyond Ten:

100 valences	百価	ひゃっか	*hyak-ka*

Notes: none

日 — か — *ka*

Japanese: か・にち
Romanized: *ka/nichi*
Pattern: 和 IV
Used with, or Means: the days of the month, see also 日 (*hi*)

the 1st day	一日	ついたち	*tsuitachi*
the 2nd day	二日	ふつか	*futsu-ka*
the 3rd day	三日	みっか	*mik-ka*
the 4th day	四日	よっか	*yok-ka*
the 5th day	五日	いつか	*itsu-ka*
the 6th day	六日	むいか	*mui-ka*
the 7th day	七日	なのか	*nano-ka*
the 8th day	八日	ようか	*you-ka*
the 9th day	九日	ここのか	*kokono-ka*
the 10th day	十日	とおか	*too-ka*

Irregularities or Special beyond Ten:

the 11th day	十一日	じゅういちにち	*juu-ichi-nichi*
the 12th day	十二日	じゅうににち	*juu-ni-nichi*
the 13th day	十三日	じゅうさんにち	*juu-san-nichi*
the 14th day	十四日	じゅうよっか	*juu-yok-ka*
the 15th day	十五日	じゅうごにち	*juu-go-nichi*

the 16th day	十六日	じゅうろくにち	*juu-roku-nichi*
the 17th day	十七日	じゅうななにち	*juu-nana-nichi*
the 18th day	十八日	じゅうはちにち	*juu-hachi-nichi*
the 19th day	十九日	じゅうきゅうにち	*juu-kyuu-nichi*
the 20th day	二十日	<u>はつか</u> にじゅうにち	<u>*hatsuka*</u> *ni-juu-nichi*
the 21st day	二十一日	にじゅういちにち	*ni-juu-ichi-nichi*
the 22nd day	二十二日	にじゅうににち	*ni-juu-ni-nichi*
the 23rd day	二十三日	にじゅうさんにち	*ni-juu-san-nichi*
the 24th day	二十四日	<u>にじゅうよっか</u>	<u>*ni-juu-yok-ka*</u>
the 25th day	二十五日	にじゅうごにち	*ni-juu-go-nichi*
the 26th day	二十六日	にじゅうろくにち	*ni-juu-roku-nichi*
the 27th day	二十七日	にじゅうななにち	*ni-juu-nana-nichi*
the 28th day	二十八日	にじゅうはちにち	*ni-juu-hachi-nichi*
the 29th day	二十九日	にじゅうきゅうにち	*ni-juu-kyuu-nichi*
the 30th day	三十日 晦日	さんじゅうにち <u>みそか</u>	*san-juu-nichi* <u>*misoka*</u>
the 31st day	三十一日	さんじゅういちにち	*san-juu-ichi-nichi*

Notes: This set pinpoints an exact day, such as May 5. Use 日間 to count days. Notice that *the first day of the month* is irregular: *tsuitachi* as opposed to the *hito-ka* or *ichi-nichi* that one might expect.

第〇日—だい〇か・にち—*dai-○-nichi*

Japanese: だい〇か・だい〇にち
Romanized: *dai-○-ka / dai-○-nichi*
Pattern: 漢 ∅
Used with, or Means: the Nth day (unrelated to months)

the 1st day	第一日	だいいちにち	*dai-ichi-nichi*
the 2nd day	第二日	だいふつか	*dai-futsu-ka*
the 3rd day	第三日	だいみっか	*dai-mik-ka*
the 4th day	第四日	だいよっか	*dai-yok-ka*
the 5th day	第五日	だいいつか	*dai-itsu-ka*
the 6th day	第六日	だいむいか	*dai-mui-ka*
the 7th day	第七日	だいなのか	*dai-nano-ka*
the 8th day	第八日	だいようか	*dai-you-ka*
the 9th day	第九日	だいここのか	*dai-kokono-ka*
the 10th day	第十日	だいとおか	*dai-too-ka*

Irregularities or Special beyond Ten:

the 14th day	第十四日	だいじゅうよっか	*dai-juu-yok-ka*
the 24th day	第二十四日	だいにじゅうよっか	*dai-ni-juu-yok-ka*

Notes: none

日間—かかん—ka-kan

Japanese: かかん・にちかん
Romanized: *ka-kan/nichi-kan*
Pattern: 和 IV
Used with, or Means: number of days

1 day	一日	いちにち	*ichi-nichi*
2 days	二日間	ふつかかん	*futsu-ka-kan*
3 days	三日間	みっかかん	*mik-ka-kan*
4 days	四日間	よっかかん	*yok-ka-kan*
5 days	五日間	いつかかん	*itsu-ka-kan*
6 days	六日間	むいかかん	*mui-ka-kan*
7 days	七日間	なのかかん	*nano-ka-kan*
8 days	八日間	ようかかん	*you-ka-kan*
9 days	九日間	ここのかかん	*kokono-ka-kan*
10 days	十日間	とおかかん	*too-ka-kan*

Irregularities or Special beyond Ten:

11 days	十一日間	じゅういちにちかん	*juu-ichi-nichi-kan*
14 days	十四日間	じゅうよっかかん	*juu-yok-ka-kan*
20 days	二十日間	はつかかん	*hatsuka-kan*
24 days	二十四日間	にじゅうよっか	*ni-juu-yok-ka-kan*

Notes: Use this to count the number of days. Notice that *one day* is irregular: just *ichi-nich* as opposed to the *tsuitachi-kan* or *ichi-nichi-kan* that one might expect.

架—か—*ka*

Japanese: か
Romanized: *ka*
Pattern: 漢 K
Used with, or Means: folding screens (屏風 *byoubu*), framed pictures; frames

1 folding screen	一架	いっか	<u>*ik-ka*</u>
2 folding screens	二架	にか	*ni-ka*
3 folding screens	三架	さんか	*san-ka*
4 folding screens	四架	よんか	*yon-ka*
5 folding screens	五架	ごか	*go-ka*
6 folding screens	六架	<u>ろっか</u>	<u>*rok-ka*</u>
7 folding screens	七架	ななか	*nana-ka*
8 folding screens	八架	<u>はっか</u>	<u>*hak-ka*</u>
9 folding screens	九架	きゅうか	*kyuu-ka*
10 folding screens	十架	<u>じゅっか</u> <u>じっか</u>	<u>*juk-ka*</u> <u>*jik-ka*</u>

Irregularities or Special beyond Ten:

100 folding screens	百架	<u>ひゃっか</u>	<u>*hyak-ka*</u>

Notes: none

箇 — か — *ka*

Japanese: か
Romanized: *ka*
Pattern: 漢 K
Used with, or Means: items, places, units of time, see also 個 (*ko*)

1 unit	一箇	いっか	*ik-ka*
2 units	二箇	にか	*ni-ka*
3 units	三箇	さんか	*san-ka*
4 units	四箇	よんか	*yon-ka*
5 units	五箇	ごか	*go-ka*
6 units	六箇	ろっか	*rok-ka*
7 units	七箇	ななか	*nana-ka*
8 units	八箇	はっか / はちか	*hak-ka* / *hachi-ka*
9 units	九箇	きゅうか	*kyuu-ka*
10 units	十箇	じゅっか / じっか	*juk-ka* / *jik-ka*

Irregularities or Special beyond Ten:

100 units	百箇	ひゃっか	*hyak-ka*

Notes: none

荷 — か — *ka*

Japanese: か
Romanized: *ka*
Pattern: 漢 K
Used with, or Means: loads, burdens; tubs, buckets (桶 *oke*)

1 load	一荷	いっか	*ik-ka*
2 loads	二荷	にか	*ni-ka*
3 loads	三荷	さんか	*san-ka*
4 loads	四荷	よんか	*yon-ka*
5 loads	五荷	ごか	*go-ka*
6 loads	六荷	ろっか	*rok-ka*
7 loads	七荷	ななか	*nana-ka*
8 loads	八荷	はっか / はちか	*hak-ka* / *hachi-ka*
9 loads	九荷	きゅうか	*kyuu-ka*
10 loads	十荷	じゅっか / じっか	*juk-ka* / *jik-ka*

Irregularities or Special beyond Ten:

100 loads	百荷	ひゃっか	*hyak-ka*

Notes: none

菓 — か — *ka*

Japanese: か
Romanized: *ka*
Pattern: 漢 K
Used with, or Means: fruits

1 fruit	一菓	いっか	*ik-ka*
2 fruits	二菓	にか	*ni-ka*
3 fruits	三菓	さんか	*san-ka*
4 fruits	四菓	よんか	*yon-ka*
5 fruits	五菓	ごか	*go-ka*
6 fruits	六菓	ろっか	*rok-ka*
7 fruits	七菓	ななか	*nana-ka*
8 fruits	八菓	はっか / はちか	*hak-ka* / *hachi-ka*
9 fruits	九菓	きゅうか	*kyuu-ka*
10 fruits	十菓	じゅっか / じっか	*juk-ka* / *jik-ka*

Irregularities or Special beyond Ten:

100 fruits	百菓	ひゃっか	*hyak-ka*

Notes: none

課—か—ka

Japanese: か
Romanized: *ka*
Pattern: 漢 K
Used with, or Means: chapters; lessons; sections; departments, divisions

1 chapter	一課	いっか	*ik-ka*
2 chapters	二課	にか	*ni-ka*
3 chapters	三課	さんか	*san-ka*
4 chapters	四課	よんか	*yon-ka*
5 chapters	五課	ごか	*go-ka*
6 chapters	六課	ろっか	*rok-ka*
7 chapters	七課	ななか	*nana-ka*
8 chapters	八課	はっか / はちか	*hak-ka* / *hachi-ka*
9 chapters	九課	きゅうか	*kyuu-ka*
10 chapters	十課	じゅっか / じっか	*juk-ka* / *jik-ka*

Irregularities or Special beyond Ten:

100 chapters	百課	ひゃっか	*hyak-ka*

Notes: none

顆・果 — か — *ka*

Japanese: か
Romanized: *ka*
Pattern: 漢 K
Used with, or Means: fruits, jewels, small round things, hanko (name stamps/seals), see also 粒 (*tsubu*), see also 玉 (*tama*)

1 jewel	一顆・果	いっか	*ik-ka*
2 jewels	二顆・果	にか	*ni-ka*
3 jewels	三顆・果	さんか	*san-ka*
4 jewels	四顆・果	よんか	*yon-ka*
5 jewels	五顆・果	ごか	*go-ka*
6 jewels	六顆・果	ろっか	*rok-ka*
7 jewels	七顆・果	ななか	*nana-ka*
8 jewels	八顆・果	はっか / はちか	*hak-ka* / *hachi-ka*
9 jewels	九顆・果	きゅうか	*kyuu-ka*
10 jewels	十顆・果	じゅっか / じっか	*juk-ka* / *jik-ka*

Irregularities or Special beyond Ten:

100 jewels	百顆・果	ひゃっか	*hyak-ka*

Notes: none

河—が—*ga*

Japanese: が
Romanized: *ga*
Pattern: 漢 ∅

Used with, or Means: rivers, streams, see also 河川 (*kasen*), see also 本 (*hon*)

1 river	一河	いちが	*ichi-ga*
2 rivers	二河	にが	*ni-ga*
3 rivers	三河	さんが	*san-ga*
4 rivers	四河	よんが	*yon-ga*
5 rivers	五河	ごが	*go-ga*
6 rivers	六河	ろくが	*roku-ga*
7 rivers	七河	ななが	*nana-ga*
8 rivers	八河	はちが	*hachi-ga*
9 rivers	九河	きゅうが	*kyuu-ga*
10 rivers	十河	じゅうが	*juu-ga*

Irregularities or Special beyond Ten: none
Notes: none

カートン—*kaaton*

Japanese: かあとん
Romanized: *kaaton*
Pattern: 漢 K
Used with, or Means: cartons (milk, cigarettes)

1 carton	1 カートン	いっかあとん いちかあとん	*ik-kaaton* *ichi-kaaton*
2 cartons	2 カートン	にかあとん	*ni-kaaton*
3 cartons	3 カートン	さんかあとん	*san-kaaton*
4 cartons	4 カートン	よんかあとん	*yon-kaaton*
5 cartons	5 カートン	ごかあとん	*go-kaaton*
6 cartons	6 カートン	ろっかあとん ろくかあとん	*rok-kaaton* *roku-kaaton*
7 cartons	7 カートン	ななかあとん	*nana-kaaton*
8 cartons	8 カートン	はっかあとん はちかあとん	*hak-kaaton* *hachi-kaaton*
9 cartons	9 カートン	きゅうかあとん	*kyuu-kaaton*
10 cartons	10 カートン	じゅっかあとん じっかあとん	*juk-kaaton* *jik-kaaton*

Irregularities or Special beyond Ten:

100 cartons	100 カートン	ひゃっかあとん ひゃくかあとん	*hyak-kaaton* *hyaku-kaaton*

Notes: none

回 — かい — *kai*

Japanese: かい
Romanized: *kai*
Pattern: 漢 K
Used with, or Means: number of times, games, matches; innings, see also 度 (*do*), see also 遍 (*hen*), see also イニング (*iningu*)

1 time / once	一回	いっかい	*ik-kai*
2 times / twice	二回	にかい	*ni-kai*
3 times / thrice	三回	さんかい	*san-kai*
4 times	四回	よんかい	*yon-kai*
5 times	五回	ごかい	*go-kai*
6 times	六回	ろっかい	*rok-kai*
7 times	七回	ななかい	*nana-kai*
8 times	八回	はっかい / はちかい	*hak-kai* / *hachi-kai*
9 times	九回	きゅうかい	*kyuu-kai*
10 times	十回	じゅっかい / じっかい	*juk-kai* / *jik-kai*

Irregularities or Special beyond Ten:

100 times	百回	ひゃっかい	*hyak-kai*

Notes: none

貝 — かい — *kai*

Japanese: かい
Romanized: *kai*
Pattern: 和 I-K
Used with, or Means: doses of ointment 膏薬 (*kouyaku*), see also 貝 (*bai*)

1 dose	一貝	ひとかい	*hito-kai*
2 doses	二貝	ふたかい	*futa-kai*
3 doses	三貝	さんかい	*san-kai*
4 doses	四貝	よんかい	*yon-kai*
5 doses	五貝	ごかい	*go-kai*
6 doses	六貝	ろっかい	*rok-kai*
7 doses	七貝	ななかい	*nana-kai*
8 doses	八貝	はっかい / はちかい	*hak-kai* / *hachi-kai*
9 doses	九貝	きゅうかい	*kyuu-kai*
10 doses	十貝	じゅっかい / じっかい	*juk-kai* / *jik-kai*

Irregularities or Special beyond Ten:

100 doses	百貝	ひゃっかい	*hyak-kai*

Notes: In olden days, the healer would dip a small shell (hence 貝 *kai*) into the ointment to measure it out and apply it to the affected area.

海 — かい — *kai*

Japanese: かい
Romanized: *kai*
Pattern: 漢 K
Used with, or Means: (literary language) oceans, seas

1 sea	一海	いっかい	*ik-kai*
2 seas	二海	にかい	*ni-kai*
3 seas	三海	さんかい	*san-kai*
4 seas	四海	よんかい	*yon-kai*
5 seas	五海	ごかい	*go-kai*
6 seas	六海	ろっかい	*rok-kai*
7 seas	七海	ななかい	*nana-kai*
8 seas	八海	はっかい / はちかい	*hak-kai* / *hachi-kai*
9 seas	九海	きゅうかい	*kyuu-kai*
10 seas	十海	じゅっかい / じっかい	*juk-kai* / *jik-kai*

Irregularities or Special beyond Ten:

100 seas	百海	ひゃっかい	*hyak-kai*

Notes: Clearly, one could conceivably count 海 to infinity, but realistically, one would only count to a small number of them.

蓋—かい—*kai*

Japanese: かい
Romanized: *kai*
Pattern: 漢 K
Used with, or Means: hats, see also 蓋 (*gai*)

1 hat	一蓋	いっかい	*ik-kai*
2 hats	二蓋	にかい	*ni-kai*
3 hats	三蓋	さんかい	*san-kai*
4 hats	四蓋	よんかい	*yon-kai*
5 hats	五蓋	ごかい	*go-kai*
6 hats	六蓋	ろっかい	*rok-kai*
7 hats	七蓋	ななかい	*nana-kai*
8 hats	八蓋	はっかい / はちかい	*hak-kai* / *hachi-kai*
9 hats	九蓋	きゅうかい	*kyuu-kai*
10 hats	十蓋	じゅっかい / じっかい	*juk-kai* / *jik-kai*

Irregularities or Special beyond Ten:

100 hats	百蓋	ひゃっかい	*hyak-kai*

Notes: none

階—かい—*kai*

Japanese: かい
Romanized: *kai*
Pattern: 漢 K
Used with, or Means: floors, building stories

1st floor *or* 1 floor	一階	いっかい	ik-kai
2nd floor *or* 2 floors	二階	にかい	ni-kai
3rd floor *or* 3 floors	三階	さんがい	san-gai
4th floor *or* 4 floors	四階	よんかい	yon-kai
5th floor *or* 5 floors	五階	ごかい	go-kai
6th floor *or* 6 floors	六階	ろっかい	rok-kai
7th floor *or* 7 floors	七階	ななかい	nana-kai
8th floor *or* 8 floors	八階	はっかい / はちかい	hak-kai / hachi-kai
9th floor *or* 9 floors	九階	きゅうかい	kyuu-kai
10th floor *or* 10 floors	十階	じゅっかい / じっかい	juk-kai / jik-kai

Irregularities or Special beyond Ten:

13rd floor *or* 13 floors	十三階	じゅうさんがい	juu-san-gai
23rd floor *or* 23 floors	二十三階	にじゅうさんがい	ni-juu-san-gai
100th floor *or* 100 floors	百階	ひゃっかい	hyak-kai

Notes: Aside from following the 漢 K pattern, traditionally, 3 階 is *san-gai* rather than *san-kai*, though many consider *san-kai* okay. Due to inference and perhaps hypercorrection, some Japanese even say *yon-gai* instead of *yon-kai*, though *yon-kai* is correct and Japanese will likely correct you if you say *yon-gai*. Finally, any number ending in ~3 階 is ~*san-gai*, rather than ~*san-kai*.

垓—がい—*gai*

Japanese: がい
Romanized: *gai*
Pattern: 漢 ∅
Used with, or Means: 10,000 京 (*kei*), 100 quintillion, 10^{20}

10^{20}	一垓	いちがい	*ichi-gai*
2×10^{20}	二垓	にがい	*ni-gai*
3×10^{20}	三垓	さんがい	*san-gai*
4×10^{20}	四垓	よんがい	*yon-gai*
5×10^{20}	五垓	ごがい	*go-gai*
6×10^{20}	六垓	ろくがい	*roku-gai*
7×10^{20}	七垓	ななガい	*nana-gai*
8×10^{20}	八垓	はちがい	*hachi-gai*
9×10^{20}	九垓	きゅうがい	*kyuu-gai*
10^{21}	十垓	じゅうがい	*juu-gai*

Irregularities or Special beyond Ten:

10^{22}	百垓	ひゃくがい	*hyaku-gai*
10^{23}	千垓	せんがい	*sen-gai*

Notes: 10^{20} is 100 000 000 000 000 000 000

蓋—がい—*gai*

Japanese: がい
Romanized: *gai*
Pattern: 漢 ∅
Used with, or Means: lid-shaped objects such as bamboo hats, umbrellas (笠 *kasa*)

1 bamboo hat	一蓋	いちがい	*ichi-gai*
2 bamboo hats	二蓋	にがい	*ni-gai*
3 bamboo hats	三蓋	さんがい	*san-gai*
4 bamboo hats	四蓋	よんがい	*yon-gai*
5 bamboo hats	五蓋	ごがい	*go-gai*
6 bamboo hats	六蓋	ろくがい	*roku-gai*
7 bamboo hats	七蓋	なながい	*nana-gai*
8 bamboo hats	八蓋	はちがい	*hachi-gai*
9 bamboo hats	九蓋	きゅうがい	*kyuu-gai*
10 bamboo hats	十蓋	じゅうがい	*juu-gai*

Irregularities or Special beyond Ten: none
Notes: none

回忌—かいき—*kaiki*

Japanese: かいき
Romanized: *kaiki*
Pattern: 漢 K
Used with, or Means: death anniversaries

1 death anniversary	一回忌	いっかいき	*ik-kaiki*
2 death anniversaries	二回忌	にかいき	*ni-kaiki*
3 death anniversaries	三回忌	さんかいき	*san-kaiki*
4 death anniversaries	四回忌	よんかいき	*yon-kaiki*
5 death anniversaries	五回忌	ごかいき	*go-kaiki*
6 death anniversaries	六回忌	ろっかいき	*rok-kaiki*
7 death anniversaries	七回忌	ななかいき / しちかいき	*nana-kaiki* / *shichi-kaiki*
8 death anniversaries	八回忌	はっかいき / はちかいき	*hak-kaiki* / *hachi-kaiki*
9 death anniversaries	九回忌	きゅうかいき	*kyuu-kaiki*
10 death anniversaries	十回忌	じゅっかいき / じっかいき	*juk-kaiki* / *jik-kaiki*

Irregularities or Special beyond Ten:

100 death anniversaries	百回忌	ひゃっかいき	*hyak-kaiki*

Notes: none

階級—かいきゅう—*kaikyuu*

Japanese: かいきゅう
Romanized: *kaikyuu*
Pattern: 和 III-K or 漢 K
Used with, or Means: level

level 1	一階級	ひとかいきゅう いっかいきゅう	*hito-kaikyuu* *ik-kaikyuu*
level 2	二階級	ふたいきゅう にかいきゅう	*futa-kaikyuu* *ni-kaikyuu*
level 3	三階級	みかいきゅう さんかいきゅう	*mi-kaikyuu* *san-kaikyuu*
level 4	四階級	よかいきゅう よんかいきゅう	*yo-kaikyuu* *yon-kaikyuu*
level 5	五階級	ごかいきゅう	*go-kaikyuu*
level 6	六階級	ろっかいきゅう	*rok-kaikyuu*
level 7	七階級	ななかいきゅう	*nana-kaikyuu*
level 8	八階級	はっかいきゅう はちかいきゅう	*hak-kaikyuu* *hachi-kaikyuu*
level 9	九階級	きゅうかいきゅう	*kyuu-kaikyuu*
level 10	十階級	じゅっかいきゅう じっかいきゅう	*juk-kaikyuu* *jik-kaikyuu*

Irregularities or Special beyond Ten:

level 100	百階級	ひゃっかいきゅう	*hyak-kaikyuu*

Notes: none

回線—かいせん—*kaisen*

Japanese: かいせん
Romanized: *kaisen*
Pattern: 和 III-K or 漢 K
Used with, or Means: circuits (used in the telegraph/telephone, light-wave communications, and cable television industries)

1 circuit	一回線	ひとかいせん / いっかいせん	*hito-kaisen* / *ik-kaisen*
2 circuits	二回線	ふたかいせん / にかいせん	*futa-kaisen* / *ni-kaisen*
3 circuits	三回線	みかいせん / さんかいせん	*mi-kaisen* / *san-kaisen*
4 circuits	四回線	よかいせん / よんかいせん	*yo-kaisen* / *yon-kaisen*
5 circuits	五回線	ごかいせん	*go-kaisen*
6 circuits	六回線	ろっかいせん	*rok-kaisen*
7 circuits	七回線	ななかいせん	*nana-kaisen*
8 circuits	八回線	はっかいせん / はちかいせん	*hak-kaisen* / *hachi-kaisen*
9 circuits	九回線	きゅうかいせん	*kyuu-kaisen*
10 circuits	十回線	じゅっかいせん / じっかいせん	*juk-kaisen* / *jik-kaisen*

Irregularities or Special beyond Ten:

100 circuits	百回線	ひゃっかいせん	*hyak-kaisen*

Notes: none

海里・浬 —かいり— *kairi*

Japanese: かいり
Romanized: *kairi*
Pattern: 漢 K
Used with, or Means: nautical miles, around 6,076 ft/1,852 m, (symbol NM)

1 NM	一海里・浬	いっかいり / いちかいり	*ik-kairi* / *ichi-kairi*
2 NM	二海里・浬	にかいり	*ni-kairi*
3 NM	三海里・浬	さんかいり	*san-kairi*
4 NM	四海里・浬	よんかいり	*yon-kairi*
5 NM	五海里・浬	ごかいり	*go-kairi*
6 NM	六海里・浬	ろっかいり	*rok-kairi*
7 NM	七海里・浬	ななかいり	*nana-kairi*
8 NM	八海里・浬	はっかいり / はちかいり	*hak-kairi* / *hachi-kairi*
9 NM	九海里・浬	きゅうかいり	*kyuu-kairi*
10 NM	十海里・浬	じゅっかいり / じっかいり	*juk-kairi* / *jik-kairi*

Irregularities or Special beyond Ten:

100 nautical miles	百海里・浬	ひゃっかいり / ひゃくかいり	*hyak-kairi* / *hyaku-kairi*

Notes: none

角 — かく — *kaku*

Japanese: かく
Romanized: *kaku*
Pattern: 漢 K
Used with, or Means: angles

1 angle	一角	いっかく	*ik-kaku*
2 angles	二角	にかく	*ni-kaku*
3 angles	三角	さんかく	*san-kaku*
4 angles	四角	よんかく しかく	*yon-kaku* *shi-kaku*
5 angles	五角	ごかく	*go-kaku*
6 angles	六角	ろっかく	*rok-kaku*
7 angles	七角	ななかく	*nana-kaku*
8 angles	八角	はっかく はちかく	*hak-kaku* *hachi-kaku*
9 angles	九角	きゅうかく	*kyuu-kaku*
10 angles	十角	じゅっかく じっかく	*juk-kaku* *jik-kaku*

Irregularities or Special beyond Ten:

100 angles	百角	ひゃっかく	*hyak-kaku*

Notes: This counter is structurally and phonologically indistinguishable from the words for the various shapes: *sankaku* means *triangle* as well as *three angles*. Similarly, *rokkaku* means both *hexagon* and *six angles*.

The term *shikaku* means *square*, whereas *yonkaku* would mean *four angles*.

画 — かく — *kaku*

Japanese: かく
Romanized: *kaku*
Pattern: 漢 K
Used with, or Means: the number of strokes in a *kanji*, kana, or letter, see also 区 (*ku*)

1 stroke	一画	いっかく	*ik-kaku*
2 strokes	二画	にかく	*ni-kaku*
3 strokes	三画	さんかく	*san-kaku*
4 strokes	四画	よんかく	*yon-kaku*
5 strokes	五画	ごかく	*go-kaku*
6 strokes	六画	ろっかく	*rok-kaku*
7 strokes	七画	ななかく	*nana-kaku*
8 strokes	八画	はっかく / はちかく	*hak-kaku* / *hachi-kaku*
9 strokes	九画	きゅうかく	*kyuu-kaku*
10 strokes	十画	じゅっかく / じっかく	*juk-kaku* / *jik-kaku*

Irregularities or Special beyond Ten:

100 strokes	百画	ひゃっかく	*hyak-kaku*

Notes: Clearly, one could conceivably count 画 to infinity, but realistically, one would only count to 48 of them: 龘 (トウ *tou*), which means *the appearance of a dragon walking*, and is the *kanji* with the most strokes.

龘

61

郭 — かく — *kaku*

Japanese: かく
Romanized: *kaku*
Pattern: 漢 K
Used with, or Means: enclosures, the grounds within the surrounding walls

1 enclosure	一郭	いっかく	*ik-kaku*
2 enclosures	二郭	にかく	*ni-kaku*
3 enclosures	三郭	さんかく	*san-kaku*
4 enclosures	四郭	よんかく	*yon-kaku*
5 enclosures	五郭	ごかく	*go-kaku*
6 enclosures	六郭	ろっかく	*rok-kaku*
7 enclosures	七郭	ななかく	*nana-kaku*
8 enclosures	八郭	はっかく / はちかく	*hak-kaku* / *hachi-kaku*
9 enclosures	九郭	きゅうかく	*kyuu-kaku*
10 enclosures	十郭	じゅっかく / じっかく	*juk-kaku* / *jik-kaku*

Irregularities or Special beyond Ten:

100 enclosures	百郭	ひゃっかく	*hyak-kaku*

Notes: none

岳 — がく — *gaku*

Japanese: がく
Romanized: *gaku*
Pattern: 漢 Ø
Used with, or Means: (polite) number of climbs or scenic spots on famous mountains

1 climb	一岳	いちがく	*ichi-gaku*
2 climbs	二岳	にがく	*ni-gaku*
3 climbs	三岳	さんがく	*san-gaku*
4 climbs	四岳	よんがく	*yon-gaku*
5 climbs	五岳	ごがく	*go-gaku*
6 climbs	六岳	ろくがく	*roku-gaku*
7 climbs	七岳	ななงがく	*nana-gaku*
8 climbs	八岳	はちがく	*hachi-gaku*
9 climbs	九岳	きゅうがく	*kyuu-gaku*
10 climbs	十岳	じゅうがく	*juu-gaku*

Irregularities or Special beyond Ten: none
Notes: 四岳 (*shigaku*, also written as 四嶽), is a mountain in China.

楽節—がくせつ—*gakusetsu*

Japanese: がくせつ
Romanized: *gakusetsu*
Pattern: 漢 Ø
Used with, or Means: musical passages, sections

1 musical passage	一楽節	いちがくせつ	*ichi-gakusetsu*
2 musical passages	二楽節	にがくせつ	*ni-gakusetsu*
3 musical passages	三楽節	さんがくせつ	*san-gakusetsu*
4 musical passages	四楽節	よんがくせつ	*yon-gakusetsu*
5 musical passages	五楽節	ごがくせつ	*go-gakusetsu*
6 musical passages	六楽節	ろくがくせつ	*roku-gakusetsu*
7 musical passages	七楽節	ななかくせつ	*nana-gakusetsu*
8 musical passages	八楽節	はちがくせつ	*hachi-gakusetsu*
9 musical passages	九楽節	きゅうがくせつ	*kyuu-gakusetsu*
10 musical passages	十楽節	じゅうがくせつ	*juu-gakusetsu*

Irregularities or Special beyond Ten: none
Notes: none

学年—がくねん—*gakunen*

Japanese: がくねん
Romanized: *gakunen*
Pattern: 漢 ∅
Used with, or Means: school years

1 school year	一学年	いちがくねん	*ichi-gakunen*
2 school years	二学年	にがくねん	*ni-gakunen*
3 school years	三学年	さんがくねん	*san-gakunen*
4 school years	四学年	よんがくねん	*yon-gakunen*
5 school years	五学年	ごがくねん	*go-gakunen*
6 school years	六学年	ろくがくねん	*roku-gakunen*
7 school years	七学年	なながくねん	*nana-gakunen*
8 school years	八学年	はちがくねん	*hachi-gakunen*
9 school years	九学年	きゅうがくねん	*kyuu-gakunen*
10 school years	十学年	じゅうがくねん	*juu-gakunen*

Irregularities or Special beyond Ten: none

Notes: Clearly, one could conceivably count 学年 to infinity, but realistically, one would only count up to about 12 or 16 of them.

片・片ら—かけ（ら）—*kake*

Japanese: かけ
Romanized: *kake*
Pattern: 和 II-K or 漢 K
Used with, or Means: shards; slices of bread; pats of butter; cloves of garlic, lily bulbs, see also 片 (*hen*)

1 bulb	一片・片ら	ひとかけ（ら）	*hito-kake(ra)*
2 bulbs	二片・片ら	ふたかけ（ら）	*futa-kake(ra)*
3 bulbs	三片・片ら	さんかけ（ら） みかけ（ら）	*san-kake(ra)* *mi-kakera(ra)*
4 bulbs	四片・片ら	よんかけ（ら）	*yon-kake(ra)*
5 bulbs	五片・片ら	ごかけ（ら）	*go-kake(ra)*
6 bulbs	六片・片ら	ろっかけ（ら）	*rok-kake(ra)*
7 bulbs	七片・片ら	ななかけ（ら）	*nana-kake(ra)*
8 bulbs	八片・片ら	はっかけ（ら） はちかけ（ら）	*hak-kake(ra)* *hachi-kake(ra)*
9 bulbs	九片・片ら	きゅうかけ（ら）	*kyuu-kake(ra)*
10 bulbs	十片・片ら	じゅっかけ（ら） じっかけ（ら）	*juk-kake(ra)* *jik-kake(ra)*

Irregularities or Special beyond Ten:

100 bulbs	百片・片ら	ひゃっかけ（ら）	*hyak-kake(ra)*

Notes: none

掛け—かけ—*kake*

Japanese: かけ
Romanized: *kake*
Pattern: 和 I-K
Used with, or Means: collars (襟 *eri*), strings (弦 *gen*)

1 string	一掛け	ひとかけ	hito-kake
2 strings	二掛け	ふたかけ	futa-kake
3 strings	三掛け	さんかけ	san-kake
4 strings	四掛け	よんかけ	yon-kake
5 strings	五掛け	ごかけ	go-kake
6 strings	六掛け	ろっかけ	rok-kake
7 strings	七掛け	ななかけ	nana-kake
8 strings	八掛け	はっかけ / はちかけ	hak-kake / hachi-kake
9 strings	九掛け	きゅうかけ	kyuu-kake
10 strings	十掛け	じゅっかけ / じっかけ	juk-kake / jik-kake

Irregularities or Special beyond Ten:

100 strings	百掛け	ひゃっかけ	hyak-kake

Notes: none

掛け—かけ—*kake*

Japanese: かけ
Romanized: *kake*
Pattern: 漢 K
Used with, or Means: rate or percentage of a transaction price (symbol: %)

1%	一掛け	いっかけ	*ik-kake*
2%	二掛け	にかけ	*ni-kake*
3%	三掛け	さんかけ	*san-kake*
4%	四掛け	よんかけ	*yon-kake*
5%	五掛け	ごかけ	*go-kake*
6%	六掛け	ろっかけ	*rok-kake*
7%	七掛け	ななかけ / なながけ	*nana-kake* / *nana-gake*
8%	八掛け	はっかけ / はちかけ	*hak-kake* / *hachi-kake*
9%	九掛け	きゅうかけ	*kyuu-kake*
10%	十掛け	じゅっかけ / じっかけ	*juk-kake* / *jik-kake*

Irregularities or Special beyond Ten:

100%	百掛け	ひゃっかけ	*hyak-kake*

Notes: none

懸け—かけ—*kake*

Japanese: かけ
Romanized: *kake*
Pattern: 和 I-K
Used with, or Means: the number of suitcase bags hanging on one's shoulder

1 bag	一懸け	ひとかけ	*hito-kake*
2 bags	二懸け	ふたかけ	*futa-kake*
3 bags	三懸け	さんかけ	*san-kake*
4 bags	四懸け	よんかけ	*yon-kake*
5 bags	五懸け	ごかけ	*go-kake*
6 bags	六懸け	ろっかけ	*rok-kake*
7 bags	七懸け	ななかけ	*nana-kake*
8 bags	八懸け	はっかけ / はちかけ	*hak-kake* / *hachi-kake*
9 bags	九懸け	きゅうかけ	*kyuu-kake*
10 bags	十懸け	じゅっかけ / じっかけ	*juk-kake* / *jik-kake*

Irregularities or Special beyond Ten:

100 bags	百懸け	ひゃっかけ	*hyak-kake*

Notes: none

籠・篭—かご—*kago*

Japanese: かご
Romanized: *kago*
Pattern: 和 I-K
Used with, or Means: baskets, fruits

1 basket	一籠・篭	ひとかご	*hito-kago*
2 baskets	二籠・篭	ふたかご	*futa-kago*
3 baskets	三籠・篭	さんかご	*san-kago*
4 baskets	四籠・篭	よんかご	*yon-kago*
5 baskets	五籠・篭	ごかご	*go-kago*
6 baskets	六籠・篭	ろっかご	*rok-kago*
7 baskets	七籠・篭	ななかご	*nana-kago*
8 baskets	八籠・篭	はっかご はちかご	*hak-kago* *hachi-kago*
9 baskets	九籠・篭	きゅうかご	*kyuu-kago*
10 baskets	十籠・篭	じゅっかご じっかご	*juk-kago* *jik-kago*

Irregularities or Special beyond Ten:

100 baskets	百籠・篭	ひゃっかご ひゃくかご	*hyak-kago* *hyaku-kago*

Notes: none

ヶ国 — かこく — *ka-koku*

Japanese: かこく
Romanized: *ka-koku*
Pattern: 漢 K
Used with, or Means: countries

1 country	一ヶ国	いっかこく	*ik-ka-koku*
2 countries	二ヶ国	にかこく	*ni-ka-koku*
3 countries	三ヶ国	さんかこく	*san-ka-koku*
4 countries	四ヶ国	よんかこく	*yon-ka-koku*
5 countries	五ヶ国	ごかこく	*go-ka-koku*
6 countries	六ヶ国	ろっかこく	*rok-ka-koku*
7 countries	七ヶ国	ななかこく	*nana-ka-koku*
8 countries	八ヶ国	はっかこく はちかこく	*hak-ka-koku* *hachi-ka-koku*
9 countries	九ヶ国	きゅうかこく	*kyuu-ka-koku*
10 countries	十ヶ国	じゅっかこく じっかこく	*juk-ka-koku* *jik-ka-koku*

Irregularities or Special beyond Ten:

100 countries	百ヶ国	ひゃっかこく	*hyak-ka-koku*

Notes: see ヶ月.

ヶ国語—かこくご—*ka-kokugo*

Japanese: かこくご
Romanized: *ka-kokugo*
Pattern: 漢 K
Used with, or Means: (national) languages

1 language	一ヶ国語	いっかこくご	*ik-ka-koku-go*
2 languages	二ヶ国語	にかこくご	*ni-ka-koku-go*
3 languages	三ヶ国語	さんかこくご	*san-ka-koku-go*
4 languages	四ヶ国語	よんかこくご	*yon-ka-koku-go*
5 languages	五ヶ国語	ごかこくご	*go-ka-koku-go*
6 languages	六ヶ国語	ろっかこくご	*rok-ka-koku-go*
7 languages	七ヶ国語	ななかこくご	*nana-ka-koku-go*
8 languages	八ヶ国語	はっかこくご はちかこくご	*hak-ka-koku-go* *hachi-ka-koku-go*
9 languages	九ヶ国語	きゅうかこくご	*kyuu-ka-koku-go*
10 languages	十ヶ国語	じゅっかこくご じっかこくご	*juk-ka-koku-go* *jik-ka-koku-go*

Irregularities or Special beyond Ten:

100 languages	百ヶ国語	ひゃっかこくご	*hyak-ka-koku-go*

Notes: see ヶ月.

72

襲—かさね—*kasane*

Japanese: かさね
Romanized: *kasane*
Pattern: 和 I-K or 漢 K
Used with, or Means: sets of Japanese clothing, see also 重 (*e*), see also 重 (*juu*), see also 重ね (*kasane*)

1 set	一襲	いっかさね ひとかさね	*ik-kasane* *hito-kasane*
2 sets	二襲	にかさね ふたかさね	*ni-kasane* *futa-kasane*
3 sets	三襲	さんかさね	*san-kasane*
4 sets	四襲	よんかさね	*yon-kasane*
5 sets	五襲	ごかさね	*go-kasane*
6 sets	六襲	ろっかさね	*rok-kasane*
7 sets	七襲	ななかさね	*nana-kasane*
8 sets	八襲	はっかさね はちかさね	*hak-kasane* *hachi-kasane*
9 sets	九襲	きゅうかさね	*kyuu-kasane*
10 sets	十襲	じゅっかさね じっかさね	*juk-kasane* *jik-kasane*

Irregularities or Special beyond Ten:

100 sets	百襲	ひゃっかさね	*hyak-kasane*

Notes: none

重ね—かさね—*kasane*

Japanese: かさね
Romanized: *kasane*
Pattern: 和 I-K
Used with, or Means: *mochi* (鏡餅 *kagami mochi*), tiered boxes (重箱 *juubako*), layers of clothing, see also 重 (*e*), see also 重 (*juu*), see also 襲 (*kasane*)

1 layer	一重ね	ひとかさね	*hito-kasane*
2 layers	二重ね	ふたかさね	*futa-kasane*
3 layers	三重ね	さんかさね	*san-kasane*
4 layers	四重ね	よんかさね	*yon-kasane*
5 layers	五重ね	ごかさね	*go-kasane*
6 layers	六重ね	ろっかさね	*rok-kasane*
7 layers	七重ね	ななかさね	*nana-kasane*
8 layers	八重ね	はっかさね / はちかさね	*hak-kasane* / *hachi-kasane*
9 layers	九重ね	きゅうかさね	*kyuu-kasane*
10 layers	十重ね	じゅっかさね / じっかさね	*juk-kasane* / *jik-kasane*

Irregularities or Special beyond Ten:

100 layers	百重ね	ひゃっかさね / ひゃくかさね	*hyak-kasane* / *hyaku-kasane*

Notes: none

ヶ所 — かしょ — *ka-sho*

Japanese: かしょ
Romanized: *ka-sho*
Pattern: 漢 K
Used with, or Means: places (箇所 *kasho*)

1 place	一箇所	いっかしょ	*ik-ka-sho*
2 places	二箇所	にかしょ	*ni-ka-sho*
3 places	三箇所	さんかしょ	*san-ka-sho*
4 places	四箇所	よんかしょ	*yon-ka-sho*
5 places	五箇所	ごかしょ	*go-ka-sho*
6 places	六箇所	ろっかしょ	*rok-ka-sho*
7 places	七箇所	ななかしょ	*nana-ka-sho*
8 places	八箇所	はっかしょ / はちかしょ	*hak-ka-sho* / *hachi-ka-sho*
9 places	九箇所	きゅうかしょ	*kyuu-ka-sho*
10 places	十箇所	じゅっかしょ / じっかしょ	*juk-ka-sho* / *jik-ka-sho*

Irregularities or Special beyond Ten:

100 places	百箇所	ひゃっかしょ	*hyak-ka-sho*

Notes: see ヶ月.

ヶ条—かじょう—*ka-jou*

Japanese: かじょう
Romanized: *ka-jou*
Pattern: 漢 K
Used with, or Means: items, errors, articles (箇条 *kajou*)

1 item	一ヶ条	いっかじょう	*ik-ka-jou*
2 items	二ヶ条	にかじょう	*ni-ka-jou*
3 items	三ヶ条	さんかじょう	*san-ka-jou*
4 items	四ヶ条	よんかじょう	*yon-ka-jou*
5 items	五ヶ条	ごかじょう	*go-ka-jou*
6 items	六ヶ条	ろっかじょう	*rok-ka-jou*
7 items	七ヶ条	ななかじょう	*nana-ka-jou*
8 items	八ヶ条	はっかじょう / はちかじょう	*hak-ka-jou* / *hachi-ka-jou*
9 items	九ヶ条	きゅうかじょう	*kyuu-ka-jou*
10 items	十ヶ条	じゅっかじょう / じっかじょう	*juk-ka-jou* / *jik-ka-jou*

Irregularities or Special beyond Ten:

100 items	百ヶ条	ひゃっかじょう	*hyak-ka-jou*

Notes: see ヶ月.

頭—かしら—*kashira*

Japanese: かしら
Romanized: *kashira*
Pattern: 和 I-K
Used with, or Means: helmets, headgear worn by nobles in court dress (烏帽子 *eboshi*); masks, faces (面 *omote*)

1 helmet	一頭	ひとかしら	*hito-kashira*
2 helmets	二頭	ふたかしら	*futa-kashira*
3 helmets	三頭	さんかしら	*san-kashira*
4 helmets	四頭	よんかしら	*yon-kashira*
5 helmets	五頭	ごかしら	*go-kashira*
6 helmets	六頭	ろっかしら	*rok-kashira*
7 helmets	七頭	ななかしら	*nana-kashira*
8 helmets	八頭	はっかしら / はちかしら	*hak-kashira* / *hachi-kashira*
9 helmets	九頭	きゅうかしら	*kyuu-kashira*
10 helmets	十頭	じゅっかしら / じっかしら	*juk-kashira* / *jik-kashira*

Irregularities or Special beyond Ten:

100 helmets	百頭	ひゃっかしら	*hyak-kashira*

Notes: none

綛・桛 — かせ — *kase*

Japanese: かせ
Romanized: *kase*
Pattern: 和 I-K
Used with, or Means: threads wound on skeins, items wound on a frame

1 thread	一綛・桛	ひとかせ	*hito-kase*
2 threads	二綛・桛	ふたかせ	*futa-kase*
3 threads	三綛・桛	さんかせ	*san-kase*
4 threads	四綛・桛	よんかせ	*yon-kase*
5 threads	五綛・桛	ごかせ	*go-kase*
6 threads	六綛・桛	ろっかせ	*rok-kase*
7 threads	七綛・桛	ななかせ	*nana-kase*
8 threads	八綛・桛	はっかせ / はちかせ	*hak-kase* / *hachi-kase*
9 threads	九綛・桛	きゅうかせ	*kyuu-kase*
10 threads	十綛・桛	じゅっかせ / じっかせ	*juk-kase* / *jik-kase*

Irregularities or Special beyond Ten:

100 threads	百綛・桛	ひゃっかせ	*hyak-kase*

Notes: none

河川—かせん—*kasen*

Japanese: かせん
Romanized: *kasen*
Pattern: 漢 K
Used with, or Means: rivers, streams, see also 河 (*ga*), see also 本 (*hon*)

1 river	一河川	いっかせん	*ik-kasen*
2 rivers	二河川	にかせん	*ni-kasen*
3 rivers	三河川	さんかせん	*san-kasen*
4 rivers	四河川	よんかせん	*yon-kasen*
5 rivers	五河川	ごかせん	*go-kasen*
6 rivers	六河川	ろっかせん	*rok-kasen*
7 rivers	七河川	ななかせん	*nana-kasen*
8 rivers	八河川	はっかせん / はちかせん	*hak-kasen* / *hachi-kasen*
9 rivers	九河川	きゅうかせん	*kyuu-kasen*
10 rivers	十河川	じゅっかせん / じっかせん	*juk-kasen* / *jik-kasen*

Irregularities or Special beyond Ten:

100 rivers	百河川	ひゃっかせん	*hyak-kasen*

Notes: none

画素 — がそ — *gaso*

Japanese: がそ
Romanized: *gaso*
Pattern: 漢
Used with, or Means: image pixels

1 pixel	一画素	いちがそ	*ichi-gaso*
2 pixels	二画素	にがそ	*ni-gaso*
3 pixels	三画素	さんがそ	*san-gaso*
4 pixels	四画素	よんがそ	*yon-gaso*
5 pixels	五画素	ごがそ	*go-gaso*
6 pixels	六画素	ろくがそ	*roku-gaso*
7 pixels	七画素	ななγそ	*nana-gaso*
8 pixels	八画素	はちがそ	*hachi-gaso*
9 pixels	九画素	きゅうがそ	*kyuu-gaso*
10 pixels	十画素	じゅうがそ	*juu-gaso*

Irregularities or Special beyond Ten: none
Notes: none

家族—かぞく—*kazoku*

Japanese: かぞく
Romanized: *kazoku*
Pattern: 漢 K/和 I-K
Used with, or Means: families

1 family	一家族	いっかぞく ひとかぞく いちかぞく	*ik-kazoku* *hito-kazoku* *ichi-kazoku*
2 families	二家族	にかぞく ふたかぞく	*ni-kazoku* *futa-kazoku*
3 families	三家族	さんかぞく	*san-kazoku*
4 families	四家族	よんかぞく	*yon-kazoku*
5 families	五家族	ごかぞく	*go-kazoku*
6 families	六家族	ろっかぞく ろくかぞく	*rok-kazoku* *roku-kazoku*
7 families	七家族	ななかぞく	*nana-kazoku*
8 families	八家族	はっかぞく はちかぞく	*hak-kazoku* *hachi-kazoku*
9 families	九家族	きゅうかぞく	*kyuu-kazoku*
10 families	十家族	じゅっかぞく じっかぞく	*juk-kazoku* *jik-kazoku*

Irregularities or Special beyond Ten:

100 families	百家族	ひゃっかぞく	*hyak-kazoku*

Notes: none

方 — かた — *kata*

Japanese: かた
Romanized: *kata*
Pattern: 和 II-K
Used with, or Means: people, saints (honorific)

1 person	一方	ひとかた	*hito-kata*
2 people	二方	ふたかた	*futa-kata*
3 people	三方	さんかた みかた	*san-kata* *mi-kata*
4 people	四方	よんかた	*yon-kata*
5 people	五方	ごかた	*go-kata*
6 people	六方	ろっかた	*rok-kata*
7 people	七方	ななかた	*nana-kata*
8 people	八方	はっかた はちかた	*hak-kata* *hachi-kata*
9 people	九方	きゅうかた	*kyuu-kata*
10 people	十方	じゅっかた じっかた	*juk-kata* *jik-kata*

Irregularities or Special beyond Ten:

100 people	百方	ひゃっかた	*hyak-kata*

Notes: One may also use 方 to refer to the general times of day: 一方 is *morning*, 二方 is *noon/afternoon*, and 三方 is *night*.

肩—かた—*kata*

Japanese: かた
Romanized: *kata*
Pattern: 和 I-K
Used with, or Means: bundles of crab legs, a unit of volume of wood

1 bundle	一肩	ひとかた	*hito-kata*
2 bundles	二肩	ふたかた	*futa-kata*
3 bundles	三肩	さんかた	*san-kata*
4 bundles	四肩	よんかた	*yon-kata*
5 bundles	五肩	ごかた	*go-kata*
6 bundles	六肩	ろっかた	*rok-kata*
7 bundles	七肩	ななかた	*nana-kata*
8 bundles	八肩	はっかた / はちかた	*hak-kata* / *hachi-kata*
9 bundles	九肩	きゅうかた	*kyuu-kata*
10 bundles	十肩	じゅっかた / じっかた	*juk-kata* / *jik-kata*

Irregularities or Special beyond Ten:

100 bundles	百肩	ひゃっかた	*hyak-kata*

Notes: none

型—かた・がた—*kata*

Japanese: かた・がた
Romanized: *kata/gata*
Pattern: 漢 K/Ø
Used with, or Means: watch size, television/computer monitor screen size

size 1	一型	いっかた・いちがた	*ik-kata*/ *ichi-gata*
size 2	二型	にかた・にがた	*ni-kata*/ *ni-gata*
size 3	三型	さんかた・さんがた	*san-kata*/ *san-gata*
size 4	四型	よんかた・よんがた	*yon-kata*/ *yon-gata*
size 5	五型	ごかた・ごがた	*go-kata*/ *go-gata*
size 6	六型	ろっかた・ろくがた	*rok-kata*/ *roku-gata*
size 7	七型	ななかた・なながた	*nana-kata*/ *nana-gata*
size 8	八型	はっかた・はちがた はちかた	*hak-kata*/ *hachi-gata* *hachi-kata*
size 9	九型	きゅうかた・きゅうがた	*kyuu-kata*/ *kyuu-gata*
size 10	十型	じゅっかた・じゅうがた じっかた	*juk-kata*/ *juu-gata* *jik-kata*

Irregularities or Special beyond Ten:

size 100	百型	ひゃっかた・ひゃくがた	*hyak-kata*/ *hyaku-gata*

Notes: Japanese measure the 型 of a television screen or computer monitor in inches, despite being an almost fully metricated country. Thus a 10型 television screen is a 10-inch screen.

片食—かたけ—*katake*

Japanese: かたけ
Romanized: *katake*
Pattern: 和 I-K
Used with, or Means: meals per day (from the Edo period when two meals per day were usual)

| 一 meal | 1 片食 | ひとかたけ | *hito-katake* |
| 二 meals | 2 片食 | ふたかたけ | *futa-katake* |

Irregularities or Special beyond Ten: none
Notes: none

担げ—かたげ—*katage*

Japanese: かたげ
Romanized: *katage*
Pattern: 和 I-K
Used with, or Means: the number of trips one makes carrying loads (for example, filling up a bushel full of grapes, carrying it to a cart and going back out to the vineyard to fill it up again).

1 trip	一担げ	ひとかたげ	*hito-katage*
2 trips	二担げ	ふたかたげ	*futa-katage*
3 trips	三担げ	さんかたげ	*san-katage*
4 trips	四担げ	よんかたげ	*yon-katage*
5 trips	五担げ	ごかたげ	*go-katage*
6 trips	六担げ	ろっかたげ / ろくかたげ	*rok-katage* / *roku-katage*
7 trips	七担げ	ななかたげ	*nana-katage*
8 trips	八担げ	はっかたげ / はちかたげ	*hak-katage* / *hachi-katage*
9 trips	九担げ	きゅうかたげ	*kyuu-katage*
10 trips	十担げ	じゅっかたげ / じっかたげ	*juk-katage* / *jik-katage*

Irregularities or Special beyond Ten:

100 trips	百担げ	ひゃっかたげ	*hyak-katage*

Notes: none

片付 — かたづけ — *katazuke*

Japanese: かたづけ
Romanized: *katazuke*
Pattern: 和 I-K
Used with, or Means: a tidying up of a place

| 1 tidying | 一片付け | ひとかたづけ | *hito-katazuke* |

Irregularities or Special beyond Ten: none
Notes: This is one of several counters with just one instance.

塊—かたまり—*katamari*

Japanese: かたまり
Romanized: *katamari*
Pattern: 和 I-K
Used with, or Means: lumped objects

1 lumped object	一塊	ひとかたまり	*hito-katamari*
2 lumped objects	二塊	ふたかたまり	*futa-katamari*
3 lumped objects	三塊	さんかたまり	*san-katamari*
4 lumped objects	四塊	よんかたまり	*yon-katamari*
5 lumped objects	五塊	ごかたまり	*go-katamari*
6 lumped objects	六塊	ろっかたまり	*rok-katamari*
7 lumped objects	七塊	ななかたまり	*nana-katamari*
8 lumped objects	八塊	はっかたまり / はちかたまり	*hak-katamari* / *hachi-katamari*
9 lumped objects	九塊	きゅうかたまり	*kyuu-katamari*
10 lumped objects	十塊	じゅっかたまり / じっかたまり	*juk-katamari* / *jik-katamari*

Irregularities or Special beyond Ten:

100 lumped objects	百塊	ひゃっかたまり	*hyak-katamari*

Notes: none

括—かつ—*katsu*

Japanese: かつ
Romanized: *katsu*
Pattern: 漢 K
Used with, or Means: *katsu*, a unit of silk packaging

1 *katsu*	一括	いっかつ	*ik-katsu*
2 *katsu*	二括	にかつ	*ni-katsu*
3 *katsu*	三括	さんかつ	*san-katsu*
4 *katsu*	四括	よんかつ	*yon-katsu*
5 *katsu*	五括	ごかつ	*go-katsu*
6 *katsu*	六括	ろっかつ	*rok-katsu*
7 *katsu*	七括	ななかつ	*nana-katsu*
8 *katsu*	八括	はっかつ / はちかつ	*hak-katsu* / *hachi-katsu*
9 *katsu*	九括	きゅうかつ	*kyuu-katsu*
10 *katsu*	十括	じゅっかつ / じっかつ	*juk-katsu* / *jik-katsu*

Irregularities or Special beyond Ten:

100 *katsu*	百括	ひゃっかつ	*hyak-katsu*

Notes: none

月 — がつ — *gatsu*

Japanese: がつ
Romanized: *gatsu*
Pattern: 漢 Ø (see Notes)
Used with, or Means: the months of the year

January	一月	いちがつ	*Ichigatsu*
February	二月	にがつ	*Nigatsu*
March	三月	さんがつ	*Sangatsu*
April	四月	<u>し</u>がつ	<u>*Shigatsu*</u>
May	五月	ごがつ	*Gogatsu*
June	六月	ろくがつ	*Rokugatsu*
July	七月	<u>しち</u>がつ	<u>*Shichigatsu*</u>
August	八月	はちがつ	*Hachigatsu*
September	九月	<u>く</u>がつ	<u>*Kugatsu*</u>
October	十月	じゅうがつ	*Juugatsu*
November	十一月	じゅういちがつ	*Juuichigatsu*
December	十二月	じゅうにがつ	*Juunigatsu*

Irregularities or Special beyond Ten: none
Notes:

Japanese Months before January 1, 1873

Before Japan adopted the Gregorian calendar in 1873, it had its own set of months based on the lunar calendar. Although the 1st month of this calendar starts *in* January, it can start as late as the 3rd week thereof, so it is not accurate to equate them on a one-to-one basis.

    See the next page for a chart featuring those months and their meanings.

Mutsuki (1st month)	睦月	むつき	*Affection Month*
Kisaragi (2nd month) *Kinusaragi*	如月 衣更着	きさらぎ きぬさらぎ	*Clothes Changing*
Yayoi (3rd month)	弥生	やよい	*New Life, Spring*
Uzuki (4th month)	卯月	うづき	*U-Flower Month*
Satsuki (5th month) *Sanaetsuki*	皐月 早苗月	さつき さなえつき	*Early Rice- Planting Month*
Minazuki (6th month)	水無月	みなづき	*Water Month*
Fumizuki (7th month)	文月	ふみづき	*Book Month*
Hazuki (8th month)	葉月	はづき	*Month of Leaves*
Nagatsuki (9th month)	長月	ながつき	*Long Month*
Kannazuki (10th month) *Kaminazuki*	神無月	かんなづき かみなづき	*Month without Gods*
Shimotsuki (11th month)	霜月	しもつき	*Frost Month*
Shiwasu (12th month)	師走	しわす	*Running Priests*

    Many people misinterpret 水無月 (*minazuki*) as the *Month without Water* because 無 means *lack, without*. However, they only used that *kanji* in this case for its sound—the sound of a particle that means *of*, not *without*.

    Although it is possible that the same phenomenon is occurring in the name of 神無月 (*kannazuki*), that is probably not the case. The Japanese believe that all the gods leave their shrines and travel to Izumo in Shimane Prefecture for a yearly retreat-of-the-gods. It would make sense that this month is in fact the *month without gods* rather than the *month of gods*. In Izumo, however, they call the same month 神有月 or 神在月 (かみありづき *kamiarizuki*—the month *with* gods/month of the gods' presence).

    The 卯 of 卯月 is from 卯の花 (うのはな *u-no-hana*), a Deutzia flower. The last month, 師走, means *running priests*. This refers to all the running around they do busily preparing for the New Year's festivals.

ヶ月・箇月—かげつ—*ka-getsu*

Japanese: かげつ
Romanized: *ka-getsu*
Pattern: 漢 K
Used with, or Means: number of months, see also 月 (*tsuki*)

1 month	一ヶ月・箇月	<u>いっかげつ</u>	<u>*ik-ka-getsu*</u>
2 months	二ヶ月・箇月	にかげつ	*ni-ka-getsu*
3 months	三ヶ月・箇月	さんかげつ	*san-ka-getsu*
4 months	四ヶ月・箇月	よんかげつ	*yon-ka-getsu*
5 months	五ヶ月・箇月	ごかげつ	*go-ka-getsu*
6 months	六ヶ月・箇月	<u>ろっかげつ</u>	<u>*rok-ka-getsu*</u>
7 months	七ヶ月・箇月	ななかげつ	*nana-ka-getsu*
8 months	八ヶ月・箇月	<u>はっかげつ</u> <u>はちかげつ</u>	<u>*hak-ka-getsu*</u> <u>*hachi-ka-getsu*</u>
9 months	九ヶ月・箇月	きゅうかげつ	*kyuu-ka-getsu*
10 months	十ヶ月・箇月	<u>じゅっかげつ</u> <u>じっかげつ</u>	<u>*juk-ka-getsu*</u> <u>*jik-ka-getsu*</u>

Irregularities or Special beyond Ten:

100 months	百ヶ月・箇月	ひゃっかげつ	*hyak-ka-getsu*

Notes: Japanese normally abbreviate 箇 using a small katakana ヶ in modern Japanese. Alternatively, one can also see 個, hiragana か, small katakana ヵ and full-size katakana カ & ケ, although only か is similarly frequent.

学期—がっき—*gakki*

Japanese: がっき
Romanized: *gakki*
Pattern: 漢 Ø
Used with, or Means: terms, semesters

1 semester	一学期	いちがっき	*ichi-gakki*
2 semesters	二学期	にがっき	*ni-gakki*
3 semesters	三学期	さんがっき	*san-gakki*
4 semesters	四学期	よんがっき	*yon-gakki*
5 semesters	五学期	ごがっき	*go-gakki*
6 semesters	六学期	ろくがっき	*roku-gakki*
7 semesters	七学期	ななががっき	*nana-gakki*
8 semesters	八学期	はちがっき	*hachi-gakki*
9 semesters	九学期	きゅうがっき	*kyuu-gakki*
10 semesters	十学期	じゅうがっき	*juu-gakki*

Irregularities or Special beyond Ten: none

Notes: Clearly, one could conceivably count 学期 to infinity, but realistically, one would normally count two of them—first semester and second semester, and maybe a third if the school works on a trimester system.

学級—がっきゅう—*gakkyuu*

Japanese: がっきゅう
Romanized: *gakkyuu*
Pattern: 漢 Ø
Used with, or Means: grade levels (in pre-university education)

1 grade level	一学級	いちがっきゅう	*ichi-gakkyuu*
2 grade levels	二学級	にがっきゅう	*ni-gakkyuu*
3 grade levels	三学級	さんがっきゅう	*san-gakkyuu*
4 grade levels	四学級	よんがっきゅう	*yon-gakkyuu*
5 grade levels	五学級	ごがっきゅう	*go-gakkyuu*
6 grade levels	六学級	ろくがっきゅう	*roku-gakkyuu*
7 grade levels	七学級	ながっきゅう	*nana-gakkyuu*
8 grade levels	八学級	はちがっきゅう	*hachi-gakkyuu*
9 grade levels	九学級	きゅうがっきゅう	*kyuu-gakkyuu*
10 grade levels	十学級	じゅうがっきゅう	*juu-gakkyuu*

Irregularities or Special beyond Ten: none

Notes: Clearly, one could conceivably count 学級 to infinity, but realistically, one would only count up to six of them—first grade through sixth grade. In Japan, one's *gakkyuu* resets to one in middle (junior high) school (first through third), and again in high school (first through third).

角形—かっけい—*kakkei*

Japanese: かっけい
Romanized: *kakkei*
Pattern: 漢 K
Used with, or Means: N-sided figure, N-agon

	∅	一角形	いっかっけい	*ik-kakkei*
digon[1]		二角形	にかっけい	*ni-kakkei*
triangle		三角形	さんかっけい	*san-kakkei*
square		四角形	しかっけい / よんかっけい	*shi-kakkei* / *yon-kakkei*
pentagon		五角形	ごかっけい	*go-kakkei*
hexagon		六角形	ろっかっけい	*rok-kakkei*
heptagon		七角形	ななかっけい	*nana-kakkei*
octagon		八角形	はっかっけい / はちかっけい	*hak-kakkei* / *hachi-kakkei*
nonagon		九角形	きゅうかっけい	*kyuu-kakkei*
decagon		十角形	じゅっかっけい / じっかっけい	*juk-kakkei* / *jik-kakkei*

Irregularities or Special beyond Ten:

Hectogon	百角形	ひゃっかっけい	*hyak-kakkei*

Notes: Unlike 角 by itself, 角形 only refers to a shape and not to a number of angles. Thus, 三角形 can only mean *triangle*, but not *three angles*, and 六角形 can only mean *hexagon*, but not *six angles*. Furthermore, notice that 一角形 is not possible. 二角形 is not a possible shape in Euclidian geometry, but exists in spherical geometry.

Notice the special reading for square.

---

[1] A digon is a two-angled shape that can only exist on a sphere by drawing two lines from pole to pole. The shape formed by those two lines is a digon. The shape formed by those two lines is a digon.

カット—*katto*

Japanese: かっと
Romanized: *katto*
Pattern: 漢 K
Used with, or Means: cuts (as in a cake)

1 cut	1 カット	いっかっと / いちかっと	*ik-katto* / *ichi-katto*
2 cuts	2 カット	にかっと	*ni-katto*
2 cuts	3 カット	さんかっと	*san-katto*
4 cuts	4 カット	よんかっと	*yon-katto*
5 cuts	5 カット	ごかっと	*go-katto*
6 cuts	6 カット	ろっかっと / ろくかっと	*rok-katto* / *roku-katto*
7 cuts	7 カット	ななかっと	*nana-katto*
8 cuts	8 カット	はっかっと / はちかっと	*hak-katto* / *hachi-katto*
9 cuts	9 カット	きゅうかっと	*kyuu-katto*
10 cuts	10 カット	じゅっかっと / じっかっと	*juk-katto* / *jik-katto*

Irregularities or Special beyond Ten:

100 cuts	100 カット	ひゃっかっと / ひゃくかっと	*hyak-katto* / *hyaku-katto*

Notes: none

cup—カップ—*kappu*

Japanese: かっぷ
Romanized: *kappu*
Pattern: 漢 K
Used with, or Means: cups (symbol: cup), a unit of volume, about 0.23659 L

1 cup	1 カップ	いっかっぷ いちかっぷ	*ik-kappu* *ichi-kappu*
2 cups	2 カップ	にかっぷ	*ni-kappu*
3 cups	3 カップ	さんかっぷ	*san-kappu*
4 cups	4 カップ	よんかっぷ	*yon-kappu*
5 cups	5 カップ	ごかっぷ	*go-kappu*
6 cups	6 カップ	ろっかっぷ ろくかっぷ	*rok-kappu* *roku-kappu*
7 cups	7 カップ	ななかっぷ	*nana-kappu*
8 cups	8 カップ	はっかっぷ はちかっぷ	*hak-kappu* *hachi-kappu*
9 cups	9 カップ	きゅうかっぷ	*kyuu-kappu*
10 cups	10 カップ	じゅっかっぷ じっかっぷ	*juk-kappu* *jik-kappu*

Irregularities or Special beyond Ten:

100 cups	100 カップ	ひゃっかっぷ ひゃくかっぷ	*hyak- kappu* *hyaku-kappu*

Notes: none

ヶ年 — かねん — ka-nen

Japanese: かねん
Romanized: *ka-nen*
Pattern: 漢 K
Used with, or Means: number of years

1 year	一ヶ年	いっかねん	*ik-ka-nen*
2 years	二ヶ年	にかねん	*ni-ka-nen*
3 years	三ヶ年	さんかねん	*san-ka-nen*
4 years	四ヶ年	よんかねん	*yon-ka-nen*
5 years	五ヶ年	ごかねん	*go-ka-nen*
6 years	六ヶ年	ろっかねん	*rok-ka-nen*
7 years	七ヶ年	ななかねん	*nana-ka-nen*
8 years	八ヶ年	はっかねん / はちかねん	*hak-ka-nen* / *hachi-ka-ken*
9 years	九ヶ年	きゅうかねん	*kyuu-ka-nen*
10 years	十ヶ年	じゅっかねん / じっかねん	*juk-ka-nen* / *jik-ka-nen*

Irregularities or Special beyond Ten:

100 years	百ヶ年	ひゃっかねん	*hyak-ka-nen*

Notes: see ヶ月.

株—かぶ—*kabu*

Japanese: かぶ
Romanized: *kabu*
Pattern: 和 I-K
Used with, or Means: stocks, shares; plants, shrubs, trees, see also 株 (*shu*)

1 share	一株	ひとかぶ	*hito-kabu*
2 shares	二株	ふたかぶ	*futa-kabu*
3 shares	三株	さんかぶ	*san-kabu*
4 shares	四株	よんかぶ	*yon-kabu*
5 shares	五株	ごかぶ	*go-kabu*
6 shares	六株	ろっかぶ ろくかぶ	*rok-kabu* *roku-kabu*
7 shares	七株	ななかぶ	*nana-kabu*
8 shares	八株	はっかぶ はちかぶ	*hak-kabu* *hachi-kabu*
9 shares	九株	きゅうかぶ	*kyuu-kabu*
10 shares	十株	じゅっかぶ じっかぶ じゅうかぶ	*juk-kabu* *jik-kabu* *juu-kabu*

Irregularities or Special beyond Ten:

100 shares	百株	ひゃっかぶ ひゃくかぶ	*hyak-kabu* *hyaku-kabu*

Notes: none

花弁—かべん—*kaben*

Japanese: かべん
Romanized: *kaben*
Pattern: 漢 K
Used with, or Means: flower petals

1 petal	一花弁	いっかべん	*ik-kaben*
2 petals	二花弁	にかべん	*ni-kaben*
3 petals	三花弁	さんかべん	*san-kaben*
4 petals	四花弁	よんかべん	*yon-kaben*
5 petals	五花弁	ごかべん	*go-kaben*
6 petals	六花弁	ろっかべん ろくかべん	*rok-kaben* *roku-kaben*
7 petals	七花弁	ななかべん	*nana-kaben*
8 petals	八花弁	はっかべん はちかべん	*hak-kaben* *hachi-kaben*
9 petals	九花弁	きゅうかべん	*kyuu-kaben*
10 petals	十花弁	じゅっかべん じっかべん じゅうかべん	*juk-kaben* *jik-kaben* *juu-kaben*

Irregularities or Special beyond Ten:

100 petals	百花弁	ひゃっかべん ひゃくかべん	*hyak-kaben* *hyaku-kaben*

Notes: none

釜—かま—*kama*

Japanese: かま
Romanized: *kama*
Pattern: 和 III-K or 和 I-K
Used with, or Means: pots, kettles, cauldrons

1 pot	一釜	ひとかま	*hito-kama*
2 pots	二釜	ふたかま	*futa-kama*
3 pots	三釜	みかま さんかま	*mi-kama* *san-kama*
4 pots	四釜	よかま よんかま	*yo-kama* *yon-kama*
5 pots	五釜	ごかま	*go-kama*
6 pots	六釜	ろっかま ろくかま	*rok-kama* *roku-kama*
7 pots	七釜	ななかま	*nana-kama*
8 pots	八釜	はっかま はちかま	*hak-kama* *hachi-kama*
9 pots	九釜	きゅうかま	*kyuu-kama*
10 pots	十釜	じゅっかま じっかま	*juk-kama* *jik-kama*

Irregularities or Special beyond Ten:

100 pots	百釜	ひゃっかま ひゃくかま	*hyak-kama* *hyaku-kama*

Notes: none

叺—かます—*kamasu*

Japanese: かます
Romanized: *kamasu*
Pattern: 和 I-K
Used with, or Means: bags of straw

1 bag of straw	一叺	ひとかます	*hito-kamasu*
2 bags of straw	二叺	ふたかます	*futa-kamasu*
3 bags of straw	三叺	さんかます	*san-kamasu*
4 bags of straw	四叺	よんかます	*yon-kamasu*
5 bags of straw	五叺	ごかます	*go-kamasu*
6 bags of straw	六叺	ろっかます / ろくかます	*rok-kamasu* / *roku-kamasu*
7 bags of straw	七叺	ななかます	*nana-kamasu*
8 bags of straw	八叺	はっかます / ろくかます	*hak-kamasu* / *hachi-kamasu*
9 bags of straw	九叺	きゅうかます	*kyuu-kamasu*
10 bags of straw	十叺	じゅっかます / じっかます / じゅうかます	*juk-kamasu* / *jik-kamasu* / *juu-kamasu*

Irregularities or Special beyond Ten:

100 bags of straw	百叺	ひゃっかます / ひゃくかます	*hyak-kamasu* / *hyaku-kamasu*

Notes: none

瓶・甕—かめ—*kame*

Japanese: かめ
Romanized: *kame*
Pattern: 和 II-K or 和 I-K
Used with, or Means: jars, jugs, urns, vases, vats

1 jar	一瓶・甕	ひとかめ		*hito-kame*
2 jars	二瓶・甕	ふたかめ		*futa-kame*
3 jars	三瓶・甕	みかめ さんかめ		*mi-kame* *san-kame*
4 jars	四瓶・甕	よんかめ		*yon-kame*
5 jars	五瓶・甕	ごかめ		*go-kame*
6 jars	六瓶・甕	ろっかめ ろくかめ		*rok-kame* *roku-kame*
7 jars	七瓶・甕	ななかめ		*nana-kame*
8 jars	八瓶・甕	はっかめ はちかめ		*hak-kame* *hachi-kame*
9 jars	九瓶・甕	きゅうかめ		*kyuu-kame*
10 jars	十瓶・甕	じゅっかめ じっかめ		*juk-kame* *jik-kame*

Irregularities or Special beyond Ten:

100 jars	百瓶・甕	ひゃっかめ ひゃくかめ	*hyak-kame* *hyaku-kame*

Notes: none

日目 — かめ — *kame*

Japanese: かめ
Romanized: *kame*
Pattern: 和 IV-K
Used with, or Means: ordinal days (unrelated to months)

1st day	一日目	いちにちめ	*ichi-nichi-me*
2nd day	二日目	ふつかめ	*futa-ka-me*
3rd day	三日目	みっかめ	*mik-ka-me*
4th day	四日目	よっかめ	*yok-ka-me*
5th day	五日目	いつかめ	*go-ka-me*
6th day	六日目	むいかめ	*mui-ka-me*
7th day	七日目	なのかめ	*nano-ka-me*
8th day	八日目	ようかめ	*you-ka-me*
9th day	九日目	ここのかめ	*kokono-ka-me*
10th day	十日目	とおかめ	*too-ka-me*

Irregularities or Special beyond Ten:

14th day	十四日目	じゅうよっかめ	*juu-yok-ka-me*
24th day	二十四日目	にじゅうよっかめ	*ni-juu-yok-ka-me*
100th day	百日目	ひゃくにちめ	*hyaku-nichi-me*

Notes: none

柄・幹—から—*kara*

Japanese: から
Romanized: *kara*
Pattern: 漢 K
Used with, or Means: long, slender weapons such as spears, swords, and guns; formerly, a counter for containers with a folding fan pattern decoration, see also 柄 (*e*), see also 柄 (*hei*)

1 weapon	一柄・幹	いっから いちから	*ik-kara* *ichi-kara*
2 weapons	二柄・幹	にから	*ni-kara*
3 weapons	三柄・幹	さんから	*san-kara*
4 weapons	四柄・幹	よんから	*yon-kara*
5 weapons	五柄・幹	ごから	*go-kara*
6 weapons	六柄・幹	ろっから ろくから	*rok-kara* *roku-kara*
7 weapons	七柄・幹	ななから	*nana-kara*
8 weapons	八柄・幹	はっから はちから	*hak-kara* *hachi-kara*
9 weapons	九柄・幹	きゅうから	*kyuu-kara*
10 weapons	十柄・幹	じゅっから じっから	*juk-kara* *jik-kara*

Irregularities or Special beyond Ten:

100 weapons	百柄・幹	ひゃっから	*hyak-kara*

Notes: none

カラー—*karaa*

Japanese: からあ
Romanized: *karaa*
Pattern: 漢 K
Used with, or Means: colors, see also 色 (*iro*), see also 色 (*shoku*)

1 color	1 カラー	いっからあ / いちからあ	*ik-karaa* / *ichi-karaa*
2 colors	2 カラー	にからあ	*ni-karaa*
3 colors	3 カラー	さんからあ	*san-karaa*
4 colors	4 カラー	よんからあ	*yon-karaa*
5 colors	5 カラー	ごからあ	*go-karaa*
6 colors	6 カラー	ろっからあ / ろくからあ	*rok-karaa* / *roku-karaa*
7 colors	7 カラー	ななからあ	*nana-karaa*
8 colors	8 カラー	はっからあ / はちからあ	*hak-karaa* / *hachi-karaa*
9 colors	9 カラー	きゅうからあ	*kyuu-karaa*
10 colors	10 カラー	じゅっからあ / じっからあ	*juk-karaa* / *jik-karaa*

Irregularities or Special beyond Ten:

100 colors	100 カラー	ひゃっからあ / ひゃくからあ	*hyak-karaa* / *hyaku-karaa*

Notes: none

CD/kt—カラット—*karatto*

Japanese: カラット
Romanized: *karatto*
Pattern: 漢 K
Used with, or Means: carats (symbol: CD), unit of weight for weighing gemstones such as diamonds, 0.00706 oz/0.20001 g; karat (symbol: kt), a unit of purity of gold, $\text{kt} = 24 \left(\frac{\text{Mass of Pure Gold}}{\text{Total Mass of the Material Being Measured}} \right)$, see also 金 (*kin*)

1 CD/kt	1 カラット	いっからっと いちからっと	*ik-karatto* *ichi-karatto*
2 CD/kt	2 カラット	にからっと	*ni-karatto*
3 CD/kt	3 カラット	さんからっと	*san-karatto*
4 CD/kt	4 カラット	よんからっと	*yon-karatto*
5 CD/kt	5 カラット	ごからっと	*go-karatto*
6 CD/kt	6 カラット	ろっからっと ろくからっと	*rok-karatto* *roku-karatto*
7 CD/kt	7 カラット	ななからっと	*nana-karatto*
8 CD/kt	8 カラット	はっからっと はちからっと	*hak-karatto* *hachi-karatto*
9 CD/kt	9 カラット	きゅうからっと	*kyuu-karatto*
10 CD/kt	10 カラット	じゅっからっと じっからっと	*juk-karatto* *jik-karatto*

Irregularities or Special beyond Ten:

100 CD/kt	100 カラット	ひゃっからっと ひゃくからっと	*hyak-karatto* *hyaku-karatto*

Notes: none

cal—カロリー—*karorii*

Japanese: カロリー
Romanized: *karorii*
Pattern: 漢 K
Used with, or Means: calories (symbol: cal), the energy needed to increase the temperature of 1 g of water by 1° C; see Notes

1 cal	1 カロリー	いっかろりい いちかろりい	*ik-karorii* *ichi-karorii*
2 cal	2 カロリー	にかろりい	*ni-karorii*
3 cal	3 カロリー	さんかろりい	*san-karorii*
4 cal	4 カロリー	よんかろりい	*yon-karorii*
5 cal	5 カロリー	ごかろりい	*go-karorii*
6 cal	6 カロリー	ろっかろりい ろくかろりい	*rok-karorii* *roku-karorii*
7 cal	7 カロリー	ななかろりい	*nana-karorii*
8 cal	8 カロリー	はっかろりい はちかろりい	*hak-karorii* *hachi-karorii*
9 cal	9 カロリー	きゅうかろりい	*kyuu-karorii*
10 cal	10 カロリー	じゅっかろりい じっかろりい	*juk-karorii* *jik-karorii*

Irregularities or Special beyond Ten:

100 cal	100 カロリー	ひゃっかろりい ひゃくかろりい	*hyak-karorii* *hyaku-karorii*

Notes: There is a difference between a calorie (cal) and a Calorie (Cal). A Calorie is 1000 calories, and many refer to it as a kilocalorie or kcal, instead. Here, I chose to give just the basic measurement.

gal—ガロン—*garon*

Japanese: ガロン
Romanized: *garon*
Pattern: 漢 ∅
Used with, or Means: gallons (symbol: gal), a unit of volume, 128 fl oz/3.78541 L

1 gal	1 ガロン	いちがろん	*ichi-garon*
2 gal	2 ガロン	にがろん	*ni-garon*
3 gal	3 ガロン	さんがろん	*san-garon*
4 gal	4 ガロン	よんがろん	*yon-garon*
5 gal	5 ガロン	ごがろん	*go-garon*
6 gal	6 ガロン	ろくがろん	*roku-garon*
7 gal	7 ガロン	ななガろん	*nana-garon*
8 gal	8 ガロン	はちがろん	*hachi-garon*
9 gal	9 ガロン	きゅうがろん	*kyuu-garon*
10 gal	10 ガロン	じゅうがろん	*juu-garon*

Irregularities or Special beyond Ten: none
Notes: none

航—かわら—*kawara*

Japanese: かわら
Romanized: *kawara*
Pattern: 和 I-K
Used with, or Means: formerly a way of counting boats

1 boat	一航	ひとかわら	<u>*hito-kawara*</u>
2 boats	二航	<u>ふたかわら</u>	<u>*futa-kawara*</u>
3 boats	三航	さんかわら	*san-kawara*
4 boats	四航	よんかわら	*yon-kawara*
5 boats	五航	ごかわら	*go-kawara*
6 boats	六航	<u>ろっかわら</u> <u>ろくかわら</u>	<u>*rok-kawara*</u> <u>*roku-kawara*</u>
7 boats	七航	ななかわら	*nana-kawara*
8 boats	八航	<u>はっかわら</u> はちかわら	<u>*hak-kawara*</u> *hachi-kawara*
9 boats	九航	きゅうかわら	*kyuu-kawara*
10 boats	十航	<u>じゅっかわら</u> <u>じっかわら</u>	<u>*juk-kawara*</u> <u>*jik-kawara*</u>

Irregularities or Special beyond Ten:

100 cans	百航	<u>ひゃっかわら</u> <u>ひゃくかわら</u>	<u>*hyak-kawara*</u> <u>*hyaku-kawara*</u>

Notes: none

缶・罐 — かん — *kan*

Japanese: かん
Romanized: *kan*
Pattern: 和 I-K
Used with, or Means: cans of *nori* (海苔 seaweed), tea, canned goods, soda can (空き缶 *akikan*)

1 can	一缶・罐	ひとかん	*hito-kan*
2 cans	二缶・罐	ふたかん	*futa-kan*
3 cans	三缶・罐	さんかん	*san-kan*
4 cans	四缶・罐	よんかん	*yon-kan*
5 cans	五缶・罐	ごかん	*go-kan*
6 cans	六缶・罐	ろっかん	*rok-kan*
7 cans	七缶・罐	ななかん	*nana-kan*
8 cans	八缶・罐	はっかん / はちかん	*hak-kan* / *hachi-kan*
9 cans	九缶・罐	きゅうかん	*kyuu-kan*
10 cans	十缶・罐	じゅっかん / じっかん	*juk-kan* / *jik-kan*

Irregularities or Special beyond Ten:

100 cans	百缶・罐	ひゃっかん	*hyak-kan*

Notes: none

冠—かん—kan

Japanese: かん
Romanized: *kan*
Pattern: 漢 K
Used with, or Means: championship wins, tournaments; a player's overall wins

1 win	一冠	いっかん	*ik-kan*
2 wins	二冠	にかん	*ni-kan*
3 wins	三冠	さんかん	*san-kan*
4 wins	四冠	よんかん	*yon-kan*
5 wins	五冠	ごかん	*go-kan*
6 wins	六冠	ろっかん	*rok-kan*
7 wins	七冠	ななかん	*nana-kan*
8 wins	八冠	はっかん / はちかん	*hak-kan* / *hachi-kan*
9 wins	九冠	きゅうかん	*kyuu-kan*
10 wins	十冠	じゅっかん / じっかん	*juk-kan* / *jik-kan*

Irregularities or Special beyond Ten:

100 wins	百冠	ひゃっかん	*hyak-kan*

Notes: none

巻―かん―*kan*

Japanese: かん
Romanized: *kan*
Pattern: 漢 K
Used with, or Means: books of a single work, volumes, reels of a film

1 volume	一巻	いっかん	*ik-kan*
2 volumes	二巻	にかん	*ni-kan*
3 volumes	三巻	さんかん	*san-kan*
4 volumes	四巻	よんかん	*yon-kan*
5 volumes	五巻	ごかん	*go-kan*
6 volumes	六巻	ろっかん	*rok-kan*
7 volumes	七巻	ななかん	*nana-kan*
8 volumes	八巻	はっかん / はちかん	*hak-kan* / *hachi-kan*
9 volumes	九巻	きゅうかん	*kyuu-kan*
10 volumes	十巻	じゅっかん / じっかん	*juk-kan* / *jik-kan*

Irregularities or Special beyond Ten:

100 volumes	百巻	ひゃっかん	*hyak-kan*

Notes: none

竿 — かん — *kan*

Japanese: かん
Romanized: *kan*
Pattern: 漢 K
Used with, or Means: bamboo poles, bamboo stalks, see also 棹 (*sao*)

1 bamboo pole	一竿	いっかん	*ik-kan*
2 bamboo poles	二竿	にかん	*ni-kan*
3 bamboo poles	三竿	さんかん	*san-kan*
4 bamboo poles	四竿	よんかん	*yon-kan*
5 bamboo poles	五竿	ごかん	*go-kan*
6 bamboo poles	六竿	ろっかん	*rok-kan*
7 bamboo poles	七竿	ななかん	*nana-kan*
8 bamboo poles	八竿	はっかん / はちかん	*hak-kan* / *hachi-kan*
9 bamboo poles	九竿	きゅうかん	*kyuu-kan*
10 bamboo poles	十竿	じゅっかん / じっかん	*juk-kan* / *jik-kan*

Irregularities or Special beyond Ten:

100 bamboo poles	百竿	ひゃっかん	*hyak-kan*

Notes: none

款 — かん — kan

Japanese: かん
Romanized: *kan*
Pattern: 漢 K
Used with, or Means: articles, subsections

1 article	一款	いっかん	*ik-kan*
2 articles	二款	にかん	*ni-kan*
3 articles	三款	さんかん	*san-kan*
4 articles	四款	よんかん	*yon-kan*
5 articles	五款	ごかん	*go-kan*
6 articles	六款	ろっかん	*rok-kan*
7 articles	七款	ななかん	*nana-kan*
8 articles	八款	はっかん / はちかん	*hak-kan* / *hachi-kan*
9 articles	九款	きゅうかん	*kyuu-kan*
10 articles	十款	じゅっかん / じっかん	*juk-kan* / *jik-kan*

Irregularities or Special beyond Ten:

100 articles	百款	ひゃっかん	*hyak-kan*

Notes: none

管—かん—*kan*

Japanese: かん
Romanized: *kan*
Pattern: 漢 K
Used with, or Means: wind instruments

1 instrument	一管	いっかん	*ik-kan*
2 instruments	二管	にかん	*ni-kan*
3 instruments	三管	さんかん	*san-kan*
4 instruments	四管	よんかん	*yon-kan*
5 instruments	五管	ごかん	*go-kan*
6 instruments	六管	ろっかん	*rok-kan*
7 instruments	七管	ななかん	*nana-kan*
8 instruments	八管	はっかん はちかん	*hak-kan* *hachi-kan*
9 instruments	九管	きゅうかん	*kyuu-kan*
10 instruments	十管	じゅっかん じっかん	*juk-kan* *jik-kan*

Irregularities or Special beyond Ten:

100 instruments	百管	ひゃっかん	*hyak-kan*

Notes: none

艦 — かん — *kan*

Japanese: かん
Romanized: *kan*
Pattern: 漢 K
Used with, or Means: warships

1 warship	一艦	いっかん	*ik-kan*
2 warships	二艦	にかん	*ni-kan*
3 warships	三艦	さんかん	*san-kan*
4 warships	四艦	よんかん	*yon-kan*
5 warships	五艦	ごかん	*go-kan*
6 warships	六艦	ろっかん	*rok-kan*
7 warships	七艦	ななかん	*nana-kan*
8 warships	八艦	はっかん / はちかん	*hak-kan* / *hachi-kan*
9 warships	九艦	きゅうかん	*kyuu-kan*
10 warships	十艦	じゅっかん / じっかん	*juk-kan* / *jik-kan*

Irregularities or Special beyond Ten:

100 warships	百艦	ひゃっかん	*hyak-kan*

Notes: none

館—かん—*kan*

Japanese: かん
Romanized: *kan*
Pattern: 漢 K
Used with, or Means: (literary language) museums, libraries, theaters, inns

1 museum	一館	いっかん	*ik-kan*
2 museums	二館	にかん	*ni-kan*
3 museums	3館	さんかん	*san-kan*
4 museums	四館	よんかん	*yon-kan*
5 museums	五館	ごかん	*go-kan*
6 museums	六館	ろっかん	*rok-kan*
7 museums	七館	ななかん	*nana-kan*
8 museums	八館	はっかん はちかん	*hak-kan* *hachi-kan*
9 museums	九館	きゅうかん	*kyuu-kan*
10 museums	十館	じゅっかん じっかん	*juk-kan* *jik-kan*

Irregularities or Special beyond Ten:

100 museums	百館	ひゃっかん	*hyak-kan*

Notes: none

貫—かん—*kan*

Japanese: かん
Romanized: *kan*
Pattern: 漢 K

Used with, or Means: pieces of *nigiri-zushi*; *kan*, a unit of weight, 1,000 匁 (*monme*), 132.27736 oz (8.26733 lb)/3,750 g; *kan*, former monetary unit, 1,000 文 (*mon*) (960 *mon* during the Edo period)

1 piece of *nigiri*	一貫	いっかん	ik-kan
2 pieces of *nigiri*	二貫	にかん	ni-kan
3 pieces of *nigiri*	三貫	さんがん さんかん	san-gan san-kan
4 pieces of *nigiri*	四貫	よんかん	yon-kan
5 pieces of *nigiri*	五貫	ごかん	go-kan
6 pieces of *nigiri*	六貫	ろっかん	rok-kan
7 pieces of *nigiri*	七貫	ななかん	nana-kan
8 pieces of *nigiri*	八貫	はっかん はちかん	hak-kan hachi-kan
9 pieces of *nigiri*	九貫	きゅうかん	kyuu-kan
10 pieces of *nigiri*	十貫	じゅっかん じっかん	juk-kan jik-kan

Irregularities or Special beyond Ten:

100 pieces of *nigiri*	百貫	ひゃっかん	hyak-kan
1,000 pieces of *nigiri*	千貫	せんがん せんかん	sen-gan sen-kan

Notes: Notice that with three and one thousand, *kan* changes to *gan*, but can remain as *kan*.

貫目―かんめ―*kamme*

Japanese: かんめ
Romanized: *kamme*
Pattern: 漢 K

Used with, or Means: *kamme*, a unit of weight, 1,000 匁 (*monme*), 132.27736 oz (8.26733 lb)/3,750 g; *kamme*, former monetary unit, 1,000 文 (*mon*) (960 *mon* during the Edo period)

1 *kamme*	一貫目	いっかんめ	*ik-kamme*
2 *kamme*	二貫目	にかんめ	*ni-kamme*
3 *kamme*	三貫目	さんかんめ さんがんめ	*san-kamme* *san-ganmme*
4 *kamme*	四貫目	よんかんめ	*yon-kamme*
5 *kamme*	五貫目	ごかんめ	*go-kamme*
6 *kamme*	六貫目	ろっかんめ	*rok-kamme*
7 *kamme*	七貫目	ななかんめ	*nana-kamme*
8 *kamme*	八貫目	はっかんめ はちかんめ	*hak-kamme* *hachi-kamme*
9 *kamme*	九貫目	きゅうかんめ	*kyuu-kamme*
10 *kamme*	十貫目	じゅっかんめ じっかんめ	*juk-kamme* *jik-kamme*

Irregularities or Special beyond Ten:

100 *kamme*	百貫目	ひゃっかんめ	*hyak-kamme*

Notes: none

澗 — かん — *kan*

Japanese: かん
Romanized: *kan*
Pattern: 漢 K
Used with, or Means: 10,000 溝 (*kou*), 1 undecillion, 10^{36}

10^{36}	一澗	いっかん	*ik-kan*
2×10^{36}	二澗	にかん	*ni-kan*
3×10^{36}	三澗	さんかん	*san-kan*
4×10^{36}	四澗	よんかん	*yon-kan*
5×10^{36}	五澗	ごかん	*go-kan*
6×10^{36}	六澗	ろっかん	*rok-kan*
7×10^{36}	七澗	ななかん	*nana-kan*
8×10^{36}	八澗	はっかん	*hak-kan*
9×10^{36}	九澗	きゅうかん	*kyuu-kan*
10^{37}	十澗	じゅっかん / じっかん	*juk-kan* / *jik-kan*

Irregularities or Special beyond Ten:

10^{38}	百澗	ひゃっかん	*hyak-kan*
10^{39}	千澗	せんかん	*sen-kan*

Notes: 10^{36} is 1 000 000 000 000 000 000 000 000 000 000 000 000

き・ぎ—Ki/Gi
寸—き—ki

Japanese: き
Romanized: *ki*
Pattern: 和 I-K
Used with, or Means: *ki*, a unit of height, 4 尺 (*shaku*), 47.72131 in (3.97678 ft)/1.21212 m; the height of a horse, see also 寸 (*sun*)

1 *ki*	一寸	ひとき	hito-ki
2 *ki*	二寸	ふたき	futa-ki
3 *ki*	三寸	さんき	san-ki
4 *ki*	四寸	よんき	yon-ki
5 *ki*	五寸	ごき	go-ki
6 *ki*	六寸	ろっき	rok-ki
7 *ki*	七寸	ななき	nana-ki
8 *ki*	八寸	はっき	hak-ki
9 *ki*	九寸	きゅうき	kyuu-ki
10 *ki*	十寸	じゅっき / じっき / とき	juk-ki / jik-ki / toki

Irregularities or Special beyond Ten:

100 *ki*	百寸	ひゃっき	hyak-ki

Notes: none

匹・疋 — き・ぎ — *ki/gi*

Japanese: き・ぎ
Romanized: *ki/gi*
Pattern: 和 I-K
Used with, or Means: a former measure of bolts of cloth 2 反 (*tan*) in size

1 *ki/gi*	一匹・疋	ひとき・ひとぎ		hito-ki/hito-gi
2 *ki/gi*	二匹・疋	ふたき・ふたぎ		futa-ki/futa-gi
3 *ki/gi*	三匹・疋	さんき・さんぎ		san-ki/san-gi
4 *ki/gi*	四匹・疋	よんき・よんぎ		yon-ki/yon-gi
5 *ki/gi*	五匹・疋	ごき・ごぎ		go-ki/go-gi
6 *ki/gi*	六匹・疋	ろっき・ろくぎ		rok-ki/roku-gi
7 *ki/gi*	七匹・疋	ななき・ななぎ		nana-ki/nana-gi
8 *ki/gi*	八匹・疋	はっき・はちぎ		hak-ki/hachi-gi
9 *ki/gi*	九匹・疋	きゅうき・きゅうぎ		kyuu-ki/kyuu-gi
10 *ki/gi*	十匹・疋	じゅっき / じっき・ / じゅうぎ		juk-ki / jik-ki/ juu-gi

Irregularities or Special beyond Ten:

100 *ki/gi*	百匹・疋	ひゃっき・ひゃくぎ		hyak-ki/hyaku-gi

Notes: none

季 — き — *ki*

Japanese: き
Romanized: *ki*
Pattern: 漢 K
Used with, or Means: seasons

1 season	一季	いっき	*ik-ki*
2 seasons	二季	にき	*ni-ki*
3 seasons	三季	さんき	*san-ki*
4 seasons / the four seasons	四季	よんき / しき	*yon-ki* / *shiki*
5 seasons	五季	ごき	*go-ki*
6 seasons	六季	ろっき	*rok-ki*
7 seasons	七季	ななき	*nana-ki*
8 seasons	八季	はっき / はちき	*hak-ki* / *hachi-ki*
9 seasons	九季	きゅうき	*kyuu-ki*
10 seasons	十季	じゅっき / じっき	*juk-ki* / *jik-ki*

Irregularities or Special beyond Ten:

100 seasons	百季	ひゃっき	*hyak-ki*

Notes: Clearly, one could conceivably count 季 to infinity, but realistically, one would only count to four of them, since they correspond to the the four seasons of the year.

紀 — き — *ki*

Japanese: き
Romanized: *ki*
Pattern: 漢 K
Used with, or Means: twelve-year periods

1 twelve-year period	一紀	いっき	*ik-ki*
2 twelve-year periods	二紀	にき	*ni-ki*
3 twelve-year periods	三紀	さんき	*san-ki*
4 twelve-year periods	四紀	よんき	*yon-ki*
5 twelve-year periods	五紀	ごき	*go-ki*
6 twelve-year periods	六紀	ろっき	*rok-ki*
7 twelve-year periods	七紀	ななき	*nana-ki*
8 twelve-year periods	八紀	はっき / はちき	*hak-ki* / *hachi-ki*
9 twelve-year periods	九紀	きゅうき	*kyuu-ki*
10 twelve-year periods	十紀	じゅっき / じっき	*juk-ki* / *jik-ki*

Irregularities or Special beyond Ten:

100 twelve-year periods	百紀	ひゃっき	*hyak-ki*

Notes: none

基 — き — *ki*

Japanese: き
Romanized: *ki*
Pattern: 漢 K
Used with, or Means: machines, elevators, gravestones, stone monuments, placed things, *torii*, screens, dressing table, wreaths, CPUs, reactors, dams, see also 機 (*ki*)

1 machine	一基	いっき	<u>*ik-ki*</u>
2 machines	二基	にき	*ni-ki*
3 machines	三基	さんき	*san-ki*
4 machines	四基	よんき	*yon-ki*
5 machines	五基	ごき	*go-ki*
6 machines	六基	<u>ろっき</u>	<u>*rok-ki*</u>
7 machines	七基	ななき	*nana-ki*
8 machines	八基	<u>はっき</u> <u>はちき</u>	<u>*hak-ki*</u> <u>*hachi-ki*</u>
9 machines	九基	きゅうき	*kyuu-ki*
10 machines	十基	<u>じゅっき</u> <u>じっき</u>	<u>*juk-ki*</u> <u>*jik-ki*</u>

Irregularities or Special beyond Ten:

100 machines	百基	ひゃっき	<u>*hyak-ki*</u>

Notes: none

期 — き — *ki*

Japanese: き
Romanized: *ki*
Pattern: 漢 K
Used with, or Means: terms (in school)

1 term	一期	いっき	*ik-ki*
2 terms	二期	にき	*ni-ki*
3 terms	三期	さんき	*san-ki*
4 terms	四期	よんき	*yon-ki*
5 terms	五期	ごき	*go-ki*
6 terms	六期	ろっき	*rok-ki*
7 terms	七期	ななき	*nana-ki*
8 terms	八期	はっき / はちき	*hak-ki* / *hachi-ki*
9 terms	九期	きゅうき	*kyuu-ki*
10 terms	十期	じゅっき / じっき	*juk-ki* / *jik-ki*

Irregularities or Special beyond Ten:

100 terms	百期	ひゃっき	*hyak-ki*

Notes: Clearly, one could conceivably count 期 to infinity, but realistically, one would only count to four of them, since they correspond to the the four quarters of a school year (half a semester).

機 — き — *ki*

Japanese: き
Romanized: *ki*
Pattern: 漢 K
Used with, or Means: planes, aircraft; heavy machinery; (professional/technical jargon) the smallest unit of the Air Force (a *Section*, in the US Air Force)

1 plane	一機	いっき	*ik-ki*
2 planes	二機	にき	*ni-ki*
3 planes	三機	さんき	*san-ki*
4 planes	四機	よんき	*yon-ki*
5 planes	五機	ごき	*go-ki*
6 planes	六機	ろっき	*rok-ki*
7 planes	七機	ななき	*nana-ki*
8 planes	八機	はっき / はちき	*hak-ki* / *hachi-ki*
9 planes	九機	きゅうき	*kyuu-ki*
10 planes	十機	じゅっき / じっき	*juk-ki* / *jik-ki*

Irregularities or Special beyond Ten:

100 planes	百機	ひゃっき	*hyak-ki*

Notes: none

騎 — き — *ki*

Japanese: き
Romanized: *ki*
Pattern: 漢 K
Used with, or Means: horsemen, (mounted) horses

1 horseman	一騎	いっき	*ik-ki*
2 horsemen	二騎	にき	*ni-ki*
3 horsemen	三騎	さんき	*san-ki*
4 horsemen	四騎	よんき	*yon-ki*
5 horsemen	五騎	ごき	*go-ki*
6 horsemen	六騎	ろっき	*rok-ki*
7 horsemen	七騎	ななき	*nana-ki*
8 horsemen	八騎	はっき / はちき	*hak-ki* / *hachi-ki*
9 horsemen	九騎	きゅうき	*kyuu-ki*
10 horsemen	十騎	じゅっき / じっき	*juk-ki* / *jik-ki*

Irregularities or Special beyond Ten:

100 horsemen	百騎	ひゃっき	*hyak-ki*

Notes: none

129

簣 — き — *ki*

Japanese: き
Romanized: *ki*
Pattern: 漢 K
Used with, or Means: earth-carrying baskets

1 basket	一簣	いっき	*ik-ki*
2 baskets	二簣	にき	*ni-ki*
3 baskets	三簣	さんき	*san-ki*
4 baskets	四簣	よんき	*yon-ki*
5 baskets	五簣	ごき	*go-ki*
6 baskets	六簣	ろっき	*rok-ki*
7 baskets	七簣	ななき	*nana-ki*
8 baskets	八簣	はっき / はちき	*hak-ki* / *hachi-ki*
9 baskets	九簣	きゅうき	*kyuu-ki*
10 baskets	十簣	じゅっき / じっき	*juk-ki* / *jik-ki*

Irregularities or Special beyond Ten:

100 baskets	百簣	ひゃっき	*hyak-ki*

Notes: none

饋 ― き ― *ki*

Japanese: き
Romanized: *ki*
Pattern: 漢 K
Used with, or Means: food rations

1 food ration	一饋	いっき	*ik-ki*
2 food rations	二饋	にき	*ni-ki*
3 food rations	三饋	さんき	*san-ki*
4 food rations	四饋	よんき	*yon-ki*
5 food rations	五饋	ごき	*go-ki*
6 food rations	六饋	ろっき	*rok-ki*
7 food rations	七饋	ななき	*nana-ki*
8 food rations	八饋	はっき / はちき	*hak-ki* / *hachi-ki*
9 food rations	九饋	きゅうき	*kyuu-ki*
10 food rations	十饋	じゅっき / じっき	*juk-ki* / *jik-ki*

Irregularities or Special beyond Ten:

100 food rations	百饋	ひゃっき	*hyak-ki*

Notes: none

儀 — ぎ — *gi*

Japanese: ぎ
Romanized: *gi*
Pattern: 漢 K
Used with, or Means: matters, affairs, circumstances, see also 件 (*ken*)

1 matter	一儀	いちぎ	*ichi-gi*
2 matters	二儀	にぎ	*ni-gi*
3 matters	三儀	さんぎ	*san-gi*
4 matters	四儀	よんぎ	*yon-gi*
5 matters	五儀	ごぎ	*go-gi*
6 matters	六儀	ろくぎ	*roku-gi*
7 matters	七儀	ななぎ	*nana-gi*
8 matters	八儀	はちぎ	*hachi-gi*
9 matters	九儀	きゅうぎ	*kyuu-gi*
10 matters	十儀	じゅうぎ	*juu-gi*

Irregularities or Special beyond Ten: none
Notes: none

気圧—きあつ—*kiatsu*

Japanese: きあつ
Romanized: *kiatsu*
Pattern: 漢 K
Used with, or Means: bars (symbol: bar), a unit of atmospheric pressure, 100 kilopascals (100 kPa)

1 bar	一気圧	いっきあつ / いちきあつ	*ik-kiatsu* / *ichi-kiatsu*
2 bar	二気圧	にきあつ	*ni-kiatsu*
3 bar	三気圧	さんきあつ	*san-kiatsu*
4 bar	四気圧	よんきあつ	*yon-kiatsu*
5 bar	五気圧	ごきあつ	*go-kiatsu*
6 bar	六気圧	ろっきあつ	*rok-kiatsu*
7 bar	七気圧	ななきあつ	*nana-kiatsu*
8 bar	八気圧	はっきあつ / はちきあつ	*hak-kiatsu* / *hachi-kiatsu*
9 bar	九気圧	きゅうきあつ	*kyuu-kiatsu*
10 bar	十気圧	じゅっきあつ / じっきあつ	*juk-kiatsu* / *jik-kiatsu*

Irregularities or Special beyond Ten:

100 bar	百気圧	ひゃっきあつ	*hyak-kiatsu*

Notes: none

掬 — きく — *kiku*

Japanese: きく
Romanized: *kiku*
Pattern: 漢 K
Used with, or Means: the amount of water that one can scoop up in two hands, see also 杯 (*hai*), see also 掬い (*sukui*)

1 handful	一掬	いっきく	*ik-kiku*
2 handfuls	二掬	にきく	*ni-kiku*
3 handfuls	三掬	さんきく	*san-kiku*
4 handfuls	四掬	よんきく	*yon-kiku*
5 handfuls	五掬	ごきく	*go-kiku*
6 handfuls	六掬	ろっきく	*rok-kiku*
7 handfuls	七掬	ななきく	*nana-kiku*
8 handfuls	八掬	はっきく / はちきく	*hak-kiku* / *hachi-kiku*
9 handfuls	九掬	きゅうきく	*kyuu-kiku*
10 handfuls	十掬	じゅっきく / じっきく	*juk-kiku* / *jik-kiku*

Irregularities or Special beyond Ten:

100 handfuls	百掬	ひゃっきく	*hyak-kiku*

Notes: none

機種—きしゅ—*kishu*

Japanese: きしゅ
Romanized: *kishu*
Pattern: 漢 K
Used with, or Means: types of equipment

1 type of equipment	一機種	いっきしゅ	*ik-kishu*
2 types of equipment	二機種	にきしゅ	*ni-kishu*
3 types of equipment	三機種	さんきしゅ	*san-kishu*
4 types of equipment	四機種	よんきしゅ	*yon-kishu*
5 types of equipment	五機種	ごきしゅ	*go-kishu*
6 types of equipment	六機種	ろっきしゅ	*rok-kishu*
7 types of equipment	七機種	ななきしゅ	*nana-kishu*
8 types of equipment	八機種	はっきしゅ / はちきしゅ	*hak-kishu* / *hachi-kishu*
9 types of equipment	九機種	きゅうきしゅ	*kyuu-kishu*
10 types of equipment	十機種	じゅっきしゅ / じっきしゅ	*juk-kishu* / *jik-kishu*

Irregularities or Special beyond Ten:

100 types of equipment	百機種	ひゃっきしゅ	*hyak-kishu*

Notes: none

段・常—きだ—*kida*

Japanese: きだ
Romanized: *kida*
Pattern: 和 I-K
Used with, or Means: a size of cloth; a unit of farm area; formerly things broken in half

1 *kida*	一段・常	ひときだ	*hito-kida*
2 *kida*	二段・常	ふたきだ	*futa-kida*
3 *kida*	三段・常	さんきだ	*san-kida*
4 *kida*	四段・常	よんきだ	*yon-kida*
5 *kida*	五段・常	ごきだ	*go-kida*
6 *kida*	六段・常	ろっきだ	*rok-kida*
7 *kida*	七段・常	ななきだ	*nana-kida*
8 *kida*	八段・常	はっきだ / はちきだ	*hak-kida* / *hachi-kida*
9 *kida*	九段・常	きゅうきだ	*kyuu-kida*
10 *kida*	十段・常	じゅっきだ / じっきだ	*juk-kida* / *jik-kida*

Irregularities or Special beyond Ten:

100 *kida*	百段・常	ひゃっきだ	*hyak-kida*

Notes: none

規定—きてい—*kitei*

Japanese: きてい
Romanized: *kitei*
Pattern: 漢 K
Used with, or Means: provisions of a law; (chemistry) Normality (symbol: N): a measure of the concentration of a solution in terms of Gram Equivalents Liters of Solution

1 provision	一規定	いっきてい / いちきてい	*ik-kitei* / *ichi-kitei*
2 provisions	二規定	にきてい	*ni-kitei*
3 provisions	三規定	さんきてい	*san-kitei*
4 provisions	四規定	よんきてい	*yon-kitei*
5 provisions	五規定	ごきてい	*go-kitei*
6 provisions	六規定	ろっきてい	*rok-kitei*
7 provisions	七規定	ななきてい	*nana-kitei*
8 provisions	八規定	はっきてい / はちきてい	*hak-kitei* / *hachi-kitei*
9 provisions	九規定	きゅうきてい	*kyuu-kitei*
10 provisions	十規定	じゅっきてい / じっきてい	*juk-kitei* / *jik-kitei*

Irregularities or Special beyond Ten:

100 provisions	百規定	ひゃっきてい	*hyak-kitei*

Notes: none

気筒—きとう—*kitou*

Japanese: きとう
Romanized: *kitou*
Pattern: 漢 K
Used with, or Means: engine cylinders

1 cylinder	一気筒	いっきとう	*ik-kitou*
2 cylinders	二気筒	にきとう	*ni-kitou*
3 cylinders	三気筒	さんきとう	*san-kitou*
4 cylinders	四気筒	よんきとう	*yon-kitou*
5 cylinders	五気筒	ごきとう	*go-kitou*
6 cylinders	六気筒	ろっきとう	*rok-kitou*
7 cylinders	七気筒	ななきとう	*nana-kitou*
8 cylinders	八気筒	はっきとう / はちきとう	*hak-kitou* / *hachi-kitou*
9 cylinders	九気筒	きゅうきとう	*kyuu-kitou*
10 cylinders	十気筒	じゅっきとう / じっきとう	*juk-kitou* / *jik-kitou*

Irregularities or Special beyond Ten:

100 cylinders	百気筒	ひゃっきとう	*hyak-kitou*

Notes: Clearly, one could conceivably count 気筒 to infinity, but realistically, one would only count to about 16 of them, since there are only so many cylinders that can fit in an engine.

客 — きゃく — *kyaku*

Japanese: きゃく
Romanized: *kyaku*
Pattern: 漢 K
Used with, or Means: utensils, teacup, and saucer set for receiving guests

1 teacup set	一客	いっきゃく	*ik-kyaku*
2 teacup sets	二客	にきゃく	*ni-kyaku*
3 teacup sets	三客	さんきゃく	*san-kyaku*
4 teacup sets	四客	よんきゃく	*yon-kyaku*
5 teacup sets	五客	ごきゃく	*go-kyaku*
6 teacup sets	六客	ろっきゃく	*rok-kyaku*
7 teacup sets	七客	ななきゃく	*nana-kyaku*
8 teacup sets	八客	はっきゃく	*hak-kyaku*
9 teacup sets	九客	きゅうきゃく	*kyuu-kyaku*
10 teacup sets	十客	じゅっきゃく / じっきゃく	*juk-kyaku* / *jik-kyaku*

Irregularities or Special beyond Ten:

100 teacup sets	百客	ひゃっきゃく	*hyak-kyaku*

Notes: none

脚 — きゃく — *kyaku*

Japanese: きゃく
Romanized: *kyaku*
Pattern: 漢 K
Used with, or Means: legged furniture: chairs, desks, tables, armrests; horseshoes, see also 台 (*dai*)

1 chair	一脚	いっきゃく	*ik-kyaku*
2 chairs	二脚	にきゃく	*ni-kyaku*
3 chairs	三脚	さんきゃく	*san-kyaku*
4 chairs	四脚	よんきゃく	*yon-kyaku*
5 chairs	五脚	ごきゃく	*go-kyaku*
6 chairs	六脚	ろっきゃく	*rok-kyaku*
7 chairs	七脚	ななきゃく	*nana-kyaku*
8 chairs	八脚	はっきゃく	*hak-kyaku*
9 chairs	九脚	きゅうきゃく	*kyuu-kyaku*
10 chairs	十脚	じゅっきゃく / じっきゃく	*juk-kyaku* / *jik-kyaku*

Irregularities or Special beyond Ten:

100 chairs	百脚	ひゃっきゃく	*hyak-kyaku*

Notes: A three-legged-race in Japanese is 二人三脚 (*ni-nin-san-kyaku*).

弓 — きゅう — *kyuu*

Japanese: きゅう
Romanized: *kyuu*
Pattern: 漢 K

Used with, or Means: an ancient Chinese unit of length; the length of a bow: 6 尺 (*shaku*), 71.58 in/1.818 m; a land-surveying unit: 8 尺 (*shaku*), 173.509 in/2.424 m

1 *kyuu*	一弓	いっきゅう	*ik-kyuu*
2 *kyuu*	二弓	にきゅう	*ni-kyuu*
3 *kyuu*	三弓	さんきゅう	*san-kyuu*
4 *kyuu*	四弓	よんきゅう	*yon-kyuu*
5 *kyuu*	五弓	ごきゅう	*go-kyuu*
6 *kyuu*	六弓	ろっきゅう	*rok-kyuu*
7 *kyuu*	七弓	ななきゅう	*nana-kyuu*
8 *kyuu*	八弓	はっきゅう	*hak-kyuu*
9 *kyuu*	九弓	きゅうきゅう	*kyuu-kyuu*
10 *kyuu*	十弓	じゅっきゅう / じっきゅう	*juk-kyuu* / *jik-kyuu*

Irregularities or Special beyond Ten:

100 *kyuu*	百弓	ひゃっきゅう	*hyak-kyuu*

Notes: none

丘 — きゅう — *kyuu*

Japanese: きゅう
Romanized: *kyuu*
Pattern: 漢 K
Used with, or Means: (literary language) hills (丘 *oka*, 丘陵 *kyuuryou*)

1 hill	一丘	いっきゅう	*ik-kyuu*
2 hills	二丘	にきゅう	*ni-kyuu*
3 hills	三丘	さんきゅう	*san-kyuu*
4 hills	四丘	よんきゅう	*yon-kyuu*
5 hills	五丘	ごきゅう	*go-kyuu*
6 hills	六丘	ろっきゅう	*rok-kyuu*
7 hills	七丘	ななきゅう	*nana-kyuu*
8 hills	八丘	はっきゅう	*hak-kyuu*
9 hills	九丘	きゅうきゅう	*kyuu-kyuu*
10 hills	十丘	じゅっきゅう / じっきゅう	*juk-kyuu* / *jik-kyuu*

Irregularities or Special beyond Ten:

100 hills	百丘	ひゃっきゅう	*hyak-kyuu*

Notes: none

級—きゅう—*kyuu*

Japanese: きゅう
Romanized: *kyuu*
Pattern: 漢 K

Used with, or Means: ordering, class, grade, see also 段 (*dan*); in typesetting/photosetting, letter size (symbol: Q), points (as in 12-point font), see also ポイント (*pointo*)

1st level	一級 初級	いっきゅう しょきゅう	ik-*kyuu* sho-*kyuu*
2nd level	二級	にきゅう	ni-*kyuu*
3rd level	三級	さんきゅう	san-*kyuu*
4th level	四級	よんきゅう	yon-*kyuu*
5th level	五級	ごきゅう	go-*kyuu*
6th level	六級	ろっきゅう	rok-*kyuu*
7th level	七級	ななきゅう	nana-*kyuu*
8th level	八級	はっきゅう	hak-*kyuu*
9th level	九級	きゅうきゅう	kyuu-*kyuu*
10th level	十級	じゅっきゅう じっきゅう	juk-*kyuu* jik-*kyuu*

Irregularities or Special beyond Ten:

100th level	百級	ひゃっきゅう	hyak-*kyuu*

Notes: The ordering, from best to worst, might go either way. For example, the 日本語能力試験 (Japanese Language Proficiency Test) has five levels (級), where 一級 is the highest level and hardest test you can take, and 五級 is the lowest level and easiest test. On the other hand, in video games, you *start* at 一級, and as you progress, your 級-number increases, rather than decreases.

球 — きゅう — *kyuu*

Japanese: きゅう
Romanized: *kyuu*
Pattern: 漢 K
Used with, or Means: balls, larger, round 個 (*ko*); pitches (baseball)

1 ball	一球	いっきゅう	*ik-kyuu*
2 balls	二球	にきゅう	*ni-kyuu*
3 balls	三球	さんきゅう	*san-kyuu*
4 balls	四球	よんきゅう	*yon-kyuu*
5 balls	五球	ごきゅう	*go-kyuu*
6 balls	六球	ろっきゅう	*rok-kyuu*
7 balls	七球	ななきゅう	*nana-kyuu*
8 balls	八球	はっきゅう	*hak-kyuu*
9 balls	九球	きゅうきゅう	*kyuu-kyuu*
10 balls	十球	じゅっきゅう / じっきゅう	*juk-kyuu* / *jik-kyuu*

Irregularities or Special beyond Ten:

100 balls	百球	ひゃっきゅう	*hyak-kyuu*

Notes: none

京 — きょう — *kyou*

Japanese: きょう
Romanized: *kyou*
Pattern: 漢 K
Used with, or Means: 10,000 兆 *(chou)*, 10 quadrillion, 10^{16}

10^{16}	一京	いっきょう	*ik-kyou*
2×10^{16}	二京	にきょう	*ni-kyou*
3×10^{16}	三京	さんきょう	*san-kyou*
4×10^{16}	四京	よんきょう	*yon-kyou*
5×10^{16}	五京	ごきょう	*go-kyou*
6×10^{16}	六京	ろっきょう	*rok-kyou*
7×10^{16}	七京	ななきょう	*nana-kyou*
8×10^{16}	八京	はっきょう / はちきょう	*hak-kyou* / *hachi-kyou*
9×10^{16}	九京	きゅうきょう	*kyuu-kyou*
10^{17}	十京	じゅっきょう / じっきょう	*juk-kyou* / *jik-kyou*

Irregularities or Special beyond Ten:

10^{18}	百京	ひゃっきょう	*hyak-kyou*
10^{19}	千京	せんきょう	*sen-kyou*

Notes: 10^{16} is 10 000 000 000 000 000

橋—きょう—*kyou*

Japanese: きょう
Romanized: *kyou*
Pattern: 漢 K
Used with, or Means: (literary language) bridges (橋 *hashi*), wharfs, jetties, piers (桟橋 *sankyou*)

1 bridge	一橋	いっきょう	*ik-kyou*
2 bridges	二橋	にきょう	*ni-kyou*
3 bridges	三橋	さんきょう	*san-kyou*
4 bridges	四橋	よんきょう	*yon-kyou*
5 bridges	五橋	ごきょう	*go-kyou*
6 bridges	六橋	ろっきょう	*rok-kyou*
7 bridges	七橋	ななきょう	*nana-kyou*
8 bridges	八橋	はっきょう はちきょう	*hak-kyou* *hachi-kyou*
9 bridges	九橋	きゅうきょう	*kyuu-kyou*
10 bridges	十橋	じゅっきょう じっきょう	*juk-kyou* *jik-kyou*

Irregularities or Special beyond Ten:

100 bridges	百橋	ひゃっきょう	*hyak-kyou*

Notes: none

行 — ぎょう — *gyou*

Japanese: ぎょう
Romanized: *gyou*
Pattern: 漢 ∅
Used with, or Means: lines of text, see also 行 (*kudari*)

1 line	一行	いちぎょう	*ichi-gyou*
2 lines	二行	にぎょう	*ni-gyou*
3 lines	三行	さんぎょう	*san-gyou*
4 lines	四行	よんぎょう	*yon-gyou*
5 lines	五行	ごぎょう	*go-gyou*
6 lines	六行	ろくぎょう	*roku-gyou*
7 lines	七行	ななぎょう	*nana-gyou*
8 lines	八行	はちぎょう	*hachi-gyou*
9 lines	九行	きゅうぎょう	*kyuu-gyou*
10 lines	十行	じゅうぎょう	*juu-gyou*

Irregularities or Special beyond Ten: none
Notes: none

曲 —— きょく —— *kyoku*

Japanese: きょく
Romanized: *kyoku*
Pattern: 漢 K
Used with, or Means: pieces of music, songs, tunes, dances

1 song	一曲	いっきょく	*ik-kyoku*
2 songs	二曲	にきょく	*ni-kyoku*
3 songs	三曲	さんきょく	*san-kyoku*
4 songs	四曲	よんきょく	*yon-kyoku*
5 songs	五曲	ごきょく	*go-kyoku*
6 songs	六曲	ろっきょく	*rok-kyoku*
7 songs	七曲	ななきょく	*nana-kyoku*
8 songs	八曲	はっきょく / はちきょく	*hak-kyoku* / *hachi-kyoku*
9 songs	九曲	きゅうきょく	*kyuu-kyoku*
10 songs	十曲	じゅっきょく / じっきょく	*juk-kyoku* / *jik-kyoku*

Irregularities or Special beyond Ten:

100 songs	百曲	ひゃっきょく	*hyak-kyoku*

Notes: none

局 — きょく — *kyoku*

Japanese: きょく
Romanized: *kyoku*
Pattern: 漢 K
Used with, or Means: board game matches (chess, igo, shogi, mahjong); game boards (chess, igo, shougi, majong); radio stations, television stations; post offices

station 1	一局	いっきょく	*ik-kyoku*
station 2	二局	にきょく	*ni-kyoku*
station 3	三局	さんきょく	*san-kyoku*
station 4	四局	よんきょく	*yon-kyoku*
station 5	五局	ごきょく	*go-kyoku*
station 6	六局	ろっきょく	*rok-kyoku*
station 7	七局	ななきょく	*nana-kyoku*
station 8	八局	はっきょく / はちきょく	*hak-kyoku* / *hachi-kyoku*
station 9	九局	きゅうきょく	*kyuu-kyoku*
station 10	十局	じゅっきょく / じっきょく	*juk-kyoku* / *jik-kyoku*

Irregularities or Special beyond Ten:

station 100	百局	ひゃっきょく	*hyak-kyoku*

Notes: none

切り・限―きり―*kiri*

Japanese: きり
Romanized: *kiri*
Pattern: 和 I-K
Used with, or Means: same as 切れ (*kire*)

1 slice	一切り・限	ひときり	*hito-kiri*
2 slices	二切り・限	ふたきり	*futa-kiri*
3 slices	三切り・限	さんきり	*san-kiri*
4 slices	四切り・限	よんきり	*yon-kiri*
5 slices	五切り・限	ごきり	*go-kiri*
6 slices	六切り・限	ろっきり	*rok-kiri*
7 slices	七切り・限	ななきり	*nana-kiri*
8 slices	八切り・限	はっきり / はちきり	*hak-kiri* / *hachi-kiri*
9 slices	九切り・限	きゅうきり	*kyuu-kiri*
10 slices	十切り・限	じゅっきり / じっきり	*juk-kiri* / *jik-kiri*

Irregularities or Special beyond Ten:

100 slices	百切り・限	ひゃっきり	*hyak-kiri*

Notes: none

切れ—きれ—*kire*

Japanese: きれ
Romanized: *kire*
Pattern: 和 I-K or 和 III-K
Used with, or Means: slices, cuts, pieces, bits, strips; a small ovular, golden coin during the Edo period (小判 *koban*); a unit of volume in the concrete and stone masonry business equal to a 才 (*sai*, 0.06100 fl oz/0.001804 L)

slices	kanji	kana	romanized
1 slice	一切れ	ひときれ	*hito-kire*
2 slices	二切れ	ふたきれ	*futa-kire*
3 slices	三切れ	さんきれ / みきれ	*san-kire* / *mi-kire*
4 slices	四切れ	よんきれ / よきれ	*yon-kire* / *yo-kire*
5 slices	五切れ	ごきれ	*go-kire*
6 slices	六切れ	ろっきれ / ろくきれ	*rok-kire* / *roku-kire*
7 slices	七切れ	ななきれ	*nana-kire*
8 slices	八切れ	はっきれ / はちきれ	*hak-kire* / *hachi-kire*
9 slices	九切れ	きゅうきれ	*kyuu-kire*
10 slices	十切れ	じゅっきれ / じっきれ	*juk-kire* / *jik-kire*

Irregularities or Special beyond Ten:

100 slices	百切れ	ひゃっきれ	*hyak-kire*

Notes: none

瓩・キログラム—きろぐらむ—*kiro-guramu*

Japanese: キログラム
Romanized: *kiro-guramu*
Pattern: 漢 K
Used with, or Means: kilograms (S. I. symbol: kg), a unit of mass, 1,000 g (35.27396 oz, 2.20462 lb)

1 kg	一瓩・キログラム	いちきろぐらむ	*ichi-kiro-guramu*
2 kg	二瓩・キログラム	にきろぐらむ	*ni-kiro-guramu*
3 kg	三瓩・キログラム	さんきろぐらむ	*san-kiro-guramu*
4 kg	四瓩・キログラム	よんきろぐらむ	*yon-kiro-guramu*
5 kg	五瓩・キログラム	ごきろぐらむ	*go-kiro-guramu*
6 kg	六瓩・キログラム	ろっきろぐらむ	*rok-kiro-guramu*
7 kg	七瓩・キログラム	ななきろぐらむ	*nana-kiro-guramu*
8 kg	八瓩・キログラム	はっきろぐらむ はちきろぐらむ	*hak-kiro-guramu* *hachi-kiro-guramu*
9 kg	九瓩・キログラム	きゅうきろぐらむ	*kyuu-kiro-guramu*
10 kg	十瓩・キログラム	じゅっきろぐらむ じっきろぐらむ	*juk-kiro-guramu* *jik-kiro-guramu*

Irregularities or Special beyond Ten:

100 kg	百瓩・キログラム	ひゃっきろぐらむ	*hyak-kiro-guramu*

Notes: none

粁・キロメートル—きろめえとる—*kiro-meetoru*

Japanese: キロメートル
Romanized: *kiro-meetoru*
Pattern: 漢 K
Used with, or Means: kilometers (S. I. symbol: km), a unit of length, 1,000 m (3,280.83990 ft)

1 km	一粁・キロメートル	いちきろめえとる	*ichi-kiro-meetoru*
2 km	二粁・キロメートル	にきろめえとる	*ni-kiro-meetoru*
3 km	三粁・キロメートル	さんきろめえとる	*san-kiro-meetoru*
4 km	四粁・キロメートル	よんきろめえとる	*yon-kiro-meetoru*
5 km	五粁・キロメートル	ごきろめえとる	*go-kiro-meetoru*
6 km	六粁・キロメートル	ろっきろめえとる	*rok-kiro-meetoru*
7 km	七粁・キロメートル	ななきろめえとる	*nana-kiro-meetoru*
8 km	八粁・キロメートル	はっきろめえとる / はちきろめえとる	*hak-kiro-meetoru* / *hachi-kiro-meetoru*
9 km	九粁・キロメートル	きゅうきろめえとる	*kyuu-kiro-meetoru*
10 km	十粁・キロメートル	じゅっきろめえとる / じっきろめえとる	*juk-kiro-meetoru* / *jik-kiro-meetoru*

Irregularities or Special beyond Ten:

100 km	百粁・キロメートル	ひゃっきろめえとる	*hyak-kiro-meetoru*

Notes: none

竏・キロリットル―きろりっとる―*kiro-rittoru*

Japanese: キロリットル
Romanized: *kiro-rittoru*
Pattern: 漢 K
Used with, or Means: kiloliters (S. I. symbol: kL), a unit of volume, 1,000 L (33,814.02270 fl oz, 264.17205 gal)

1 kL	一竏・キロリットル	いちきろりっとる	*ichi-kiro-rittoru*
2 kL	二竏・キロリットル	にきろりっとる	*ni-kiro-rittoru*
3 kL	三竏・キロリットル	さんきろりっとる	*san-kiro-rittoru*
4 kL	四竏・キロリットル	よんきろりっとる	*yon-kiro-rittoru*
5 kL	五竏・キロリットル	ごきろりっとる	*go-kiro-rittoru*
6 kL	六竏・キロリットル	ろっきろりっとる	*rok-kiro-rittoru*
7 kL	七竏・キロリットル	ななきろりっとる	*nana-kiro-rittoru*
8 kL	八竏・キロリットル	はっきろりっとる はちきろりっとる	*hak-kiro-rittoru* *hachi-kiro-rittoru*
9 kL	九竏・キロリットル	きゅうきろりっとる	*kyuu-kiro-rittoru*
10 kL	十竏・キロリットル	じゅっきろりっとる じっきろりっとる	*juk-kiro-rittoru* *jik-kiro-rittoru*

Irregularities or Special beyond Ten:

100 kL	百竏・キロリットル	ひゃっきろりっとる	*hyak-kiro-rittoru*

Notes: none

斤 — きん — *kin*

Japanese: きん
Romanized: *kin*
Pattern: 漢 K

Used with, or Means: *kin*, a former unit of weight, 160 匁 (*monme*), 21.16438 oz (1.32277 lb)/600 g; loaves of bread

1 *kin*	一斤	いっきん	*ik-kin*
2 *kin*	二斤	にきん	*ni-kin*
3 *kin*	三斤	さんきん さんぎん	*san-kin* *san-gin*
4 *kin*	四斤	よんきん	*yon-kin*
5 *kin*	五斤	ごきん	*go-kin*
6 *kin*	六斤	ろっきん	*rok-kin*
7 *kin*	七斤	ななきん	*nana-kin*
8 *kin*	八斤	はっきん はちきん	*hak-kin* *hachi-kin*
9 *kin*	九斤	きゅうきん	*kyuu-kin*
10 *kin*	十斤	じゅっきん じっきん	*juk-kin* *jik-kin*

Irregularities or Special beyond Ten:

100 *kin*	百斤	ひゃっきん	*hyak-kin*

Notes: none

金 — きん — *kin*

Japanese: きん
Romanized: *kin*
Pattern: 漢 K
Used with, or Means: karat (symbol: kt), a unit of purity of gold, kt = $24 \left(\frac{\text{Mass of Pure Gold}}{\text{Total Mass of the Material Being Measured}} \right)$, see also カラット (*karatto*)

1 kt	一金	いっきん	*ik-kin*
2 kt	二金	にきん	*ni-kin*
3 kt	三金	さんきん	*san-kin*
4 kt	四金	よんきん	*yon-kin*
5 kt	五金	ごきん	*go-kin*
6 kt	六金	ろっきん	*rok-kin*
7 kt	七金	ななきん	*nana-kin*
8 kt	八金	はっきん / はちきん	*hak-kin* / *hachi-kin*
9 kt	九金	きゅうきん	*kyuu-kin*
10 kt	十金	じゅっきん / じっきん	*juk-kin* / *jik-kin*

Irregularities or Special beyond Ten:

100 kt	百金	ひゃっきん	*hyak-kin*

Notes: none

く・ぐ—*Ku/Gu*
区—く—*ku*

Japanese: く
Romanized: *ku*
Pattern: 漢 K
Used with, or Means: sections, city districts, wards

1 section	一区	いっく	*ik-ku*
2 sections	二区	にく	*ni-ku*
3 sections	三区	さんく	*san-ku*
4 sections	四区	よんく	*yon-ku*
5 sections	五区	ごく	*go-ku*
6 sections	六区	ろっく	*rok-ku*
7 sections	七区	ななく	*nana-ku*
8 sections	八区	はっく / はちく	*hak-ku* / *hachi-ku*
9 sections	九区	きゅうく	*kyuu-ku*
10 sections	十区	じゅっく / じっく	*juk-ku* / *jik-ku*

Irregularities or Special beyond Ten:

100 sections	百区	ひゃっく	*hyak-ku*

Notes: none

口 — く — *ku*

Japanese: く
Romanized: *ku*
Pattern: 漢 K
Used with, or Means: swords (刀 *katana*), razors (剃刀 *kamisori*), kettles (釜 *kama*), pots, dishes (皿 *sara*), see also 口 (*kuchi*), see also 口 (*kou*), see also 蓋 (*san*)

1 sword	一口	いっく	*ik-ku*
2 swords	二口	にく	*ni-ku*
3 swords	三口	さんく	*san-ku*
4 swords	四口	よんく	*yon-ku*
5 swords	五口	ごく	*go-ku*
6 swords	六口	ろっく	*rok-ku*
7 swords	七口	ななく	*nana-ku*
8 swords	八口	はっく / はちく	*hak-ku* / *hachi-ku*
9 swords	九口	きゅうく	*kyuu-ku*
10 swords	十口	じゅっく / じっく	*juk-ku* / *jik-ku*

Irregularities or Special beyond Ten:

100 swords	百口	ひゃっく	*hyak-ku*

Notes: none

句 — く — *ku*

Japanese: く
Romanized: *ku*
Pattern: 漢 K
Used with, or Means: *haiku* (5-7-5 poem), *senryuu* (comical haiku)

1 *haiku*	一句	いっく	*ik-ku*
2 *haiku*	二句	にく	*ni-ku*
3 *haiku*	三句	さんく	*san-ku*
4 *haiku*	四句	よんく	*yon-ku*
5 *haiku*	五句	ごく	*go-ku*
6 *haiku*	六句	ろっく	*rok-ku*
7 *haiku*	七句	ななく	*nana-ku*
8 *haiku*	八句	はっく / はちく	*hak-ku* / *hachi-ku*
9 *haiku*	九句	きゅうく	*kyuu-ku*
10 *haiku*	十句	じゅっく / じっく	*juk-ku* / *jik-ku*

Irregularities or Special beyond Ten:

100 *haiku*	百句	ひゃっく	*hyak-ku*

Notes: none

躯・軀—く—ku

Japanese: く
Romanized: *ku*
Pattern: 漢 K
Used with, or Means: statues (of gods, Buddhas), bronze statues (銅像 *douzou*), see also 体 (*tai*)

1 statue	一躯・軀	いっく	*ik-ku*
2 statues	二躯・軀	にく	*ni-ku*
3 statues	三躯・軀	さんく	*san-ku*
4 statues	四躯・軀	よんく	*yon-ku*
5 statues	五躯・軀	ごく	*go-ku*
6 statues	六躯・軀	ろっく	*rok-ku*
7 statues	七躯・軀	ななく	*nana-ku*
8 statues	八躯・軀	はっく / はちく	*hak-ku* / *hachi-ku*
9 statues	九躯・軀	きゅうく	*kyuu-ku*
10 statues	十躯・軀	じゅっく / じっく	*juk-ku* / *jik-ku*

Irregularities or Special beyond Ten:

100 statues	百躯・軀	ひゃっく	*hyak-ku*

Notes: none

駒 — く — ku

Japanese: く
Romanized: *ku*
Pattern: 漢 K
Used with, or Means: same as コマ (*koma*)

1 frame	一駒	いっく	*ik-ku*
2 frames	二駒	にく	*ni-ku*
3 frames	三駒	さんく	*san-ku*
4 frames	四駒	よんく	*yon-ku*
5 frames	五駒	ごく	*go-ku*
6 frames	六駒	ろっく	*rok-ku*
7 frames	七駒	ななく	*nana-ku*
8 frames	八駒	はっく	*hak-ku*
9 frames	九駒	きゅうく	*kyuu-ku*
10 frames	十駒	じゅっく / じっく	*juk-ku* / *jik-ku*

Irregularities or Special beyond Ten:

100 statues	百駒	ひゃっく	*hyak-ku*

Notes: none

具 — ぐ — *gu*

Japanese: ぐ
Romanized: *gu*
Pattern: 漢 ∅
Used with, or Means: sets of articles, as in suits of armor, prayer beads (数珠 *juzu*), palanquins (駕籠 *kago*)

1 suit of armor	一具	いちぐ	*ichi-gu*
2 suits of armor	二具	にぐ	*ni-gu*
3 suits of armor	三具	さんぐ	*san-gu*
4 suits of armor	四具	よんぐ	*yon-gu*
5 suits of armor	五具	ごぐ	*go-gu*
6 suits of armor	六具	ろくぐ	*roku-gu*
7 suits of armor	七具	ななぐ	*nana-gu*
8 suits of armor	八具	はちぐ	*hachi-gu*
9 suits of armor	九具	きゅうぐ	*kyuu-gu*
10 suits of armor	十具	じゅうぐ	*juu-gu*

Irregularities or Special beyond Ten: none
Notes: none

クール—*kuuru*

Japanese: くうる
Romanized: *kuuru*
Pattern: 漢 K
Used with, or Means: seasons of a serialized television show (クール is from the French word *cours* [kuːʁ], meaning *course*, as in, *a show has run its course*).

1 season	1クール	いっくうる いちくうる	*ik-kuuru* *ichi-kuuru*
2 seasons	2クール	にくうる	*ni-kuuru*
3 seasons	3クール	さんくうる	*san-kuuru*
4 seasons	4クール	よんくうる	*yon-kuuru*
5 seasons	5クール	ごくうる	*go-kuuru*
6 seasons	6クール	ろっくうる	*rok-kuuru*
7 seasons	7クール	ななくうる	*nana-kuuru*
8 seasons	8クール	はっくうる はちくうる	*hak-kuuru* *hachi-kuuru*
9 seasons	9クール	きゅうくうる	*kyuu-kuuru*
10 seasons	10クール	じゅっくうる じっくうる じゅうくうる	*juk-kuuru* *jik-kuuru* *juu-kuuru*

Irregularities or Special beyond Ten:

100 seasons	100クール	ひゃっくうる ひゃくくうる	*hyak-kuuru* *hyaku-kuuru*

Notes: none

区画 — くかく — *kukaku*

Japanese: くかく
Romanized: *kukaku*
Pattern: 和 II-K or 漢 K
Used with, or Means: divisions, sections, boundaries, compartments, areas, blocks; punctuated, cut off, or divided things

1 division	一区画	ひとくかく いっくかく いちくかく	*hito-kukaku* *ik-kukaku* *ichi-kukaku*
2 divisions	二区画	ふたくかく にくかく	*futa-kukaku* *ni-kukaku*
3 divisions	三区画	みくかく さんくかく	*mi-kukaku* *san-kukaku*
4 divisions	四区画	よんくかく	*yon-kukaku*
5 divisions	五区画	ごくかく	*go-kukaku*
6 divisions	六区画	ろっくかく	*rok-kukaku*
7 divisions	七区画	ななくかく	*nana-kukaku*
8 divisions	八区画	はっくかく はちくかく	*hak-kukaku* *hachi-kukaku*
9 divisions	九区画	きゅうくかく	*kyuu-kukaku*
10 divisions	十区画	じゅっくかく じっくかく じゅうくかく	*juk-kukaku* *jik-kukaku* *juu-kukaku*

Irregularities or Special beyond Ten:

100 divisions	百区画	ひゃっくかく	*hyak-kukaku*

Notes: none

区間—くかん—*kukan*

Japanese: くかん
Romanized: *kukan*
Pattern: 和 II-K or 漢 K
Used with, or Means: sections between two points (such as between two stations for calculating fare)

1 section	一区間	ひとくかん いっくかん いちくかん	*hito-kukan* *ik-kukan* *ichi-kukan*
2 sections	二区間	ふたくかん にくかん	*futa-kukan* *ni-kukan*
3 sections	三区間	みくかん さんくかん	*mi-kukan* *san-kukan*
4 sections	四区間	よんくかん	*yon-kukan*
5 sections	五区間	ごくかん	*go-kukan*
6 sections	六区間	ろっくかん	*rok-kukan*
7 sections	七区間	ななくかん	*nana-kukan*
8 sections	八区間	はっくかん はちくかん	*hak-kukan* *hachi-kukan*
9 sections	九区間	きゅうくかん	*kyuu-kukan*
10 sections	十区間	じゅっくかん じっくかん じゅうくかん	*juk-kukan* *jik-kukan* *juu-kukan*

Irregularities or Special beyond Ten:

100 sections	百区間	ひゃっくかん	*hyak-kukan*

Notes: none

茎 — く き — *kuki*

Japanese: く き
Romanized: *kuki*
Pattern: 和 II-K or 和 I-K
Used with, or Means: writing brushes (筆 *fude*)

1 writing brush	一茎	ひとくき	*hito-kuki*
2 writing brushes	二茎	ふたくき	*futa-kuki*
3 writing brushes	三茎	みくき / さんくき	*mi-kuki* / *san-kuki*
4 writing brushes	四茎	よんくき	*yon-kuki*
5 writing brushes	五茎	ごくき	*go-kuki*
6 writing brushes	六茎	ろっくき	*rok-kuki*
7 writing brushes	七茎	ななくき	*nana-kuki*
8 writing brushes	八茎	はっくき / はちくき	*hak-kuki* / *hachi-kuki*
9 writing brushes	九茎	きゅうくき	*kyuu-kuki*
10 writing brushes	十茎	じゅっくき / じっくき / じゅうくき	*juk-kuki* / *jik-kuki* / *juu-kuki*

Irregularities or Special beyond Ten:

100 writing brushes	百茎	ひゃっくき	*hyak-kuki*

Notes: none

括り —— くくり —— *kukuri*

Japanese: くくり
Romanized: *kukuri*
Pattern: 和 II-K
Used with, or Means: bundles of papers

1 bundle	一括り	ひとくくり	hito-kukuri
2 bundles	二括り	ふたくくり	futa-kukuri
3 bundles	三括り	みくくり	mi-kukuri
		さんくくり	san-kukuri
4 bundles	四括り	よんくくり	yon-kukuri
5 bundles	五括り	ごくくり	go-kukuri
6 bundles	六括り	ろっくくり	rok-kukuri
		ろくくくり	roku-kukuri
7 bundles	七括り	ななくくり	nana-kukuri
8 bundles	八括り	はっくくり	hak-kukuri
		はちくくり	hachi-kukuri
9 bundles	九括り	きゅうくくり	kyuu-kukuri
10 bundles	十括り	じゅっくくり	juk-kukuri
		じっくくり	jik-kukuri
		じゅうくくり	juu-kukuri

Irregularities or Special beyond Ten:

100 bundles	百括り	ひゃっくくり	hyak-kukuri
		ひゃくくくり	hyaku-kukuri

Notes: none

鎖—くさり—*kusari*

Japanese: くさり
Romanized: *kusari*
Pattern: 和 II-K or 和 I-K
Used with, or Means: chain links, section of a sequence

1 link	一鎖	ひとくさり	*hito-kusari*
2 links	二鎖	ふたくさり	*futa-kusari*
3 links	三鎖	みくさり さんくさり	*mi-kusari* *san-kusari*
4 links	四鎖	よんくさり	*yon-kusari*
5 links	五鎖	ごくさり	*go-kusari*
6 links	六鎖	ろっくさり ろくくさり	*rok-kusari* *roku-kusari*
7 links	七鎖	ななくさり	*nana-kusari*
8 links	八鎖	はっくさり はちくさり	*hak-kusari* *hachi-kusari*
9 links	九鎖	きゅうくさり	*kyuu-kusari*
10 links	十鎖	じゅっくさり じっくさり じゅうくさり	*juk-kusari* *jik-kusari* *juu-kusari*

Irregularities or Special beyond Ten:

100 links	百鎖	ひゃっくさり ひゃくくさり	*hyak-kusari* *hyaku-kusari*

Notes: none

串 — く し — *kushi*

Japanese: くし
Romanized: *kushi*
Pattern: 和 II-K or 和 I-K
Used with, or Means: food served on spits, skewers such as *dango* (団子), kebabs, see also 本 (*hon*) for counting sticks of such foods

1 skewer	一串	ひとくし	*hito-kushi*
2 skewers	二串	ふたくし	*futa-kushi*
3 skewers	三串	みくし さんくし	*mi-kushi* *san-kushi*
4 skewers	四串	よんくし	*yon-kushi*
5 skewers	五串	ごくし	*go-kushi*
6 skewers	六串	ろっくし	*rok-kushi*
7 skewers	七串	ななくし	*nana-kushi*
8 skewers	八串	はっくし はちくし	*hak-kushi* *hachi-kushi*
9 skewers	九串	きゅうくし	*kyuu-kushi*
10 skewers	十串	じゅっくし じっくし じゅうくし	*juk-kushi* *jik-kushi* *juu-kushi*

Irregularities or Special beyond Ten:

100 skewers	百串	ひゃっくし ひゃくくし	*hyak-kushi* *hyaku-kushi*

Notes: none

癖 — くせ — *kuse*

Japanese: くせ
Romanized: *kuse*
Pattern: 和 II-K or 和 I-K
Used with, or Means: actions that are out-of-the-ordinary

1 action	一癖	ひとくせ	*hito-kuse*
2 actions	二癖	ふたくせ	*futa-kuse*
3 actions	三癖	みくせ / さんくせ	*mi-kuse* / *san-kuse*
4 actions	四癖	よんくせ	*yon-kuse*
5 actions	五癖	ごくせ	*go-kuse*
6 actions	六癖	ろっくせ	*rok-kuse*
7 actions	七癖	ななくせ	*nana-kuse*
8 actions	八癖	はっくせ / はちくせ	*hak-kuse* / *hachi-kuse*
9 actions	九癖	きゅうくせ	*kyuu-kuse*
10 actions	十癖	じゅっくせ / じっくせ	*juk-kuse* / *jik-kuse*

Irregularities or Special beyond Ten:

100 actions	百癖	ひゃっくせ	*hyak-kuse*

Notes: none

行 — くだり — *kudari*

Japanese: くだり
Romanized: *kudari*
Pattern: 和 II-K
Used with, or Means: (literary language) same as 行 (*gyou*), see also 流れ (*nagare*)

1 line	一行	ひとくだり	*hito-kudari*
2 lines	二行	ふたくだり	*futa-kudari*
3 lines	三行	みくだり さんくだり	*mi-kudari* *san-kudari*
4 lines	四行	よんくだり	*yon-kudari*
5 lines	五行	ごくだり	*go-kudari*
6 lines	六行	ろっくだり ろくくだり	*rok-kudari* *roku-kudari*
7 lines	七行	ななくだり	*nana-kudari*
8 lines	八行	はっくだり はちくだり	*hak-kudari* *hachi-kudari*
9 lines	九行	きゅうくだり	*kyuu-kudari*
10 lines	十行	じゅっくだり じっくだり じゅうくだり	*juk-kudari* *jik-kudari* *juu-kudari*

Irregularities or Special beyond Ten:

100 lines	百行	ひゃっくだり ひゃくくだり	*hyak-kudari* *hyaku-kudari*

Notes: none

領・襲 — くだり — *kudari*

Japanese: くだり
Romanized: *kudari*
Pattern: 和 II-K or 和 I-K
Used with, or Means: sets of clothing

1 set	一領・襲	ひとくだり	*hito-kudari*
2 sets	二領・襲	ふたくだり	*futa-kudari*
3 sets	三領・襲	みくだり / さんくだり	*mi-kudari* / *san-kudari*
4 sets	四領・襲	よんくだり	*yon-kudari*
5 sets	五領・襲	ごくだり	*go-kudari*
6 sets	六領・襲	ろっくだり / ろくくだり	*rok-kudari* / *roku-kudari*
7 sets	七領・襲	ななくだり	*nana-kudari*
8 sets	八領・襲	はっくだり / はちくだり	*hak-kudari* / *hachi-kudari*
9 sets	九領・襲	きゅうくだり	*kyuu-kudari*
10 sets	十領・襲	じゅっくだり / じっくだり / じゅうくだり	*juk-kudari* / *jik-kudari* / *juu-kudari*

Irregularities or Special beyond Ten:

100 sets	百領・襲	ひゃっくだり / ひゃくくだり	*hyak-kudari* / *hyaku-kudari*

Notes: none

口 — くち — *kuchi*

Japanese: くち
Romanized: *kuchi*
Pattern: 和 II-K or 和 I-K
Used with, or Means: mouthfuls; drinks (liquor); (Bank) accounts, donations; shares, units, bites

1 mouthful	一口	ひとくち	*hito-kuchi*
2 mouthfuls	二口	ふたくち	*futa-kuchi*
3 mouthfuls	三口	みくち / さんくち	*mi-kuchi* / *san-kuchi*
4 mouthfuls	四口	よんくち	*yon-kuchi*
5 mouthfuls	五口	ごくち	*go-kuchi*
6 mouthfuls	六口	ろっくち	*rok-kuchi*
7 mouthfuls	七口	ななくち	*nana-kuchi*
8 mouthfuls	八口	はっくち / はちくち	*hak-kuchi* / *hachi-kuchi*
9 mouthfuls	九口	きゅうくち	*kyuu-kuchi*
10 mouthfuls	十口	じゅっくち / じっくち	*juk-kuchi* / *jik-kuchi*

Irregularities or Special beyond Ten:

100 mouthfuls	百口	ひゃっくち	*hyak-kuchi*

Notes: none

組—くみ—*kumi*

Japanese: くみ
Romanized: *kumi*
Pattern: 和 II-K
Used with, or Means: sets, suits, sake cups in sets of three, tiered boxes, plates, bowls, groups of people, see also 揃い (*sorori*)

1 group	一組	ひとくみ	*hito-kumi*
2 groups	二組	ふたくみ	*futa-kumi*
3 groups	三組	さんくみ	*san-kumi*
4 groups	四組	よんくみ	*yon-kumi*
5 groups	五組	ごくみ	*go-kumi*
6 groups	六組	ろっくみ	*rok-kumi*
7 groups	七組	ななくみ	*nana-kumi*
8 groups	八組	はっくみ / はちくみ	*hak-kumi* / *hachi-kumi*
9 groups	九組	きゅうくみ	*kyuu-kumi*
10 groups	十組	じゅっくみ / じっくみ	*juk-kumi* / *jik-kumi*

Irregularities or Special beyond Ten:

100 groups	百組	ひゃっくみ	*hyak-kumi*

Notes: Schools subdivide their grade levels into 組 (*gumi*) of about 30 children. Therefore, two divisions of the third grade might be 3年A組 and 3年B組. Elementary schools in Japan tend to use the *Iroha* poem[2] for

---

[2] The *Iroha* poem reads: いろはにほへと ちりぬるを わかよたれそ つねならむ うゐのおくやま けふこえて あさきゆめみし ゑひもせす (*i-ro-ha-ni-ho-he-to chi-ri-nu-ru-[w]o wa-ka-yo-ta-re-so tsu-ne-na-ra-mu u-[w]i-no-o-ku-ya-ma ke-fu-ko-e-te a-sa-ki-yu-me-mi-shi [w]e-hi-mo-se-su*) in archaic Japanese and reads 色は匂へど 散りぬるを 我が世誰ぞ 常ならむ 有為の奥山 今日越えて 浅き夢見じ 酔ひもせず (*Iro wa nioedo // Chirinuru o // Wa ga yo tare zo*

their gumis: い組, ろ組, は組, and so on. Middle schools tend to use the letters of the Roman alphabet: A組, B組, C組, and so on. High schools tend to use numbers: 1組, 2組, 3組 and so on. However, rather than *hito-gumi* or *futa-gumi*, they use *ichi-kumi* and *ni-kumi* for classes. Finally, kindergartens use cute, themed names such as flower names, animals, etc ...

When using 組 to mean *a group of N people*, it becomes *gumi*. Thus, 二人組 (*futari-gumi*), 三人組 (*san-nin-gumi*), 四人組 (*yon-nin-gumi*), and so on, is correct. Along with *futari-gumi*, one can also say *ni-nin-gumi*. Obviously, you could not have a 一人組 (*hitori-gumi*).

// *Tsune naramu* // *Ui no okuyama* // *Kyou koete* // *Asaki yume miji* // *Ei mo sezu*) in modern Japanese. It translates "Even the blossoming flowers // Will eventually scatter // Who in our world // Is unchanging? // The deep mountains of vanity, // We cross them today // And we shall not see superficial dreams // Nor be deluded." The poem is important because it contained all of the original *kana* used exactly once, and so it used to be used to "alphabetize" the *kana*.

位—くらい—*kurai*

Japanese: くらい
Romanized: *kurai*
Pattern: 漢 ∅
Used with, or Means: class; N's place

1's place	一の位	いちのくらい	*ichi-no-kurai*
10's place	十の位	じゅうのくらい	*juu-no-kurai*
100's place	百の位	ひゃくのくらい	*hyaku-no-kurai*
1,000's place	千の位	せんのくらい	*sen-no-kurai*
10,000's place	万の位	まんのくらい	*man-no-kurai*

Irregularities or Special beyond Ten: none
Notes: Although this would otherwise follow the 漢 K pattern, because of the interposed の, the *k* in *kurai* has no effect upon the numbers preceding it.

クラス—*kurasu*

Japanese: くらす
Romanized: *kurasu*
Pattern: 和 I-K
Used with, or Means: classes (in school), see also 組 (*kumi*)

1 class	1クラス	ひとくらす	*hito-kurasu*
2 classes	2クラス	ふたくらす	*futa-kurasu*
3 classes	3クラス	さんくらす	*san-kurasu*
4 classes	4クラス	よんくらす	*yon-kurasu*
5 classes	5クラス	ごくらす	*go-kurasu*
6 classes	6クラス	ろっくらす ろくくらす	*rok-kurasu* *roku-kurasu*
7 classes	7クラス	ななくらす	*nana-kurasu*
8 classes	8クラス	はっくらす はちくらす	*hak-kurasu* *hachi-kurasu*
9 classes	9クラス	きゅうくらす	*kyuu-kurasu*
10 classes	10クラス	じゅっくらす じっくらす じゅうくらす	*juk-kurasu* *jik-kurasu* *juu-kurasu*

Irregularities or Special beyond Ten:

100 classes	100クラス	ひゃっくらす ひゃくくらす	*hyak-kurasu* *hyaku-kurasu*

Notes: none

瓦・グラム—ぐらむ—*guramu*

Japanese: グラム
Romanized: *guramu*
Pattern: 漢 Ø
Used with, or Means: grams (S. I. symbol: g), 1 g (0.03527 oz)

1 g	一瓦・グラム	いちぐらむ	*ichi-guramu*
2 g	二瓦・グラム	にぐらむ	*ni-guramu*
3 g	三瓦・グラム	さんぐらむ	*san-guramu*
4 g	四瓦・グラム	よんぐらむ	*yon-guramu*
5 g	五瓦・グラム	ごぐらむ	*go-guramu*
6 g	六瓦・グラム	ろくぐらむ	*roku-guramu*
7 g	七瓦・グラム	ななぐらむ	*nana-guramu*
8 g	八瓦・グラム	はっぐらむ	*hachi-guramu*
9 g	九瓦・グラム	きゅうぐらむ	*kyuu-guramu*
10 g	十瓦・グラム	じゅうぐらむ	*juu-guramu*

Irregularities or Special beyond Ten: none
Notes: none

グループ—*guruupu*

Japanese: ぐるうぷ
Romanized: *guruupu*
Pattern: 和 I or 漢 ∅
Used with, or Means: groups, same as 組 (*kumi*)

1 group	1グループ	ひとぐるうぷ いちぐるうぷ	*hito-guruupu* *ichi-guruupu*
2 groups	2グループ	ふたぐるうぷ にぐるうぷ	*futa-guruupu* *ni-guruupu*
3 groups	3グループ	さんぐるうぷ	*san-guruupu*
4 groups	4グループ	よんぐるうぷ	*yon-guruupu*
5 groups	5グループ	ごぐるうぷ	*go-guruupu*
6 groups	6グループ	ろくぐるうぷ	*roku-guruupu*
7 groups	7グループ	ななぐるうぷ	*nana-guruupu*
8 groups	8グループ	はちぐるうぷ	*hachi-guruupu*
9 groups	9グループ	きゅうぐるうぷ	*kyuu-guruupu*
10 groups	10グループ	じゅうぐるうぷ	*juu-guruupu*

Irregularities or Special beyond Ten: none
Notes: none

車分—くるまふん—*kuruma-fun*

Japanese: くるまふん
Romanized: *kuruma-fun*
Pattern: 和 III-K
Used with, or Means: travel-time (in minutes) to a destination (for cars or buses)

1 minute	一車分	ひとくるまふん	*hito-kuruma-fun*
2 minutes	二車分	ふたくるまふん	*futa-kuruma-fun*
3 minutes	三車分	みくるまふん	*mi-kuruma-fun*
4 minutes	四車分	よくるまふん	*yo-kuruma-fun*
5 minutes	五車分	ごくるまふん	*go-kuruma-fun*
6 minutes	六車分	ろっくるまふん	*rok-kuruma-fun*
7 minutes	七車分	ななくるまふん	*nana-kuruma-fun*
8 minutes	八車分	はっくるまふん	*hak-kuruma-fun*
9 minutes	九車分	きゅうくるまふん	*kyuu-kuruma-fun*
10 minutes	十車分	じゅっくるまふん じっくるまふん	*juk-kuruma-fun* *jik-kuruma-fun*

Irregularities or Special beyond Ten:

100 minutes	百車分	ひゃっくるまふん	*hyak-kuruma-fun*

Notes: none

クローネ—*kuroone*

Japanese: くろおね
Romanized: *kuroone*
Pattern: 漢 K
Used with, or Means: *krones*, Danish and Norwegian monetary unit

1 *krone*	1 クローネ	いちくろおね	*ichi-kuroone*
2 *krones*	2 クローネ	にくろおね	*ni-kuroone*
3 *krones*	3 クローネ	さんくろおね	*san-kuroone*
4 *krones*	4 クローネ	よんくろおね	*yon-kuroone*
5 *krones*	5 クローネ	ごくろおね	*go-kuroone*
6 *krones*	6 クローネ	ろっくろおね	*rok-kuroone*
7 *krones*	7 クローネ	ななくろおね	*nana-kuroone*
8 *krones*	8 クローネ	はちくろおね	*hachi-kuroone*
9 *krones*	9 クローネ	きゅうくろおね	*kyuu-kuroone*
10 *krones*	10 クローネ	じゅっくろおね / じっくろおね	*juk-kuroone* / *jik-kuroone*

Irregularities or Special beyond Ten:

100 *krones* 100 クローネ ひゃっくろおね *hyak-kuroone*

Notes: none

グロス—*gurosu*

Japanese: ぐろす
Romanized: *gurosu*
Pattern: 漢 ∅
Used with, or Means: gross (12 dozen), 144

1 gross	1グロス	いちぐろす	*ichi-gurosu*
2 gross	2グロス	にぐろす	*ni-gurosu*
3 gross	3グロス	さんぐろす	*san-gurosu*
4 gross	4グロス	よんぐろす	*yon-gurosu*
5 gross	5グロス	ごぐろす	*go-gurosu*
6 gross	6グロス	ろくぐろす	*roku-gurosu*
7 gross	7グロス	ななぐろす	*nana-gurosu*
8 gross	8グロス	はちぐろす	*hachi-gurosu*
9 gross	9グロス	きゅうぐろす	*kyuu-gurosu*
10 gross	10グロス	じゅうぐろす	*juu-gurosu*

Irregularities or Special beyond Ten: none
Notes: none

軍—ぐん—*gun*

Japanese: ぐん
Romanized: *gun*
Pattern: 漢 ∅
Used with, or Means: armies; winning teams (professional sports)

1 winning team	一軍	いちぐん	*ichi-gun*
2 winning teams	二軍	にぐん	*ni-gun*
3 winning teams	三軍	さんぐん	*san-gun*
4 winning teams	四軍	よんぐん	*yon-gun*
5 winning teams	五軍	ごぐん	*go-gun*
6 winning teams	六軍	ろくぐん	*roku-gun*
7 winning teams	七軍	ななぐん	*nana-gun*
8 winning teams	八軍	はちぐん	*hachi-gun*
9 winning teams	九軍	きゅうぐん	*kyuu-gun*
10 winning teams	十軍	じゅうぐん	*juu-gun*

Iregunlarities or Special beyond Ten: none
Notes: none

群 — ぐん — *gun*

Japanese: ぐん
Romanized: *gun*
Pattern: 漢 ∅
Used with, or Means: groups, crowds, flocks, herds, bevies, schools, swarms, clusters (of stars), clumps, see also 団 (*dan*)

1 flock	一群	いちぐん	*ichi-gun*
2 flocks	二群	にぐん	*ni-gun*
3 flocks	三群	さんぐん	*san-gun*
4 flocks	四群	よんぐん	*yon-gun*
5 flocks	五群	ごぐん	*go-gun*
6 flocks	六群	ろくぐん	*roku-gun*
7 flocks	七群	ななぐん	*nana-gun*
8 flocks	八群	はちぐん	*hachi-gun*
9 flocks	九群	きゅうぐん	*kyuu-gun*
10 flocks	十群	じゅうぐん	*juu-gun*

Irregunlarities or Special beyond Ten: none
Notes: none

け・げ—Ke/Ge
茎—けい—kei

Japanese: けい
Romanized: kei
Pattern: 漢 K
Used with, or Means: long and narrow objects (rare), hanging lanterns (灯籠 *touron*), writing brushes (筆 *fude*)

1 lantern	一茎	いっけい	*ik-kei*
2 lanterns	二茎	にけい	*ni-kei*
3 lanterns	三茎	さんけい	*san-kei*
4 lanterns	四茎	よんけい	*yon-kei*
5 lanterns	五茎	ごけい	*go-kei*
6 lanterns	六茎	ろっけい	*rok-kei*
7 lanterns	七茎	ななけい	*nana-kei*
8 lanterns	八茎	はっけい / はちけい	*hak-kei* / *hachi-kei*
9 lanterns	九茎	きゅうけい	*kyuu-kei*
10 lanterns	十茎	じゅっけい / じっけい	*juk-kei* / *jik-kei*

Irregularities or Special beyond Ten:

100 lanterns	百茎	ひゃっけい	*hyak-kei*

Notes: none

景 — けい — *kei*

Japanese: けい
Romanized: *kei*
Pattern: 漢 K
Used with, or Means: scenes, sections of a play; (literary language) scenery, landscapes

1 scene	一景	いっけい	*ik-kei*
2 scenes	二景	にけい	*ni-kei*
3 scenes	三景	さんけい	*san-kei*
4 scenes	四景	よんけい	*yon-kei*
5 scenes	五景	ごけい	*go-kei*
6 scenes	六景	ろっけい	*rok-kei*
7 scenes	七景	ななけい	*nana-kei*
8 scenes	八景	はっけい / はちけい	*hak-kei* / *hachi-kei*
9 scenes	九景	きゅうけい	*kyuu-kei*
10 scenes	十景	じゅっけい / じっけい	*juk-kei* / *jik-kei*

Irregularities or Special beyond Ten:

100 scenes	百景	ひゃっけい	*hyak-kei*

Notes: none

京—けい—*kei*

Japanese: けい
Romanized: *kei*
Pattern: 漢 K
Used with, or Means: 10,000 兆 (*chou*), 10 quadrillion, 10¹⁶

10¹⁶	一京	いっけい	*ik-kei*
2×10¹⁶	二京	にけい	*ni-kei*
3×10¹⁶	三京	さんけい	*san-kei*
4×10¹⁶	四京	よんけい	*yon-kei*
5×10¹⁶	五京	ごけい	*go-kei*
6×10¹⁶	六京	ろっけい	*rok-kei*
7×10¹⁶	七京	ななけい	*nana-kei*
8×10¹⁶	八京	はっけい / はちけい	*hak-kei* / *hachi-kei*
9×10¹⁶	九京	きゅうけい	*kyuu-kei*
10¹⁷	十京	じゅっけい / じっけい	*juk-kei* / *jik-kei*

Irregularities or Special beyond Ten:

10¹⁸	百京	ひゃっけい	*hyak-kei*
10¹⁹	千京	せんけい	*sen-kei*

Notes: 10¹⁶ is 10 000 000 000 000 000

圭 — けい — *kei*

Japanese: けい
Romanized: *kei*
Pattern: 漢 K

Used with, or Means: *kei*; unit of volume, 10 升 (*shou*), 609.971 fl oz (4.765 gal)/18.039 L

1 *kei*	一圭	いっけい	*ik-kei*
2 *kei*	二圭	にけい	*ni-kei*
3 *kei*	三圭	さんけい	*san-kei*
4 *kei*	四圭	よんけい	*yon-kei*
5 *kei*	五圭	ごけい	*go-kei*
6 *kei*	六圭	ろっけい	*rok-kei*
7 *kei*	七圭	ななけい	*nana-kei*
8 *kei*	八圭	はっけい / はちけい	*hak-kei* / *hachi-kei*
9 *kei*	九圭	きゅうけい	*kyuu-kei*
10 *kei*	十圭	じゅっけい / じっけい	*juk-kei* / *jik-kei*

Irregularities or Special beyond Ten:

100 scenes 百圭 ひゃっけい *hyak-kei*

Notes: none

芸 — げい — *gei*

Japanese: げい
Romanized: *gei*
Pattern: 漢 ∅
Used with, or Means: talents, arts

1 talent	一芸	いちげい	*ichi-gei*
2 talents	二芸	にげい	*ni-gei*
3 talents	三芸	さんげい	*san-gei*
4 talents	四芸	よんげい	*yon-gei*
5 talents	五芸	ごげい	*go-gei*
6 talents	六芸	ろくげい	*roku-gei*
7 talents	七芸	ななげい	*nana-gei*
8 talents	八芸	はちげい	*hachi-gei*
9 talents	九芸	きゅうげい	*kyuu-gei*
10 talents	十芸	じゅうげい	*juu-gei*

Irregularities or Special beyond Ten: none
Notes: none

系統—けいとう—*keitou*

Japanese: けいとう
Romanized: *keitou*
Pattern: 漢 K or 漢 ∅
Used with, or Means: systems

1 system	一系統	いっけいとう	*ik-keitou*
		いちけいとう	*ichi-keitou*
2 systems	二系統	にけいとう	*ni-keitou*
3 systems	三系統	さんけいとう	*san-keitou*
4 systems	四系統	よんけいとう	*yon-keitou*
5 systems	五系統	ごけいとう	*go-keitou*
6 systems	六系統	ろっけいとう	*rok-keitou*
		ろくけいとう	*roku-keitou*
7 systems	七系統	ななけいとう	*nana-keitou*
8 systems	八系統	はっけいとう	*hak-keitou*
		はちけいとう	*hachi-keitou*
9 systems	九系統	きゅうけいとう	*kyuu-keitou*
10 systems	十系統	じゅっけいとう	*juk-keitou*
		じっけいとう	*jik-keitou*
		じゅうけいとう	*juu-keitou*

Irregularities or Special beyond Ten:

100 systems	百系統	ひゃっけいとう	*hyak-keitou*
		ひゃくけいとう	*hyaku-keitou*

Notes: none

ゲーム—*geemu*

Japanese: げえむ
Romanized: *geemu*
Pattern: 漢 ∅
Used with, or Means: games

1 game	1 ゲーム	いちげえむ	*ichi-geemu*
2 games	2 ゲーム	にげえむ	*ni-geemu*
3 games	3 ゲーム	さんげえむ	*san-geemu*
4 games	4 ゲーム	よんげえむ	*yon-geemu*
5 games	5 ゲーム	ごげえむ	*go-geemu*
6 games	6 ゲーム	ろくげえむ	*roku-geemu*
7 games	7 ゲーム	ななげえむ	*nana-geemu*
8 games	8 ゲーム	はちげえむ	*hachi-geemu*
9 games	9 ゲーム	きゅうげえむ	*kyuu-geemu*
10 games	10 ゲーム	じゅうげえむ	*juu-geemu*

Irregularities or Special beyond Ten: none
Notes: none

桁—けた—*keta*

Japanese: けた
Romanized: *keta*
Pattern: 和 III-K or 漢 K
Used with, or Means: digits (as in numbers), class

1 digit/1st class	一桁	ひとけた / いっけいた	*hito-keta* / *ik-keta*
2 digits/2nd class	二桁	ふたけた / にけた	*futa-keta* / *ni-keta*
3 digits/3rd class	三桁	みけた / さんけた	*mi-keta* / *san-keta*
4 digits/4th class	四桁	よけた / よんけた	*yo-keta* / *yon-keta*
5 digits/5th class	五桁	ごけた	*go-keta*
6 digits/6th class	六桁	ろっけた	*rok-keta*
7 digits/7th class	七桁	ななけた	*nana-keta*
8 digits/8th class	八桁	はっけた / はちけた	*hak-keta* / *hachi-keta*
9 digits/9th class	九桁	きゅうけた	*kyuu-keta*
10 digits/10th class	十桁	じゅっけた / じっけた	*juk-keta* / *jik-keta*

Irregularities or Special beyond Ten:

100 digits/100th class	百桁	ひゃっけた	*hyak-keta*

Notes: none

穴—けつ—*ketsu*

Japanese: けつ
Romanized: *ketsu*
Pattern: 漢 K
Used with, or Means: holes

1 hole	一穴	いっけつ	<u>*ik-ketsu*</u>
2 holes	二穴	にけつ	*ni-ketsu*
3 holes	三穴	さんけつ	*san-ketsu*
4 holes	四穴	よんけつ	*yon-ketsu*
5 holes	五穴	ごけつ	*go-ketsu*
6 holes	六穴	ろっけつ	<u>*rok-ketsu*</u>
7 holes	七穴	ななけつ	*nana-ketsu*
8 holes	八穴	はっけつ / はちけつ	<u>*hak-ketsu*</u> / <u>*hachi-ketsu*</u>
9 holes	九穴	きゅうけつ	*kyuu-ketsu*
10 holes	十穴	じゅっけつ / じっけつ	<u>*juk-ketsu*</u> / <u>*jik-ketsu*</u>

Irregularities or Special beyond Ten: none

100 holes	百穴	ひゃっけつ	<u>*hyak-ketsu*</u>

Notes: none

193

月 — げつ — *getsu*

Japanese: げつ
Romanized: *getsu*
Pattern: 漢 K
Used with, or Means: months, see also ヶ月 (*ka-getsu*), see also 月 (*tsuki*)

1 month	一月	いちげつ	*ichi-getsu*
2 months	二月	にげつ	*ni-getsu*
3 months	三月	さんげつ	*san-getsu*
4 months	四月	よんげつ	*yon-getsu*
5 months	五月	ごげつ	*go-getsu*
6 months	六月	ろくげつ	*roku-getsu*
7 months	七月	ななげつ	*nana-getsu*
8 months	八月	はちげつ	*hachi-getsu*
9 months	九月	きゅうげつ	*kyuu-getsu*
10 months	十月	じゅうげつ	*juu-getsu*

Irregularities or Special beyond Ten: none
Notes: none

犬—けん—*ken*

Japanese: けん
Romanized: *ken*
Pattern: 漢 K
Used with, or Means: (literary language) dogs, see also 匹 (*hiki*)

1 dog	一犬	いっけん	*ik-ken*
2 dogs	二犬	にけん	*ni-ken*
3 dogs	三犬	さんけん	*san-ken*
4 dogs	四犬	よんけん	*yon-ken*
5 dogs	五犬	ごけん	*go-ken*
6 dogs	六犬	ろっけん	*rok-ken*
7 dogs	七犬	ななけん	*nana-ken*
8 dogs	八犬	はっけん	*hak-ken*
9 dogs	九犬	きゅうけん	*kyuu-ken*
10 dogs	十犬	じゅっけん / じっけん	*juk-ken* / *jik-ken*

Irregularities or Special beyond Ten: none

100 dogs	百犬	ひゃっけん	*hyak-ken*

Notes: Outside of literature or poetry, one uses 匹 (*hiki*) to count dogs, not 犬 (*ken*).

件 — けん — ken

Japanese: けん
Romanized: ken
Pattern: 漢 K
Used with, or Means: cases, matters, affairs, bills, measures; real estate

1 matter	一件	いっけん	ik-ken
2 matters	二件	にけん	ni-ken
3 matters	三件	さんけん	san-ken
4 matters	四件	よんけん	yon-ken
5 matters	五件	ごけん	go-ken
6 matters	六件	ろっけん	rok-ken
7 matters	七件	ななけん	nana-ken
8 matters	八件	はっけん / はちけん	hak-ken / hachi-ken
9 matters	九件	きゅうけん	kyuu-ken
10 matters	十件	じゅっけん / じっけん	juk-ken / jik-ken

Irregularities or Special beyond Ten: none

100 matters	百件	ひゃっけん	hyak-ken

Notes: none

間 — けん — *ken*

Japanese: けん
Romanized: *ken*
Pattern: 漢 K

Used with, or Means: *ken*, a unit of length, 6 尺 (*shaku*), 71.58196 in (5.96516 ft)/1.81818 m, see also 間 (*ma*)

1 *ken*	一間	いっけん	*ik-ken*
2 *ken*	二間	にけん	*ni-ken*
3 *ken*	三間	さんけん	*san-ken*
4 *ken*	四間	よんけん	*yon-ken*
5 *ken*	五間	ごけん	*go-ken*
6 *ken*	六間	ろっけん	*rok-ken*
7 *ken*	七間	ななけん	*nana-ken*
8 *ken*	八間	はっけん / はちけん	*hak-ken* / *hachi-ken*
9 *ken*	九間	きゅうけん	*kyuu-ken*
10 *ken*	十間	じゅっけん / じっけん	*juk-ken* / *jik-ken*

Irregularities or Special beyond Ten: none

100 *ken*	百間	ひゃっけん	*hyak-ken*

Notes: A *ken* is the distance between two pillars. In traditional architecture, this distance was typically the same throughout a single building in order to obtain other proportions (for example, the height of a room might be one half of that building's *ken*, or a room might be three of that buidling's *ken* wide), but it also became its own unit of length. People also began calling it a 京間 (*kyouma*) after the Edo period.

軒—けん—ken

Japanese: けん
Romanized: *ken*
Pattern: 漢 K
Used with, or Means: buildings, houses, private homes, see also 戸 (*ko*), see also 棟 (*tou*); shops, restaurants, see also 店 (*ten*)

1 building	一軒	いっけん	<u>*ik-ken*</u>
2 buildings	二軒	にけん	*ni-ken*
3 buildings	三軒	さんけん さんげん	*san-ken* <u>*san-gen*</u>
4 buildings	四軒	よんけん	*yon-ken*
5 buildings	五軒	ごけん	*go-ken*
6 buildings	六軒	ろっけん	<u>*rok-ken*</u>
7 buildings	七軒	ななけん	*nana-ken*
8 buildings	八軒	はっけん はちけん	<u>*hak-ken*</u> <u>*hachi-ken*</u>
9 buildings	九軒	きゅうけん	*kyuu-ken*
10 buildings	十軒	じゅっけん じっけん	<u>*juk-ken*</u> <u>*jik-ken*</u>

Irregularities or Special beyond Ten: none

100 buildings	百軒	ひゃっけん	<u>*hyak-ken*</u>

Notes: none

鍵 — けん — *ken*

Japanese: けん
Romanized: *ken*
Pattern: 漢 K
Used with, or Means: keys, piano keys

1 key	一鍵	いっけん	*ik-ken*
2 keys	二鍵	にけん	*ni-ken*
3 keys	三鍵	さんけん	*san-ken*
		さんげん	*san-gen*
4 keys	四鍵	よんけん	*yon-ken*
5 keys	五鍵	ごけん	*go-ken*
6 keys	六鍵	ろっけん	*rok-ken*
7 keys	七鍵	ななけん	*nana-ken*
8 keys	八鍵	はっけん	*hak-ken*
		はちけん	*hachi-ken*
9 keys	九鍵	きゅうけん	*kyuu-ken*
10 keys	十鍵	じゅっけん	*juk-ken*
		じっけん	*jik-ken*

Irregularities or Special beyond Ten: none

100 keys	百鍵	ひゃっけん	*hyak-ken*

Notes: none

剣 — けん — *ken*

Japanese: けん
Romanized: *ken*
Pattern: 漢 K
Used with, or Means: *katana*, Japanese swords, so-called "samurai swords"

1 sword	一剣	いっけん	*ik-ken*
2 swords	二剣	にけん	*ni-ken*
3 swords	三剣	さんけん	*san-ken*
4 swords	四剣	よんけん	*yon-ken*
5 swords	五剣	ごけん	*go-ken*
6 swords	六剣	ろっけん	*rok-ken*
7 swords	七剣	ななけん	*nana-ken*
8 swords	八剣	はっけん / はちけん	*hak-ken* / *hachi-ken*
9 swords	九剣	きゅうけん	*kyuu-ken*
10 swords	十剣	じゅっけん / じっけん	*juk-ken* / *jik-ken*

Irregularities or Special beyond Ten: none

100 swords	百剣	ひゃっけん	*hyak-ken*

Notes: none

元 — げん — *gen*

Japanese: げん
Romanized: *gen*
Pattern: 漢 Ø
Used with, or Means: *gen*, a Chinese monetary unit; year numbers; dimensions, places

1 *gen*	一元	いちげん	*ichi-gen*
2 *gen*	二元	にげん	*ni-gen*
3 *gen*	三元	さんげん	*san-gen*
4 *gen*	四元	よんげん	*yon-gen*
5 *gen*	五元	ごげん	*go-gen*
6 *gen*	六元	ろくげん	*roku-gen*
7 *gen*	七元	ななげん	*nana-gen*
8 *gen*	八元	はちげん	*hachi-gen*
9 *gen*	九元	きゅうげん	*kyuu-gen*
10 *gen*	十元	じゅうげん	*juu-gen*

Irregularities or Special beyond Ten: none
Notes: none

弦—げん—*gen*

Japanese: げん
Romanized: *gen*
Pattern: 漢 ∅
Used with, or Means: strings (chords)

1 string	一弦	いちげん	*ichi-gen*
2 strings	二弦	にげん	*ni-gen*
3 strings	三弦	さんげん	*san-gen*
4 strings	四弦	よんげん	*yon-gen*
5 strings	五弦	ごげん	*go-gen*
6 strings	六弦	ろくげん	*roku-gen*
7 strings	七弦	ななげん	*nana-gen*
8 strings	八弦	はちげん	*hachi-gen*
9 strings	九弦	きゅうげん	*kyuu-gen*
10 strings	十弦	じゅうげん	*juu-gen*

Irregularities or Special beyond Ten: none
Notes: none

言 — げん — *gen*

Japanese: げん
Romanized: *gen*
Pattern: 漢 ∅
Used with, or Means: words, see also 言 (*koto*)

1 word	一言	いちげん	*ichi-gen*
2 words	二言	にげん	*ni-gen*
3 words	三言	さんげん	*san-gen*
4 words	四言	よんげん	*yon-gen*
5 words	五言	ごげん	*go-gen*
6 words	六言	ろくげん	*roku-gen*
7 words	七言	ななげん	*nana-gen*
8 words	八言	はちげん	*hachi-gen*
9 words	九言	きゅうげん	*kyuu-gen*
10 words	十言	じゅうげん	*juu-gen*

Irregularities or Special beyond Ten: none
Notes: none

限—げん—*gen*

Japanese: げん
Romanized: *gen*
Pattern: 漢 ∅
Used with, or Means: class periods (primarily in college, university), see also 時限 (*jigen*), see also 齣 (*koma*)

period 1	一限	いちげん	*ichi-gen*
period 2	二限	にげん	*ni-gen*
period 3	三限	さんげん	*san-gen*
period 4	四限	よんげん	*yon-gen*
period 5	五限	ごげん	*go-gen*
period 6	六限	ろくげん	*roku-gen*
period 7	七限	ななげん	*nana-gen*
period 8	八限	はちげん	*hachi-gen*
period 9	九限	きゅうげん	*kyuu-gen*
period 10	十限	じゅうげん	*juu-gen*

Irregularities or Special beyond Ten: none
Notes: none

原子—げんし—*genshi*

Japanese: げんし
Romanized: *genshi*
Pattern: 漢 ∅
Used with, or Means: atoms

1 atom	一原子	いちげんし	*ichi-genshi*
2 atoms	二原子	にげんし	*ni-genshi*
3 atoms	三原子	さんげんし	*san-genshi*
4 atoms	四原子	よんげんし	*yon-genshi*
5 atoms	五原子	ごげんし	*go-genshi*
6 atoms	六原子	ろくげんし	*roku-genshi*
7 atoms	七原子	ななげんし	*nana-genshi*
8 atoms	八原子	はちげんし	*hachi-genshi*
9 atoms	九原子	きゅうげんし	*kyuu-genshi*
10 atoms	十原子	じゅうげんし	*juu-genshi*

Irregularities or Special beyond Ten: none
Notes: none

こ・ご —Ko/Go
戸 — こ — ko

Japanese: こ
Romanized: *ko*
Pattern: 漢 K
Used with, or Means: houses, households, see also 軒 (*ken*), see also 棟 (*tou*), see also 世帯 (*setai*)

1 house	一戸	いっこ	*ik-ko*
2 houses	二戸	にこ	*ni-ko*
3 houses	三戸	さんこ	*san-ko*
4 houses	四戸	よんこ	*yon-ko*
5 houses	五戸	ごこ	*go-ko*
6 houses	六戸	ろっこ	*rok-ko*
7 houses	七戸	ななこ	*nana-ko*
8 houses	八戸	はっこ / はちこ	*hak-ko* / *hachi-ko*
9 houses	九戸	きゅうこ	*kyuu-ko*
10 houses	十戸	じゅっこ / じっこ	*juk-ko* / *jik-ko*

Irregularities or Special beyond Ten: none

100 houses	百戸	ひゃっこ	*hyak-ko*

Notes: none

個・箇・个・ヶ ― こ ― *ko*

Japanese: こ
Romanized: *ko*
Pattern: 漢 K
Used with, or Means: general articles, goods, luggage, hats, items, small artifacts, fruits, mochi; 個 is also used for military units

1 small item	一個・箇・个・ヶ	いっこ	*ik-ko*
2 small items	二個・箇・个・ヶ	にこ	*ni-ko*
3 small items	三個・箇・个・ヶ	さんこ	*san-ko*
4 small items	四個・箇・个・ヶ	よんこ	*yon-ko*
5 small items	五個・箇・个・ヶ	ごこ	*go-ko*
6 small items	六個・箇・个・ヶ	ろっこ	*rok-ko*
7 small items	七個・箇・个・ヶ	ななこ	*nana-ko*
8 small items	八個・箇・个・ヶ	はっこ / はちこ	*hak-ko* / *hachi-ko*
9 small items	九個・箇・个・ヶ	きゅうこ	*kyuu-ko*
10 small items	十個・箇・个・ヶ	じゅっこ / じっこ	*juk-ko* / *jik-ko*

Irregularities or Special beyond Ten: none

100 small items	百個・箇・个・ヶ	ひゃっこ	*hyak-ko*

Notes: none

絇 — こ — ko

Japanese: こ
Romanized: ko
Pattern: 漢 K
Used with, or Means: threads

1 thread	一絇	いっこ	ik-ko
2 threads	二絇	にこ	ni-ko
3 threads	三絇	さんこ	san-ko
4 threads	四絇	よんこ	yon-ko
5 threads	五絇	ごこ	go-ko
6 threads	六絇	ろっこ	rok-ko
7 threads	七絇	ななこ	nana-ko
8 threads	八絇	はっこ / はちこ	hak-ko / hachi-ko
9 threads	九絇	きゅうこ	kyuu-ko
10 threads	十絇	じゅっこ / じっこ	juk-ko / jik-ko

Irregularities or Special beyond Ten: none

100 threads	百絇	ひゃっこ	hyak-ko

Notes: none

湖 — こ — *ko*

Japanese: こ
Romanized: *ko*
Pattern: 漢 K
Used with, or Means: (literary language) lakes

1 lake	一湖	いっこ	*ik-ko*
2 lakes	二湖	にこ	*ni-ko*
3 lakes	三湖	さんこ	*san-ko*
4 lakes	四湖	よんこ	*yon-ko*
5 lakes	五湖	ごこ	*go-ko*
6 lakes	六湖	ろっこ	*rok-ko*
7 lakes	七湖	ななこ	*nana-ko*
8 lakes	八湖	はっこ / はちこ	*hak-ko* / *hachi-ko*
9 lakes	九湖	きゅうこ	*kyuu-ko*
10 lakes	十湖	じゅっこ / じっこ	*juk-ko* / *jik-ko*

Irregularities or Special beyond Ten: none

100 lakes	百湖	ひゃっこ	*hyak-ko*

Notes: none

209

壺 — こ — *ko*

Japanese: こ
Romanized: *ko*
Pattern: 漢 K
Used with, or Means: jars 壺 (*tsubo*)

1 jar	一壺	いっこ	*ik-ko*
2 jars	二壺	にこ	*ni-ko*
3 jars	三壺	さんこ	*san-ko*
4 jars	四壺	よんこ	*yon-ko*
5 jars	五壺	ごこ	*go-ko*
6 jars	六壺	ろっこ	*rok-ko*
7 jars	七壺	ななこ	*nana-ko*
8 jars	八壺	はっこ / はちこ	*hak-ko* / *hachi-ko*
9 jars	九壺	きゅうこ	*kyuu-ko*
10 jars	十壺	じゅっこ / じっこ	*juk-ko* / *jik-ko*

Irregularities or Special beyond Ten: none

100 jars	百壺	ひゃっこ	*hyak-ko*

Notes: none

語 — ご — go

Japanese: ご
Romanized: *go*
Pattern: 漢 ∅
Used with, or Means: words, languages

1 word	一語	いちご	*ichi-go*
2 words	二語	にご	*ni-go*
3 words	三語	さんご	*san-go*
4 words	四語	よんご	*yon-go*
5 words	五語	ごご	*go-go*
6 words	六語	ろくご	*roku-go*
7 words	七語	ななご	*nana-go*
8 words	八語	はちご	*hachi-go*
9 words	九語	きゅうご	*kyuu-go*
10 words	十語	じゅうご	*juu-go*

Irregularities or Special beyond Ten: none
Notes: none

口 — こう — *kou*

Japanese: こう
Romanized: *kou*
Pattern: 漢 K
Used with, or Means: kettles, pots, teacups, plates, bowls, see also 蓋 (*san*), see also 口 (*ku*); bells; swords, see also 口 (*kuchi*), see also 口 (*furi*)

1 pot	一口	いっこう	*ik-kou*
2 pots	二口	にこう	*ni-kou*
3 pots	三口	さんこう	*san-kou*
4 pots	四口	よんこう	*yon-kou*
5 pots	五口	ごこう	*go-kou*
6 pots	六口	ろっこう	*rok-kou*
7 pots	七口	ななこう	*nana-kou*
8 pots	八口	はっこう / はちこう	*hak-kou* / *hachi-kou*
9 pots	九口	きゅうこう	*kyuu-kou*
10 pots	十口	じゅっこう / じっこう	*juk-kou* / *jik-kou*

Irregularities or Special beyond Ten: none

100 pots	百口	ひゃっこう	*hyak-kou*

Notes: none

行 — こう — *kou*

Japanese: こう
Romanized: *kou*
Pattern: 漢 K
Used with, or Means: banks

1 bank	一行	いっこう	*ik-kou*
2 banks	二行	にこう	*ni-kou*
3 banks	三行	さんこう	*san-kou*
4 banks	四行	よんこう	*yon-kou*
5 banks	五行	ごこう	*go-kou*
6 banks	六行	ろっこう	*rok-kou*
7 banks	七行	ななこう	*nana-kou*
8 banks	八行	はっこう	*hak-kou*
9 banks	九行	きゅうこう	*kyuu-kou*
10 banks	十行	じゅっこう / じっこう	*juk-kou* / *jik-kou*

Irregularities or Special beyond Ten: none

100 banks	百行	ひゃっこう	*hyak-kou*

Notes: none

更 — こう — *kou*

Japanese: こう
Romanized: *kou*
Pattern: 漢 K
Used with, or Means: watches of the night, lateness of the night, night-shifts

1st watch	一更	いっこう	*ik-kou*
2nd watch	二更	にこう	*ni-kou*
3rd watch	三更	さんこう	*san-kou*
4th watch	四更	よんこう	*yon-kou*
5th watch	五更	ごこう	*go-kou*
6th watch	六更	ろっこう	*rok-kou*
7th watch	七更	ななこう	*nana-kou*
8th watch	八更	はっこう	*hak-kou*
9th watch	九更	きゅうこう	*kyuu-kou*
10th watch	十更	じゅっこう / じっこう	*juk-kou* / *jik-kou*

Irregularities or Special beyond Ten: none

100th watch	百更	ひゃっこう	*hyak-kou*

Notes: Clearly, one could conceivably count 更 to infinity, but realistically, one would only count to three or four of them.

岬 — こう — *kou*

Japanese: こう
Romanized: *kou*
Pattern: 漢 K
Used with, or Means: (literary language) capes (as in Cape Cod)

1 cape	一岬	いっこう	*ik-kou*
2 capes	二岬	にこう	*ni-kou*
3 capes	三岬	さんこう	*san-kou*
4 capes	四岬	よんこう	*yon-kou*
5 capes	五岬	ごこう	*go-kou*
6 capes	六岬	ろっこう	*rok-kou*
7 capes	七岬	ななこう	*nana-kou*
8 capes	八岬	はっこう / はちこう	*hak-kou* / *hachi-kou*
9 capes	九岬	きゅうこう	*kyuu-kou*
10 capes	十岬	じゅっこう / じっこう	*juk-kou* / *jik-kou*

Irregularities or Special beyond Ten: none

100 capes	百岬	ひゃっこう	*hyak-kou*

Notes: none

校 — こう — *kou*

Japanese: こう
Romanized: *kou*
Pattern: 漢 K
Used with, or Means: schools; proofs (printing corrections), manuscript drafts, see Notes

1 school 1st proof	一校	いっこう 初校	*ik-kou* *shokou*
2 schools 2nd proof	二校	にこう 再校	*ni-kou* *saikou*
3 schools	三校	さんこう	*san-kou*
4 schools	四校	よんこう	*yon-kou*
5 schools	五校	ごこう	*go-kou*
6 schools	六校	ろっこう	*rok-kou*
7 schools	七校	ななこう	*nana-kou*
8 schools	八校	はっこう はちこう	*hak-kou* *hachi-kou*
9 schools	九校	きゅうこう	*kyuu-kou*
10 schools	十校	じゅっこう じっこう	*juk-kou* *jik-kou*

Irregularities or Special beyond Ten: none

100 schools	百校	ひゃっこう	*hyak-kou*

Notes: For printing corrections, use the special first and second words, 初校 (*shokou*) and 再校 (*saikou*) rather than *ikkou*, *nikou*. For schools, use *ikkou*, *nikou*, respectively.

216

項 — こう — *kou*

Japanese: こう
Romanized: *kou*
Pattern: 漢 K
Used with, or Means: provisions, articles of a law; clauses of a sentence; polynomial classes, see also 項目 (*koumoku*)

1 article	一項	いっこう	*ik-kou*
2 articles	二項	にこう	*ni-kou*
3 articles	三項	さんこう	*san-kou*
4 articles	四項	よんこう	*yon-kou*
5 articles	五項	ごこう	*go-kou*
6 articles	六項	ろっこう	*rok-kou*
7 articles	七項	ななこう	*nana-kou*
8 articles	八項	はっこう / はちこう	*hak-kou* / *hachi-kou*
9 articles	九項	きゅうこう	*kyuu-kou*
10 articles	十項	じゅっこう / じっこう	*juk-kou* / *jik-kou*

Irregularities or Special beyond Ten: none

100 articles	百項	ひゃっこう	*hyak-kou*

Notes: none

稿 — こう — *kou*

Japanese: こう
Romanized: *kou*
Pattern: 漢 K
Used with, or Means: manuscript drafts

1 draft	一稿	いっこう / 初稿	*ik-kou* / *shokou*
2 drafts	二稿	にこう / 再稿	*ni-kou* / *saikou*
3 drafts	三稿	さんこう	*san-kou*
4 drafts	四稿	よんこう	*yon-kou*
5 drafts	五稿	ごこう	*go-kou*
6 drafts	六稿	ろっこう	*rok-kou*
7 drafts	七稿	ななこう	*nana-kou*
8 drafts	八稿	はっこう / はちこう	*hak-kou* / *hachi-kou*
9 drafts	九稿	きゅうこう	*kyuu-kou*
10 drafts	十稿	じゅっこう / じっこう	*juk-kou* / *jik-kou*

Irregularities or Special beyond Ten: none

100 drafts	百稿	ひゃっこう	*hyak-kou*

Notes: none

218

講 — こう — *kou*

Japanese: こう
Romanized: *kou*
Pattern: 漢 K
Used with, or Means: lectures

1 lecture	一講	いっこう	*ik-kou*
2 lectures	二講	にこう	*ni-kou*
3 lectures	三講	さんこう	*san-kou*
4 lectures	四講	よんこう	*yon-kou*
5 lectures	五講	ごこう	*go-kou*
6 lectures	六講	ろっこう	*rok-kou*
7 lectures	七講	ななこう	*nana-kou*
8 lectures	八講	はっこう / はちこう	*hak-kou* / *hachi-kou*
9 lectures	九講	きゅうこう	*kyuu-kou*
10 lectures	十講	じゅっこう / じっこう	*juk-kou* / *jik-kou*

Irregularities or Special beyond Ten: none

100 lectures	百講	ひゃっこう	*hyak-kou*

Notes: none

溝 — こう — *kou*

Japanese: こう
Romanized: *kou*
Pattern: 漢 K
Used with, or Means: 10,000 穣 (*jou*), 100 nonillion, 10^{32}

10^{32}	一溝	いっこう	*ik-kou*
2×10^{32}	二溝	にこう	*ni-kou*
3×10^{32}	三溝	さんこう	*san-kou*
4×10^{32}	四溝	よんこう	*yon-kou*
5×10^{32}	五溝	ごこう	*go-kou*
6×10^{32}	六溝	ろっこう	*rok-kou*
7×10^{32}	七溝	ななこう	*nana-kou*
8×10^{32}	八溝	はっこう / はちこう	*hak-kou* / *hachi-kou*
9×10^{32}	九溝	きゅうこう	*kyuu-kou*
10^{33}	十溝	じゅっこう / じっこう	*juk-kou* / *jik-kou*

Irregularities or Special beyond Ten:

10^{34}	百溝	ひゃっこう	*hyak-kou*
10^{35}	千溝	せんこう	*sen-kou*

Notes: 10^{32} is 100 000 000 000 000 000 000 000 000 000 000

号 — ごう — *gou*

Japanese: ごう
Romanized: *gou*
Pattern: 漢 ∅
Used with, or Means: #, No., number, issue; dress size

No. 1	一号	いちごう	*ichi-gou*
No. 2	二号	にごう	*ni-gou*
No. 3	三号	さんごう	*san-gou*
No. 4	四号	よんごう	*yon-gou*
No. 5	五号	ごごう	*go-gou*
No. 6	六号	ろくごう	*roku-gou*
No. 7	七号	ななごう	*nana-gou*
No. 8	八号	はちごう	*hachi-gou*
No. 9	九号	きゅうごう	*kyuu-gou*
No. 10	十号	じゅうごう	*juu-gou*

Irregularities or Special beyond Ten: none
Notes: none

合 — ごう — *gou*

Japanese: ごう
Romanized: *gou*
Pattern: 漢 ∅

Used with, or Means: cups of rice, lidded utensils or receptacles, incense containers (香合 *kougou*); engagements (especially in fencing matches); *gou*, a unit of area, 1/10th of a 坪 (*tsubo*), 512.39772 in² (3.55832 ft²)/0.33058 m²; *gou*, a unit of volume, 1/10th of a 升 (*shou*), 6.09973 fl oz/0.18039 L

1 cup of rice	一合	いちごう	*ichi-gou*
2 cups of rice	二合	にごう	*ni-gou*
3 cups of rice	三合	さんごう	*san-gou*
4 cups of rice	四合	よんごう	*yon-gou*
5 cups of rice	五合	ごごう	*go-gou*
6 cups of rice	六合	ろくごう	*roku-gou*
7 cups of rice	七合	ななごう	*nana-gou*
8 cups of rice	八合	はちごう	*hachi-gou*
9 cups of rice	九合	きゅうごう	*kyuu-gou*
10 cups of rice	十合	じゅうごう	*juu-gou*

Irregularities or Special beyond Ten: none
Notes: none

盒 — ごう — *gou*

Japanese: ごう
Romanized: *gou*
Pattern: 漢 ∅
Used with, or Means: incense containers (香盒 *kougou*)

1 incense container	一盒	いちごう	*ichi-gou*
2 incense containers	二盒	にごう	*ni-gou*
3 incense containers	三盒	さんごう	*san-gou*
4 incense containers	四盒	よんごう	*yon-gou*
5 incense containers	五盒	ごごう	*go-gou*
6 incense containers	六盒	ろくごう	*roku-gou*
7 incense containers	七盒	ななごう	*nana-gou*
8 incense containers	八盒	はちごう	*hachi-gou*
9 incense containers	九盒	きゅうごう	*kyuu-gou*
10 incense containers	十盒	じゅうごう	*juu-gou*

Irregularities or Special beyond Ten: none
Notes: none

航海—こうかい—*koukai*

Japanese: こうかい
Romanized: *koukai*
Pattern: 漢 K
Used with, or Means: sea voyages

1 sea voyage	一航海	いっこうかい いちこうかい	*ik-koukai* *ichi-koukai*
2 sea voyages	二航海	にこうかい	*ni-koukai*
3 sea voyages	三航海	さんこうかい	*san-koukai*
4 sea voyages	四航海	よんこうかい	*yon-koukai*
5 sea voyages	五航海	ごこうかい	*go-koukai*
6 sea voyages	六航海	ろっこうかい	*rok-koukai*
7 sea voyages	七航海	ななこうかい	*nana-koukai*
8 sea voyages	八航海	はっこうかい はちこうかい	*hak-koukai* *hachi-koukai*
9 sea voyages	九航海	きゅうこうかい	*kyuu-koukai*
10 sea voyages	十航海	じゅっこうかい じっこうかい	*juk-koukai* *jik-koukai*

Irregularities or Special beyond Ten:

100 sea voyages	百航海	ひゃっこうかい ひゃくこうかい	*hyak-koukai* *hyaku-koukai*

Notes: none

恒河沙 — ごうがしゃ — *gougasha*

Japanese: ごうがしゃ
Romanized: *gougasha*
Pattern: 漢 ∅
Used with, or Means: 10,000 極 (*goku*), 10 sexdecillion, 10^{52}

10^{52}	一恒河沙	いちごうがしゃ	*ichi-gougasha*
2×10^{52}	二恒河沙	にごうがしゃ	*ni-gougasha*
3×10^{52}	三恒河沙	さんごうがしゃ	*san-gougasha*
4×10^{52}	四恒河沙	よんごうがしゃ	*yon-gougasha*
5×10^{52}	五恒河沙	ごごうがしゃ	*go-gougasha*
6×10^{52}	六恒河沙	ろくごうがしゃ	*roku-gougasha*
7×10^{52}	七恒河沙	ななごうがしゃ	*nana-gougasha*
8×10^{52}	八恒河沙	はちごうがしゃ	*hachi-gougasha*
9×10^{52}	九恒河沙	きゅうごうがしゃ	*kyuu-gougasha*
10^{53}	十恒河沙	じゅうごうがしゃ	*juu-gougasha*

Irregularities or Special beyond Ten:

10^{54}	百恒河沙	ひゃくごうがしゃ	*hyaku-gougasha*
10^{55}	千恒河沙	せんごうがしゃ	*sen-gougasha*

Notes: 10^{52} is 10 000 000 000 000 000 000 000 000 000 000 000 000 000 000 000 000 000

号車―ごうしゃ―*gousha*

Japanese: ごうしゃ
Romanized: *gousha*
Pattern: 漢 Ø
Used with, or Means: train car numbers

Car No. 1	一号車	いちごうしゃ	*ichi-gousha*
Car No. 2	二号車	にごうしゃ	*ni-gousha*
Car No. 3	三号車	さんごうしゃ	*san-gousha*
Car No. 4	四号車	よんごうしゃ	*yon-gousha*
Car No. 5	五号車	ごごうしゃ	*go-gousha*
Car No. 6	六号車	ろくごうしゃ	*roku-gousha*
Car No. 7	七号車	ななごうしゃ	*nana-gousha*
Car No. 8	八号車	はちごうしゃ	*hachi-gousha*
Car No. 9	九号車	きゅうごうしゃ	*kyuu-gousha*
Car No. 10	十号車	じゅうごうしゃ	*juu-gousha*

Irregularities or Special beyond Ten: none
Notes: none

工程—こうてい—*koutei*

Japanese: こうてい
Romanized: *koutei*
Pattern: 漢 K
Used with, or Means: work hours

1 work hour	一工程	いっこうてい いちこうてい	*ik-koutei* *ichi-koutei*
2 work hours	二工程	にこうてい	*ni-koutei*
3 work hours	三工程	さんこうてい	*san-koutei*
4 work hours	四工程	よんこうてい	*yon-koutei*
5 work hours	五工程	ごこうてい	*go-koutei*
6 work hours	六工程	ろっこうてい ろくこうてい	*rok-koutei* *roku-koutei*
7 work hours	七工程	ななこうてい	*nana-koutei*
8 work hours	八工程	はっこうてい はちこうてい	*hak-koutei* *hachi-koutei*
9 work hours	九工程	きゅうこうてい	*kyuu-koutei*
10 work hours	十工程	じゅっこうてい じっこうてい	*juk-koutei* *jik-koutei*

Irregularities or Special beyond Ten: none

100 work hours	百工程	ひゃっこうてい ひゃくこうてい	*hyak-koutei* *hyaku-koutei*

Notes: none

光年—こうねん—*kounen*

Japanese: こうねん
Romanized: *kounen*
Pattern: 漢 K
Used with, or Means: lightyears

1 lightyear	一光年	いっこうねん いちこうねん	*ik-kounen* *ichi-kounen*
2 lightyears	二光年	にこうねん	*ni-kounen*
3 lightyears	三光年	さんこうねん	*san-kounen*
4 lightyears	四光年	よんこうねん	*yon-kounen*
5 lightyears	五光年	ごこうねん	*go-kounen*
6 lightyears	六光年	ろっこうねん	*rok-kounen*
7 lightyears	七光年	ななこうねん	*nana-kounen*
8 lightyears	八光年	はっこうねん はちこうねん	*hak-kounen* *hachi-kounen*
9 lightyears	九光年	きゅうこうねん	*kyuu-kounen*
10 lightyears	十光年	じゅっこうねん じっこうねん	*juk-kounen* *jik-kounen*

Irregularities or Special beyond Ten:

100 lightyears	百光年	ひゃっこうねん ひゃくこうねん	*hyak-kounen* *hyaku-kounen*

Notes: none

項目—こうもく—*koumoku*

Japanese: こうもく
Romanized: *koumoku*
Pattern: 漢 K
Used with, or Means: items, clauses, see also 項 (*kou*)

1 clause	一項目	いっこうもく / いちこうもく	*ik-koumoku* / *ichi-koumoku*
2 clauses	二項目	にこうもく	*ni-koumoku*
3 clauses	三項目	さんこうもく	*san-koumoku*
4 clauses	四項目	よんこうもく	*yon-koumoku*
5 clauses	五項目	ごこうもく	*go-koumoku*
6 clauses	六項目	ろっこうもく	*rok-koumoku*
7 clauses	七項目	ななこうもく	*nana-koumoku*
8 clauses	八項目	はっこうもく / はちこうもく	*hak-koumoku* / *hachi-koumoku*
9 clauses	九項目	きゅうこうもく	*kyuu-koumoku*
10 clauses	十項目	じゅっこうもく / じっこうもく	*juk-koumoku* / *jik-koumoku*

Irregularities or Special beyond Ten:

100 clauses	百項目	ひゃっこうもく / ひゃくこうもく	*hyak-koumoku* / *hyaku-koumoku*

Notes: none

声 — こえ — *koe*

Japanese: こえ
Romanized: *koe*
Pattern: 和 II-K
Used with, or Means: voices, cries, shouts, see also 声 *(sei)*

1 voice	一声	ひとこえ	*hito-koe*
2 voices	二声	ふたこえ	*futa-koe*
3 voices	三声	みこえ	*mi-koe*
4 voices	四声	よんこえ	*yon-koe*
5 voices	五声	ごこえ	*go-koe*
6 voices	六声	ろっこえ	*rok-koe*
7 voices	七声	ななこえ	*nana-koe*
8 voices	八声	はっこえ / はちこえ	*hak-koe* / *hachi-koe*
9 voices	九声	きゅうこえ	*kyuu-koe*
10 voices	十声	じゅっこえ / じっこえ	*juk-koe* / *jik-koe*

Irregularities or Special beyond Ten:

100 voices	百声	ひゃっこえ	*hyak-koe*

Notes: none

ゴール—*gooru*

Japanese: ごおる
Romanized: *gooru*
Pattern: 漢 ∅
Used with, or Means: goals, baskets, scores, points won, runs

1 goal	1ゴール	いちごおる	*ichi-gooru*
2 goals	2ゴール	にごおる	*ni-gooru*
3 goals	3ゴール	さんごおる	*san-gooru*
4 goals	4ゴール	よんごおる	*yon-gooru*
5 goals	5ゴール	ごごおる	*go-gooru*
6 goals	6ゴール	ろくごおる	*roku-gooru*
7 goals	7ゴール	ななごおる	*nana-gooru*
8 goals	8ゴール	はちごおる	*hachi-gooru*
9 goals	9ゴール	きゅうごおる	*kyuu-gooru*
10 goals	10ゴール	じゅうごおる	*juu-gooru*

Irregularities or Special beyond Ten: none
Notes: none

石 — こく — *koku*

Japanese: こく
Romanized: *koku*
Pattern: 漢 K

Used with, or Means: *koku*; a unit of volume: 100 升 (*shou*), 6,099.73467 fl oz (381.23342 pt, 47.65418 gal)/180.39068 L; traditionally, the amount of rice consumed by one person in one year

1 *koku*	一石	いっこく	*ik-koku*
2 *koku*	二石	にこく	*ni-koku*
3 *koku*	三石	さんこく	*san-koku*
4 *koku*	四石	よんこく	*yon-koku*
5 *koku*	五石	ごこく	*go-koku*
6 *koku*	六石	ろっこく	*rok-koku*
7 *koku*	七石	ななこく	*nana-koku*
8 *koku*	八石	はっこく	*hak-koku*
9 *koku*	九石	きゅうこく	*kyuu-koku*
10 *koku*	十石	じゅっこく / じっこく	*juk-koku* / *jik-koku*

Irregularities or Special beyond Ten:

100 *koku*	百石	ひゃっこく	*hyak-koku*

Notes: none

国 — こく — *koku*

Japanese: こく
Romanized: *koku*
Pattern: 漢 K
Used with, or Means: countries

1 country	一国	いっこく	*ik-koku*
2 countries	二国	にこく	*ni-koku*
3 countries	三国	さんこく	*san-koku*
4 countries	四国	よんこく	*yon-koku*
5 countries	五国	ごこく	*go-koku*
6 countries	六国	ろっこく	*rok-koku*
7 countries	七国	ななこく	*nana-koku*
8 countries	八国	はっこく	*hak-koku*
9 countries	九国	きゅうこく	*kyuu-koku*
10 countries	十国	じゅっこく じっこく	*juk-koku* *jik-koku*

Irregularities or Special beyond Ten:

100 countries	百国	ひゃっこく	*hyak-koku*

Notes: none

極——ごく——*goku*

Japanese: ごく
Romanized: *goku*
Pattern: 漢 Ø
Used with, or Means: 10,000 載 (*sai*), 1 quindecillion, 10^{48}

10^{48}	一極	いちごく	*ichi-goku*
2×10^{48}	二極	にごく	*ni-goku*
3×10^{48}	三極	さんごく	*san-goku*
4×10^{48}	四極	よんごく	*yon-goku*
5×10^{48}	五極	ごごく	*go-goku*
6×10^{48}	六極	ろくごく	*roku-goku*
7×10^{48}	七極	ななごく	*nana-goku*
8×10^{48}	八極	はちごく	*hachi-goku*
9×10^{48}	九極	きゅうごく	*kyuu-goku*
10^{49}	十極	じゅうごく	*juu-goku*

Irregularities or Special beyond Ten:

10^{50}	百極	ひゃくごく	*hyaku-goku*
10^{51}	千極	せんごく	*sen-goku*

Notes: 10^{48} is 1 000 000 000 000 000 000 000 000 000 000 000 000 000 000 000 000

腰 —— こし —— *koshi*

Japanese: こし
Romanized: *koshi*
Pattern: 和 I-K
Used with, or Means: objects attached to the waist such as swords, 袴 (*hakama*) (pleated pants), quiver, etc . . .

1 *hakama*	一腰	ひとこし	*hito-koshi*
2 *hakama*	二腰	ふたこし	*futa-koshi*
3 *hakama*	三腰	さんこし	*san-koshi*
4 *hakama*	四腰	よんこし	*yon-koshi*
5 *hakama*	五腰	ごこし	*go-koshi*
6 *hakama*	六腰	ろっこし	*rok-koshi*
7 *hakama*	七腰	ななこし	*nana-koshi*
8 *hakama*	八腰	はっこし / はちこし	*hak-koshi* / *hachi-koshi*
9 *hakama*	九腰	きゅうこし	*kyuu-koshi*
10 *hakama*	十腰	じゅっこし / じっこし	*juk-koshi* / *jik-koshi*

Irregularities or Special beyond Ten:

100 *hakama*	百腰	ひゃっこし / ひゃくこし	*hyak-koshi* / *hyaku-koshi*

Notes: none

個体——こたい——*kotai*

Japanese: こたい
Romanized: *kotai*
Pattern: 漢 K
Used with, or Means: (professional/technical jargon) number of living subjects of a scientific study, research project

1 animal	一個体	いっこたい / いちこたい	*ik-kotai* / *ichi-kotai*
2 animals	二個体	にこたい	*ni-kotai*
3 animals	三個体	さんこたい	*san-kotai*
4 animals	四個体	よんこたい	*yon-kotai*
5 animals	五個体	ごこたい	*go-kotai*
6 animals	六個体	ろっこたい / ろくこたい	*rok-kotai* / *roku-kotai*
7 animals	七個体	ななこたい	*nana-kotai*
8 animals	八個体	はっこたい / はちこたい	*hak-kotai* / *hachi-kotai*
9 animals	九個体	きゅうこたい	*kyuu-kotai*
10 animals	十個体	じゅっこたい / じっこたい	*juk-kotai* / *jik-kotai*

Irregularities or Special beyond Ten:

100 animals	百個体	ひゃっこたい / ひゃくこたい	*hyak-kotai* / *hyaku-kotai*

Notes: none

忽—こつ—*kotsu*

Japanese: こつ
Romanized: *kotsu*
Pattern: 漢 K
Used with, or Means: 1/100,000th, 10^{-5}

10^{-5}	一忽	いっこつ	*ik-kotsu*
2×10^{-5}	二忽	にこつ	*ni-kotsu*
3×10^{-5}	三忽	さんこつ	*san-kotsu*
4×10^{-5}	四忽	よんこつ	*yon-kotsu*
5×10^{-5}	五忽	ごこつ	*go-kotsu*
6×10^{-5}	六忽	ろっこつ	*rok-kotsu*
7×10^{-5}	七忽	ななこつ	*nana-kotsu*
8×10^{-5}	八忽	はっこつ	*hak-kotsu*
9×10^{-5}	九忽	きゅうこつ	*kyuu-kotsu*
10^{-4}	十忽	じゅっこつ / じっこつ	*juk-kotsu* / *jik-kotsu*

Irregularities or Special beyond Ten:

10^{-3}	百忽	ひゃっこつ	*hyak-kotsu*
10^{-2}	千忽	せんこつ	*sen-kotsu*

Notes: none

言 — こと — *koto*

Japanese: こと
Romanized: *koto*
Pattern: 和 II-K or 和 I-K
Used with, or Means: words, see also 言 (*gon*)

1 word	一言	ひとこと	*ik-koto*
2 words	二言	ふたこと	*futa-koto*
3 words	三言	みこと / さんこと	*mi-koto* / *san-koto*
4 words	四言	よんこと	*yon-koto*
5 words	五言	ごこと	*go-koto*
6 words	六言	ろっこと	*rok-koto*
7 words	七言	ななこと	*nana-koto*
8 words	八言	はっこと	*hak-koto*
9 words	九言	きゅうこと	*kyuu-koto*
10 words	十言	じゅっこと / じっこと	*juk-koto* / *jik-koto*

Irregularities or Special beyond Ten:

100 words	百言	ひゃっこと	*hyak-koto*

Notes: none

コペック—kopekku

Japanese: こぺっく
Romanized: *kopekku*
Pattern: 漢 K
Used with, or Means: *kopek*, копейка, Russian monetary unit

1 *kopek*	1 コペック	いちこぺっく	*ichi-kopekku*
2 *kopeks*	2 コペック	にこぺっく	*ni-kopekku*
3 *kopeks*	3 コペック	さんこぺっく	*san-kopekku*
4 *kopeks*	4 コペック	よんこぺっく	*yon-kopekku*
5 *kopeks*	5 コペック	ごこぺっく	*go-kopekku*
6 *kopeks*	6 コペック	ろっこぺっく	*rok-kopekku*
7 *kopeks*	7 コペック	ななこぺっく	*nana-kopekku*
8 *kopeks*	8 コペック	はっこぺっく はちこぺっく	*hak-kopekku* *hachi-kopekku*
9 *kopeks*	9 コペック	きゅうこぺっく	*kyuu-kopekku*
10 *kopeks*	10 コペック	じゅっこぺっく じっこぺっく じゅうこぺっく	*juk-kopekku* *jik-kopekku* *juu-kopekku*

Irregularities or Special beyond Ten:

100 *kopeks*	100 コペック	ひゃっこぺっく	*hyak-kopekku*

Notes: none

小間—*koma*

Japanese: こま
Romanized: *koma*
Pattern: 和 III-K
Used with, or Means: a tax levied on Edo[3] merchants equal to 20 坪 (tsubo)/歩 (bu), 102,486.205 in² (711.6 ft²)/66.12 m²

1 *koma*	一小間	ひとこま	*hito-koma*
2 *koma*	二小間	ふたこま	*futa-koma*
3 *koma*	三小間	みこま	*mi-koma*
4 *koma*	四小間	よこま	*yo-koma*
5 *koma*	五小間	ごこま	*go-koma*
6 *koma*	六小間	ろっこま	*rok-koma*
7 *koma*	七小間	ななこま	*nana-koma*
8 *koma*	八小間	はっこま	*hak-koma*
9 *koma*	九小間	きゅうこま	*kyuu-koma*
10 *koma*	十小間	じゅっこま / じっこま	*juk-koma* / *jik-koma*

Irregularities or Special beyond Ten:

100 *koma*	百小間	ひゃっこま	*hyak-koma*

Notes: none

---

[3] Edo (江戸) is the old name of Tokyo (東京).

コマ・駒・齣——こま—*koma*

Japanese: こま
Romanized: *koma*
Pattern: 和 I-K
Used with, or Means: movie scenes, shows, shorts, cartoon frames, panels, see also 場 (*ba*), see also 幕 (*maku*), see also 限 (*gen*); classes (授業 *jugyou*)

1 scene	一コマ・駒・齣	ひとこま	*hito-koma*
2 scenes	二コマ・駒・齣	ふたこま	*futa-koma*
3 scenes	三コマ・駒・齣	さんこま	*san-koma*
4 scenes	四コマ・駒・齣	よんこま	*yon-koma*
5 scenes	五コマ・駒・齣	ごこま	*go-koma*
6 scenes	六コマ・駒・齣	ろっこま	*rok-koma*
7 scenes	七コマ・駒・齣	ななこま	*nana-koma*
8 scenes	八コマ・駒・齣	はっこま はちこま	*hak-koma* *hachi-koma*
9 scenes	九コマ・駒・齣	きゅうこま	*kyuu-koma*
10 scenes	十コマ・駒・齣	じゅっこま じっこま	*juk-koma* *jik-koma*

Irregularities or Special beyond Ten:

100 scenes	百コマ・駒・齣	ひゃっこま ひゃくこま	*hyak-koma* *hyaku-koma*

Notes: Virtually no one uses 齣 nowadays.

梱 ― こり ― *kori*

Japanese: こり
Romanized: *kori*
Pattern: 和 II-K
Used with, or Means: raw silk (thread) (生糸 *kiito*), luggage (荷物 *nimotsu*)

1 silk thread	一梱	ひとこり	*hito-kori*
2 silk threads	二梱	ふたこり	*futa-kori*
3 silk threads	三梱	みこり	*mi-kori*
4 silk threads	四梱	よんこり	*yon-kori*
5 silk threads	五梱	ごこり	*go-kori*
6 silk threads	六梱	ろっこり	*rok-kori*
7 silk threads	七梱	ななこり	*nana-kori*
8 silk threads	八梱	はっこり	*hak-kori*
9 silk threads	九梱	きゅうこり	*kyuu-kori*
10 silk threads	十梱	じゅっこり	*juk-kori*
		じっこり	*jik-kori*

Irregularities or Special beyond Ten:

100 silk threads 百コマ・駒・齣 ひゃっこり *hyak-kori*

Notes: none

両・塊 — ころ — *koro*

Japanese: ころ
Romanized: *koro*
Pattern: 和 III-K
Used with, or Means: chunks of raw fish, see also さく (*saku*)

1 chunk	一両・塊	ひところ	*hito-koro*
2 chunks	二両・塊	ふたころ	*futa-koro*
3 chunks	三両・塊	みころ	*mi-koro*
4 chunks	四両・塊	よころ	*yo-koro*
5 chunks	五両・塊	ごころ	*go-koro*
6 chunks	六両・塊	ろっころ	*rok-koro*
7 chunks	七両・塊	ななころ	*nana-koro*
8 chunks	八両・塊	はっころ	*hak-koro*
9 chunks	九両・塊	きゅうころ	*kyuu-koro*
10 chunks	十両・塊	じゅっころ じっころ	*juk-koro* *jik-koro*

Irregularities or Special beyond Ten:

100 chunks	百両・塊	ひゃっころ	*hyak-koro*

Notes: none

喉 — こん — *kon*

Japanese: こん
Romanized: *kon*
Pattern: 漢 K
Used with, or Means: fish, see also 尾 (*bi*), see also 匹 (*hiki*)

1 fish	一喉	いっこん	*ik-kon*
2 fish	二喉	にこん	*ni-kon*
3 fish	三喉	さんこん	*san-kon*
4 fish	四喉	よんこん	*yon-kon*
5 fish	五喉	ごこん	*go-kon*
6 fish	六喉	ろっこん	*rok-kon*
7 fish	七喉	ななこん	*nana-kon*
8 fish	八喉	はっこん	*hak-kon*
9 fish	九喉	きゅうこん	*kyuu-kon*
10 fish	十喉	じゅっこん じっこん	*juk-kon* *jik-kon*

Irregularities or Special beyond Ten:

100 fish	百喉	ひゃっこん	*hyak-kon*

Notes: none

献 — こん — *kon*

Japanese: こん
Romanized: *kon*
Pattern: 漢 K
Used with, or Means: *sake* offerings

1 *sake* offering	一献	いっこん	*ik-kon*
2 *sake* offerings	二献	にこん	*ni-kon*
3 *sake* offerings	三献	さんこん	*san-kon*
4 *sake* offerings	四献	よんこん	*yon-kon*
5 *sake* offerings	五献	ごこん	*go-kon*
6 *sake* offerings	六献	ろっこん	*rok-kon*
7 *sake* offerings	七献	ななこん	*nana-kon*
8 *sake* offerings	八献	はっこん	*hak-kon*
9 *sake* offerings	九献	きゅうこん	*kyuu-kon*
10 *sake* offerings	十献	じゅっこん / じっこん	*juk-kon* / *jik-kon*

Irregularities or Special beyond Ten:

100 *sake* offerings	百献	ひゃっこん	*hyak-kon*

Notes: none

言―ごん―*gon*

Japanese: ごん
Romanized: *gon*
Pattern: 漢 Ø
Used with, or Means: words, letters, see also 言 (*koto*)

1 word	一言	いちごん	*ichi-gon*
2 words	二言	にごん	*ni-gon*
3 words	三言	さんごん	*san-gon*
4 words	四言	よんごん	*yon-gon*
5 words	五言	ごごん	*go-gon*
6 words	六言	ろくごん	*roku-gon*
7 words	七言	ななごん	*nana-gon*
8 words	八言	はちごん	*hachi-gon*
9 words	九言	きゅうごん	*kyuu-gon*
10 words	十言	じゅうごん	*juu-gon*

Irregularities or Special beyond Ten: none
Notes: 武士(男)に二言はない (*bushi [otoko] ni nigon wa nai*) is an expression that means, "You've got my word on it!" Literally it translates as "A (real) warrior (or man) need not be told to do something a second time."

さ・ざ—Sa/Za
座—ざ—za

Japanese: ざ
Romanized: za
Pattern: 漢 ∅
Used with, or Means: Shinto shrines, seated statues, gods; tall mountains; forests

1 statue	一座	いちざ	ichi-za
2 statues	二座	にざ	ni-za
3 statues	三座	さんざ	san-za
4 statues	四座	よんざ	yon-za
5 statues	五座	ござ	go-za
6 statues	六座	ろくざ	roku-za
7 statues	七座	ななざ	nana-za
8 statues	八座	はちざ	hachi-za
9 statues	九座	きゅうざ	kyuu-za
10 statues	十座	じゅうざ	juu-za

Irregularities or Special beyond Ten: none
Notes: none

才 — さい — *sai*

Japanese: さい
Romanized: *sai*
Pattern: 漢 S

Used with, or Means: *sai*, a unit of volume, 1/1,000th of a 升 (*shou*), 0.0609973467 fl oz/0.0018039068 L

1 *sai*	一才	いっさい	*is-sai*
2 *sai*	二才	にさい	*ni-sai*
3 *sai*	三才	さんさい	*san-sai*
4 *sai*	四才	よんさい	*yon-sai*
5 *sai*	五才	ごさい	*go-sai*
6 *sai*	六才	ろくさい	*roku-sai*
7 *sai*	七才	ななさい	*nana-sai*
8 *sai*	八才	はっさい / はちさい	*has-sai* / *hachi-sai*
9 *sai*	九才	きゅうさい	*kyuu-sai*
10 *sai*	十才	じゅっさい / じっさい	*jus-sai* / *jis-sai*

Irregularities or Special beyond Ten: none
Notes: none

菜—さい—*sai*

Japanese: さい
Romanized: *sai*
Pattern: 漢 S
Used with, or Means: dishes of food

1 dish	一菜	いっさい	<u>*is-sai*</u>
2 dishes	二菜	にさい	*ni-sai*
3 dishes	三菜	さんさい	*san-sai*
4 dishes	四菜	よんさい	*yon-sai*
5 dishes	五菜	ごさい	*go-sai*
6 dishes	六菜	ろくさい	*roku-sai*
7 dishes	七菜	ななさい	*nana-sai*
8 dishes	八菜	<u>はっさい</u> <u>はちさい</u>	<u>*has-sai*</u> <u>*hachi-sai*</u>
9 dishes	九菜	きゅうさい	*kyuu-sai*
10 dishes	十菜	<u>じゅっさい</u> <u>じっさい</u>	<u>*jus-sai*</u> <u>*jis-sai*</u>

Irregularities or Special beyond Ten: none
Notes: none

彩 — さい — *sai*

Japanese: さい
Romanized: *sai*
Pattern: 漢 S
Used with, or Means: (polite) colors, hues, tints, see also 色 (*iro*), see also 色 (*shoku*)

1 hue	一彩	いっさい	*is-sai*
2 hues	二彩	にさい	*ni-sai*
3 hues	三彩	さんさい	*san-sai*
4 hues	四彩	よんさい	*yon-sai*
5 hues	五彩	ごさい	*go-sai*
6 hues	六彩	ろくさい	*roku-sai*
7 hues	七彩	ななさい	*nana-sai*
8 hues	八彩	はっさい / はちさい	*has-sai* / *hachi-sai*
9 hues	九彩	きゅうさい	*kyuu-sai*
10 hues	十彩	じゅっさい / じっさい	*jus-sai* / *jis-sai*

Irregularities or Special beyond Ten: none
Notes: none

歳・才—さい—*sai*

Japanese: さい
Romanized: *sai*
Pattern: 漢 S
Used with, or Means: N years old

1 year old	一歳・才	いっさい	*is-sai*
2 years old	二歳・才	にさい	*ni-sai*
3 years old	三歳・才	さんさい	*san-sai*
4 years old	四歳・才	よんさい	*yon-sai*
5 years old	五歳・才	ごさい	*go-sai*
6 years old	六歳・才	ろくさい	*roku-sai*
7 years old	七歳・才	ななさい	*nana-sai*
8 years old	八歳・才	はっさい	*has-sai*
9 years old	九歳・才	きゅうさい	*kyuu-sai*
10 years old	十歳・才	じゅっさい / じっさい	*jus-sai* / *jis-sai*

Irregularities or Special beyond Ten:

20 years old	20歳・才	はたち / にじゅっさい	*hatachi* / *ni-jus-sai*

Notes: Although *Hatachi* is common, somewhat less common, but nonetheless correct, are the multiples of ten after twenty, which follow their own pattern and only go up to eighty (see next page).

Furthermore, there are a set of significant birthdays which, rather than numbers, have special names (also see next page).

十路 — そじ — *soji*

Japanese: そじ
Romanized: *soji*
Pattern: 和 IV
Used with, or Means: Nty years old

30 years old	三十路	みそじ	*mi-soji*
40 years old	四十路	よそじ	*yo-soji*
50 years old	五十路	いそじ	*i-soji*
60 years old	六十路	むそじ	*mu-soji*
70 years old	七十路	ななそじ	*nana-soji*
80 years old	八十路	やそじ	*ya-soji*

Significant Birthdays with Special Names:

60th birthday	還暦	かんれき	*kanreki*
70th birthday	古希	こき	*koki*
77th birthday	喜寿	きじゅ	*kiju*
80th birthday	傘寿	さんじゅ	*sanju*
88th birthday	米寿	べいじゅ	*beiju*
90th birthday	卒寿	そつじゅ	*sotsuju*
99th birthday	白寿	はくじゅ	*hakuju*
108th birthday	茶寿	ちゃじゅ	*chaju*
111th birthday	皇寿	こうじゅ	*kouju*
	川寿	せんじゅ	*senju*

載—さい—*sai*

Japanese: さい
Romanized: *sai*
Pattern: 漢 S
Used with, or Means: 10,000 正 (*sei*), 100 tredecillion, 10^{44}, years (archaic)

10^{44}	一載	いっさい	*is-sai*
2×10^{44}	二載	にさい	*ni-sai*
3×10^{44}	三載	さんさい	*san-sai*
4×10^{44}	四載	よんさい	*yon-sai*
5×10^{44}	五載	ごさい	*go-sai*
6×10^{44}	六載	ろくさい	*roku-sai*
7×10^{44}	七載	ななさい	*nana-sai*
8×10^{44}	八載	はっさい / はちさい	*has-sai* / *hachi-sai*
9×10^{44}	九載	きゅうさい	*kyuu-sai*
10^{45}	十載	じゅっさい / じっさい	*jus-sai* / *jis-sai*

Irregularities or Special beyond Ten:

10^{46}	百載	ひゃくさい	*hyaku-sai*
10^{47}	千載	せんさい	*sen-sai*

Notes: 10^{44} is 100 000 000 000 000 000 000 000 000 000 000 000 000 000 000

剤 — ざい — *zai*

Japanese: ざい
Romanized: *zai*
Pattern: 漢 ∅
Used with, or Means: doses of medicine

1 dose	一剤	いちざい	*ichi-zai*
2 doses	二剤	にざい	*ni-zai*
3 doses	三剤	さんざい	*san-zai*
4 doses	四剤	よんざい	*yon-zai*
5 doses	五剤	ござい	*go-zai*
6 doses	六剤	ろくざい	*roku-zai*
7 doses	七剤	ななざい	*nana-zai*
8 doses	八剤	はちざい	*hachi-zai*
9 doses	九剤	きゅうざい	*kyuu-zai*
10 doses	十剤	じゅうざい	*juu-zai*

Irregularities or Special beyond Ten: none
Notes: none

c—サイクル—*saikuru*

Japanese: サイクル
Romanized: *saikuru*
Pattern: 漢 S
Used with, or Means: cycles[4] (symbol: c)

1 c	1 サイクル	いっさいくる	*is-saikuru*
		いちさいくる	*ichi-saikuru*
2 c	2 サイクル	にさいくる	*ni-saikuru*
3 c	3 サイクル	さんさいくる	*san-saikuru*
4 c	4 サイクル	よんさいくる	*yon-saikuru*
5 c	5 サイクル	ごさいくる	*go-saikuru*
6 c	6 サイクル	ろくさいくる	*roku-saikuru*
7 c	7 サイクル	ななさいくる	*nana-saikuru*
8 c	8 サイクル	はっさいくる	*has-saikuru*
		はちさいくる	*hachi-saikuru*
9 c	9 サイクル	きゅうさいくる	*kyuu-saikuru*
10 c	10 サイクル	じゅっさいくる	*jus-saikuru*
		じっさいくる	*jis-saikuru*

Irregularities or Special beyond Ten: none
Notes: none

---

[4] Unlike its S. I. equivalent, the hertz (hz), cycles (c) are not S. I. units; although, there is a 1 to 1 ratio between cycles per second and hertz. However, cycles are just one half of the hertz equation because hertz are cycles *per second*.

竿・棹 — さお — *sao*

Japanese: さお
Romanized: *sao*
Pattern: 和 I-S
Used with, or Means: chests, chests of drawers, drawers, cupboards; shamisen; flags, poles, see also 竿 (*kan*), see also 本 (*hon*)

1 drawer	一竿・棹	ひとさお	*hito-sao*
2 drawers	二竿・棹	ふたさお	*futa-sao*
3 drawers	三竿・棹	さんさお	*san-sao*
4 drawers	四竿・棹	よんさお	*yon-sao*
5 drawers	五竿・棹	ごさお	*go-sao*
6 drawers	六竿・棹	ろくさお	*roku-sao*
7 drawers	七竿・棹	ななさお	*nana-sao*
8 drawers	八竿・棹	はっさお / はちさお	*has-sao* / *hachi-sao*
9 drawers	九竿・棹	きゅうさお	*kyuu-sao*
10 drawers	十竿・棹	じゅっさお / じっさお	*jus-sao* / *jis-sao*

Irregularities or Special beyond Ten: none
Notes: none

尺—さか—*saka*

Japanese: さか
Romanized: *saka*
Pattern: 和 I-S
Used with, or Means: same as 尺 (*shaku*)

1 *shaku*	一尺	ひとさか	*hito-saka*
2 *shaku*	二尺	ふたさか	*futa-saka*
3 *shaku*	三尺	さんさか	*san-saka*
4 *shaku*	四尺	よんさか	*yon-saka*
5 *shaku*	五尺	ごさか	*go-saka*
6 *shaku*	六尺	ろくさか	*roku-saka*
7 *shaku*	七尺	ななさか	*nana-saka*
8 *shaku*	八尺	はっさか / はちさか	*has-saka* / *hachi-saka*
9 *shaku*	九尺	きゅうさか	*kyuu-saka*
10 *shaku*	十尺	じゅっさか / じっさか	*jus-saka* / *jis-saka*

Irregularities or Special beyond Ten: none
Notes: none

さく —*saku*

Japanese: さく
Romanized: *saku*
Pattern: 和 I-S
Used with, or Means: block of fish prepared for sashimi, half a fish, see also 両・塊 (*koro*), see also 切れ (*kire*)

1 fish block	一さく	ひとさく	*hito-saku*
2 fish blocks	二さく	ふたさく	*futa-saku*
3 fish blocks	三さく	さんさく	*san-saku*
4 fish blocks	四さく	よんさく	*yon-saku*
5 fish blocks	五さく	ごさく	*go-saku*
6 fish blocks	六さく	ろくさく	*roku-saku*
7 fish blocks	七さく	ななさく	*nana-saku*
8 fish blocks	八さく	はっさく / はちさく	*has-saku* / *hachi-saku*
9 fish blocks	九さく	きゅうさく	*kyuu-saku*
10 fish blocks	十さく	じゅっさく / じっさく	*jus-saku* / *jis-saku*

Irregularities or Special beyond Ten: none
Notes: none

作 — さく — *saku*

Japanese: さく
Romanized: *saku*
Pattern: 漢 S
Used with, or Means: films, works, works of art, works of literature, see also 作品 (*sakuhin*)

1 film	一作	いっさく	*is-saku*
2 films	二作	にさく	*ni-saku*
3 films	三作	さんさく	*san-saku*
4 films	四作	よんさく	*yon-saku*
5 films	五作	ごさく	*go-saku*
6 films	六作	ろくさく	*roku-saku*
7 films	七作	ななさく	*nana-saku*
8 films	八作	はっさく / はちさく	*has-saku* / *hachi-saku*
9 films	九作	きゅうさく	*kyuu-saku*
10 films	十作	じゅっさく / じっさく	*jus-saku* / *jis-saku*

Irregularities or Special beyond Ten: none
Notes: none

作品—さくひん—*sakuhin*

Japanese: さくひん
Romanized: *sakuhin*
Pattern: 漢 S
Used with, or Means: works, works of art, works of literature, see also 作 (*saku*)

1 work	一作品	いっさくひん	*is-sakuhin*
2 works	二作品	にさくひん	*ni-sakuhin*
3 works	三作品	さんさくひん	*san-sakuhin*
4 works	四作品	よんさくひん	*yon-sakuhin*
5 works	五作品	ごさくひん	*go-sakuhin*
6 works	六作品	ろくさくひん	*roku-sakuhin*
7 works	七作品	ななさくひん	*nana-sakuhin*
8 works	八作品	はっさくひん はちさくひん	*has-sakuhin* *hachi-sakuhin*
9 works	九作品	きゅうさくひん	*kyuu-sakuhin*
10 works	十作品	じゅっさくひん じっさくひん	*jus-sakuhin* *jis-sakuhin*

Irregularities or Special beyond Ten: none
Notes: none

下げ—さげ—*sage*

Japanese: さげ
Romanized: *sage*
Pattern: 和 I-S
Used with, or Means: *hakama* (袴)[5]

1 *hakama*	一下げ	ひとさげ	*hito-sage*
2 *hakama*	二下げ	ふたさげ	*futa-sage*
3 *hakama*	三下げ	さんさげ	*san-sage*
4 *hakama*	四下げ	よんさげ	*yon-sage*
5 *hakama*	五下げ	ごさげ	*go-sage*
6 *hakama*	六下げ	ろくさげ	*roku-sage*
7 *hakama*	七下げ	ななさげ	*nana-sage*
8 *hakama*	八下げ	はっさげ / はちさげ	*has-sage* / *hachi-sage*
9 *hakama*	九下げ	きゅうさげ	*kyuu-sage*
10 *hakama*	十下げ	じゅっさげ / じっさげ	*jus-sage* / *jis-sage*

Irregularities or Special beyond Ten: none
Notes: none

---

[5] A hakama is a formal, divided or pleated skirt worn by *aikido/kyuudo* practitioners (black), *kannushi*/shrine priests (light blue), and *miko*/shrine maidens (red).

提げ — さげ — *sage*

Japanese: さげ
Romanized: *sage*
Pattern: 和 I-S
Used with, or Means: the number of *sake* bottles (徳利 *tokuri/tokkuri*); *sake* decanters (銚子 *choushi*) that one is carrying

1 sake bottle	一提げ	ひとさげ	*hito-sage*
2 sake bottles	二提げ	ふたさげ	*futa-sage*
3 sake bottles	三提げ	さんさげ	*san-sage*
4 sake bottles	四提げ	よんさげ	*yon-sage*
5 sake bottles	五提げ	ごさげ	*go-sage*
6 sake bottles	六提げ	ろくさげ	*roku-sage*
7 sake bottles	七提げ	ななさげ	*nana-sage*
8 sake bottles	八提げ	はっさげ / はちさげ	*has-sage* / *hachi-sage*
9 sake bottles	九提げ	きゅうさげ	*kyuu-sage*
10 sake bottles	十提げ	じゅっさげ / じっさげ	*jus-sage* / *jis-sage*

Irregularities or Special beyond Ten: none
Notes: none

差し — さし — *sashi*

Japanese: さし
Romanized: *sashi*
Pattern: 和 I-S
Used with, or Means: dances, *Noh* (能) dances, flowers for *Ikebana*

1 dance	一差し	ひとさし	*hito-sashi*
2 dances	二差し	ふたさし	*futa-sashi*
3 dances	三差し	さんさし	*san-sashi*
4 dances	四差し	よんさし	*yon-sashi*
5 dances	五差し	ごさし	*go-sashi*
6 dances	六差し	ろくさし	*roku-sashi*
7 dances	七差し	ななさし	*nana-sashi*
8 dances	八差し	はっさし / はちさし	*has-sashi* / *hachi-sashi*
9 dances	九差し	きゅうさし	*kyuu-sashi*
10 dances	十差し	じゅっさし / じっさし	*jus-sashi* / *jis-sashi*

Irregularities or Special beyond Ten: none
Notes: none

点し—さし—*sashi*

Japanese: さし
Romanized: *sashi*
Pattern: 和 I-S
Used with, or Means: eye drops (目薬 *megusuri*)

1 drop	一点し	ひとさし	*hito-sashi*
2 drops	二点し	ふたさし	*futa-sashi*
3 drops	三点し	さんさし	*san-sashi*
4 drops	四点し	よんさし	*yon-sashi*
5 drops	五点し	ごさし	*go-sashi*
6 drops	六点し	ろくさし	*roku-sashi*
7 drops	七点し	ななさし	*nana-sashi*
8 drops	八点し	はっさし / はちさし	*has-sashi* / *hachi-sashi*
9 drops	九点し	きゅうさし	*kyuu-sashi*
10 drops	十点し	じゅっさし / じっさし	*jus-sashi* / *jis-sashi*

Irregularities or Special beyond Ten: none
Notes: none

匙 — さじ — *saji*

Japanese: さじ
Romanized: *saji*
Pattern: 和 I-S
Used with, or Means: spoons, spoonfuls

1 spoonful	一匙	ひとさじ	*hito-saji*
2 spoonfuls	二匙	ふたさじ	*futa-saji*
3 spoonfuls	三匙	さんさじ	*san-saji*
4 spoonfuls	四匙	よんさじ	*yon-saji*
5 spoonfuls	五匙	ごさじ	*go-saji*
6 spoonfuls	六匙	ろくさじ	*roku-saji*
7 spoonfuls	七匙	ななさじ	*nana-saji*
8 spoonfuls	八匙	はっさじ / はちさじ	*has-saji* / *hachi-saji*
9 spoonfuls	九匙	きゅうさじ	*kyuu-saji*
10 spoonfuls	十匙	じゅっさじ / じっさじ	*jus-saji* / *jis-saji*

Irregularities or Special beyond Ten: none
Notes: none

冊 — さつ — *satsu*

Japanese: さつ
Romanized: *satsu*
Pattern: 漢 S
Used with, or Means: books, volumes, magazines, copies

1 book	一冊	いっさつ	*is-satsu*
2 books	二冊	にさつ	*ni-satsu*
3 books	三冊	さんさつ	*san-satsu*
4 books	四冊	よんさつ	*yon-satsu*
5 books	五冊	ごさつ	*go-satsu*
6 books	六冊	ろくさつ	*roku-satsu*
7 books	七冊	ななさつ	*nana-satsu*
8 books	八冊	はっさつ / はちさつ	*has-satsu* / *hachi-satsu*
9 books	九冊	きゅうさつ	*kyuu-satsu*
10 books	十冊	じゅっさつ / じっさつ	*jus-satsu* / *jis-satsu*

Irregularities or Special beyond Ten: none
Notes: none

札—さつ—*satsu*

Japanese: さつ
Romanized: *satsu*
Pattern: 漢 S
Used with, or Means: notes, bills (as in 千円札 *sen-en-satsu*—a thousand-yen note, or 千ドル札 *sen-doru-satsu*—a thousand dollar bill), bonds (finance), papers, letters, documents; *fuda*[6] (札)

1 document	一札	いっさつ	*is-satsu*
2 documents	二札	にさつ	*ni-satsu*
3 documents	三札	さんさつ	*san-satsu*
4 documents	四札	よんさつ	*yon-satsu*
5 documents	五札	ごさつ	*go-satsu*
6 documents	六札	ろくさつ	*roku-satsu*
7 documents	七札	ななさつ	*nana-satsu*
8 documents	八札	はっさつ / はちさつ	*has-satsu* / *hachi-satsu*
9 documents	九札	きゅうさつ	*kyuu-satsu*
10 documents	十札	じゅっさつ / じっさつ	*jus-satsu* / *jis-satsu*

Irregularities or Special beyond Ten: none
Notes: none

---

[6] A *fuda* is a talisman that one can buy at a shrine and insert into ones family shrine at home. It is usually a plaque of wood about six to twelve inches long, a quarter of an inch thick, and an inch-and-a-half wide, wrapped in paper, on which the name of a shrine's god is written.

刷 — さつ — *satsu*

Japanese: さつ
Romanized: *satsu*
Pattern: 漢 S
Used with, or Means: prints, copies, see also 刷り (*suri*)

1 print	一刷	いっさつ	*is-satsu*
2 prints	二刷	にさつ	*ni-satsu*
3 prints	三刷	さんさつ	*san-satsu*
4 prints	四刷	よんさつ	*yon-satsu*
5 prints	五刷	ごさつ	*go-satsu*
6 prints	六刷	ろくさつ	*roku-satsu*
7 prints	七刷	ななさつ	*nana-satsu*
8 prints	八刷	はっさつ はちさつ	*has-satsu* *hachi-satsu*
9 prints	九刷	きゅうさつ	*kyuu-satsu*
10 prints	十刷	じゅっさつ じっさつ	*jus-satsu* *jis-satsu*

Irregularities or Special beyond Ten: none
Notes: none

撮—さつ—*satsu*

Japanese: さつ
Romanized: *satsu*
Pattern: 漢 S

Used with, or Means: *satsu*; a unit of volume, 1 升 (*shou*), 60.99735 fl oz/1.80391 L

1 *satsu*	一撮	いっさつ	*is-satsu*
2 *satsu*	二撮	にさつ	*ni-satsu*
3 *satsu*	三撮	さんさつ	*san-satsu*
4 *satsu*	四撮	よんさつ	*yon-satsu*
5 *satsu*	五撮	ごさつ	*go-satsu*
6 *satsu*	六撮	ろくさつ	*roku-satsu*
7 *satsu*	七撮	ななさつ	*nana-satsu*
8 *satsu*	八撮	はっさつ / はちさつ	*has-satsu* / *hachi-satsu*
9 *satsu*	九撮	きゅうさつ	*kyuu-satsu*
10 *satsu*	十撮	じゅっさつ / じっさつ	*jus-satsu* / *jis-satsu*

Irregularities or Special beyond Ten: none
Notes: none

莢—さや—*saya*

Japanese: さや
Romanized: *saya*
Pattern: 和 II-S or 和 I-S
Used with, or Means: bean shells, pods, hulls

1 bean shell	一莢	ひとさや	hito-saya
2 bean shells	二莢	ふたさや	futa-saya
3 bean shells	三莢	みさや さんさや	mi-saya san-saya
4 bean shells	四莢	よんさや	yon-saya
5 bean shells	五莢	ごさや	go-saya
6 bean shells	六莢	ろくさや	roku-saya
7 bean shells	七莢	ななさや	nana-saya
8 bean shells	八莢	はっさや はちさや	has-saya hachi-saya
9 bean shells	九莢	きゅうさや	kyuu-saya
10 bean shells	十莢	じゅっさや じっさや	jus-saya jis-saya

Irregularities or Special beyond Ten: none
Notes: none

皿・盤 — さら — *sara*

Japanese: さら
Romanized: *sara*
Pattern: 和 III-S or 和 I-S
Used with, or Means: plates, helpings, sashimi, see also 品 (*hin*)

1 plate	一皿・盤	ひとさら	*hito-sara*
2 plates	二皿・盤	ふたさら	*futa-sara*
3 plates	三皿・盤	みさら / さんさら	*mi-sara* / *san-sara*
4 plates	四皿・盤	よさら / よんさら	*yo-sara* / *yon-sara*
5 plates	五皿・盤	ごさら	*go-sara*
6 plates	六皿・盤	ろくさら	*roku-sara*
7 plates	七皿・盤	ななさら	*nana-sara*
8 plates	八皿・盤	はっさら / はちさら	*has-sara* / *hachi-sara*
9 plates	九皿・盤	きゅうさら	*kyuu-sara*
10 plates	十皿・盤	じゅっさら / じっさら	*jus-sara* / *jis-sara*

Irregularities or Special beyond Ten: none
Notes: none

盞—さん—san

Japanese: さん
Romanized: *san*
Pattern: 漢 S
Used with, or Means: *sake* glasses, see also 杯 (*hai*), see also 口 (*ku*), see also 口 (*kou*)

1 *sake* glass	一盞	いっさん	*is-san*
2 *sake* glasses	二盞	にさん	*ni-san*
3 *sake* glasses	三盞	さんさん	*san-san*
4 *sake* glasses	四盞	よんさん	*yon-san*
5 *sake* glasses	五盞	ごさん	*go-san*
6 *sake* glasses	六盞	ろくさん	*roku-san*
7 *sake* glasses	七盞	ななさん	*nana-san*
8 *sake* glasses	八盞	はっさん	*has-san*
9 *sake* glasses	九盞	きゅうさん	*kyuu-san*
10 *sake* glasses	十盞	じゅっさん / じっさん	*jus-san* / *jis-san*

Irregularities or Special beyond Ten: none
Notes: none

山 — ざん — *zan*

Japanese: ざん
Romanized: *zan*
Pattern: 漢 ∅
Used with, or Means: temples (寺院 *jiin*), see also 寺 (*ji*); mountain climbs, see also 山 (*yama*)

1 temple	一山	いちざん	*ichi-zan*
2 temples	二山	にざん	*ni-zan*
3 temples	三山	さんざん	*san-zan*
4 temples	四山	よんざん	*yon-zan*
5 temples	五山	ござん	*go-zan*
6 temples	六山	ろくざん	*roku-zan*
7 temples	七山	ななざん	*nana-zan*
8 temples	八山	はちざん	*hachi-zan*
9 temples	九山	きゅうざん	*kyuu-zan*
10 temples	十山	じゅうざん	*juu-zan*

Irregularities or Special beyond Ten: none
Notes: none

し・じ—Shi/Ji
市—し—shi

Japanese: し
Romanized: *shi*
Pattern: 漢 S
Used with, or Means: cities

1 city	一市	いっし	*is-shi*
2 cities	二市	にし	*ni-shi*
3 cities	三市	さんし	*san-shi*
4 cities	四市	よんし	*yon-shi*
5 cities	五市	ごし	*go-shi*
6 cities	六市	ろくし	*roku-shi*
7 cities	七市	ななし	*nana-shi*
8 cities	八市	はっし	*has-shi*
9 cities	九市	きゅうし	*kyuu-shi*
10 cities	十市	じゅっし / じっし	*jus-shi* / *jis-shi*

Irregularities or Special beyond Ten: none
Notes: none

子 — し — *shi*

Japanese: し
Romanized: *shi*
Pattern: 漢 S
Used with, or Means: *Go* stones

1 *Go* stone	一子	いっし	*is-shi*
2 *Go* stones	二子	にし	*ni-shi*
3 *Go* stones	三子	さんし	*san-shi*
4 *Go* stones	四子	よんし	*yon-shi*
5 *Go* stones	五子	ごし	*go-shi*
6 *Go* stones	六子	ろくし	*roku-shi*
7 *Go* stones	七子	ななし	*nana-shi*
8 *Go* stones	八子	はっし	*has-shi*
9 *Go* stones	九子	きゅうし	*kyuu-shi*
10 *Go* stones	十子	じゅっし / じっし	*jus-shi* / *jis-shi*

Irregularities or Special beyond Ten: none

Notes: 囲碁 (*Igo*), or *Go* is a game somewhat similar to checkers. Typical *Go* boards sport a 19×19 grid. Players place black or white, smooth, flattened, round stones on each of the intersections. The goal is to surround an opponant's piece(s) with one on all sides.

枝 — し — *shi*

Japanese: し
Romanized: *shi*
Pattern: 漢 S
Used with, or Means: slender objects, halberds (rare)

1 halberd	一枝	<u>いっし</u>	<u>*is-shi*</u>
2 halberds	二枝	にし	*ni-shi*
3 halberds	三枝	さんし	*san-shi*
4 halberds	四枝	よんし	*yon-shi*
5 halberds	五枝	ごし	*go-shi*
6 halberds	六枝	ろくし	*roku-shi*
7 halberds	七枝	ななし	*nana-shi*
8 halberds	八枝	<u>はっし</u>	<u>*has-shi*</u>
9 halberds	九枝	きゅうし	*kyuu-shi*
10 halberds	十枝	じゅっし じっし	*jus-shi* *jis-shi*

Irregularities or Special beyond Ten: none
Notes: none

指 — し — *shi*

Japanese: し
Romanized: *shi*
Pattern: 漢 S
Used with, or Means: fingers, see also 本 (*hon*)

1 finger	一指	いっし	*is-shi*
2 fingers	二指	にし	*ni-shi*
3 fingers	三指	さんし	*san-shi*
4 fingers	四指	よんし	*yon-shi*
5 fingers	五指	ごし	*go-shi*
6 fingers	六指	ろくし	*roku-shi*
7 fingers	七指	ななし	*nana-shi*
8 fingers	八指	はっし	*has-shi*
9 fingers	九指	きゅうし	*kyuu-shi*
10 fingers	10指	じゅっし じっし	*jus-shi* *jis-shi*

Irregularities or Special beyond Ten: none
Notes: none

紙 — し — *shi*

Japanese: し
Romanized: *shi*
Pattern: 漢 S
Used with, or Means: newspaper subscriptions; kinds of newspaper, see also 部 (*bu*), see also 誌 (*shi*)

1 subscription	一紙	いっし	*is-shi*
2 subscriptions	二紙	にし	*ni-shi*
3 subscriptions	三紙	さんし	*san-shi*
4 subscriptions	四紙	よんし	*yon-shi*
5 subscriptions	五紙	ごし	*go-shi*
6 subscriptions	六紙	ろくし	*roku-shi*
7 subscriptions	七紙	ななし	*nana-shi*
8 subscriptions	八紙	はっし	*has-shi*
9 subscriptions	九紙	きゅうし	*kyuu-shi*
10 subscriptions	十紙	じゅっし / じっし	*jus-shi* / *jis-shi*

Irregularities or Special beyond Ten: none
Notes: 紙 (*shi*) counts mainly subscriptions and *kinds of* newspapers, whereas typically, the number of newspapers themselves is counted with 部 (*bu*).

誌 — し — *shi*

Japanese: し
Romanized: *shi*
Pattern: 漢 S
Used with, or Means: magazines, see also 部 (*bu*), see also 紙 (*shi*)

1 magazine	一誌	いっし	*is-shi*
2 magazines	二誌	にし	*ni-shi*
3 magazines	三誌	さんし	*san-shi*
4 magazines	四誌	よんし	*yon-shi*
5 magazines	五誌	ごし	*go-shi*
6 magazines	六誌	ろくし	*roku-shi*
7 magazines	七誌	ななし	*nana-shi*
8 magazines	八誌	はっし	*has-shi*
9 magazines	九誌	きゅうし	*kyuu-shi*
10 magazines	十誌	じゅっし / じっし	*jus-shi* / *jis-shi*

Irregularities or Special beyond Ten: none
Notes: none

歯 — し — *shi*

Japanese: し
Romanized: *shi*
Pattern: 漢 S
Used with, or Means: (professional/technical jargon) teeth, see also 本 (*hon*)

1 tooth	一歯	いっし	*is-shi*
2 teeth	二歯	にし	*ni-shi*
3 teeth	三歯	さんし	*san-shi*
4 teeth	四歯	よんし	*yon-shi*
5 teeth	五歯	ごし	*go-shi*
6 teeth	六歯	ろくし	*roku-shi*
7 teeth	七歯	ななし	*nana-shi*
8 teeth	八歯	はっし	*has-shi*
9 teeth	九歯	きゅうし	*kyuu-shi*
10 teeth	十歯	じゅっし / じっし	*jus-shi* / *jis-shi*

Irregularities or Special beyond Ten: none

Notes: Most Japanese use 本 (*hon*) to count teeth, but add 第 (*dai*) in front of ○歯 (N-*shi*): 第一歯 (*dai-is-shi*), 第二歯 (*dai-ni-shi*), and so on, to count *which* tooth in the mouth it is: *the first tooth, the second tooth,* respectively.

翅 — し — *shi*

Japanese: し
Romanized: *shi*
Pattern: 漢 S
Used with, or Means: birds

1 bird	一翅	いっし	<u>*is-shi*</u>
2 birds	二翅	にし	*ni-shi*
3 birds	三翅	さんし	*san-shi*
4 birds	四翅	よんし	*yon-shi*
5 birds	五翅	ごし	*go-shi*
6 birds	六翅	ろくし	*roku-shi*
7 birds	七翅	ななし	*nana-shi*
8 birds	八翅	はっし	<u>*has-shi*</u>
9 birds	九翅	きゅうし	*kyuu-shi*
10 birds	十翅	じゅっし じっし	<u>*jus-shi*</u> <u>*jis-shi*</u>

Irregularities or Special beyond Ten: none
Notes: none

詩 — し — *shi*

Japanese: し
Romanized: *shi*
Pattern: 漢 S
Used with, or Means: Chinese poems

1 Chinese poem	一詩	いっし	*is-shi*
2 Chinese poems	二詩	にし	*ni-shi*
3 Chinese poems	三詩	さんし	*san-shi*
4 Chinese poems	四詩	よんし	*yon-shi*
5 Chinese poems	五詩	ごし	*go-shi*
6 Chinese poems	六詩	ろくし	*roku-shi*
7 Chinese poems	七詩	ななし	*nana-shi*
8 Chinese poems	八詩	はっし	*has-shi*
9 Chinese poems	九詩	きゅうし	*kyuu-shi*
10 Chinese poems	十詩	じゅっし / じっし	*jus-shi* / *jis-shi*

Irregularities or Special beyond Ten: none
Notes: none

秄・秭 — し — *shi*

Japanese: し
Romanized: *shi*
Pattern: 漢 S
Used with, or Means: 10,000 垓 (*gai*), 1 septillion, 10^{24}

10^{24}	一秄・秭	いっし	*is-shi*
2×10^{24}	二秄・秭	にし	*ni-shi*
3×10^{24}	三秄・秭	さんし	*san-shi*
4×10^{24}	四秄・秭	よんし	*yon-shi*
5×10^{24}	五秄・秭	ごし	*go-shi*
6×10^{24}	六秄・秭	ろくし	*roku-shi*
7×10^{24}	七秄・秭	ななし	*nana-shi*
8×10^{24}	八秄・秭	はっし	*has-shi*
9×10^{24}	九秄・秭	きゅうし	*kyuu-shi*
10^{25}	十秄・秭	じゅっし / じっし	*jus-shi* / *jis-shi*

Irregularities or Special beyond Ten:

10^{26}	百秄・秭	ひゃくし	*hyaku-shi*
10^{27}	千秄・秭	せんし	*sen-shi*

Notes: 10^{24} is 1 000 000 000 000 000 000 000 000

糸 — し — *shi*

Japanese: し
Romanized: *shi*
Pattern: 漢 S
Used with, or Means: 1/10,000th (later 1/100,000th), 10^{-4} (later 10^{-5})

10^{-4} (later 10^{-5})	一糸	いっし	*is-shi*
2×10^{-4} (later 2×10^{-5})	二糸	にし	*ni-shi*
3×10^{-4} (later 3×10^{-5})	三糸	さんし	*san-shi*
4×10^{-4} (later 4×10^{-5})	四糸	よんし	*yon-shi*
5×10^{-4} (later 5×10^{-5})	五糸	ごし	*go-shi*
6×10^{-4} (later 6×10^{-5})	六糸	ろくし	*roku-shi*
7×10^{-4} (later 7×10^{-5})	七糸	ななし	*nana-shi*
8×10^{-4} (later 8×10^{-5})	八糸	はっし	*has-shi*
9×10^{-4} (later 9×10^{-5})	九糸	きゅうし	*kyuu-shi*
10^{-3} (later 10^{-4})	十糸	じゅっし / じっし	*jus-shi* / *jis-shi*

Irregularities or Special beyond Ten:

10^{-2} (later 10^{-3})	百糸	ひゃくし	*hyaku-shi*
10^{-1} (later 10^{-2})	千糸	せんし	*sen-shi*

Notes: none

児 — じ — *ji*

Japanese: じ
Romanized: *ji*
Pattern: 漢 ∅
Used with, or Means: children

1 child	一児	いちじ	*ichi-ji*
2 children	二児	にじ	*ni-ji*
3 children	三児	さんじ	*san-ji*
4 children	四児	よんじ	*yon-ji*
5 children	五児	ごじ	*go-ji*
6 children	六児	ろくじ	*roku-ji*
7 children	七児	ななじ	*nana-ji*
8 children	八児	はちじ	*hachi-ji*
9 children	九児	きゅうじ	*kyuu-ji*
10 children	十児	じゅうじ	*juu-ji*

Irregularities or Special beyond Ten: none
Notes: none

字 — じ — *ji*

Japanese: じ
Romanized: *ji*
Pattern: 漢 ∅
Used with, or Means: characters, letters, *kanji*, *kana*, glyphs, see also 文字 (*moji*)

1 glyph	一字	いちじ	*ichi-ji*
2 glyphs	二字	にじ	*ni-ji*
3 glyphs	三字	さんじ	*san-ji*
4 glyphs	四字	よんじ	*yon-ji*
5 glyphs	五字	ごじ	*go-ji*
6 glyphs	六字	ろくじ	*roku-ji*
7 glyphs	七字	ななじ	*nana-ji*
8 glyphs	八字	はちじ	*hachi-ji*
9 glyphs	九字	きゅうじ	*kyuu-ji*
10 glyphs	十字	じゅうじ	*juu-ji*

Irregularities or Special beyond Ten: none
Notes: none

寺 — じ — *ji*

Japanese: じ
Romanized: *ji*
Pattern: 漢 Ø
Used with, or Means: Buddhist temples, see also 山 (*zan*)

1 temple	一寺	いちじ	*ichi-ji*
2 temples	二寺	にじ	*ni-ji*
3 temples	三寺	さんじ	*san-ji*
4 temples	四寺	よんじ	*yon-ji*
5 temples	五寺	ごじ	*go-ji*
6 temples	六寺	ろくじ	*roku-ji*
7 temples	七寺	ななじ	*nana-ji*
8 temples	八寺	はちじ	*hachi-ji*
9 temples	九寺	きゅうじ	*kyuu-ji*
10 temples	十寺	じゅうじ	*juu-ji*

Irregularities or Special beyond Ten: none
Notes: none

時 — じ — *ji*

Japanese: じ
Romanized: *ji*
Pattern: 漢 Ø
Used with, or Means: N o'clock; hours of the day

1 o'clock	一時	いちじ	*ichi-ji*
2 o'clock	二時	にじ	*ni-ji*
3 o'clock	三時	さんじ	*san-ji*
4 o'clock	四時	<u>よじ</u>	<u>*yo-ji*</u>
5 o'clock	五時	ごじ	*go-ji*
6 o'clock	六時	ろくじ	*roku-ji*
7 o'clock	七時	<u>しちじ</u> <u>ななじ</u>	<u>*shichi-ji*</u> <u>*nana-ji*</u>
8 o'clock	八時	はちじ	*hachi-ji*
9 o'clock	九時	<u>くじ</u>	<u>*ku-ji*</u>
10 o'clock	十時	じゅうじ	*juu-ji*
11 o'clock	十一時	じゅういちじ	*juu-ichi-ji*
12 o'clock	十二時	じゅうにじ	*juu-ni-ji*

Irregularities or Special beyond Twelve: See Notes.

Notes: A. M. is 午前 (*gozen*), P. M. is 午後 (*gogo*). Thus, 午前 9 時 (*gozen ku-ji*) is nine A. M. whilst 午後 9 時 (*gogo ku-ji*) is nine P. M. However, many Japanese choose to use the 24-hour clock instead. Train and bus companies will write all their schedules using a 24-hour clock.

Some even go beyond 24 hours: the idea being that, rather than going to sleep and waking up extremely early the next morning for something scheduled around two or three A. M., you would just stay awake until then.

Late-night television programming schedules tend to follow this pattern, listing a show for Monday night at 26-o'clock rather than two A. M. on Tuesday morning. The schedule will reset itself around five A. M. when the early risers are getting up to watch the weather and traffic reports.

13 o'clock (1 P. M.)	十三時	じゅうさんじ	juu-san-ji
14 o'clock (2 P. M.)	十四時	じゅうよじ	juu-yo-ji
15 o'clock (3 P. M.)	十五時	じゅうごじ	juu-go-ji
16 o'clock (4 P. M.)	十六時	じゅうろくじ	juu-roku-ji
17 o'clock (5 P. M.)	十七時	じゅうななじ	juu-nana-ji
18 o'clock (6 P. M.)	十八時	じゅうはちじ	juu-hachi-ji
19 o'clock (7 P. M.)	十九時	じゅうくじ	juu-ku-ji
20 o'clock (8 P. M.)	二十時	にじゅうじ	ni-juu-ji
21 o'clock (9 P. M.)	二十一時	にじゅういちじ	ni-juu-ichi-ji
22 o'clock (10 P. M.)	二十二時	にじゅうにじ	ni-juu-ni-ji
23 o'clock (11 P. M.)	二十三時	にじゅうさんじ	ni-juu-san-ji
24 o'clock (12 A. M.) 0 o'clock[7]	二十四時 零時	にじゅうよじ れいじ	ni-juu-yo-ji rei-ji

---

[7] Due to the way train and bus schedules are arranged, you are likely to see 0 時 rather than 24 時, followed by a series of numbers representing the minutes at the top of a posted schedule:

0 時	05	15	25	35	45	55
1 時	03	12	21	30	39	48	57
2 時	09		25		41		57

... And so on ...

時間—じかん—ji-kan

Japanese: じかん
Romanized: *ji-kan*
Pattern: 漢 ∅
Used with, or Means: number of hours, see also 時限 (*jigen*)

1 hour	一時間	いちじかん	*ichi-ji-kan*
2 hours	二時間	にじかん	*ni-ji-kan*
3 hours	三時間	さんじかん	*san-ji-kan*
4 hours	四時間	よんじかん	*yon-ji-kan*
5 hours	五時間	ごじかん	*go-ji-kan*
6 hours	六時間	ろくじかん	*roku-ji-kan*
7 hours	七時間	ななじかん	*nana-ji-kan*
8 hours	八時間	はちじかん	*hachi-ji-kan*
9 hours	九時間	きゅうじかん	*kyuu-ji-kan*
10 hours	十時間	じゅうじかん	*juu-ji-kan*

Irregularities or Special beyond Ten: none
Notes: none

次 — じ — *ji*

Japanese: じ
Romanized: *ji*
Pattern: 漢 ∅
Used with, or Means: numerical order, number of times

1st in line	一次	いちじ	*ichi-ji*
2nd in line	二次	にじ	*ni-ji*
3rd in line	三次	さんじ	*san-ji*
4th in line	四次	よんじ	*yon-ji*
5th in line	五次	ごじ	*go-ji*
6th in line	六次	ろくじ	*roku-ji*
7th in line	七次	ななじ	*nana-ji*
8th in line	八次	はちじ	*hachi-ji*
9th in line	九次	きゅうじ	*kyuu-ji*
10th in line	十次	じゅうじ	*juu-ji*

Irregularities or Special beyond Ten: none
Notes: none

耳 — じ — *ji*

Japanese: じ
Romanized: *ji*
Pattern: 漢 ∅
Used with, or Means: pairs of rabbits

1 pair of rabbits	一耳	いちじ	*ichi-ji*
2 pairs of rabbits	二耳	にじ	*ni-ji*
3 pairs of rabbits	三耳	さんじ	*san-ji*
4 pairs of rabbits	四耳	よんじ	*yon-ji*
5 pairs of rabbits	五耳	ごじ	*go-ji*
6 pairs of rabbits	六耳	ろくじ	*roku-ji*
7 pairs of rabbits	七耳	ななじ	*nana-ji*
8 pairs of rabbits	八耳	はちじ	*hachi-ji*
9 pairs of rabbits	九耳	きゅうじ	*kyuu-ji*
10 pairs of rabbits	十耳	じゅうじ	*juu-ji*

Irregularities or Special beyond Ten: none
Notes: none

試合—しあい—*shiai*

Japanese: しあい
Romanized: *shiai*
Pattern: 漢 S or 和 I-S
Used with, or Means: matches, sporting events, competitions

1 match	一試合	いっしあい いちしあい ひとしあい	*is-shiai* *ichi-shiai* *hito-shiai*
2 matches	二試合	にしあい ふたしあい	*ni-shiai* *futa-shiai*
3 matches	三試合	さんしあい	*san-shiai*
4 matches	四試合	よんしあい	*yon-shiai*
5 matches	五試合	ごしあい	*go-shiai*
6 matches	六試合	ろくしあい	*roku-shiai*
7 matches	七試合	ななしあい	*nana-shiai*
8 matches	八試合	はっしあい はちしあい	*has-shiai* *hachi-shiai*
9 matches	九試合	きゅうしあい	*kyuu-shiai*
10 matches	十試合	じゅっしあい じっしあい	*jus-shiai* *jis-shiai*

Irregularities or Special beyond Ten: none
Notes: none

cc—シーシー—*shiishii*

Japanese: シーシー
Romanized: *shiishii*
Pattern: 漢 S or 漢 Ø
Used with, or Means: cubic centimeters (S. I. symbol: cc)

1 cc	1 シーシー	いっしいしい いちしいしい	*is-shiishii* *ichi-shiishii*
2 cc	2 シーシー	にしいしい	*ni-shiishii*
3 cc	3 シーシー	さんしいしい	*san-shiishii*
4 cc	4 シーシー	よんしいしい	*yon-shiishii*
5 cc	5 シーシー	ごしいしい	*go-shiishii*
6 cc	6 シーシー	ろくしいしい	*roku-shiishii*
7 cc	7 シーシー	ななしいしい	*nana-shiishii*
8 cc	8 シーシー	はっしいしい はちしいしい	*has-shiishii* *hachi-shiishii*
9 cc	9 シーシー	きゅうしいしい	*kyuu-shiishii*
10 cc	10 シーシー	じゅっしいしい じっしいしい	*jus-shiishii* *jis-shiishii*

Irregularities or Special beyond Ten: none
Notes: none

シーズン—*shiizun*

Japanese: しいずん
Romanized: *shiizun*
Pattern: 和 I-S or 漢 Ø
Used with, or Means: sports seasons

1 season	1 シーズン	ひとしいずん いちしいずん	*hito-shiizun* *ichi-shiizun*
2 seasons	2 シーズン	ふたしいずん にしいずん	*futa-shiizun* *ni-shiizun*
3 seasons	3 シーズン	さんしいずん	*san-shiizun*
4 seasons	4 シーズン	よんしいずん	*yon-shiizun*
5 seasons	5 シーズン	ごしいずん	*go-shiizun*
6 seasons	6 シーズン	ろくしいずん	*roku-shiizun*
7 seasons	7 シーズン	ななしいずん	*nana-shiizun*
8 seasons	8 シーズン	はっしいずん	*has-shiizun*
9 seasons	9 シーズン	きゅうしいずん	*kyuu-shiizun*
10 seasons	10 シーズン	じゅっしいずん じっしいずん	*jus-shiizun* *jis-shiizun*

Irregularities or Special beyond Ten: none
Notes: none

シート—*shiito*

Japanese: しいと
Romanized: *shiito*
Pattern: 漢 S
Used with, or Means: seats, sheets (of paper)

1 seat	1 シート	いっしいと いちしいと	*is-shiito* *ichi-shiito*
2 seats	2 シート	にしいと	*ni-shiito*
3 seats	3 シート	さんしいと	*san-shiito*
4 seats	4 シート	よんしいと	*yon-shiito*
5 seats	5 シート	ごしいと	*go-shiito*
6 seats	6 シート	ろくしいと	*roku-shiito*
7 seats	7 シート	ななしいと	*nana-shiito*
8 seats	8 シート	はっしいと はちしいと	*has-shiito* *hachi-shiito*
9 seats	9 シート	きゅうしいと	*kyuu-shiito*
10 seats	10 シート	じゅっしいと じっしいと	*jus-shiito* *jis-shiito*

Irregularities or Special beyond Ten: none
Notes: none

入―しお―*shio*

Japanese: しお
Romanized: *shio*
Pattern: 和 I-S
Used with, or Means: the number of times one soaks fabrics in dyes to dye them

1 soak	一入	ひとしお	*hito-shio*
2 soaks	二入	ふたしお	*futa-shio*
3 soaks	三入	さんしお	*san-shio*
4 soaks	四入	よんしお	*yon-shio*
5 soaks	五入	ごしお	*go-shio*
6 soaks	六入	ろくしお	*roku-shio*
7 soaks	七入	ななしお	*nana-shio*
8 soaks	八入	はっしお	*has-shio*
9 soaks	九入	きゅうしお	*kyuu-shio*
10 soaks	十入	じゅっしお じっしお	*jus-shio* *jis-shio*

Irregularities or Special beyond Ten: none
Notes: none

塩—しお—*shio*

Japanese: しお
Romanized: *shio*
Pattern: 和 I-S
Used with, or Means: shakes of salt, see also 振り *(furi)*

1 shake	一塩	ひとしお	*hito-shio*
2 shakes	二塩	ふたしお	*futa-shio*
3 shakes	三塩	さんしお	*san-shio*
4 shakes	四塩	よんしお	*yon-shio*
5 shakes	五塩	ごしお	*go-shio*
6 shakes	六塩	ろくしお	*roku-shio*
7 shakes	七塩	ななしお	*nana-shio*
8 shakes	八塩	はっしお	*has-shio*
9 shakes	九塩	きゅうしお	*kyuu-shio*
10 shakes	十塩	じゅっしお じっしお	*jus-shio* *jis-shio*

Irregularities or Special beyond Ten: none
Notes: none

式 — しき — *shiki*

Japanese: しき
Romanized: *shiki*
Pattern: 和 III-S or 漢 S
Used with, or Means: sets of things, such as furniture, documents

1 set	一式	ひとしき いっしき	*hito-shiki* *is-shiki*
2 sets	二式	ふたしき にしき	*futa-shiki* *ni-shiki*
3 sets	三式	みしき さんしき	*mi-shiki* *san-shiki*
4 sets	四式	よしき よんしき	*yo-shiki* *yon-shiki*
5 sets	五式	ごしき	*go-shiki*
6 sets	六式	ろくしき	*roku-shiki*
7 sets	七式	ななしき	*nana-shiki*
8 sets	八式	はっしき	*has-shiki*
9 sets	九式	きゅうしき	*kyuu-shiki*
10 sets	十式	じゅっしき じっしき	*jus-shiki* *jis-shiki*

Irregularities or Special beyond Ten: none
Notes: none

軸—じく—*jiku*

Japanese: じく
Romanized: *jiku*
Pattern: 漢 ∅
Used with, or Means: scrolls, see also 幅 (*fuku*)

1 scroll	一軸	いちじく	*ichi-jiku*
2 scrolls	二軸	にじく	*ni-jiku*
3 scrolls	三軸	さんじく	*san-jiku*
4 scrolls	四軸	よんじく	*yon-jiku*
5 scrolls	五軸	ごじく	*go-jiku*
6 scrolls	六軸	ろくじく	*roku-jiku*
7 scrolls	七軸	ななじく	*nana-jiku*
8 scrolls	八軸	はちじく	*hachi-jiku*
9 scrolls	九軸	きゅうじく	*kyuu-jiku*
10 scrolls	十軸	じゅうじく	*juu-jiku*

Irregularities or Special beyond Ten: none
Notes: none

時限—じげん—*jigen*

Japanese: じげん
Romanized: *jigen*
Pattern: 漢 ∅
Used with, or Means: N[th] hour, N[th] period

1st period	一時限	いちじげん	*ichi-jigen*
2nd period	二時限	にじげん	*ni-jigen*
3rd period	三時限	さんじげん	*san-jigen*
4th period	四時限	よんじげん	*yon-jigen*
5th period	五時限	ごじげん	*go-jigen*
6th period	六時限	ろくじげん	*roku-jigen*
7th period	七時限	ななじげん	*nana-jigen*
8th period	八時限	はちじげん	*hachi-jigen*
9th period	九時限	きゅうじげん	*kyuu-jigen*
10th period	十時限	じゅうじげん	*juu-jigen*

Irregularities or Special beyond Ten: none
Notes: none

次元—じげん—*jigen*

Japanese: じげん
Romanized: *jigen*
Pattern: 漢 ∅
Used with, or Means: dimensions; dimensional

1 dimensional	一次元	いちじげん	*ichi-jigen*
2 dimensional	二次元	にじげん	*ni-jigen*
3 dimensional	三次元	さんじげん	*san-jigen*
4 dimensional	四次元	よんじげん	*yon-jigen*
5 dimensional	五次元	ごじげん	*go-jigen*
6 dimensional	六次元	ろくじげん	*roku-jigen*
7 dimensional	七次元	ななじげん	*nana-jigen*
8 dimensional	八次元	はちじげん	*hachi-jigen*
9 dimensional	九次元	きゅうじげん	*kyuu-jigen*
10 dimensional	十次元	じゅうじげん	*juu-jigen*

Irregularities or Special beyond Ten: none
Notes: none

雫・滴 — しずく — *shizuku*

Japanese: しずく
Romanized: *shizuku*
Pattern: 和 III-S or 和 I-S
Used with, or Means: drops of liquid, rain drops, see also 滴 (*teki*), see also 点 (*ten*)

1 drop	一雫・滴	ひとしずく	*hito-shizuku*
2 drops	二雫・滴	ふたしずく	*futa-shizuku*
3 drops	三雫・滴	みしずく さんしずく	*mi-shizuku* *san-shizuku*
4 drops	四雫・滴	よしずく よんしずく	*yo-shizuku* *yon-shizuku*
5 drops	五雫・滴	ごしずく	*go-shizuku*
6 drops	六雫・滴	ろくしずく	*roku-shizuku*
7 drops	七雫・滴	ななしずく	*nana-shizuku*
8 drops	八雫・滴	はっしずく はちしずく	*has-shizuku* *hachi-shizuku*
9 drops	九雫・滴	きゅうしずく	*kyuu-shizuku*
10 drops	十雫・滴	じゅっしずく じっしずく	*jus-shizuku* *jis-shizuku*

Irregularities or Special beyond Ten: none
Notes: none

室—しつ—*shitsu*

Japanese: しつ
Romanized: *shitsu*
Pattern: 漢 S
Used with, or Means: rooms

1 room	一室	いっしつ	<u>*is-shitsu*</u>
2 rooms	二室	にしつ	*ni-shitsu*
3 rooms	三室	さんしつ	*san-shitsu*
4 rooms	四室	よんしつ	*yon-shitsu*
5 rooms	五室	ごしつ	*go-shitsu*
6 rooms	六室	ろくしつ	*roku-shitsu*
7 rooms	七室	ななしつ	*nana-shitsu*
8 rooms	八室	<u>はっしつ</u>	<u>*has-shitsu*</u>
9 rooms	九室	きゅうしつ	*kyuu-shitsu*
10 rooms	十室	じゅっしつ じっしつ	*jus-shitsu* *jis-shitsu*

Irregularities or Special beyond Ten: none
Notes: none

品—しな—*shina*

Japanese: しな
Romanized: *shina*
Pattern: 和 III-S
Used with, or Means: meal courses, gifts, see also 品 (*hin*)

1 course	一品	ひとしな	*hito-shina*
2 courses	二品	ふたしな	*futa-shina*
3 courses	三品	みしな	*mi-shina*
4 courses	四品	よしな	*yo-shina*
5 courses	五品	ごしな	*go-shina*
6 courses	六品	ろくしな	*roku-shina*
7 courses	七品	ななしな	*nana-shina*
8 courses	八品	はっしな / はちしな	*has-shina* / *hachi-shina*
9 courses	九品	きゅうしな	*kyuu-shina*
10 courses	十品	じゅっしな / じっしな	*jus-shina* / *jis-shina*

Irregularities or Special beyond Ten: none
Notes: none

締め—しめ—*shime*

Japanese: しめ
Romanized: *shime*
Pattern: 和 I-S
Used with, or Means: paper reams, bundles

1 ream	一締め	ひとしめ	*hito-shime*
2 reams	二締め	ふたしめ	*futa-shime*
3 reams	三締め	さんしめ	*san-shime*
4 reams	四締め	よんしめ	*yon-shime*
5 reams	五締め	ごしめ	*go-shime*
6 reams	六締め	ろくしめ	*roku-shime*
7 reams	七締め	ななしめ	*nana-shime*
8 reams	八締め	はっしめ	*has-shime*
9 reams	九締め	きゅうしめ	*kyuu-shime*
10 reams	十締め	じゅっしめ / じっしめ	*jus-shime* / *jis-shime*

Irregularities or Special beyond Ten: none
Notes: none

社—しゃ—*sha*

Japanese: しゃ
Romanized: *sha*
Pattern: 漢 S
Used with, or Means: companies; Shinto shrines, see also 社 (*yashiro*)

1 company	一社	いっしゃ	*is-sha*
2 companies	二社	にしゃ	*ni-sha*
3 companies	三社	さんしゃ	*san-sha*
4 companies	四社	よんしゃ	*yon-sha*
5 companies	五社	ごしゃ	*go-sha*
6 companies	六社	ろくしゃ	*roku-sha*
7 companies	七社	ななしゃ	*nana-sha*
8 companies	八社	はっしゃ / はちしゃ	*has-sha* / *hachi-sha*
9 companies	九社	きゅうしゃ	*kyuu-sha*
10 companies	十社	じゅっしゃ / じっしゃ	*jus-sha* / *jis-sha*

Irregularities or Special beyond Ten: none
Notes: none

車—しゃ—*sha*

Japanese: しゃ
Romanized: *sha*
Pattern: 漢 S
Used with, or Means: cars, see also 台 (*dai*); freight train cars, see also 号車 (*gousha*)

1 car	一車	いっしゃ	*is-sha*
2 cars	二車	にしゃ	*ni-sha*
3 cars	三車	さんしゃ	*san-sha*
4 cars	四車	よんしゃ	*yon-sha*
5 cars	五車	ごしゃ	*go-sha*
6 cars	六車	ろくしゃ	*roku-sha*
7 cars	七車	ななしゃ	*nana-sha*
8 cars	八車	はっしゃ	*has-sha*
9 cars	九車	きゅうしゃ	*kyuu-sha*
10 cars	十車	じゅっしゃ / じっしゃ	*jus-sha* / *jis-sha*

Irregularities or Special beyond Ten: none
Notes: none

者 — しゃ — *sha*

Japanese: しゃ
Romanized: *sha*
Pattern: 漢 S
Used with, or Means: the number of people involved in an activity (a 3-person discussion); the number of runners, batters in a baseball inning

1 person	一者	いっしゃ	*is-sha*
2 persons	二者	にしゃ	*ni-sha*
3 persons	三者	さんしゃ	*san-sha*
4 persons	四者	よんしゃ	*yon-sha*
5 persons	五者	ごしゃ	*go-sha*
6 persons	六者	ろくしゃ	*roku-sha*
7 persons	七者	ななしゃ	*nana-sha*
8 persons	八者	はっしゃ	*has-sha*
9 persons	九者	きゅうしゃ	*kyuu-sha*
10 persons	十者	じゅっしゃ じっしゃ	*jus-sha* *jis-sha*

Irregularities or Special beyond Ten: none

Notes: Typically for baseball games, they will use 走者 (*sousha—runner*) and 打者 (*dasha—batter*). These are not really counters, but you will hear or read about 第一走者 (*dai-ichi-sousha—the first runner* [notice how it is not *dai-is-sousha*, but *dai-ichi-sousha*]) or 第二打者 (*dai-ni-dasha—the second batter*), and so on.

沙 — しゃ — *sha*

Japanese: しゃ
Romanized: *sha*
Pattern: 漢 S
Used with, or Means: 1/100,000,000th, 10⁻⁸

10⁻⁸	一沙	いっしゃ	*is-sha*
2×10⁻⁸	二沙	にしゃ	*ni-sha*
3×10⁻⁸	三沙	さんしゃ	*san-sha*
4×10⁻⁸	四沙	よんしゃ	*yon-sha*
5×10⁻⁸	五沙	ごしゃ	*go-sha*
6×10⁻⁸	六沙	ろくしゃ	*roku-sha*
7×10⁻⁸	七沙	ななしゃ	*nana-sha*
8×10⁻⁸	八沙	はっしゃ	*has-sha*
9×10⁻⁸	九沙	きゅうしゃ	*kyuu-sha*
10⁻⁷	十沙	じゅっしゃ / じっしゃ	*jus-sha* / *jis-sha*

Irregularities or Special beyond Ten:

10⁻⁶	百沙	ひゃくしゃ	*hyaku-sha*
2×10⁻⁵	千沙	せんしゃ	*sen-sha*

Notes: none

勺 — しゃく — *shaku*

Japanese: しゃく
Romanized: *shaku*
Pattern: 漢 S

Used with, or Means: *shaku*, a unit of area, 1/100th of a 坪 (*tsubo*), 51.23977 in²/0.03306 m²; *shaku*, a unit of volume, 1/100th of a 升 (*shou*), 0.60997 fl oz/0.01804 L

1 *shaku*	一勺	いっしゃく	*is-shaku*
2 *shaku*	二勺	にしゃく	*ni-shaku*
3 *shaku*	三勺	さんしゃく	*san-shaku*
4 *shaku*	四勺	よんしゃく	*yon-shaku*
5 *shaku*	五勺	ごしゃく	*go-shaku*
6 *shaku*	六勺	ろくしゃく	*roku-shaku*
7 *shaku*	七勺	ななしゃく	*nana-shaku*
8 *shaku*	八勺	はっしゃく	*has-shaku*
9 *shaku*	九勺	きゅうしゃく	*kyuu-shaku*
10 *shaku*	十勺	じゅっしゃく / じっしゃく	*jus-shaku* / *jis-shaku*

Irregularities or Special beyond Ten: none
Notes: none

尺—しゃく—*shaku*

Japanese: しゃく
Romanized: *shaku*
Pattern: 漢 S
Used with, or Means: *shaku*, a unit of length: 11.93033 in/0.30303 m; a length of cloth

1 *shaku*	一尺	いっしゃく	*is-shaku*
2 *shaku*	二尺	にしゃく	*ni-shaku*
3 *shaku*	三尺	さんしゃく	*san-shaku*
4 *shaku*	四尺	よんしゃく	*yon-shaku*
5 *shaku*	五尺	ごしゃく	*go-shaku*
6 *shaku*	六尺	ろくしゃく	*roku-shaku*
7 *shaku*	七尺	ななしゃく	*nana-shaku*
8 *shaku*	八尺	はっしゃく	*has-shaku*
9 *shaku*	九尺	きゅうしゃく	*kyuu-shaku*
10 *shaku*	十尺	じゅっしゃく じっしゃく	*jus-shaku* *jis-shaku*

Irregularities or Special beyond Ten: none
Notes: none

隻 — しゃく — *shaku*

Japanese: しゃく
Romanized: *shaku*
Pattern: 漢 S
Used with, or Means: sides of a folding screen; formerly the number of arrows, birds, fish; large ships, warships, same as 隻 (*seki*)

1 large ship	一隻	いっしゃく	*is-shaku*
2 large ships	二隻	にしゃく	*ni-shaku*
3 large ships	三隻	さんしゃく	*san-shaku*
4 large ships	四隻	よんしゃく	*yon-shaku*
5 large ships	五隻	ごしゃく	*go-shaku*
6 large ships	六隻	ろくしゃく	*roku-shaku*
7 large ships	七隻	ななしゃく	*nana-shaku*
8 large ships	八隻	はっしゃく	*has-shaku*
9 large ships	九隻	きゅうしゃく	*kyuu-shaku*
10 large ships	十隻	じゅっしゃく / じっしゃく	*jus-shaku* / *jis-shaku*

Irregularities or Special beyond Ten: none
Notes: none

車線 — しゃせん — *shasen*

Japanese: しゃせん
Romanized: *shasen*
Pattern: 漢 S
Used with, or Means: traffic lanes

1 lane	一車線	いっしゃせん	*is-shasen*
2 lanes	二車線	にしゃせん	*ni-shasen*
3 lanes	三車線	さんしゃせん	*san-shasen*
4 lanes	四車線	よんしゃせん	*yon-shasen*
5 lanes	五車線	ごしゃせん	*go-shasen*
6 lanes	六車線	ろくしゃせん	*roku-shasen*
7 lanes	七車線	ななしゃせん	*nana-shasen*
8 lanes	八車線	はっしゃせん	*has-shasen*
9 lanes	九車線	きゅうしゃせん	*kyuu-shasen*
10 lanes	十車線	じゅっしゃせん じっしゃせん	*jus-shasen* *jis-shasen*

Irregularities or Special beyond Ten: none
Notes: none

炷 — しゅ — *shu*

Japanese: しゅ
Romanized: *shu*
Pattern: 漢 S
Used with, or Means: formerly the number of burning incense sticks; (polite) incense sticks

1 incense stick	一炷	いっしゅ	*is-shu*
2 incense sticks	二炷	にしゅ	*ni-shu*
3 incense sticks	三炷	さんしゅ	*san-shu*
4 incense sticks	四炷	よんしゅ	*yon-shu*
5 incense sticks	五炷	ごしゅ	*go-shu*
6 incense sticks	六炷	ろくしゅ	*roku-shu*
7 incense sticks	七炷	ななしゅ	*nana-shu*
8 incense sticks	八炷	はっしゅ	*has-shu*
9 incense sticks	九炷	きゅうしゅ	*kyuu-shu*
10 incense sticks	十炷	じゅっしゅ / じっしゅ	*jus-shu* / *jis-shu*

Irregularities or Special beyond Ten: none
Notes: none

首 — しゅ — *shu*

Japanese: しゅ
Romanized: *shu*
Pattern: 漢 S
Used with, or Means: Chinese poems, *waka* poems, *tanka* poems, pieces

1 poem	一首	いっしゅ	*is-shu*
2 poems	二首	にしゅ	*ni-shu*
3 poems	三首	さんしゅ	*san-shu*
4 poems	四首	よんしゅ	*yon-shu*
5 poems	五首	ごしゅ	*go-shu*
6 poems	六首	ろくしゅ	*roku-shu*
7 poems	七首	ななしゅ	*nana-shu*
8 poems	八首	はっしゅ	*has-shu*
9 poems	九首	きゅうしゅ	*kyuu-shu*
10 poems	十首	じゅっしゅ / じっしゅ	*jus-shu* / *jis-shu*

Irregularities or Special beyond Ten: none
Notes: none

朱 — しゅ — *shu*

Japanese: しゅ
Romanized: *shu*
Pattern: 漢 S
Used with, or Means: *shu* former monetary unit, 1/16th of a 両 (*ryou*)

1 *shu*	一朱	いっしゅ	*is-shu*
2 *shu*	二朱	にしゅ	*ni-shu*
3 *shu*	三朱	さんしゅ	*san-shu*
4 *shu*	四朱	よんしゅ	*yon-shu*
5 *shu*	五朱	ごしゅ	*go-shu*
6 *shu*	六朱	ろくしゅ	*roku-shu*
7 *shu*	七朱	ななしゅ	*nana-shu*
8 *shu*	八朱	はっしゅ	*has-shu*
9 *shu*	九朱	きゅうしゅ	*kyuu-shu*
10 *shu*	十朱	じゅっしゅ / じっしゅ	*jus-shu* / *jis-shu*

Irregularities or Special beyond Ten: none
Notes: none

株—しゅ—*shu*

Japanese: しゅ
Romanized: *shu*
Pattern: 漢 S
Used with, or Means: plants, trees, see also 株 (*kabu*)

1 plant	一株	いっしゅ	*is-shu*
2 plants	二株	にしゅ	*ni-shu*
3 plants	三株	さんしゅ	*san-shu*
4 plants	四株	よんしゅ	*yon-shu*
5 plants	五株	ごしゅ	*go-shu*
6 plants	六株	ろくしゅ	*roku-shu*
7 plants	七株	ななしゅ	*nana-shu*
8 plants	八株	はっしゅ	*has-shu*
9 plants	九株	きゅうしゅ	*kyuu-shu*
10 plants	十株	じゅっしゅ / じっしゅ	*jus-shu* / *jis-shu*

Irregularities or Special beyond Ten: none
Notes: none

種 — しゅ — *shu*

Japanese: しゅ
Romanized: *shu*
Pattern: 漢 S
Used with, or Means: sorts, kinds, varieties, sports events, see also 種類 (*shurui*)

1 kind	一種	いっしゅ	*is-shu*
2 kinds	二種	にしゅ	*ni-shu*
3 kinds	三種	さんしゅ	*san-shu*
4 kinds	四種	よんしゅ	*yon-shu*
5 kinds	五種	ごしゅ	*go-shu*
6 kinds	六種	ろくしゅ	*roku-shu*
7 kinds	七種	ななしゅ	*nana-shu*
8 kinds	八種	はっしゅ	*has-shu*
9 kinds	九種	きゅうしゅ	*kyuu-shu*
10 kinds	十種	じゅっしゅ / じっしゅ	*jus-shu* / *jis-shu*

Irregularities or Special beyond Ten: none
Notes: none

樹 — じゅ — *ju*

Japanese: じゅ
Romanized: *ju*
Pattern: 漢 Ø
Used with, or Means: trees, see also 本 (*hon*)

1 tree	一樹	いちじゅ	*ichi-ju*
2 trees	二樹	にじゅ	*ni-ju*
3 trees	三樹	さんじゅ	*san-ju*
4 trees	四樹	よんじゅ	*yon-ju*
5 trees	五樹	ごじゅ	*go-ju*
6 trees	六樹	ろくじゅ	*roku-ju*
7 trees	七樹	ななじゅ	*nana-ju*
8 trees	八樹	はちじゅ	*hachi-ju*
9 trees	九樹	きゅうじゅ	*kyuu-ju*
10 trees	十樹	じゅうじゅ	*juu-ju*

Irregularities or Special beyond Ten: none
Notes: none

舟 — しゅう — *shuu*

Japanese: しゅう
Romanized: *shuu*
Pattern: 漢 S
Used with, or Means: (polite) boats, see also 隻 (*seki*), see also 艘 (*sou*)

1 boat	一舟	いっしゅう	*is-shuu*
2 boats	二舟	にしゅう	*ni-shuu*
3 boats	三舟	さんしゅう	*san-shuu*
4 boats	四舟	よんしゅう	*yon-shuu*
5 boats	五舟	ごしゅう	*go-shuu*
6 boats	六舟	ろくしゅう	*roku-shuu*
7 boats	七舟	ななしゅう	*nana-shuu*
8 boats	八舟	はっしゅう	*has-shuu*
9 boats	九舟	きゅうしゅう	*kyuu-shuu*
10 boats	十舟	じゅっしゅう じっしゅう	*jus-shuu* *jis-shuu*

Irregularities or Special beyond Ten: none
Notes: none

周 — しゅう — *shuu*

Japanese: しゅう
Romanized: *shuu*
Pattern: 漢 S
Used with, or Means: rounds, circuits, laps (around a track)

1 lap	一周	いっしゅう	*is-shuu*
2 laps	二周	にしゅう	*ni-shuu*
3 laps	三周	さんしゅう	*san-shuu*
4 laps	四周	よんしゅう	*yon-shuu*
5 laps	五周	ごしゅう	*go-shuu*
6 laps	六周	ろくしゅう	*roku-shuu*
7 laps	七周	ななしゅう	*nana-shuu*
8 laps	八周	はっしゅう	*has-shuu*
9 laps	九周	きゅうしゅう	*kyuu-shuu*
10 laps	十周	じゅっしゅう / じっしゅう	*jus-shuu* / *jis-shuu*

Irregularities or Special beyond Ten: none
Notes: none

第○週 — だい○しゅう — *dai-○-shuu*

Japanese: だい○しゅう
Romanized: *shuu*
Pattern: 漢 S
Used with, or Means: order of weeks (in a month)

week 1	第一週	だいいっしゅう	*dai-is-shuu*
week 2	第二週	だいにしゅう	*dai-ni-shuu*
week 3	第三週	だいさんしゅう	*dai-san-shuu*
week 4	第四週	だいよんしゅう	*dai-yon-shuu*
week 5	第五週	だいごしゅう	*dai-go-shuu*

Irregularities or Special beyond Ten: none
Notes: There can only be up to five weeks in a month.

週間—しゅうかん—*shuu-kan*

Japanese: しゅうかん
Romanized: *shuu-kan*
Pattern: 漢 S
Used with, or Means: number of weeks

1 week	一週間	いっしゅうかん	*is-shuu-kan*
2 weeks	二週間	にしゅうかん	*ni-shuu-kan*
3 weeks	三週間	さんしゅうかん	*san-shuu-kan*
4 weeks	四週間	よんしゅうかん	*yon-shuu-kan*
5 weeks	五週間	ごしゅうかん	*go-shuu-kan*
6 weeks	六週間	ろくしゅうかん	*roku-shuu-kan*
7 weeks	七週間	ななしゅうかん	*nana-shuu-kan*
8 weeks	八週間	はっしゅうかん	*has-shuu-kan*
9 weeks	九週間	きゅうしゅうかん	*kyuu-shuu-kan*
10 weeks	十週間	じゅっしゅうかん じっしゅうかん	*jus-shuu-kan* *jis-shuu-kan*

Irregularities or Special beyond Ten: none
Notes: none

十 — じゅう — *juu*

Japanese: じゅう
Romanized: *juu*
Pattern: 漢 ∅
Used with, or Means: 10, ten, 10[1]

10	十	じゅう	*juu*
20	二十	にじゅう	*ni-juu*
30	三十	さんじゅう	*san-juu*
40	四十	よんじゅう	*yon-juu*
50	五十	ごじゅう	*go-juu*
60	六十	ろくじゅう	*roku-juu*
70	七十	ななじゅう	*nana-juu*
80	八十	はちじゅう	*hachi-juu*
90	九十	きゅうじゅう	*kyuu-juu*

Irregularities or Special beyond Ten: none
Notes: 十十 (*juu-juu*) does not exist because that would be 百 (*hyaku*).

什 — じゅう — *juu*

Japanese: じゅう
Romanized: *juu*
Pattern: 漢 ∅
Used with, or Means: Chinese poems

1 poem	一什	いちじゅう	*ichi-juu*
2 poems	二什	にじゅう	*ni-juu*
3 poems	三什	さんじゅう	*san-juu*
4 poems	四什	よんじゅう	*yon-juu*
5 poems	五什	ごじゅう	*go-juu*
6 poems	六什	ろくじゅう	*roku-juu*
7 poems	七什	ななじゅう	*nana-juu*
8 poems	八什	はちじゅう	*hachi-juu*
9 poems	九什	きゅうじゅう	*kyuu-juu*
10 poems	十什	じゅうじゅう	*juu-juu*

Irregularities or Special beyond Ten: none
Notes: none

汁 — じゅう — *juu*

Japanese: じゅう
Romanized: *juu*
Pattern: 漢 ∅
Used with, or Means: bowls of soup

1 bowl of soup	一汁	いちじゅう	*ichi-juu*
2 bowls of soup	二汁	にじゅう	*ni-juu*
3 bowls of soup	三汁	さんじゅう	*san-juu*
4 bowls of soup	四汁	よんじゅう	*yon-juu*
5 bowls of soup	五汁	ごじゅう	*go-juu*
6 bowls of soup	六汁	ろくじゅう	*roku-juu*
7 bowls of soup	七汁	ななじゅう	*nana-juu*
8 bowls of soup	八汁	はちじゅう	*hachi-juu*
9 bowls of soup	九汁	きゅうじゅう	*kyuu-juu*
10 bowls of soup	十汁	じゅうじゅう	*juu-juu*

Irregularities or Special beyond Ten: none
Notes: none

重 — じゅう — *juu*

Japanese: じゅう
Romanized: *juu*
Pattern: 漢 ∅
Used with, or Means: folds, layers, plies, tiered boxes (重箱 *juubako*), see also 重 (*e*), see also 重ね (*kasane*), see also 襲 (*kasane*)

1 fold	一重	いちじゅう	*ichi-juu*
2 folds	二重	にじゅう	*ni-juu*
3 folds	三重	さんじゅう	*san-juu*
4 folds	四重	よんじゅう	*yon-juu*
5 folds	五重	ごじゅう	*go-juu*
6 folds	六重	ろくじゅう	*roku-juu*
7 folds	七重	ななじゅう	*nana-juu*
8 folds	八重	はちじゅう	*hachi-juu*
9 folds	九重	きゅうじゅう	*kyuu-juu*
10 folds	十重	じゅうじゅう	*juu-juu*

Irregularities or Special beyond Ten: none
Notes: none

銃—じゅう—*juu*

Japanese: じゅう
Romanized: *juu*
Pattern: 漢 Ø
Used with, or Means: (literary language) guns, see also 挺・丁 (*chou*), see also 挺 (*tei*)

1 gun	一銃	いちじゅう	*ichi-juu*
2 guns	二銃	にじゅう	*ni-juu*
3 guns	三銃	さんじゅう	*san-juu*
4 guns	四銃	よんじゅう	*yon-juu*
5 guns	五銃	ごじゅう	*go-juu*
6 guns	六銃	ろくじゅう	*roku-juu*
7 guns	七銃	ななじゅう	*nana-juu*
8 guns	八銃	はちじゅう	*hachi-juu*
9 guns	九銃	きゅうじゅう	*kyuu-juu*
10 guns	十銃	じゅうじゅう	*juu-juu*

Irregularities or Special beyond Ten: none
Notes: none

周忌—しゅうき—*shuuki*

Japanese: しゅうき
Romanized: *shuuki*
Pattern: 漢 S
Used with, or Means: death anniversaries

1 death anniversary	一周忌	いっしゅうき	*is-shuuki*
2 death anniversaries	二周忌	にしゅうき	*ni-shuuki*
3 death anniversaries	三周忌	さんしゅうき	*san-shuuki*
4 death anniversaries	四周忌	よんしゅうき	*yon-shuuki*
5 death anniversaries	五周忌	ごしゅうき	*go-shuuki*
6 death anniversaries	六周忌	ろくしゅうき	*roku-shuuki*
7 death anniversaries	七周忌	ななしゅうき	*nana-shuuki*
8 death anniversaries	八周忌	はっしゅうき	*has-shuuki*
9 death anniversaries	九周忌	きゅうしゅうき	*kyuu-shuuki*
10 death anniversaries	十周忌	じゅっしゅうき じっしゅうき	*jus-shuuki* *jis-shuuki*

Irregularities or Special beyond Ten: none
Notes: none

周年 — しゅうねん — *shuunen*

Japanese: しゅうねん
Romanized: *shuunen*
Pattern: 漢 S
Used with, or Means: years in a row, continuous years; years after an event

1 continuous year	一周年	いっしゅうねん	*is-shuunen*
2 continuous years	二周年	にしゅうねん	*ni-shuunen*
3 continuous years	三周年	さんしゅうねん	*san-shuunen*
4 continuous years	四周年	よんしゅうねん	*yon-shuunen*
5 continuous years	五周年	ごしゅうねん	*go-shuunen*
6 continuous years	六周年	ろくしゅうねん	*roku-shuunen*
7 continuous years	七周年	ななしゅうねん	*nana-shuunen*
8 continuous years	八周年	はっしゅうねん	*has-shuunen*
9 continuous years	九周年	きゅうしゅうねん	*kyuu-shuunen*
10 continuous years	十周年	じゅっしゅうねん じっしゅうねん	*jus-shuunen* *jis-shuunen*

Irregularities or Special beyond Ten: none
Notes: none

宿—しゅく—*shuku*

Japanese: しゅく
Romanized: *shuku*
Pattern: 漢 S
Used with, or Means: night's stay; same as 泊 (*haku*); a station on the Toukai Highway, see Notes in 次 (*tsugi*)

1 night's stay	一宿	いっしゅく	*is-shuku*
2 nights' stay	二宿	にしゅく	*ni-shuku*
3 nights' stay	三宿	さんしゅく	*san-shuku*
4 nights' stay	四宿	よんしゅく	*yon-shuku*
5 nights' stay	五宿	ごしゅく	*go-shuku*
6 nights' stay	六宿	ろくしゅく	*roku-shuku*
7 nights' stay	七宿	ななしゅく	*nana-shuku*
8 nights' stay	八宿	はっしゅく	*has-shuku*
9 nights' stay	九宿	きゅうしゅく	*kyuu-shuku*
10 nights' stay	十宿	じゅっしゅく じっしゅく	*jus-shuku* *jis-shuku*

Irregularities or Special beyond Ten: none
Notes: 泊 (*haku*) is used more often.

種目―しゅもく―*shumoku*

Japanese: しゅもく
Romanized: *shumoku*
Pattern: 和 III-S or 漢 S
Used with, or Means: items of business; events

1 item of business	一種目	ひとしゅもく / いっしゅもく	*hito-shumoku* / *is-shumoku*
2 items of business	二種目	ふたしゅもく / にしゅもく	*futa-shumoku* / *ni-shumoku*
3 items of business	三種目	さんしゅもく	*mi-shumoku*
4 items of business	四種目	よんしゅもく	*yo-shumoku*
5 items of business	五種目	ごしゅもく	*go-shumoku*
6 items of business	六種目	ろくしゅもく	*roku-shumoku*
7 items of business	七種目	ななしゅもく	*nana-shumoku*
8 items of business	八種目	はっしゅもく	*has-shumoku*
9 items of business	九種目	きゅうしゅもく	*kyuu-shumoku*
10 items of business	十種目	じゅっしゅもく / じっしゅもく	*jus-shumoku* / *jis-shumoku*

Irregularities or Special beyond Ten: none
Notes: none

種類—しゅるい—*shurui*

Japanese: しゅるい
Romanized: *shurui*
Pattern: 漢 S
Used with, or Means: sorts, kinds, see also 種 (*shu*)

1 kind	一種類	いっしゅるい	*is-shurui*
2 kinds	二種類	にしゅるい	*ni-shurui*
3 kinds	三種類	さんしゅるい	*san-shurui*
4 kinds	四種類	よんしゅるい	*yon-shurui*
5 kinds	五種類	ごしゅるい	*go-shurui*
6 kinds	六種類	ろくしゅるい	*roku-shurui*
7 kinds	七種類	ななしゅるい	*nana-shurui*
8 kinds	八種類	はっしゅるい	*has-shurui*
9 kinds	九種類	きゅうしゅるい	*kyuu-shurui*
10 kinds	十種類	じゅっしゅるい じっしゅるい	*jus-shurui* *jis-shurui*

Irregularities or Special beyond Ten: none
Notes: none

巡 —じゅん— *jun*

Japanese: じゅん
Romanized: *jun*
Pattern: 漢 Ø
Used with, or Means: patrols, rounds

1 patrol	一巡	いちじゅん <u>ひとまわり</u>	*ichi-jun* <u>*hito-mawari*</u>
2 patrols	二巡	にじゅん	*ni-jun*
3 patrols	三巡	さんじゅん	*san-jun*
4 patrols	四巡	よんじゅん	*yon-jun*
5 patrols	五巡	ごじゅん	*go-jun*
6 patrols	六巡	ろくじゅん	*roku-jun*
7 patrols	七巡	ななじゅん	*nana-jun*
8 patrols	八巡	はちじゅん	*hachi-jun*
9 patrols	九巡	きゅうじゅん	*kyuu-jun*
10 patrols	十巡	じゅうじゅん	*juu-jun*

Irregularities or Special beyond Ten: none
Notes: none

旬―じゅん―jun

Japanese: じゅん
Romanized: *jun*
Pattern: 漢 ∅
Used with, or Means: ten-day periods

1 ten-day period	一旬	いちじゅん	*ichi-jun*
2 ten-day periods	二旬	にじゅん	*ni-jun*
3 ten-day periods	三旬	さんじゅん	*san-jun*
4 ten-day periods	四旬	よんじゅん	*yon-jun*
5 ten-day periods	五旬	ごじゅん	*go-jun*
6 ten-day periods	六旬	ろくじゅん	*roku-jun*
7 ten-day periods	七旬	ななじゅん	*nana-jun*
8 ten-day periods	八旬	はちじゅん	*hachi-jun*
9 ten-day periods	九旬	きゅうじゅん	*kyuu-jun*
10 ten-day periods	十旬	じゅうじゅん	*juu-jun*

Irregularities or Special beyond Ten: none
Notes: none

女 — じょ — *jo*

Japanese: じょ
Romanized: *jo*
Pattern: 漢 ∅
Used with, or Means: daughters (see Notes); girls; sisters

1 daughter	一女	いちじょ	*ichi-jo*
1st daughter	長女	ちょうじょ	*chou-jo*
2 daughters	二女	にじょ	*ni-jo*
2nd daughter	次女	じじょ	*ji-jo*
3 daughters 3rd daughter	三女	さんじょ	*san-jo*
4 daughters 4th daughter	四女	よんじょ	*yon-jo*
5 daughters 5th daughter	五女	ごじょ	*go-jo*
6 daughters 6th daughter	六女	ろくじょ	*roku-jo*
7 daughters 7th daughter	七女	ななじょ	*nana-jo*
8 daughters 8th daughter	八女	はちじょ	*hachi-jo*
9 daughters 9th daughter	九女	きゅうじょ	*kyuu-jo*
10 daughters 10th daughter	十女	じゅうじょ	*juu-jo*

Irregularities or Special beyond Ten: none
Notes: When counting daughters, your first daughter is your *chou-jo*, and second is *ji-jo*, rather than *ichi-jo* and *ni-jo*.

秭・秭—じょ—*jo*

Japanese: じょ
Romanized: *jo*
Pattern: 漢 Ø
Used with, or Means: 10,000 垓 (*gai*), 1 septillion, 10^{24}

10^{24}	一秭・秭	いちじょ	*ichi-jo*
2×10^{24}	二秭・秭	にじょ	*ni-jo*
3×10^{24}	三秭・秭	さんじょ	*san-jo*
4×10^{24}	四秭・秭	よんじょ	*yon-jo*
5×10^{24}	五秭・秭	ごじょ	*go-jo*
6×10^{24}	六秭・秭	ろくじょ	*roku-jo*
7×10^{24}	七秭・秭	ななじょ	*nana-jo*
8×10^{24}	八秭・秭	はちじょ	*hachi-jo*
9×10^{24}	九秭・秭	きゅうじょ	*kyuu-jo*
10^{25}	十秭・秭	じゅうじょ	*juu-jo*

Irregularities or Special beyond Ten:

10^{26}	百秭・秭	ひゃくじょ	*hyaku-jo*
10^{27}	千秭・秭	せんじょ	*sen-jo*

Notes: 10^{24} is 1 000 000 000 000 000 000 000 000

勝 — しょう — shou

Japanese: しょう
Romanized: shou
Pattern: 漢 S
Used with, or Means: sports wins

1 win	一勝	いっしょう	is-shou
2 wins	二勝	にしょう	ni-shou
3 wins	三勝	さんしょう	san-shou
4 wins	四勝	よんしょう	yon-shou
5 wins	五勝	ごしょう	go-shou
6 wins	六勝	ろくしょう	roku-shou
7 wins	七勝	ななしょう	nana-shou
8 wins	八勝	はっしょう	has-shou
9 wins	九勝	きゅうしょう	kyuu-shou
10 wins	十勝	じゅっしょう じっしょう	jus-shou jis-shou

Irregularities or Special beyond Ten: none
Notes: none

升 — しょう — *shou*

Japanese: しょう
Romanized: *shou*
Pattern: 漢 S
Used with, or Means: *shou*, a unit of volume, 60.99735 fl oz (3.81233 pt)/1.80391 L, see also 升 (*masu*)

1 *shou*	一升	いっしょう	*is-shou*
2 *shou*	二升	にしょう	*ni-shou*
3 *shou*	三升	さんしょう	*san-shou*
4 *shou*	四升	よんしょう	*yon-shou*
5 *shou*	五升	ごしょう	*go-shou*
6 *shou*	六升	ろくしょう	*roku-shou*
7 *shou*	七升	ななしょう	*nana-shou*
8 *shou*	八升	はっしょう	*has-shou*
9 *shou*	九升	きゅうしょう	*kyuu-shou*
10 *shou*	十升	じゅっしょう じっしょう	*jus-shou* *jis-shou*

Irregularities or Special beyond Ten: none
Notes: none

床——しょう——*shou*

Japanese: しょう
Romanized: *shou*
Pattern: 漢 S
Used with, or Means: beds, *futon* (布団)

1 bed	一床	いっしょう	*is-shou*
2 beds	二床	にしょう	*ni-shou*
3 beds	三床	さんしょう	*san-shou*
4 beds	四床	よんしょう	*yon-shou*
5 beds	五床	ごしょう	*go-shou*
6 beds	六床	ろくしょう	*roku-shou*
7 beds	七床	ななしょう	*nana-shou*
8 beds	八床	はっしょう	*has-shou*
9 beds	九床	きゅうしょう	*kyuu-shou*
10 beds	十床	じゅっしょう / じっしょう	*jus-shou* / *jis-shou*

Irregularities or Special beyond Ten: none
Notes: none

章—しょう—*shou*

Japanese: しょう
Romanized: *shou*
Pattern: 漢 S
Used with, or Means: book chapters

chapter 1	(第)一章	(だい)いっしょう	*(dai)-is-shou*
chapter 2	(第)二章	(だい)にしょう	*(dai)-ni-shou*
chapter 3	(第)三章	(だい)さんしょう	*(dai)-san-shou*
chapter 4	(第)四章	(だい)よんしょう	*(dai)-yon-shou*
chapter 5	(第)五章	(だい)ごしょう	*(dai)-go-shou*
chapter 6	(第)六章	(だい)ろくしょう	*(dai)-roku-shou*
chapter 7	(第)七章	(だい)ななしょう	*(dai)-nana-shou*
chapter 8	(第)八章	(だい)はっしょう	*(dai)-has-shou*
chapter 9	(第)九章	(だい)きゅうしょう	*(dai)-kyuu-shou*
chapter 10	(第)十章	(だい)じゅっしょう (だい)じっしょう	*(dai)-jus-shou* *(dai)-jis-shou*

Irregularities or Special beyond Ten: none
Notes: Typically, this counter is prefixed with 第 (*dai*).

抄 — しょう — *shou*

Japanese: しょう
Romanized: *shou*
Pattern: 漢 S

Used with, or Means: *shou*; a unit of volume, 1/10th of a 升 (*shou*), 6.09973 fl oz/0.18039 L

1 *shou*	一抄	いっしょう	*is-shou*
2 *shou*	二抄	にしょう	*ni-shou*
3 *shou*	三抄	さんしょう	*san-shou*
4 *shou*	四抄	よんしょう	*yon-shou*
5 *shou*	五抄	ごしょう	*go-shou*
6 *shou*	六抄	ろくしょう	*roku-shou*
7 *shou*	七抄	ななしょう	*nana-shou*
8 *shou*	八抄	はっしょう	*has-shou*
9 *shou*	九抄	きゅうしょう	*kyuu-shou*
10 *shou*	十抄	じゅっしょう / じっしょう	*jus-shou* / *jis-shou*

Irregularities or Special beyond Ten: none
Notes: none

丈 — じょう — *jou*

Japanese: じょう
Romanized: *jou*
Pattern: 漢 Ø

Used with, or Means: *jou*, a unit of length, 10 尺 (*shaku*), 119.30315 in (9.94193 ft)/3.03030 m

1 *jou*	一丈	いちじょう	*ichi-jou*
2 *jou*	二丈	にじょう	*ni-jou*
3 *jou*	三丈	さんじょう	*san-jou*
4 *jou*	四丈	よんじょう	*yon-jou*
5 *jou*	五丈	ごじょう	*go-jou*
6 *jou*	六丈	ろくじょう	*roku-jou*
7 *jou*	七丈	ななじょう	*nana-jou*
8 *jou*	八丈	はちじょう	*hachi-jou*
9 *jou*	九丈	きゅうじょう	*kyuu-jou*
10 *jou*	十丈	じゅうじょう	*juu-jou*

Irregularities or Special beyond Ten: none
Notes: none

条—じょう—*jou*

Japanese: じょう
Romanized: *jou*
Pattern: 漢 ∅
Used with, or Means: articles, sections (e.g. of the Constitution); strip-like, slender objects, 帯 (*obi*); rivers, see also 筋 (*suji*), see also 本 (*hon*); streets in Kyoto and some other cities (usually translating to *street*)

1 section	(第)一条	(だい)いちじょう	(*dai*)-*ichi-jou*
2 sections	(第)二条	(だい)にじょう	(*dai*)-*ni-jou*
3 sections	(第)三条	(だい)さんじょう	(*dai*)-*san-jou*
4 sections	(第)四条	(だい)よんじょう	(*dai*)-*yon-jou*
5 sections	(第)五条	(だい)ごじょう	(*dai*)-*go-jou*
6 sections	(第)六条	(だい)ろくじょう	(*dai*)-*roku-jou*
7 sections	(第)七条	(だい)ななじょう	(*dai*)-*nana-jou*
8 sections	(第)八条	(だい)はちじょう	(*dai*)-*hachi-jou*
9 sections	(第)九条	(だい)きゅうじょう	(*dai*)-*kyuu-jou*
10 sections	(第)十条	(だい)じゅうじょう	(*dai*)-*juu-jou*

Irregularities or Special beyond Ten: none
Notes: Typically, this counter is prefixed with 第 (*dai*).

帖—じょう—jou

Japanese: じょう
Romanized: *jou*
Pattern: 漢 ∅
Used with, or Means: quires of paper[8]; folding screens, paper-covered sliding doors (唐紙 *karakami*); volumes of Japanese books; straw mats (畳 *tatami*)

1 folding screen	一帖	いちじょう	*ichi-jou*
2 folding screens	二帖	にじょう	*ni-jou*
3 folding screens	三帖	さんじょう	*san-jou*
4 folding screens	四帖	よんじょう	*yon-jou*
5 folding screens	五帖	ごじょう	*go-jou*
6 folding screens	六帖	ろくじょう	*roku-jou*
7 folding screens	七帖	ななじょう	*nana-jou*
8 folding screens	八帖	はちじょう	*hachi-jou*
9 folding screens	九帖	きゅうじょう	*kyuu-jou*
10 folding screens	十帖	じゅうじょう	*juu-jou*

Irregularities or Special beyond Ten: none
Notes: none

---

[8] A *quire* (pronounced like *choir*) is *a set of 24 uniform sheets of paper*, a term in the bookbinding industry to refer to *a section of printed leaves in proper sequence after folding; gathering*—quire Dictionary.com *Dictionary.com Unabridged* Random House, Inc. http://dictionary.reference.com/browse/quire (accessed: August 04, 2010)

乗・乘—じょう—*jou*

Japanese: じょう
Romanized: *jou*
Pattern: 漢 ∅
Used with, or Means: (literary language) vehicles, numbers (powers)

1 car/x^1	一乗・乘	いちじょう	*ichi-jou*
2 cars/x^2	二乗・乘	にじょう / <u>じじょう</u>	*ni-jou* / <u>*ji-jou*</u>
3 cars/x^3	三乗・乘	さんじょう	*san-jou*
4 cars/x^4	四乗・乘	よんじょう	*yon-jou*
5 cars/x^5	五乗・乘	ごじょう	*go-jou*
6 cars/x^6	六乗・乘	ろくじょう	*roku-jou*
7 cars/x^7	七乗・乘	ななじょう	*nana-jou*
8 cars/x^8	八乗・乘	はちじょう	*hachi-jou*
9 cars/x^9	九乗・乘	きゅうじょう	*kyuu-jou*
10 cars/x^{10}	十乗・乘	じゅうじょう	*juu-jou*

Irregularities or Special beyond Ten: none

Notes: Although the Japanese would write 4^3 (*four to the third power*) like we would when doing math, when speaking, the Japanese would say 四の三乗 (*yon no san-jou*).

Notice the special, alternative reading of *squared*, just as we can say *x to the second power* or *x squared*.

城 — じょう — *jou*

Japanese: じょう
Romanized: *jou*
Pattern: 漢 ∅
Used with, or Means: castles

1 castle	一城	いちじょう	*ichi-jou*
2 castles	二城	にじょう	*ni-jou*
3 castles	三城	さんじょう	*san-jou*
4 castles	四城	よんじょう	*yon-jou*
5 castles	五城	ごじょう	*go-jou*
6 castles	六城	ろくじょう	*roku-jou*
7 castles	七城	ななじょう	*nana-jou*
8 castles	八城	はちじょう	*hachi-jou*
9 castles	九城	きゅうじょう	*kyuu-jou*
10 castles	十城	じゅうじょう	*juu-jou*

Irregularities or Special beyond Ten: none
Notes: none

畳—じょう—*jou*

Japanese: じょう
Romanized: *jou*
Pattern: 漢 ∅
Used with, or Means: *tatami* mats (roughly 3-foot × 6-foot mats), roomsize (see Notes); *jou*, a unit of area, ½ of a 坪 (*tsubo*), 2,561.98859 in^2 (17.79159 ft^2)/1.65289 m^2

1 *tatami* mat	一畳	いちじょう	*ichi-jou*
2 *tatami* mats	二畳	にじょう	*ni-jou*
3 *tatami* mats	三畳	さんじょう	*san-jou*
4 *tatami* mats	四畳	よんじょう	*yon-jou*
5 *tatami* mats	五畳	ごじょう	*go-jou*
6 *tatami* mats	六畳	ろくじょう	*roku-jou*
7 *tatami* mats	七畳	ななじょう	*nana-jou*
8 *tatami* mats	八畳	はちじょう	*hachi-jou*
9 *tatami* mats	九畳	きゅうじょう	*kyuu-jou*
10 *tatami* mats	十畳	じゅうじょう	*juu-jou*

Irregularities or Special beyond Ten: none
Notes: *Tatami* mats are arproximately three feet wide by six feet long. Historically, the Japanese have used the mats as a form of modular room design. Thus, rather than using square meters (or square *shaku* before they adopted the metric system), they simply say how many mats would fit into the room—even for rooms into which no one intends to place any mats!

The typical bedroom is six-mats-large, and larger rooms (like master bedrooms) tend to be eight-mats-large. See the next page for a graphical example of an eight-tatami and six-tatami room.

There are two arrangement patterns: 祝儀敷き (*shuugishiki*), which is for everyday life; and, 不祝儀敷き (*fushuugishiki*), which is for sad occasions, such as funerals.

Figure 1: Examples of Tatami Mats Arranged in the Shuugishiki Style

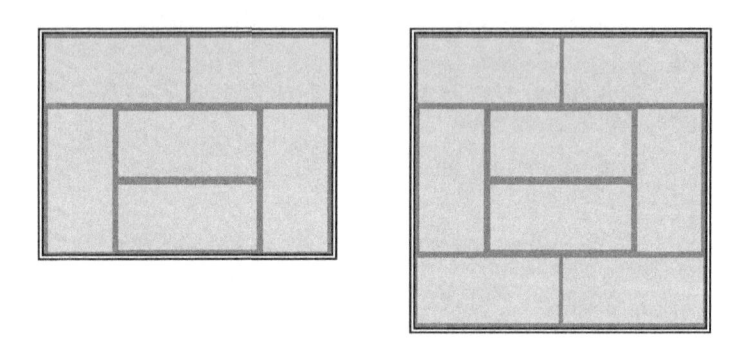

Figure 2: Examples of Tatami Mats Arranged in the Fushuugishiki Style

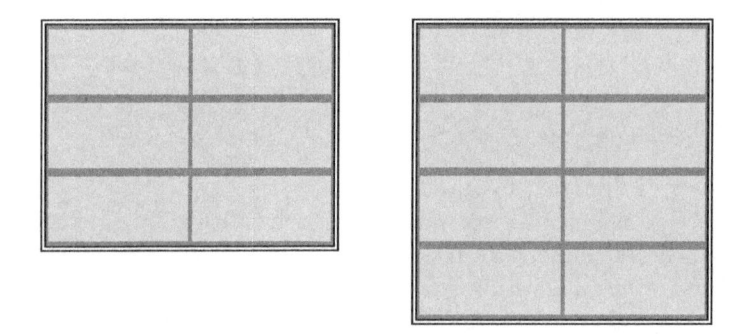

Drawings by Jason Monti © 2011

錠 —じょう— *jou*

Japanese: じょう
Romanized: *jou*
Pattern: 漢 ∅
Used with, or Means: tablets, pills

1 pill	一錠	いちじょう	*ichi-jou*
2 pills	二錠	にじょう	*ni-jou*
3 pills	三錠	さんじょう	*san-jou*
4 pills	四錠	よんじょう	*yon-jou*
5 pills	五錠	ごじょう	*go-jou*
6 pills	六錠	ろくじょう	*roku-jou*
7 pills	七錠	ななじょう	*nana-jou*
8 pills	八錠	はちじょう	*hachi-jou*
9 pills	九錠	きゅうじょう	*kyuu-jou*
10 pills	十錠	じゅうじょう	*juu-jou*

Irregularities or Special beyond Ten: none
Notes: none

穣—じょう—jou

Japanese: じょう
Romanized: *jou*
Pattern: 漢 ∅
Used with, or Means: 10,000秭・秭 (*shi/jo*), 10 octillion, 10^{28}

10^{28}	一穣	いちじょう	*ichi-jou*
$2×10^{28}$	二穣	にじょう	*ni-jou*
$3×10^{28}$	三穣	さんじょう	*san-jou*
$4×10^{28}$	四穣	よんじょう	*yon-jou*
$5×10^{28}$	五穣	ごじょう	*go-jou*
$6×10^{28}$	六穣	ろくじょう	*roku-jou*
$7×10^{28}$	七穣	ななじょう	*nana-jou*
$8×10^{28}$	八穣	はちじょう	*hachi-jou*
$9×10^{28}$	九穣	きゅうじょう	*kyuu-jou*
10^{29}	十穣	じゅうじょう	*juu-jou*

Irregularities or Special beyond Ten:

10^{30}	百穣	ひゃくじょう	*hyaku-jou*
10^{31}	千穣	せんじょう	*sen-jou*

Notes: 10^{28} is 10 000 000 000 000 000 000 000 000 000

勝負—しょうぶ—*shoubu*

Japanese: しょうぶ
Romanized: *shoubu*
Pattern: 漢 S or 和 I-S
Used with, or Means: matches, contests, games

1 match	一勝負	いっしょうぶ ひとしょうぶ	*is-shoubu* *hito-shoubu*
2 matches	二勝負	にしょうぶ ふたしょうぶ	*ni-shoubu* *futa-shoubu*
3 matches	三勝負	さんしょうぶ	*san-shoubu*
4 matches	四勝負	よんしょうぶ	*yon-shoubu*
5 matches	五勝負	ごしょうぶ	*go-shoubu*
6 matches	六勝負	ろくしょうぶ	*roku-shoubu*
7 matches	七勝負	ななしょうぶ	*nana-shoubu*
8 matches	八勝負	はっしょうぶ はちしょうぶ	*has-shoubu* *hachi-shoubu*
9 matches	九勝負	きゅうしょうぶ	*kyuu-shoubu*
10 matches	十勝負	じゅっしょうぶ じっしょうぶ	*jus-shoubu* *jis-shoubu*

Irregularities or Special beyond Ten: none
Notes: none

色―しょく―*shoku*

Japanese: しょく
Romanized: *shoku*
Pattern: 漢 S
Used with, or Means: colors, see also 色 (*iro*), see also カラー (*karaa*)

1 color	一色	いっしょく	*is-shoku*
2 colors	二色	にしょく	*ni-shoku*
3 colors	三色	さんしょく	*san-shoku*
4 colors	四色	よんしょく	*yon-shoku*
5 colors	五色	ごしょく	*go-shoku*
6 colors	六色	ろくしょく	*roku-shoku*
7 colors	七色	ななしょく	*nana-shoku*
8 colors	八色	はっしょく	*has-shoku*
9 colors	九色	きゅうしょく	*kyuu-shoku*
10 colors	十色	じゅっしょく / じっしょく	*jus-shoku* / *jis-shoku*

Irregularities or Special beyond Ten: none
Notes: none

食 — しょく — *shoku*

Japanese: しょく
Romanized: *shoku*
Pattern: 漢 S
Used with, or Means: meals

1 meal	一食	いっしょく	*is-shoku*
2 meals	二食	にしょく	*ni-shoku*
3 meals	三食	さんしょく	*san-shoku*
4 meals	四食	よんしょく	*yon-shoku*
5 meals	五食	ごしょく	*go-shoku*
6 meals	六食	ろくしょく	*roku-shoku*
7 meals	七食	ななしょく	*nana-shoku*
8 meals	八食	はっしょく	*has-shoku*
9 meals	九食	きゅうしょく	*kyuu-shoku*
10 meals	十食	じゅっしょく / じっしょく	*jus-shoku* / *jis-shoku*

Irregularities or Special beyond Ten: none
Notes: none

尻 — しり — *shiri*

Japanese: しり
Romanized: *shiri*
Pattern: 和 I-S
Used with, or Means: formerly the number of arrow feathers obtained from a single bird's tail

1 arrow feather	一尻	ひとしり	*hito-shiri*
2 arrow feathers	二尻	ふたしり	*futa-shiri*
3 arrow feathers	三尻	さんしり	*san-shiri*
4 arrow feathers	四尻	よんしり	*yon-shiri*
5 arrow feathers	五尻	ごしり	*go-shiri*
6 arrow feathers	六尻	ろくしり	*roku-shiri*
7 arrow feathers	七尻	ななしり	*nana-shiri*
8 arrow feathers	八尻	はっしり	*has-shiri*
9 arrow feathers	九尻	きゅうしり	*kyuu-shiri*
10 arrow feathers	十尻	じゅっしり じっしり	*jus-shiri* *jis-shiri*

Irregularities or Special beyond Ten: none
Notes: none

シリング—*shiringu*

Japanese: しりんぐ
Romanized: *shiringu*
Pattern: 漢 S
Used with, or Means: shillings, former British monetary unit

1 shilling	1シリング	いっしりんぐ いちしりんぐ	*is-shiringu* *ichi-shiringu*
2 shillings	2シリング	にしりんぐ	*ni-shiringu*
3 shillings	3シリング	さんしりんぐ	*san-shiringu*
4 shillings	4シリング	よんしりんぐ	*yon-shiringu*
5 shillings	5シリング	ごしりんぐ	*go-shiringu*
6 shillings	6シリング	ろくしりんぐ	*roku-shiringu*
7 shillings	7シリング	ななしりんぐ	*nana-shiringu*
8 shillings	8シリング	はっしりんぐ はちしりんぐ	*has-shiringu* *hachi-shiringu*
9 shillings	9シリング	きゅうしりんぐ	*kyuu-shiringu*
10 shillings	10シリング	じゅっしりんぐ じっしりんぐ	*jus-shiringu* *jis-shiringu*

Irregularities or Special beyond Ten: none
Notes: none

針―しん―*shin*

Japanese: しん
Romanized: *shin*
Pattern: 漢 S
Used with, or Means: needles, see 針 (*hari*)

1 needle	一針	いっしん	<u>*is-shin*</u>
2 needles	二針	にしん	*ni-shin*
3 needles	三針	さんしん	*san-shin*
4 needles	四針	よんしん	*yon-shin*
5 needles	五針	ごしん	*go-shin*
6 needles	六針	ろくしん	*roku-shin*
7 needles	七針	ななしん	*nana-shin*
8 needles	八針	<u>はっしん</u>	<u>*has-shin*</u>
9 needles	九針	きゅうしん	*kyuu-shin*
10 needles	十針	<u>じゅっしん</u> <u>じっしん</u>	<u>*jus-shin*</u> <u>*jis-shin*</u>

Irregularities or Special beyond Ten: none
Notes: 針 (*hari*) is used more often than *shin*.

審 — しん — *shin*

Japanese: しん
Romanized: *shin*
Pattern: 漢 S
Used with, or Means: judgements, (court) hearings, stages

1 hearing	(第)一審	<u>(だい)いっしん</u>	<u>*(dai)-is-shin*</u>
2 hearings	(第)二審	(だい)にしん	*(dai)-ni-shin*
3 hearings	(第)三審	(だい)さんしん	*(dai)-san-shin*
4 hearings	(第)四審	(だい)よんしん	*(dai)-yon-shin*
5 hearings	(第)五審	(だい)ごしん	*(dai)-go-shin*
6 hearings	(第)六審	(だい)ろくしん	*(dai)-roku-shin*
7 hearings	(第)七審	(だい)ななしん	*(dai)-nana-shin*
8 hearings	(第)八審	<u>(だい)はっしん</u>	<u>*(dai)-has-shin*</u>
9 hearings	(第)九審	(だい)きゅうしん	*(dai)-kyuu-shin*
10 hearings	(第)十審	<u>(だい)じゅっしん</u> <u>(だい)じっしん</u>	<u>*(dai)-jus-shin*</u> <u>*(dai)-jis-shin*</u>

Irregularities or Special beyond Ten: none
Notes: Typically, this counter is prefixed with 第 (*dai*).

陣 — じん — *jin*

Japanese: じん
Romanized: *jin*
Pattern: 漢 ∅
Used with, or Means: troops, military forces; storms, stormy weather patterns; the order of stops to a destination (busses, trains); magic circles (stars used by occultists or in fantasy for summoning or other rituals)

1 troop	(第)一陣	(だい)いちじん	*(dai)-ichi-jin*
2 troops	(第)二陣	(だい)にじん	*(dai)-ni-jin*
3 troops	(第)三陣	(だい)さんじん	*(dai)-san-jin*
4 troops	(第)四陣	(だい)よんじん	*(dai)-yon-jin*
5 troops	(第)五陣	(だい)ごじん	*(dai)-go-jin*
6 troops	(第)六陣	(だい)ろくじん	*(dai)-roku-jin*
7 troops	(第)七陣	(だい)ななじん	*(dai)-nana-jin*
8 troops	(第)八陣	(だい)はちじん	*(dai)-hachi-jin*
9 troops	(第)九陣	(だい)きゅうじん	*(dai)-kyuu-jin*
10 troops	(第)十陣	(だい)じゅうじん	*(dai)-juu-jin*

Irregularities or Special beyond Ten: none
Notes: Typically, this counter is prefixed with 第 *(dai)*.

尋・仭・仞 —じん— *jin*

Japanese: じん
Romanized: *jin*
Pattern: 漢 Ø

Used with, or Means: Japanese fathoms, *jin*, a unit of length, 6 尺 (*shaku*), 71.58196 in (5.96516 ft)/1.81818 m/0.99419 fathoms, same as 尋 (*hiro*)

1 *jin*	一尋・仭・仞	いちじん	*ichi-jin*
2 *jin*	二尋・仭・仞	にじん	*ni-jin*
3 *jin*	三尋・仭・仞	さんじん	*san-jin*
4 *jin*	四尋・仭・仞	よんじん	*yon-jin*
5 *jin*	五尋・仭・仞	ごじん	*go-jin*
6 *jin*	六尋・仭・仞	ろくじん	*roku-jin*
7 *jin*	七尋・仭・仞	ななじん	*nana-jin*
8 *jin*	八尋・仭・仞	はちじん	*hachi-jin*
9 *jin*	九尋・仭・仞	きゅうじん	*kyuu-jin*
10 *jin*	十尋・仭・仞	じゅうじん	*juu-jin*

Irregularities or Special beyond Ten: none
Notes: none

塵 — じん — *jin*

Japanese: じん
Romanized: *jin*
Pattern: 漢 S
Used with, or Means: 1/1,000,000,000th, 10^{-9}

10^{-9}	一塵	<u>いっじん</u>	<u>*is-jin*</u>
2×10^{-9}	二塵	にじん	*ni-jin*
3×10^{-9}	三塵	さんじん	*san-jin*
4×10^{-9}	四塵	よんじん	*yon-jin*
5×10^{-9}	五塵	ごじん	*go-jin*
6×10^{-9}	六塵	ろくじん	*roku-jin*
7×10^{-9}	七塵	ななじん	*nana-jin*
8×10^{-9}	八塵	<u>はちじん</u>	<u>*hachi-jin*</u>
9×10^{-9}	九塵	きゅうじん	*kyuu-jin*
10^{-8}	十塵	じゅうじん	*juu-jin*

Irregularities or Special beyond Ten:

10^{-7}	百塵	<u>いっじん</u>	<u>*is-jin*</u>
10^{-6}	千塵	にじん	*ni-jin*

Notes: none

進数—しんすう—*shinsuu*

Japanese: しんすう
Romanized: *shinsuu*
Pattern: 漢 S
Used with, or Means: counting-base, counting system (see Notes)

base 1	一進数	いっしんすう	*is-shinsuu*
base 2	二進数	にしんすう	*ni-shinsuu*
base 3	三進数	さんしんすう	*san-shinsuu*
base 4	四進数	よんしんすう	*yon-shinsuu*
base 5	五進数	ごしんすう	*go-shinsuu*
base 6	六進数	ろくしんすう	*roku-shinsuu*
base 7	七進数	ななしんすう	*nana-shinsuu*
base 8	八進数	はっしんすう	*has-shinsuu*
base 9	九進数	きゅうしんすう	*kyuu-shinsuu*
base 10	十進数	じゅっしんすう / じっしんすう	*jus-shinsuu* / *jis-shinsuu*

Irregularities or Special beyond Ten: none

Notes: *Most* people on earth count in what mathematicians call *Base-10*. This means that we count from zero to nine, then add a tens place from 10 to 99, and then add a hundreds place 100 to 999, and so on. Computers use binary (base-2), meaning they count zero to one, then 10 to 11, then 100 to 111, and so on. To abbreviate the eight ones or zeros that make up each 2-bit piece of information, computer programmers use Hexadecimal (base-16): 0, 1, 2, 3, 4, 5, 6, 7, 8, 9, a, b, c, d, e, and f; so, 00 to ff. Each numbr represents four binary digits, and two digits represent eight: c3 would be 1100 0011. C in hexadecimal is 13 in base-10 is 1100 in base-2 is 22 in base-5.

The Babylonians counted in base-60, which means that their "10" would be equal to our "60" and that to a Babylonian, a circle has 40 degrees, whereas a circle has 360 degrees to us.

親等—しんとう—*shintou*

Japanese: しんとう
Romanized: *shintou*
Pattern: 漢 S
Used with, or Means: degrees of separation in a familial relationship

1 degree	一親等	いっしんとう いちしんとう	*is-shintou* *ichi-shintou*
2 degrees	二親等	にしんとう	*ni-shintou*
3 degrees	三親等	さんしんとう	*san-shintou*
4 degrees	四親等	よんしんとう	*yon-shintou*
5 degrees	五親等	ごしんとう	*go-shintou*
6 degrees	六親等	ろくしんとう	*roku-shintou*
7 degrees	七親等	ななしんとう	*nana-shintou*
8 degrees	八親等	はっしんとう はちしんとう	*has-shintou* *hachi-shintou*
9 degrees	九親等	きゅうしんとう	*kyuu-shintou*
10 degrees	十親等	じゅっしんとう じっしんとう	*jus-shintou* *jis-shintou*

Irregularities or Special beyond Ten: none
Notes: none

進法—しんほう—*shinhou*

Japanese: しんほう
Romanized: *shinhou*
Pattern: 漢 S
Used with, or Means: counting-base, counting system, same as 進数 (*shinsuu*)

base 1	一進法	いっしんほう	*is-shinhou*
base 2	二進法	にしんほう	*ni-shinhou*
base 3	三進法	さんしんほう	*san-shinhou*
base 4	四進法	よんしんほう	*yon-shinhou*
base 5	五進法	ごしんほう	*go-shinhou*
base 6	六進法	ろくしんほう	*roku-shinhou*
base 7	七進法	ななしんほう	*nana-shinhou*
base 8	八進法	はっしんほう	*has-shinhou*
base 9	九進法	きゅうしんほう	*kyuu-shinhou*
base 10	十進法	じゅっしんほう じっしんほう	*jus-shinhou* *jis-shinhou*

Irregularities or Special beyond Ten: none
Notes: none

す・ず—Su/Zu
図—ず—zu

Japanese: ず
Romanized: zu
Pattern: 漢 Ø
Used with, or Means: dots, marks, spots, see also 点 (ten)

1 mark	一図	いちず	ichi-zu
2 marks	二図	にず	ni-zu
3 marks	三図	さんず	san-zu
4 marks	四図	よんず	yon-zu
5 marks	五図	ごず	go-zu
6 marks	六図	ろくず	roku-zu
7 marks	七図	ななず	nana-zu
8 marks	八図	はちず	hachi-zu
9 marks	九図	きゅうず	kyuu-zu
10 marks	十図	じゅうず	juu-zu

Irregularities or Special beyond Ten: none
Notes: none

頭 — ず — *zu*

Japanese: ず
Romanized: *zu*
Pattern: 漢 ∅
Used with, or Means: persons, people's heads (literally a *head count*), see also 頭 (*tou*)

1 person	一頭	いちず	*ichi-zu*
2 persons	二頭	にず	*ni-zu*
3 persons	三頭	さんず	*san-zu*
4 persons	四頭	よんず	*yon-zu*
5 persons	五頭	ごず	*go-zu*
6 persons	六頭	ろくず	*roku-zu*
7 persons	七頭	ななず	*nana-zu*
8 persons	八頭	はちず	*hachi-zu*
9 persons	九頭	きゅうず	*kyuu-zu*
10 persons	十頭	じゅうず	*juu-zu*

Irregularities or Special beyond Ten: none
Notes: Though this is the same *kanji* as *tou*, which is used for counting large animals, this usage, as a head count of people, is older.

錘 — すい — *sui*

Japanese: すい
Romanized: *sui*
Pattern: 漢 S

Used with, or Means: thread, yarn, string spinning tools, spindles (錘 *tsumu*); a unit of spinning mill, spinning wheel production output (五万錘の生産力 *go-man-sui no seisan-ryoku* 50,000 spindles of output)

1 spindle	一錘	いっすい	*is-sui*
2 spindles	二錘	にすい	*ni-sui*
3 spindles	三錘	さんすい	*san-sui*
4 spindles	四錘	よんすい	*yon-sui*
5 spindles	五錘	ごすい	*go-sui*
6 spindles	六錘	ろくすい	*roku-sui*
7 spindles	七錘	ななすい	*nana-sui*
8 spindles	八錘	はっすい	*has-sui*
9 spindles	九錘	きゅうすい	*kyuu-sui*
10 spindles	十錘	じゅっすい / じっすい	*jus-sui* / *jis-sui*

Irregularities or Special beyond Ten: none
Notes: none

据え—すえ—*sue*

Japanese: すえ
Romanized: *sue*
Pattern: 和 III-S or 和 I-S
Used with, or Means: the number of appliances, fixtures that a house has; bathtubs (浴槽 *yokusou*), bath basins (風呂桶 *furooke*)

1 fixture	一据え	ひとすえ	*hito-sue*
2 fixtures	二据え	ふたすえ	*futa-sue*
3 fixtures	三据え	みすえ / さんすえ	*mi-sue* / *san-sue*
4 fixtures	四据え	よすえ / よんすえ	*yo-sue* / *yon-sue*
5 fixtures	五据え	ごすえ	*go-sue*
6 fixtures	六据え	ろくすえ	*roku-sue*
7 fixtures	七据え	ななすえ	*nana-sue*
8 fixtures	八据え	はっすえ / はちすえ	*has-sue* / *hachi-sue*
9 fixtures	九据え	きゅうすえ	*kyuu-sue*
10 fixtures	十据え	じゅっすえ / じっすえ	*jus-sue* / *jis-sue*

Irregularities or Special beyond Ten: none
Notes: none

掬い—すくい—*sukui*

Japanese: すくい
Romanized: *sukui*
Pattern: 和 III-S or 和 I-S
Used with, or Means: the amount of a liquid or powder (flour, sugar, salt); cupfuls, spoonfuls, scoops, see also 掬 (*kiku*), see also 杯 (*hai*)

1 scoop	一掬い	ひとすくい	*hito-sukui*
2 scoops	二掬い	ふたすくい	*futa-sukui*
3 scoops	三掬い	みすくい さんすくい	*mi-sukui* *san-sukui*
4 scoops	四掬い	よすくい よんすくい	*yo-sukui* *yon-sukui*
5 scoops	五掬い	ごすくい	*go-sukui*
6 scoops	六掬い	ろくすくい	*roku-sukui*
7 scoops	七掬い	ななすくい	*nana-sukui*
8 scoops	八掬い	はっすくい はちすくい	*has-sukui* *hachi-sukui*
9 scoops	九掬い	きゅうすくい	*kyuu-sukui*
10 scoops	十掬い	じゅっすくい じっすくい じゅうすくい	*jus-sukui* *jis-sukui* *juu-sukui*

Irregularities or Special beyond Ten: none
Notes: none

筋 — すじ — *suji*

Japanese: すじ
Romanized: *suji*
Pattern: 和 III-S or 和 I-S
Used with, or Means: long, thin objects with an ill-defined shape, rays of light, smoke (like the stream of smoke arising from cigarettes), tear streaks, wrinkles, creases; arrowheads; *kimono obi*[9]; during the Edo period, loops of 100 銭[10] (*sen*) strung together equal to one 文 (*mon*); roads, rivers

1 *obi*	一筋	ひとすじ	*hito-suji*
2 *obi*	二筋	ふたすじ	*futa-suji*
3 *obi*	三筋	みすじ さんすじ	*mi-suji* *san-suji*
4 *obi*	四筋	よすじ よんすじ	*yo-suji* *yon-suji*
5 *obi*	五筋	ごすじ	*go-suji*
6 *obi*	六筋	ろくすじ	*roku-suji*
7 *obi*	七筋	ななすじ	*nana-suji*
8 *obi*	八筋	はっすじ はちすじ	*has-suji* *hachi-suji*
9 *obi*	九筋	きゅうすじ	*kyuu-suji*
10 *obi*	十筋	じゅっすじ じっすじ じゅうすじ	*jus-suji* *jis-suji* *juu-suji*

Irregularities or Special beyond Ten: none
Notes: none

---

[9] An *obi* is the wide belt-like decorative wrap that goes around a woman's waist and holds the *kimono* together.
[10] A 銭 is 1/100th of a yen.

ステージ—*suteeji*

Japanese: すてえじ
Romanized: *suteeji*
Pattern: 漢 S
Used with, or Means: performances, shows

1 performance	1 ステージ	いっすてえじ いちすでえじ	*is-suteeji* *ichi-suteeji*
2 performances	2 ステージ	にすてえじ	*ni-suteeji*
3 performances	3 ステージ	さんすてえじ	*san-suteeji*
4 performances	4 ステージ	よんすてえじ	*yon-suteeji*
5 performances	5 ステージ	ごすてえじ	*go-suteeji*
6 performances	6 ステージ	ろくすてえじ	*roku-suteeji*
7 performances	7 ステージ	ななすてえじ	*nana-suteeji*
8 performances	8 ステージ	はっすてえじ はちすてえじ	*has-suteeji* *hachi-suteeji*
9 performances	9 ステージ	きゅうすてえじ	*kyuu-suteeji*
10 performances	10 ステージ	じゅっすてえじ じっすてえじ じゅうすてえじ	*jus-suteeji* *jis-suteeji* *juu-suteeji*

Irregularities or Special beyond Ten: none
Notes: none

刷り — すり — *suri*

Japanese: すり
Romanized: *suri*
Pattern: 漢 S or 和 I-S

Used with, or Means: revisions, see 版 (*han*) for editions (when the content *does* change); printings: 第一刷発行 (*dai-is-satsu hakkou* a first printing, a first run), see also 刷 (*satsu*)

1st edition	一刷り	いっすり / ひとすり	*is-suri* / *hito-suri*
2nd edition	二刷り	にすり / ふたすり	*ni-suri* / *futa-suri*
3rd edition	三刷り	さんすり	*san-suri*
4th edition	四刷り	よんすり	*yon-suri*
5th edition	五刷り	ごすり	*go-suri*
6th edition	六刷り	ろくすり	*roku-suri*
7th edition	七刷り	ななすり	*nana-suri*
8th edition	八刷り	はっすり	*has-suri*
9th edition	九刷り	きゅうすり	*kyuu-suri*
10th edition	十刷り	じゅっすり / じっすり	*jus-suri* / *jis-suri*

Irregularities or Special beyond Ten: none

Notes: *Suri* is used for revisions or successive printings of books, as opposed to editions. In this case, the content itself does not change. Mistakes might be corrected (before the book goes public), or because of high demand, a new printing run occurs, but otherwise, there is no change to the book.

In English, if a publisher prints a copy for an author or editor to revise before going public, that copy is called a *proof* or *proof copy*.

据わり —すわり— *suwari*

Japanese: すわり
Romanized: *suwari*
Pattern: 和 III-S
Used with, or Means: pieces of *kasane-mochi* (重ね餅): layered, sticky rice-cakes

1 piece	一据わり	ひとすわり	*hito-suwari*
2 pieces	二据わり	ふたすわり	*futa-suwari*
3 pieces	三据わり	みすわり	*mi-suwari*
4 pieces	四据わり	よすわり	*yo-suwari*
5 pieces	五据わり	ごすわり	*go-suwari*
6 pieces	六据わり	ろくすわり	*roku-suwari*
7 pieces	七据わり	ななすわり	*nana-suwari*
8 pieces	八据わり	はっすわり / はちすわり	*has-suwari* / *hachi-suwari*
9 pieces	九据わり	きゅうすわり	*kyuu-suwari*
10 pieces	十据わり	じゅっすわり / じっすわり	*jus-suwari* / *jis-suwari*

Irregularities or Special beyond Ten: none
Notes: none

寸 — すん — *sun*

Japanese: すん
Romanized: *sun*
Pattern: 漢 S
Used with, or Means: *sun*; a unit of length, 1/10th of a 尺 (*shaku*), 1.1930326879 in/0.0303030303 m; length of cloth, see also 寸 (*ki*)

1 *sun*	一寸	いっすん	*is-sun*
2 *sun*	二寸	にすん	*ni-sun*
3 *sun*	三寸	さんすん	*san-sun*
4 *sun*	四寸	よんすん	*yon-sun*
5 *sun*	五寸	ごすん	*go-sun*
6 *sun*	六寸	ろくすん	*roku-sun*
7 *sun*	七寸	ななすん	*nana-sun*
8 *sun*	八寸	はっすん / はちすん	*has-sun* / *hachi-sun*
9 *sun*	九寸	きゅうすん	*kyuu-sun*
10 *sun*	十寸	じゅっすん / じっすん	*jus-sun* / *jis-sun*

Irregularities or Special beyond Ten: none
Notes: none

せ・ぜ — Se/Ze
背 — せ — se

Japanese: せ
Romanized: se
Pattern: 漢 S
Used with, or Means: (horse) saddles

1 saddle	一背	いっせ	*is-se*
2 saddles	二背	にせ	*ni-se*
3 saddles	三背	さんせ	*san-se*
4 saddles	四背	よんせ	*yon-se*
5 saddles	五背	ごせ	*go-se*
6 saddles	六背	ろくせ	*roku-se*
7 saddles	七背	ななせ	*nana-se*
8 saddles	八背	はっせ / はちせ	*has-se* / *hachi-se*
9 saddles	九背	きゅうせ	*kyuu-se*
10 saddles	十背	じゅっせ / じっせ	*jus-se* / *jis-se*

Irregularities or Special beyond Ten: none
Notes: none

畝——せ——*se*

Japanese: せ
Romanized: *se*
Pattern: 漢 S
Used with, or Means: *se*, a unit of area, 30 坪 (tsubo), 153,719.31539 in² (1,067.49525 ft²)/99.17355 m²

1 *se*	一畝	いっせ	*is-se*
2 *se*	二畝	にせ	*ni-se*
3 *se*	三畝	さんせ	*san-se*
4 *se*	四畝	よんせ	*yon-se*
5 *se*	五畝	ごせ	*go-se*
6 *se*	六畝	ろくせ	*roku-se*
7 *se*	七畝	ななせ	*nana-se*
8 *se*	八畝	はっせ / はちせ	*has-se* / *hachi-se*
9 *se*	九畝	きゅうせ	*kyuu-se*
10 *se*	十畝	じゅっせ / じっせ	*jus-se* / *jis-se*

Irregularities or Special beyond Ten: none
Notes: none

世 — せい — *sei*

Japanese: せい
Romanized: *sei*
Pattern: 漢 S
Used with, or Means: generations; monarchical reigns (ルイ 14 世 *Rui juu-yon-sei* the reign of Louis XIV); 30-year periods, see also 代 (*dai*)

1 thirty-year period	一世	いっせい	*is-sei*
2 thirty-year periods	二世	にせい	*ni-sei*
3 thirty-year periods	三世	さんせい	*san-sei*
4 thirty-year periods	四世	よんせい	*yon-sei*
5 thirty-year periods	五世	ごせい	*go-sei*
6 thirty-year periods	六世	ろくせい	*roku-sei*
7 thirty-year periods	七世	ななせい	*nana-sei*
8 thirty-year periods	八世	はっせい / はちせい	*has-sei* / *hachi-sei*
9 thirty-year periods	九世	きゅうせい	*kyuu-sei*
10 thirty-year periods	十世	じゅっせい / じっせい	*jus-sei* / *jis-sei*

Irregularities or Special beyond Ten: none
Notes: none

正—せい—sei

Japanese: せい
Romanized: sei
Pattern: 漢 S
Used with, or Means: 10,000 澗 (*kan*), 10 duodecillion, 10^{40}

10^{40}	一正	いっせい	*is-sei*
$2×10^{40}$	二正	にせい	*ni-sei*
$3×10^{40}$	三正	さんせい	*san-sei*
$4×10^{40}$	四正	よんせい	*yon-sei*
$5×10^{40}$	五正	ごせい	*go-sei*
$6×10^{40}$	六正	ろくせい	*roku-sei*
$7×10^{40}$	七正	ななせい	*nana-sei*
$8×10^{40}$	八正	はっせい	*has-sei*
$9×10^{40}$	九正	きゅうせい	*kyuu-sei*
10^{41}	十正	じゅっせい / じっせい	*jus-sei* / *jis-sei*

Irregularities or Special beyond Ten:

10^{42}	百正	ひゃくせい	*hyaku-sei*
10^{43}	千正	せんせい	*sen-sei*

Notes: 10^{40} is 10 000 000 000 000 000 000 000 000 000 000 000 000 000

声 — せい — *sei*

Japanese: せい
Romanized: *sei*
Pattern: 漢 S
Used with, or Means: voices, cries, shouts, see also 声 (*koe*)

1 shout	一声	いっせい	*is-sei*
2 shouts	二声	にせい	*ni-sei*
3 shouts	三声	さんせい	*san-sei*
4 shouts	四声	よんせい	*yon-sei*
5 shouts	五声	ごせい	*go-sei*
6 shouts	六声	ろくせい	*roku-sei*
7 shouts	七声	ななせい	*nana-sei*
8 shouts	八声	はっせい / はちせい	*has-sei* / *hachi-sei*
9 shouts	九声	きゅうせい	*kyuu-sei*
10 shouts	十声	じゅっせい / じっせい	*jus-sei* / *jis-sei*

Irregularities or Special beyond Ten: none
Notes: none

星—せい—*sei*

Japanese: せい
Romanized: *sei*
Pattern: 漢 S
Used with, or Means: (professional/technical jargon) flares, fireworks

1 flare	一星	いっせい	*is-sei*
2 flares	二星	にせい	*ni-sei*
3 flares	三星	さんせい	*san-sei*
4 flares	四星	よんせい	*yon-sei*
5 flares	五星	ごせい	*go-sei*
6 flares	六星	ろくせい	*roku-sei*
7 flares	七星	ななせい	*nana-sei*
8 flares	八星	はっせい / はちせい	*has-sei* / *hachi-sei*
9 flares	九星	きゅうせい	*kyuu-sei*
10 flares	十星	じゅっせい / じっせい	*jus-sei* / *jis-sei*

Irregularities or Special beyond Ten: none
Notes: none

世紀—せいき—*seiki*

Japanese: せいき
Romanized: *seiki*
Pattern: 漢 S
Used with, or Means: the century

1st century	一世紀	いっせいき	<u>*is-seiki*</u>
2nd century	二世紀	にせいき	*ni-seiki*
3rd century	三世紀	さんせいき	*san-seiki*
4th century	四世紀	よんせいき	*yon-seiki*
5th century	五世紀	ごせいき	*go-seiki*
6th century	六世紀	ろくせいき	*roku-seiki*
7th century	七世紀	ななせいき	*nana-seiki*
8th century	八世紀	はっせいき はちせいき	<u>*has-seiki*</u> <u>*hachi-seiki*</u>
9th century	九世紀	きゅうせいき	*kyuu-seiki*
10th century	十世紀	じゅっせいき じっせいき	<u>*jus-seiki*</u> <u>*jis-seiki*</u>

Irregularities or Special beyond Ten: none

Notes: We are currently living in 21 世紀 (*ni-juu-is-seiki*), or the 21st century.
    What we could call B. C. (*before Christ*) or B. C. E. (*before common era*) is 紀元前 (*kigenzen*); and, A. D. (*anno Domnini*) is 西暦 (*seireki*) but C. E. (*common era*) is 紀元 (*kigen*). Thus, the *first century B. C.* is 紀元前 1 世紀 (*kigenzen is-seiki*).

世紀間—せいきかん—seiki-kan

Japanese: せいきかん
Romanized: *seiki-kan*
Pattern: 漢 S
Used with, or Means: centuries

1 century	一世紀間	いっせいきかん	*is-seiki-kan*
2 centuries	二世紀間	にせいきかん	*ni-seiki-kan*
3 centuries	三世紀間	さんせいきかん	*san-seiki-kan*
4 centuries	四世紀間	よんせいきかん	*yon-seiki-kan*
5 centuries	五世紀間	ごせいきかん	*go-seiki-kan*
6 centuries	六世紀間	ろくせいきかん	*roku-seiki-kan*
7 centuries	七世紀間	ななせいきかん	*nana-seiki-kan*
8 centuries	八世紀間	はっせいきかん / はちせいきかん	*has-seiki-kan* / *hachi-seiki-kan*
9 centuries	九世紀間	きゅうせいきかん	*kyuu-seiki-kan*
10 centuries	十世紀間	じゅっせいきかん / じっせいきかん	*jus-seiki-kan* / *jis-seiki-kan*

Irregularities or Special beyond Ten: none
Notes: none

石 — せき — *seki*

Japanese: せき
Romanized: *seki*
Pattern: 漢 S
Used with, or Means: watch jewels; transistors, diodes

1 jewel	一石	いっせき	*is-seki*
2 jewels	二石	にせき	*ni-seki*
3 jewels	三石	さんせき	*san-seki*
4 jewels	四石	よんせき	*yon-seki*
5 jewels	五石	ごせき	*go-seki*
6 jewels	六石	ろくせき	*roku-seki*
7 jewels	七石	ななせき	*nana-seki*
8 jewels	八石	はっせき	*has-seki*
9 jewels	九石	きゅうせき	*kyuu-seki*
10 jewels	十石	じゅっせき じっせき	*jus-seki* *jis-seki*

Irregularities or Special beyond Ten: none
Notes: none

席 — せき — *seki*

Japanese: せき
Romanized: *seki*
Pattern: 漢 S
Used with, or Means: one's seat, place at the table, seat number in a classroom; seats; Rakugo (落語) shows; (drinking) parties (宴会 *enkai*)

1 seat	一席	いっせき	*is-seki*
2 seats	二席	にせき	*ni-seki*
3 seats	三席	さんせき	*san-seki*
4 seats	四席	よんせき	*yon-seki*
5 seats	五席	ごせき	*go-seki*
6 seats	六席	ろくせき	*roku-seki*
7 seats	七席	ななせき	*nana-seki*
8 seats	八席	はっせき / はちせき	*has-seki* / *hachi-seki*
9 seats	九席	きゅうせき	*kyuu-seki*
10 seats	十席	じゅっせき / じっせき	*jus-seki* / *jis-seki*

Irregularities or Special beyond Ten: none
Notes: none

隻 — せき — *seki*

Japanese: せき
Romanized: *seki*
Pattern: 漢 S
Used with, or Means: large ships, warships

1 warship	一隻	いっせき	<u>*is-seki*</u>
2 warships	二隻	にせき	*ni-seki*
3 warships	三隻	さんせき	*san-seki*
4 warships	四隻	よんせき	*yon-seki*
5 warships	五隻	ごせき	*go-seki*
6 warships	六隻	ろくせき	*roku-seki*
7 warships	七隻	ななせき	*nana-seki*
8 warships	八隻	はっせき はちせき	<u>*has-seki*</u> <u>*hachi-seki*</u>
9 warships	九隻	きゅうせき	*kyuu-seki*
10 warships	十隻	じゅっせき じっせき	<u>*jus-seki*</u> <u>*jis-seki*</u>

Irregularities or Special beyond Ten: none
Notes: none

関 — せき — *seki*

Japanese: せき
Romanized: *seki*
Pattern: 漢 S
Used with, or Means: (literary language) gates, barriers

1 gate	一関	いっせき	<u>*is-seki*</u>
2 gates	二関	にせき	*ni-seki*
3 gates	三関	さんせき	*san-seki*
4 gates	四関	よんせき	*yon-seki*
5 gates	五関	ごせき	*go-seki*
6 gates	六関	ろくせき	*roku-seki*
7 gates	七関	ななせき	*nana-seki*
8 gates	八関	はっせき / はちせき	<u>*has-seki*</u> / <u>*hachi-seki*</u>
9 gates	九関	きゅうせき	*kyuu-seki*
10 gates	十関	じゅっせき / じっせき	<u>*jus-seki*</u> / <u>*jis-seki*</u>

Irregularities or Special beyond Ten: none
Notes: none

齣 — せき — *seki*

Japanese: せき
Romanized: *seki*
Pattern: 漢 S
Used with, or Means: frames, same as 齣 (*koma*)

1 frame	一齣	いっせき	*is-seki*
2 frames	二齣	にせき	*ni-seki*
3 frames	三齣	さんせき	*san-seki*
4 frames	四齣	よんせき	*yon-seki*
5 frames	五齣	ごせき	*go-seki*
6 frames	六齣	ろくせき	*roku-seki*
7 frames	七齣	ななせき	*nana-seki*
8 frames	八齣	はっせき / はちせき	*has-seki* / *hachi-seki*
9 frames	九齣	きゅうせき	*kyuu-seki*
10 frames	十齣	じゅっせき / じっせき	*jus-seki* / *jis-seki*

Irregularities or Special beyond Ten: none
Notes: none

世帯 — せたい — *setai*

Japanese: せたい
Romanized: *setai*
Pattern: 漢 S
Used with, or Means: households, see also 戸 (*ko*), see also 棟 (*tou*)

1 household	一世帯	いっせたい / いちせたい	*is-setai* / *ichi-setai*
2 households	二世帯	にせたい	*ni-setai*
3 households	三世帯	さんせたい	*san-setai*
4 households	四世帯	よんせたい	*yon-setai*
5 households	五世帯	ごせたい	*go-setai*
6 households	六世帯	ろくせたい	*roku-setai*
7 households	七世帯	ななせたい	*nana-setai*
8 households	八世帯	はっせたい / はちせたい	*has-setai* / *hachi-setai*
9 households	九世帯	きゅうせたい	*kyuu-setai*
10 households	十世帯	じゅっせたい / じっせたい	*jus-setai* / *jis-setai*

Irregularities or Special beyond Ten: none
Notes: none

世代 — せだい — *sedai*

Japanese: せだい
Romanized: *sedai*
Pattern: 漢 S
Used with, or Means: generations

1 generation	一世代	いっせだい / いちせだい	*is-sedai* / *ichi-sedai*
2 generations	二世代	にせだい	*ni-sedai*
3 generations	三世代	さんせだい	*san-sedai*
4 generations	四世代	よんせだい	*yon-sedai*
5 generations	五世代	ごせだい	*go-sedai*
6 generations	六世代	ろくせだい	*roku-sedai*
7 generations	七世代	ななせだい	*nana-sedai*
8 generations	八世代	はっせだい / はちせだい	*has-sedai* / *hachi-sedai*
9 generations	九世代	きゅうせだい	*kyuu-sedai*
10 generations	十世代	じゅっせだい / じっせだい	*jus-sedai* / *jis-sedai*

Irregularities or Special beyond Ten: none
Notes: none

節—せつ—*setsu*

Japanese: せつ
Romanized: *setsu*
Pattern: 漢 S
Used with, or Means: sections of a novel, musical score; paragraphs of a document

1 section	一節	いっせつ	<u>*is-setsu*</u>
2 sections	二節	にせつ	*ni-setsu*
3 sections	三節	さんせつ	*san-setsu*
4 sections	四節	よんせつ	*yon-setsu*
5 sections	五節	ごせつ	*go-setsu*
6 sections	六節	ろくせつ	*roku-setsu*
7 sections	七節	ななせつ	*nana-setsu*
8 sections	八節	はっせつ はちせつ	<u>*has-setsu*</u> <u>*hachi-setsu*</u>
9 sections	九節	きゅうせつ	*kyuu-setsu*
10 sections	十節	じゅっせつ じっせつ	<u>*jus-setsu*</u> <u>*jis-setsu*</u>

Irregularities or Special beyond Ten: none
Notes: none

説—せつ—*setsu*

Japanese: せつ
Romanized: *setsu*
Pattern: 漢 S
Used with, or Means: theories

1 theory	一説	いっせつ	*is-setsu*
2 theories	二説	にせつ	*ni-setsu*
3 theories	三説	さんせつ	*san-setsu*
4 theories	四説	よんせつ	*yon-setsu*
5 theories	五説	ごせつ	*go-setsu*
6 theories	六説	ろくせつ	*roku-setsu*
7 theories	七説	ななせつ	*nana-setsu*
8 theories	八説	はっせつ はちせつ	*has-setsu* *hachi-setsu*
9 theories	九説	きゅうせつ	*kyuu-setsu*
10 theories	十説	じゅっせつ じっせつ	*jus-setsu* *jis-setsu*

Irregularities or Special beyond Ten: none
Notes: none

絶—ぜつ—*zetsu*

Japanese: ぜつ
Romanized: *zetsu*
Pattern: 漢 S
Used with, or Means: Chinese poems

1 Chinese poems	一絶	いちぜつ	*ichi-zetsu*
2 Chinese poems	二絶	にぜつ	*ni-zetsu*
3 Chinese poems	三絶	さんぜつ	*san-zetsu*
4 Chinese poems	四絶	よんぜつ	*yon-zetsu*
5 Chinese poems	五絶	ごぜつ	*go-zetsu*
6 Chinese poems	六絶	ろくぜつ	*roku-zetsu*
7 Chinese poems	七絶	ななぜつ	*nana-zetsu*
8 Chinese poems	八絶	はちぜつ	*hachi-zetsu*
9 Chinese poems	九絶	きゅうぜつ	*kyuu-zetsu*
10 Chinese poems	十絶	じゅうぜつ	*juu-zetsu*

Irregularities or Special beyond Ten: none
Notes: none

セット—*setto*

Japanese: せっと
Romanized: *setto*
Pattern: 漢 S
Used with, or Means: sets of clothing

1 set of clothing	1セット	いっせっと いちせっと	*is-setto* *ichi-setto*
2 sets of clothing	2セット	にせっと	*ni-setto*
3 sets of clothing	3セット	さんせっと	*san-setto*
4 sets of clothing	4セット	よんせっと	*yon-setto*
5 sets of clothing	5セット	ごせっと	*go-setto*
6 sets of clothing	6セット	ろくせっと	*roku-setto*
7 sets of clothing	7セット	ななせっと	*nana-setto*
8 sets of clothing	8セット	はっせっと はちせっと	*has-setto* *hachi-setto*
9 sets of clothing	9セット	きゅうせっと	*kyuu-setto*
10 sets of clothing	10セット	じゅっせっと じっせっと	*jus-setto* *jis-setto*

Irregularities or Special beyond Ten: none
Notes: none

千 — せん — *sen*

Japanese: せん
Romanized: *sen*
Pattern: 漢 S
Used with, or Means: thousands, 10³

1,000	一千 千	いっせん せん	<u>*is-*</u>*sen* *sen*
2,000	二千	にせん	*ni-sen*
3,000	三千	さんぜん	*san-*<u>*zen*</u>
4,000	四千	よんせん	*yon-sen*
5,000	五千	ごせん	*go-sen*
6,000	六千	ろくせん	*roku-sen*
7,000	七千	ななせん	*nana-sen*
8,000	八千	はっせん	<u>*has-*</u>*sen*
9,000	九千	きゅうせん	*kyuu-sen*

Irregularities or Special beyond Ten:

Notes: There is no 十千 (*juu-sen*) because that would be 10,000, which is 一万 (*ichi-man*). Furthermore, 一千 is rarely used: typically one just says 千 (*sen*) by itself to mean 1,000.

川—せん—*sen*

Japanese: せん
Romanized: *sen*
Pattern: 漢 S
Used with, or Means: rivers

1 river	一川	いっせん	*is-sen*
2 rivers	二川	にせん	*ni-sen*
3 rivers	三川	さんせん	*san-sen*
4 rivers	四川	よんせん	*yon-sen*
5 rivers	五川	ごせん	*go-sen*
6 rivers	六川	ろくせん	*roku-sen*
7 rivers	七川	ななせん	*nana-sen*
8 rivers	八川	はっせん	*has-sen*
9 rivers	九川	きゅうせん	*kyuu-sen*
10 rivers	十川	じゅっせん / じっせん	*jus-sen* / *jis-sen*

Irregularities or Special beyond Ten: none
Notes: none

泉 — せん — *sen*

Japanese: せん
Romanized: *sen*
Pattern: 漢 S
Used with, or Means: (literary language) fountains, (natural) springs

1 spring	一泉	いっせん	*is-sen*
2 springs	二泉	にせん	*ni-sen*
3 springs	三泉	さんせん	*san-sen*
4 springs	四泉	よんせん	*yon-sen*
5 springs	五泉	ごせん	*go-sen*
6 springs	六泉	ろくせん	*roku-sen*
7 springs	七泉	ななせん	*nana-sen*
8 springs	八泉	はっせん	*has-sen*
9 springs	九泉	きゅうせん	*kyuu-sen*
10 springs	十泉	じゅっせん / じっせん	*jus-sen* / *jis-sen*

Irregularities or Special beyond Ten: none
Notes: none

扇 — せん — sen

Japanese: せん
Romanized: *sen*
Pattern: 漢 S
Used with, or Means: doors, windows; folding screens

1 window	一扇	いっせん	*is-sen*
2 windows	二扇	にせん	*ni-sen*
3 windows	三扇	さんせん	*san-sen*
4 windows	四扇	よんせん	*yon-sen*
5 windows	五扇	ごせん	*go-sen*
6 windows	六扇	ろくせん	*roku-sen*
7 windows	七扇	ななせん	*nana-sen*
8 windows	八扇	はっせん	*has-sen*
9 windows	九扇	きゅうせん	*kyuu-sen*
10 windows	十扇	じゅっせん / じっせん	*jus-sen* / *jis-sen*

Irregularities or Special beyond Ten: none
Notes: none

戦—せん—*sen*

Japanese: せん
Romanized: *sen*
Pattern: 漢 S
Used with, or Means: wars, battles; sports matches

1 battle	(第)一戦	(だい)いっせん	(*dai*)-*is-sen*
2 battles	(第)二戦	(だい)にせん	(*dai*)-*ni-sen*
3 battles	(第)三戦	(だい)さんせん	(*dai*)-*san-sen*
4 battles	(第)四戦	(だい)よんせん	(*dai*)-*yon-sen*
5 battles	(第)五戦	(だい)ごせん	(*dai*)-*go-sen*
6 battles	(第)六戦	(だい)ろくせん	(*dai*)-*roku-sen*
7 battles	(第)七戦	(だい)ななせん	(*dai*)-*nana-sen*
8 battles	(第)八戦	(だい)はっせん	(*dai*)-*has-sen*
9 battles	(第)九戦	(だい)きゅうせん	(*dai*)-*kyuu-sen*
10 battles	(第)十戦	(だい)じゅっせん (だい)じっせん	(*dai*)-*jus-sen* (*dai*)-*jis-sen*

Irregularities or Special beyond Ten: none
Notes: none

煎 — せん — *sen*

Japanese: せん
Romanized: *sen*
Pattern: 漢 S
Used with, or Means: brews of tea (煎茶 *sencha*)

1 brew	一煎	<u>いっせん</u>	<u>*is-sen*</u>
2 brews	二煎	にせん	*ni-sen*
3 brews	三煎	さんせん	*san-sen*
4 brews	四煎	よんせん	*yon-sen*
5 brews	五煎	ごせん	*go-sen*
6 brews	六煎	ろくせん	*roku-sen*
7 brews	七煎	ななせん	*nana-sen*
8 brews	八煎	<u>はっせん</u>	<u>*has-sen*</u>
9 brews	九煎	きゅうせん	*kyuu-sen*
10 brews	十煎	<u>じゅっせん</u> <u>じっせん</u>	<u>*jus-sen*</u> <u>*jis-sen*</u>

Irregularities or Special beyond Ten: none
Notes: none

銭—せん—sen

Japanese: せん
Romanized: sen
Pattern: 漢 S
Used with, or Means: sen, former monetary unit, 1/100th of a 円 (yen), 10 厘 (rin); formerly 1/1,000th of a 貫 (kan)

1 sen	(第)一銭	(だい)いっせん	(dai)-is-sen
2 sen	(第)二銭	(だい)にせん	(dai)-ni-sen
3 sen	(第)三銭	(だい)さんせん	(dai)-san-sen
4 sen	(第)四銭	(だい)よんせん	(dai)-yon-sen
5 sen	(第)五銭	(だい)ごせん	(dai)-go-sen
6 sen	(第)六銭	(だい)ろくせん	(dai)-roku-sen
7 sen	(第)七銭	(だい)ななせん	(dai)-nana-sen
8 sen	(第)八銭	(だい)はっせん	(dai)-has-sen
9 sen	(第)九銭	(だい)きゅうせん	(dai)-kyuu-sen
10 sen	(第)十銭	(だい)じゅっせん (だい)じっせん	(dai)-jus-sen (dai)-jis-sen

Irregularities or Special beyond Ten: none
Notes: none

<u>選 — せん — *sen*</u>

Japanese: せん
Romanized: *sen*
Pattern: 漢 S
Used with, or Means: election terms

1 term	一選	<u>いっせん</u>	<u>*is-sen*</u>
2 terms	二選	にせん	*ni-sen*
3 terms	三選	さんせん	*san-sen*
4 terms	四選	よんせん	*yon-sen*
5 terms	五選	ごせん	*go-sen*
6 terms	六選	ろくせん	*roku-sen*
7 terms	七選	ななせん	*nana-sen*
8 terms	八選	<u>はっせん</u>	<u>*has-sen*</u>
9 terms	九選	きゅうせん	*kyuu-sen*
10 terms	十選	<u>じゅっせん</u> <u>じっせん</u>	<u>*jus-sen*</u> <u>*jis-sen*</u>

Irregularities or Special beyond Ten: none
Notes: none

繊—せん—sen

Japanese: せん
Romanized: *sen*
Pattern: 漢 S
Used with, or Means: 1/10,000,000th, 10^{-7}

10^{-7}	一繊	いっせん	*is-sen*
2×10^{-7}	二繊	にせん	*ni-sen*
3×10^{-7}	三繊	さんせん	*san-sen*
4×10^{-7}	四繊	よんせん	*yon-sen*
5×10^{-7}	五繊	ごせん	*go-sen*
6×10^{-7}	六繊	ろくせん	*roku-sen*
7×10^{-7}	七繊	ななせん	*nana-sen*
8×10^{-7}	八繊	はっせん	*has-sen*
9×10^{-7}	九繊	きゅうせん	*kyuu-sen*
10^{-6}	十繊	じゅっせん / じっせん	*jus-sen* / *jis-sen*

Irregularities or Special beyond Ten:

10^{-5}	百繊	ひゃくせん	*hyaku-sen*
2×10^{-4}	千繊	せんせん	*sen-sen*

Notes: none

前 — ぜん — zen

Japanese: ぜん
Romanized: zen
Pattern: 漢 S
Used with, or Means: tables, armrests (脇息 *kyousoku*); food trays (懸盤 *kakeban*); companies, shrines, small shrines (社祠 *shashi*)

1 table	一前	いちぜん	*ichi-zen*
2 tables	二前	にぜん	*ni-zen*
3 tables	三前	さんぜん	*san-zen*
4 tables	四前	よんぜん	*yon-zen*
5 tables	五前	ごぜん	*go-zen*
6 tables	六前	ろくぜん	*roku-zen*
7 tables	七前	ななぜん	*nana-zen*
8 tables	八前	はちぜん	*hachi-zen*
9 tables	九前	きゅうぜん	*kyuu-zen*
10 tables	十前	じゅうぜん	*juu-zen*

Irregularities or Special beyond Ten: none
Notes: none

膳 — ぜん — zen

Japanese: ぜん
Romanized: zen
Pattern: 漢 S
Used with, or Means: pairs of chopsticks; bowls of rice, meals; small dining tables (膳 zen), see also 飯 (han)

1 bowl of rice	一膳	いちぜん	ichi-zen
2 bowls of rice	二膳	にぜん	ni-zen
3 bowls of rice	三膳	さんぜん	san-zen
4 bowls of rice	四膳	よんぜん	yon-zen
5 bowls of rice	五膳	ごぜん	go-zen
6 bowls of rice	六膳	ろくぜん	roku-zen
7 bowls of rice	七膳	ななぜん	nana-zen
8 bowls of rice	八膳	はちぜん	hachi-zen
9 bowls of rice	九膳	きゅうぜん	kyuu-zen
10 bowls of rice	十膳	じゅうぜん	juu-zen

Irregularities or Special beyond Ten: none
Notes: none

船団—せんだん—sendan

Japanese: せんだん
Romanized: *sendan*
Pattern: 漢 S
Used with, or Means: naval fleets

1 fleet	一船団	いっせんだん いちせんだん	*is-sendan* *ichi-sendan*
2 fleets	二船団	にせんだん	*ni-sendan*
3 fleets	三船団	さんせんだん	*san-sendan*
4 fleets	四船団	よんせんだん	*yon-sendan*
5 fleets	五船団	ごせんだん	*go-sendan*
6 fleets	六船団	ろくせんだん	*roku-sendan*
7 fleets	七船団	ななせんだん	*nana-sendan*
8 fleets	八船団	はっせんだん はちせんだん	*has-sendan* *hachi-sendan*
9 fleets	九船団	きゅうせんだん	*kyuu-sendan*
10 fleets	十船団	じゅっせんだん じっせんだん じゅうせんだん	*jus-sendan* *jis-sendan* *juu-sendan*

Irregularities or Special beyond Ten: none
Notes: none

センチメートル・糎—せんちめえとる—*senchi-meetoru*

Japanese: せんちめえとる
Romanized: *senchi-meetoru*
Pattern: 漢 S
Used with, or Means: centimeters (S. I. symbol: cm), 1/100th of a meter (0.394 in)

1 cm	一センチメートル・糎	いっせんちめえとる	*is-senchi-meetoru*
2 cm	二センチメートル・糎	にせんちめえとる	*ni-senchi-meetoru*
3 cm	三センチメートル・糎	さんせんちめえとる	*san-senchi-meetoru*
4 cm	四センチメートル・糎	よんせんちめえとる	*yon-senchi-meetoru*
5 cm	五センチメートル・糎	ごせんちめえとる	*go-senchi-meetoru*
6 cm	六センチメートル・糎	ろくせんちめえとる	*roku-senchi-meetoru*
7 cm	七センチメートル・糎	ななせんちめえとる	*nana-senchi-meetoru*
8 cm	八センチメートル・糎	はっせんちめえとる	*has-senchi-meetoru*
9 cm	九センチメートル・糎	きゅうせんちめえとる	*kyuu-senchi-meetoru*
10 cm	十センチメートル・糎	じゅっせんちめえとる じっせんちめえとる	*jus-senchi-meetoru* *jis-senchi-meetoru*

Irregularities or Special beyond Ten: none
Notes: none

センチグラム・甅—せんちぐらむ—*senchi-guramu*

Japanese: せんちぐらむ
Romanized: *senchi-guramu*
Pattern: 漢 S
Used with, or Means: centigrams (S. I. symbol: cg), 1/100th of a gram (0.000353 oz)

1 cg	一センチグラム・甅	いっせんちぐらむ	*is-senchi-guramu*
2 cg	二センチグラム・甅	にせんちぐらむ	*ni-senchi-guramu*
3 cg	三センチグラム・甅	さんせんちぐらむ	*san-senchi-guramu*
4 cg	四センチグラム・甅	よんせんちぐらむ	*yon-senchi-guramu*
5 cg	五センチグラム・甅	ごせんちぐらむ	*go-senchi-guramu*
6 cg	六センチグラム・甅	ろくせんちぐらむ	*roku-senchi-guramu*
7 cg	七センチグラム・甅	ななせんちぐらむ	*nana-senchi-guramu*
8 cg	八センチグラム・甅	はっせんちぐらむ	*has-senchi-guramu*
9 cg	九センチグラム・甅	きゅうせんちぐらむ	*kyuu-senchi-guramu*
10 cg	十センチグラム・甅	じゅっせんちぐらむ じっせんちぐらむ	*jus-senchi-guramu* *jis-senchi-guramu*

Irregularities or Special beyond Ten: none
Notes: none

センチリットル・糎—せんちりっとる—*senchi-rittoru*

Japanese: せんちりっとる
Romanized: *senchi-rittoru*
Pattern: 漢 S
Used with, or Means: centiliters (S. I. symbol: cL), 1/100th of a liter (0.338 fl oz)

1 cL	一センチリットル・糎	いっせんちりっとる	*is-senchi-rittoru*
2 cL	二センチリットル・糎	にせんちりっとる	*ni-senchi-rittoru*
3 cL	三センチリットル・糎	さんせんちりっとる	*san-senchi-rittoru*
4 cL	四センチリットル・糎	よんせんちりっとる	*yon-senchi-rittoru*
5 cL	五センチリットル・糎	ごせんちりっとる	*go-senchi-rittoru*
6 cL	六センチリットル・糎	ろくせんちりっとる	*roku-senchi-rittoru*
7 cL	七センチリットル・糎	ななせんちりっとる	*nana-senchi-rittoru*
8 cL	八センチリットル・糎	はっせんちりっとる	*has-senchi-rittoru*
9 cL	九センチリットル・糎	きゅうせんちりっとる	*kyuu-senchi-rittoru*
10 cL	十センチリットル・糎	じゅっせんちりっとる じっせんちりっとる	*jus-senchi-rittoru* *jis-senchi-rittoru*

Irregularities or Special beyond Ten: none
Notes: none

セント・仙—せんと—*sento*

Japanese: せんと
Romanized: *sento*
Pattern: 漢 S
Used with, or Means: cents (symbol: ¢), 1/100th of a dollar

1 ¢	一セント・仙	いっせんと	*is-sento*
2 ¢	二セント・仙	にせんと	*ni-sento*
3 ¢	三セント・仙	さんせんと	*san-sento*
4 ¢	四セント・仙	よんせんと	*yon-sento*
5 ¢	五セント・仙	ごせんと	*go-sento*
6 ¢	六セント・仙	ろくせんと	*roku-sento*
7 ¢	七セント・仙	ななせんと	*nana-sento*
8 ¢	八セント・仙	はっせんと	*has-sento*
9 ¢	九セント・仙	きゅうせんと	*kyuu-sento*
10 ¢	十セント・仙	じゅっせんと / じっせんと	*jus-sento* / *jis-sento*

Irregularities or Special beyond Ten: none
Notes: none

そ・ぞ—So/Zo
雙・双—そう—sou

Japanese: そう
Romanized: *sou*
Pattern: 漢 S
Used with, or Means: pairs of things

1 pair	一雙・双	いっそう	*is-sou*
2 pairs	二雙・双	にそう	*ni-sou*
3 pairs	三雙・双	さんそう	*san-sou*
4 pairs	四雙・双	よんそう	*yon-sou*
5 pairs	五雙・双	ごそう	*go-sou*
6 pairs	六雙・双	ろくそう	*roku-sou*
7 pairs	七雙・双	ななそう	*nana-sou*
8 pairs	八雙・双	はっそう	*has-sou*
9 pairs	九雙・双	きゅうそう	*kyuu-sou*
10 pairs	十雙・双	じゅっそう / じっそう	*jus-sou* / *jis-sou*

Irregularities or Special beyond Ten: none
Notes: none

層 — そう — *sou*

Japanese: そう
Romanized: *sou*
Pattern: 漢 S
Used with, or Means: layers; building stories, levels

1 layer	一層	いっそう	*is-sou*
2 layers	二層	にそう	*ni-sou*
3 layers	三層	さんそう	*san-sou*
4 layers	四層	よんそう	*yon-sou*
5 layers	五層	ごそう	*go-sou*
6 layers	六層	ろくそう	*roku-sou*
7 layers	七層	ななそう	*nana-sou*
8 layers	八層	はっそう	*has-sou*
9 layers	九層	きゅうそう	*kyuu-sou*
10 layers	十層	じゅっそう / じっそう	*jus-sou* / *jis-sou*

Irregularities or Special beyond Ten: none
Notes: none

槍 — そう — *sou*

Japanese: そう
Romanized: *sou*
Pattern: 漢 S
Used with, or Means: the number of times one strikes, stabs, or jabs one's opponent with a spear, lance, or javelin (槍 *yari*)

1 jab	一槍	いっそう	*is-sou*
2 jabs	二槍	にそう	*ni-sou*
3 jabs	三槍	さんそう	*san-sou*
4 jabs	四槍	よんそう	*yon-sou*
5 jabs	五槍	ごそう	*go-sou*
6 jabs	六槍	ろくそう	*roku-sou*
7 jabs	七槍	ななそう	*nana-sou*
8 jabs	八槍	はっそう	*has-sou*
9 jabs	九槍	きゅうそう	*kyuu-sou*
10 jabs	十槍	じゅっそう / じっそう	*jus-sou* / *jis-sou*

Irregularities or Special beyond Ten: none
Notes: none

槽 — そう — *sou*

Japanese: そう
Romanized: *sou*
Pattern: 漢 S
Used with, or Means: water tanks (水槽 *suisou*), cisterns, fish tanks; bathtubs (浴槽 *yokusou*); (laundary) wash basins (洗濯層 *sentaku-sou*)

1 water tank	一槽	いっそう	*is-sou*
2 water tanks	二槽	にそう	*ni-sou*
3 water tanks	三槽	さんそう	*san-sou*
4 water tanks	四槽	よんそう	*yon-sou*
5 water tanks	五槽	ごそう	*go-sou*
6 water tanks	六槽	ろくそう	*roku-sou*
7 water tanks	七槽	ななそう	*nana-sou*
8 water tanks	八槽	はっそう	*has-sou*
9 water tanks	九槽	きゅうそう	*kyuu-sou*
10 water tanks	十槽	じゅっそう / じっそう	*jus-sou* / *jis-sou*

Irregularities or Special beyond Ten: none
Notes: none

艘 — そう — sou

Japanese: そう
Romanized: sou
Pattern: 漢 S
Used with, or Means: small boats, row-boats, see also 杯 (hai), see also 隻 (seki), see also 艇 (tei)

1 small boat	一艘	いっそう	*is-sou*
2 small boats	二艘	にそう	*ni-sou*
3 small boats	三艘	さんそう	*san-sou*
4 small boats	四艘	よんそう	*yon-sou*
5 small boats	五艘	ごそう	*go-sou*
6 small boats	六艘	ろくそう	*roku-sou*
7 small boats	七艘	ななそう	*nana-sou*
8 small boats	八艘	はっそう	*has-sou*
9 small boats	九艘	きゅうそう	*kyuu-sou*
10 small boats	十艘	じゅっそう じっそう	*jus-sou* *jis-sou*

Irregularities or Special beyond Ten: none
Notes: none

叢 — そう — *sou*

Japanese: そう
Romanized: *sou*
Pattern: 漢 S
Used with, or Means: flocks, herds, groups

1 flock	一叢	いっそう	*is-sou*
2 flocks	二叢	にそう	*ni-sou*
3 flocks	三叢	さんそう	*san-sou*
4 flocks	四叢	よんそう	*yon-sou*
5 flocks	五叢	ごそう	*go-sou*
6 flocks	六叢	ろくそう	*roku-sou*
7 flocks	七叢	ななそう	*nana-sou*
8 flocks	八叢	はっそう	*has-sou*
9 flocks	九叢	きゅうそう	*kyuu-sou*
10 flocks	十叢	じゅっそう / じっそう	*jus-sou* / *jis-sou*

Irregularities or Special beyond Ten: none
Notes: none

束 —— そく —— soku

Japanese: そく
Romanized: *soku*
Pattern: 漢 S

Used with, or Means: reams of paper, especially 半紙 (*hanshi*), equal to 200 枚 (*mai*); bundles of grain sheaves equal to 10 把 (*wa*); a unit of caught fish equal to 100 尾 (*bi* fish); a bundle of arrows equal to 20 本 (*hon*); (professional/technical jargon) a unit of arrow length; an Edo period secret term referring to 1, 10, 100, 1,000, etc . . .; Samurai topknots (髻 *motodori*), see also 把 (*wa*)

1 bundle	一束	いっそく	*is-soku*
2 bundles	二束	にそく	*ni-soku*
3 bundles	三束	さんそく	*san-soku*
4 bundles	四束	よんそく	*yon-soku*
5 bundles	五束	ごそく	*go-soku*
6 bundles	六束	ろくそく	*roku-soku*
7 bundles	七束	ななそく	*nana-soku*
8 bundles	八束	はっそく	*has-soku*
9 bundles	九束	きゅうそく	*kyuu-soku*
10 bundles	十束	じゅっそく / じっそく	*jus-soku* / *jis-soku*

Irregularities or Special beyond Ten: none

Notes: *Hanshi* is Japanese paper sized specially for calligraphy. Nowadays, *hanshi* is 25 cm wide (across the top) by 35 cm long. Traditionally, it was 1 尺 3 寸 (39 cm) wide by 2 尺 3 寸 (70 cm) long.

Kabura-ya (literally *turnip-bulb arrows*) are arrows with bulb-shaped whistles attached to their arrow-heads. Samurai used the whistles as battle signals at first, but because many believed the whistles helped ward off evil spirits, the arrows became a popular item sold at shrines during festivals. Over time, they replaced the whistle with a knob of solid wood. One can still buy these at shrines duing New Years.

足 — そく — *soku*

Japanese: そく
Romanized: *soku*
Pattern: 漢 S
Used with, or Means: pairs of shoes, socks, *tabi*, stockings; pairs of things that form a left-right set; (colloquialism) cuttlefish; the number of times one kicks the ball in the game kickball; the number of times one jumps with both feet; (see Notes)

1 pair	一足	いっそく	is-soku
2 pairs	二足	にそく	ni-soku
3 pairs	三足	さんそく さんぞく	san-soku san-zoku
4 pairs	四足	よんそく	yon-soku
5 pairs	五足	ごそく	go-soku
6 pairs	六足	ろくそく	roku-soku
7 pairs	七足	ななそく	nana-soku
8 pairs	八足	はっそく	has-soku
9 pairs	九足	きゅうそく	kyuu-soku
10 pairs	十足	じゅっそく じっそく	jus-soku jis-soku

Irregularities or Special beyond Ten: none
Notes: 一足飛び (*is-soku-tobi*) means *a single bound*.

則 — そく — *soku*

Japanese: そく
Romanized: *soku*
Pattern: 漢 S
Used with, or Means: provisions, articles, sections of a constitution, act, treaty, etc . . . (see Notes)

1st provision	(第)一則	(だい)いっそく	*(dai)-is-soku*
2nd provision	(第)二則	(だい)にそく	*(dai)-ni-soku*
3rd provision	(第)三則	(だい)さんそく	*(dai)-san-soku*
4th provision	(第)四則	(だい)よんそく	*(dai)-yon-soku*
5th provision	(第)五則	(だい)ごそく	*(dai)-go-soku*
6th provision	(第)六則	(だい)ろくそく	*(dai)-roku-soku*
7th provision	(第)七則	(だい)ななそく	*(dai)-nana-soku*
8th provision	(第)八則	*(だい)はっそく*	*(dai)-has-soku*
9th provision	(第)九則	(だい)きゅうそく	*(dai)-kyuu-soku*
10th provision	(第)十則	(だい)じゅっそく (だい)じっそく	*(dai)-jus-soku* *(dai)-jis-soku*

Irregularities or Special beyond Ten: none
Notes: Typically, this counter is prefixed with 第 (*dai*), as in, 会規の第五則 (*kaiki dai-go-soku* the fifth article of the club's by-laws).

息 — そく — *soku*

Japanese: そく
Romanized: *soku*
Pattern: 漢 S
Used with, or Means: breaths

1 breath	一息	いっそく / ひといき	*is-soku* / *hito-iki*
2 breaths	二息	にそく / ふたいき	*ni-soku* / *futa-iki*
3 breaths	三息	さんそく	*san-soku*
4 breaths	四息	よんそく	*yon-soku*
5 breaths	五息	ごそく	*go-soku*
6 breaths	六息	ろくそく	*roku-soku*
7 breaths	七息	ななそく	*nana-soku*
8 breaths	八息	はっそく	*has-soku*
9 breaths	九息	きゅうそく	*kyuu-soku*
10 breaths	十息	じゅっそく / じっそく	*jus-soku* / *jis-soku*

Irregularities or Special beyond Ten: none
Notes: One can also count "a breath" or "a couple of breaths" using the same kanji, but pronouncing it *iki*, instead of *soku*. In this case, use *hito-*, and *futa-*, respectively.

速 — そく — *soku*

Japanese: そく
Romanized: *soku*
Pattern: 漢 S
Used with, or Means: car gears (as in, *shift into 4th gear*), bicycle speeds (as in, *a 10-speed*)

1st gear	(第)一速	(だい)いっそく	(*dai*)-*is-soku*
2nd gear	(第)二速	(だい)にそく	(*dai*)-*ni-soku*
3rd gear	(第)三速	(だい)さんそく	(*dai*)-*san-soku*
4th gear	(第)四速	(だい)よんそく	(*dai*)-*yon-soku*
5th gear	(第)五速	(だい)ごそく	(*dai*)-*go-soku*
6th gear	(第)六速	(だい)ろくそく	(*dai*)-*roku-soku*
7th gear	(第)七速	(だい)ななそく	(*dai*)-*nana-soku*
8th gear	(第)八速	(だい)はっそく	(*dai*)-*has-soku*
9th gear	(第)九速	(だい)きゅうそく	(*dai*)-*kyuu-soku*
10th gear	(第)十速	(だい)じゅっそく (だい)じっそく	(*dai*)-*jus-soku* (*dai*)-*jis-soku*

Irregularities or Special beyond Ten: none
Notes: Typically, this counter is prefixed with 第 (*dai*), as in, 第三速 (*dai-san-soku* the third gear).

粟 — ぞく — zoku

Japanese: ぞく
Romanized: zoku
Pattern: 漢 Ø

Used with, or Means: zoku; a unit of volume, 100 升 (shou), 6,099.73467 fl oz (47.65418 gal)/180.39068 L; individual grains of millet

1 zoku	一粟	いちぞく	ichi-zoku
2 zoku	二粟	にぞく	ni-zoku
3 zoku	三粟	さんぞく	san-zoku
4 zoku	四粟	よんぞく	yon-zoku
5 zoku	五粟	ごぞく	go-zoku
6 zoku	六粟	ろくぞく	roku-zoku
7 zoku	七粟	ななぞく	nana-zoku
8 zoku	八粟	はちぞく	hachi-zoku
9 zoku	九粟	きゅうぞく	kyuu-zoku
10 zoku	十粟	じゅうぞく	juu-zoku

Irregularities or Special beyond Ten: none

Notes: 一粟 can also be taken literally or metaphorical. Literally, a single grain of millet, or metaphorically, something extremely small, as in, 大海の一粟 (*taikai no ichi-zoku*), which means *a drop in the bucket, a drop in the ocean*, something very small in proportion to the whole.

具—そなえ—*sonae*

Japanese: そなえ
Romanized: *sonae*
Pattern: 和 I-S
Used with, or Means: ceremonial dress (裃 *kamishimo*); surplice, stole (袈裟 *kesa*), see also 具 (*gu*)

1 surplice	一具	ひとそなえ	*hito-sonae*
2 surplices	二具	ふたそなえ	*futa-sonae*
3 surplices	三具	さんそなえ	*san-sonae*
4 surplices	四具	よんそなえ	*yon-sonae*
5 surplices	五具	ごそなえ	*go-sonae*
6 surplices	六具	ろくそなえ	*roku-sonae*
7 surplices	七具	ななそなえ	*nana-sonae*
8 surplices	八具	はっそなえ / はちそなえ	*has-sonae* / *hachi-sonae*
9 surplices	九具	きゅうそなえ	*kyuu-sonae*
10 surplices	十具	じゅっそなえ / じっそなえ	*jus-sonae* / *jis-sonae*

Irregularities or Special beyond Ten: none
Notes: none

揃い—そろい—*soroi*

Japanese: そろい
Romanized: *soroi*
Pattern: 和 II-S or 和 I-S
Used with, or Means: bedding, tea utensils; sets of things; pairs of chopsticks, see also 具 (*gu*), see also 装い (*yosoi*), see also 組 (*kumi*)

1 set	一揃い	ひとそろい	*hito-soroi*
2 sets	二揃い	ふたそろい	*futa-soroi*
3 sets	三揃い	みそろい さんそおり	*mi-soroi* *san-soroi*
4 sets	四揃い	よんそろい	*yon-soroi*
5 sets	五揃い	ごそろい	*go-soroi*
6 sets	六揃い	ろくそろい	*roku-soroi*
7 sets	七揃い	ななそろい	*nana-soroi*
8 sets	八揃い	はっそろい はちそおり	*has-soroi* *hachi-soroi*
9 sets	九揃い	きゅうそろい	*kyuu-soroi*
10 sets	十揃い	じゅっそろい じっそろい	*jus-soroi* *jis-soroi*

Irregularities or Special beyond Ten: none
Notes: 三つ揃い (*mitsu-zoroi*) means *a three piece suit*.

村 — そん — *son*

Japanese: そん
Romanized: *son*
Pattern: 漢 S
Used with, or Means: villages

1 village	一村	いっそん	*is-son*
2 villages	二村	にそん	*ni-son*
3 villages	三村	さんそん	*san-son*
4 villages	四村	よんそん	*yon-son*
5 villages	五村	ごそん	*go-son*
6 villages	六村	ろくそん	*roku-son*
7 villages	七村	ななそん	*nana-son*
8 villages	八村	はっそん	*has-son*
9 villages	九村	きゅうそん	*kyuu-son*
10 villages	十村	じゅっそん / じっそん	*jus-son* / *jis-son*

Irregularities or Special beyond Ten: none
Notes: none

尊 — そん — *son*

Japanese: そん
Romanized: *son*
Pattern: 漢 S
Used with, or Means: statues of Buddha; stone buddhist images, see also 体 (*tai*); *Jizou*[11] statues; images of the Buddha in a temple

1 Buddhist statue	一尊	いっそん	*is-son*
2 Buddhist statues	二尊	にそん	*ni-son*
3 Buddhist statues	三尊	さんそん	*san-son*
4 Buddhist statues	四尊	よんそん	*yon-son*
5 Buddhist statues	五尊	ごそん	*go-son*
6 Buddhist statues	六尊	ろくそん	*roku-son*
7 Buddhist statues	七尊	ななそん	*nana-son*
8 Buddhist statues	八尊	はっそん	*has-son*
9 Buddhist statues	九尊	きゅうそん	*kyuu-son*
10 Buddhist statues	十尊	じゅっそん じっそん	*jus-son* *jis-son*

Irregularities or Special beyond Ten: none
Notes: Typically, 体 (*tai*) is used more often to count statues.

---

[11] *Ksitigarbha* (地蔵, *Jizou* in Japanese) is the bodhisattva responsible for the safe transmigration of all souls, but especially the defenseless souls of little children. Images of him are found along the road side, at crossroads, along high mountain passes, and the entrances of graveyards—often wrapped in little red bibs. Typically, rather than one, there will be six of him in a row: one for each of the six positions on the karmic wheel—hell, hungry spirits (*gakki*), animals, humans, *ashura* (noble, fighting spirits, sometimes called demons), and gods.

た・だ—Ta/Da
打—だ—da

Japanese: だ
Romanized: *da*
Pattern: 漢 ∅
Used with, or Means: hits (in baseball)

1 hit	一打	いちだ	*ichi-da*
2 hits	二打	にだ	*ni-da*
3 hits	三打	さんだ	*san-da*
4 hits	四打	よんだ	*yon-da*
5 hits	五打	ごだ	*go-da*
6 hits	六打	ろくだ	*roku-da*
7 hits	七打	ななだ	*nana-da*
8 hits	八打	はちだ	*hachi-da*
9 hits	九打	きゅうだ	*kyuu-da*
10 hits	十打	じゅうだ	*juu-da*

Irregularities or Special beyond Ten: none
Notes: none

<h1 align="center">朶—だ—da</h1>

Japanese: だ
Romanized: da
Pattern: 漢 Ø
Used with, or Means: long, oblong chests for clothing; trees

1 chest	一朶	いちだ	ichi-da
2 chests	二朶	にだ	ni-da
3 chests	三朶	さんだ	san-da
4 chests	四朶	よんだ	yon-da
5 chests	五朶	ごだ	go-da
6 chests	六朶	ろくだ	roku-da
7 chests	七朶	ななだ	nana-da
8 chests	八朶	はちだ	hachi-da
9 chests	九朶	きゅうだ	kyuu-da
10 chests	十朶	じゅうだ	juu-da

Irregularities or Special beyond Ten: none
Notes: none

駄—だ—da

Japanese: だ
Romanized: *da*
Pattern: 漢 ∅
Used with, or Means: horseloads, see also 貫 (*kan*), see also 樽 (*taru*)

1 horseload	一駄	いちだ	*ichi-da*
2 horseloads	二駄	にだ	*ni-da*
3 horseloads	三駄	さんだ	*san-da*
4 horseloads	四駄	よんだ	*yon-da*
5 horseloads	五駄	ごだ	*go-da*
6 horseloads	六駄	ろくだ	*roku-da*
7 horseloads	七駄	ななだ	*nana-da*
8 horseloads	八駄	はちだ	*hachi-da*
9 horseloads	九駄	きゅうだ	*kyuu-da*
10 horseloads	十駄	じゅうだ	*juu-da*

Irregularities or Special beyond Ten: none
Notes: none

ダース・打—だあす—*daasu*

Japanese: だあす
Romanized: *daasu*
Pattern: 漢 ∅
Used with, or Means: dozen

1 dozen	一ダース・打	いちだあす	*ichi-daasu*
2 dozen	二ダース・打	にだあす	*ni-daasu*
3 dozen	三ダース・打	さんだあす	*san-daasu*
4 dozen	四ダース・打	よんだあす	*yon-daasu*
5 dozen	五ダース・打	ごだあす	*go-daasu*
6 dozen	六ダース・打	ろくだあす	*roku-daasu*
7 dozen	七ダース・打	ななだあす	*nana-daasu*
8 dozen	八ダース・打	はちだあす	*hachi-daasu*
9 dozen	九ダース・打	きゅうだあす	*kyuu-daasu*
10 dozen	十ダース・打	じゅうだあす	*juu-daasu*

Irregularities or Special beyond Ten: none
Notes: none

体 — たい — *tai*

Japanese: たい
Romanized: *tai*
Pattern: 漢 T
Used with, or Means: dead bodies, corpses, remains, ashes; Buddhist statues, statues of Shinto gods, see also 仏 (*butsu*), see also 尊 (*son*); mannequins; dolls

1 corpse	一体	いったい	*it-tai*
2 corpses	二体	にたい	*ni-tai*
3 corpses	三体	さんたい	*san-tai*
4 corpses	四体	よんたい	*yon-tai*
5 corpses	五体	ごたい	*go-tai*
6 corpses	六体	ろくたい	*roku-tai*
7 corpses	七体	ななたい	*nana-tai*
8 corpses	八体	はったい / はちたい	*hat-tai* / *hachi-tai*
9 corpses	九体	きゅうたい	*kyuu-tai*
10 corpses	十体	じゅったい / じったい	*jut-tai* / *jit-tai*

Irregularities or Special beyond Ten: none
Notes: none

袋—たい—*tai*

Japanese: たい
Romanized: *tai*
Pattern: 漢 T

Used with, or Means: bags, bagfuls, same as 袋 (*fukuro*); (professional/technical jargon) a unit of volume in industries and agriculture: 1 bag of cement, 1 bag of wheat, see also 袋 (*fukuro*)

1 bag	一袋	いったい	*it-tai*
2 bags	二袋	にたい	*ni-tai*
3 bags	三袋	さんたい	*san-tai*
4 bags	四袋	よんたい	*yon-tai*
5 bags	五袋	ごたい	*go-tai*
6 bags	六袋	ろくたい	*roku-tai*
7 bags	七袋	ななたい	*nana-tai*
8 bags	八袋	はったい / はちたい	*hat-tai* / *hachi-tai*
9 bags	九袋	きゅうたい	*kyuu-tai*
10 bags	十袋	じゅったい / じったい	*jut-tai* / *jit-tai*

Irregularities or Special beyond Ten: none
Notes: none

隊—たい—*tai*

Japanese: たい
Romanized: *tai*
Pattern: 漢 T
Used with, or Means: gatherings, groups of people; military forces, military units, armies, squads

1 military unit	一隊	いったい	*it-tai*
2 military units	二隊	にたい	*ni-tai*
3 military units	三隊	さんたい	*san-tai*
4 military units	四隊	よんたい	*yon-tai*
5 military units	五隊	ごたい	*go-tai*
6 military units	六隊	ろくたい	*roku-tai*
7 military units	七隊	ななたい	*nana-tai*
8 military units	八隊	はったい / はちたい	*hat-tai* / *hachi-tai*
9 military units	九隊	きゅうたい	*kyuu-tai*
10 military units	十隊	じゅったい / じったい	*jut-tai* / *jit-tai*

Irregularities or Special beyond Ten: none
Notes: none

代—だい—*dai*

Japanese: だい
Romanized: *dai*
Pattern: 漢 Ø
Used with, or Means: Nth generation

1st generation	一代	いちだい	*ichi-dai*
2nd generation	二代	にだい	*ni-dai*
3rd generation	三代	さんだい	*san-dai*
4th generation	四代	よんだい	*yon-dai*
5th generation	五代	ごだい	*go-dai*
6th generation	六代	ろくだい	*roku-dai*
7th generation	七代	ななだい	*nana-dai*
8th generation	八代	はちだい	*hachi-dai*
9th generation	九代	きゅうだい	*kyuu-dai*
10th generation	十代	じゅうだい	*juu-dai*

Irregularities or Special beyond Ten: none
Notes: none

台 — だい — dai

Japanese: だい
Romanized: *dai*
Pattern: 漢 ∅

Used with, or Means: vehicles; machines, mechanical devices, see also 基 (*ki*); pair of skis; sliding ponds; 16-page, 32-page units in printing, bookbinding; galleys

1 vehicle	一台	いちだい	*ichi-dai*
2 vehicles	二台	にだい	*ni-dai*
3 vehicles	三台	さんだい	*san-dai*
4 vehicles	四台	よんだい	*yon-dai*
5 vehicles	五台	ごだい	*go-dai*
6 vehicles	六台	ろくだい	*roku-dai*
7 vehicles	七台	ななだい	*nana-dai*
8 vehicles	八台	はちだい	*hachi-dai*
9 vehicles	九台	きゅうだい	*kyuu-dai*
10 vehicles	十台	じゅうだい	*juu-dai*

Irregularities or Special beyond Ten: none
Notes: none

弟 — だい — dai

Japanese: だい
Romanized: *dai*
Pattern: 漢 ∅
Used with, or Means: younger siblings; children

1 sibling	一弟	いちだい	*ichi-dai*
2 siblings	二弟	にだい	*ni-dai*
3 siblings	三弟	さんだい	*san-dai*
4 siblings	四弟	よんだい	*yon-dai*
5 siblings	五弟	ごだい	*go-dai*
6 siblings	六弟	ろくだい	*roku-dai*
7 siblings	七弟	ななだい	*nana-dai*
8 siblings	八弟	はちだい	*hachi-dai*
9 siblings	九弟	きゅうだい	*kyuu-dai*
10 siblings	十弟	じゅうだい	*juu-dai*

Irregularities or Special beyond Ten: none
Notes: none

第 — だい — dai

Japanese: だい
Romanized: dai
Pattern: 漢 Ø
Used with, or Means: the order in which things occur, numerical order, see also 番 (ban)

No. 1	第一	だいいち	dai-ichi
No. 2	第二	だいに	dai-ni
No. 3	第三	だいさん	dai-san
No. 4	第四	だいよん	dai-yon
No. 5	第五	だいご	dai-go
No. 6	第六	だいろく	dai-roku
No. 7	第七	だいなな	dai-nana
No. 8	第八	だいはち	dai-hachi
No. 9	第九	だいきゅう	dai-kyuu
No. 10	第十	だいじゅう	dai-juu

Irregularities or Special beyond Ten: none
Notes: Notice how the counter comes *before* the number, rather than after it. You may have noticed several other counters by now that use this counter in conjunction with them (such as 第二戦 *dai-ni-sen*). Technically, no matter what counter to which you attach 第 (*dai*), it changes its meaning from (using the above example), *two battles* (二戦 *ni-sen*) to *the second battle* (第二戦 *dai-ni-sen*).

I give some counters here as accompanied with 第 (*dai*) because that's the context in which they occur the vast majority of the time; that is to say, they typically *do not* occur alone.

題—だい—dai

Japanese: だい
Romanized: *dai*
Pattern: 漢 Ø
Used with, or Means: subjects, themes, titles, discoveries; questions, problems, tasks; Rakugo performances

1 question	一題	いちだい	*ichi-dai*
2 questions	二題	にだい	*ni-dai*
3 questions	三題	さんだい	*san-dai*
4 questions	四題	よんだい	*yon-dai*
5 questions	五題	ごだい	*go-dai*
6 questions	六題	ろくだい	*roku-dai*
7 questions	七題	ななだい	*nana-dai*
8 questions	八題	はちだい	*hachi-dai*
9 questions	九題	きゅうだい	*kyuu-dai*
10 questions	十題	じゅうだい	*juu-dai*

Irregularities or Special beyond Ten: none
Notes: none

代目―だいめ―*dai-me*

Japanese: だいめ
Romanized: *dai-me*
Pattern: 漢 ∅
Used with, or Means: generations; junior, senior, the III, etc . . ., as in 十四代目ルイ (*juu-yon-dai-me Rui* Louis XIV)

1st generation	一代目	いちだいめ	*ichi-dai-me*
2nd generation	二代目	にだいめ	*ni-dai-me*
3rd generation	三代目	さんだいめ	*san-dai-me*
4th generation	四代目	よんだいめ	*yon-dai-me*
5th generation	五代目	ごだいめ	*go-dai-me*
6th generation	六代目	ろくだいめ	*roku-dai-me*
7th generation	七代目	ななだいめ	*nana-dai-me*
8th generation	八代目	はちだいめ	*hachi-dai-me*
9th generation	九代目	きゅうだいめ	*kyuu-dai-me*
10th generation	十代目	じゅうだいめ	*juu-dai-me*

Irregularities or Special beyond Ten: none
Notes: none

卓 — たく — *taku*

Japanese: たく
Romanized: *taku*
Pattern: 漢 T
Used with, or Means: tables, dining tables, mahjong tables (雀卓 *jantaku*); stands, see also 台 (*dai*)

1 mahjong table	一卓	いったく		*it-taku*
2 mahjong tables	二卓	にたく		*ni-taku*
3 mahjong tables	三卓	さんたく		*san-taku*
4 mahjong tables	四卓	よんたく		*yon-taku*
5 mahjong tables	五卓	ごたく		*go-taku*
6 mahjong tables	六卓	ろくたく		*roku-taku*
7 mahjong tables	七卓	ななたく		*nana-taku*
8 mahjong tables	八卓	はったく / はちたく		*hat-taku* / *hachi-taku*
9 mahjong tables	九卓	きゅうたく		*kyuu-taku*
10 mahjong tables	十卓	じゅったく / じったく		*jut-taku* / *jit-taku*

Irregularities or Special beyond Ten: none
Notes: none

打席—だせき—*daseki*

Japanese: だせき
Romanized: *daseki*
Pattern: 漢 ∅
Used with, or Means: one's turn at bat (in baseball)

1st at bat	一打席	いちだせき	*ichi-daseki*
2nd at bat	二打席	にだせき	*ni-daseki*
3rd at bat	三打席	さんだせき	*san-daseki*
4th at bat	四打席	よんだせき	*yon-daseki*
5th at bat	五打席	ごだせき	*go-daseki*
6th at bat	六打席	ろくだせき	*roku-daseki*
7th at bat	七打席	ななだせき	*nana-daseki*
8th at bat	八打席	はちだせき	*hachi-daseki*
9th at bat	九打席	きゅうだせき	*kyuu-daseki*
10th at bat	十打席	じゅうだせき	*juu-daseki*

Irregularities or Special beyond Ten: none
Notes: none

立 — たて — *tate*

Japanese: たて
Romanized: *tate*
Pattern: 漢 T
Used with, or Means: consecutive defeats (連敗 *renpai*)

1 consecutive defeat	一立	いったて	<u>*it-tate*</u>
2 consecutive defeats	二立	にたて	*ni-tate*
3 consecutive defeats	三立	さんたて	*san-tate*
4 consecutive defeats	四立	よんたて	*yon-tate*
5 consecutive defeats	五立	ごたて	*go-tate*
6 consecutive defeats	六立	ろくたて	*roku-tate*
7 consecutive defeats	七立	ななたて	*nana-tate*
8 consecutive defeats	八立	はったて	<u>*hat-tate*</u>
9 consecutive defeats	九立	きゅうたて	*kyuu-tate*
10 consecutive defeats	十立	じゅったて じったて	<u>*jut-tate*</u> <u>*jit-tate*</u>

Irregularities or Special beyond Ten: none
Notes: none

立て—だて—*date*

Japanese: だて
Romanized: *date*
Pattern: 漢 ∅
Used with, or Means: carriage horses; boat oars; films at a multi-feature movie

1 oar	一立て	いちだて	*ichi-date*
2 oars	二立て	にだて	*ni-date*
3 oars	三立て	さんだて	*san-date*
4 oars	四立て	よんだて	*yon-date*
5 oars	五立て	ごだて	*go-date*
6 oars	六立て	ろくだて	*roku-date*
7 oars	七立て	ななだて	*nana-date*
8 oars	八立て	はちだて	*hachi-date*
9 oars	九立て	きゅうだて	*kyuu-date*
10 oars	十立て	じゅうだて	*juu-date*

Irregularities or Special beyond Ten: none
Notes: none

束—たば—*taba*

Japanese: たば
Romanized: *taba*
Pattern: 和 I-T
Used with, or Means: bundles, bunches; bundles of bank notes, vegetables, firewood; strings of paper cranes (千羽鶴 *sembazuru*); bunches of flowers

1 bundle	一束	ひとたば	*hito-taba*
2 bundles	二束	ふたたば	*futa-taba*
3 bundles	三束	さんたば	*san-taba*
4 bundles	四束	よんたば	*yon-taba*
5 bundles	五束	ごたば	*go-taba*
6 bundles	六束	ろくたば	*roku-taba*
7 bundles	七束	ななたば	*nana-taba*
8 bundles	八束	はったば	*hat-taba*
9 bundles	九束	きゅうたば	*kyuu-taba*
10 bundles	十束	じゅったば / じったば	*jut-taba* / *jit-taba*

Irregularities or Special beyond Ten: none
Notes: none

度—たび—*tabi*

Japanese: たび
Romanized: *tabi*
Pattern: 和 I-T or 和 III-T
Used with, or Means: number of times, same as 度 (*do*)

1 time	一度	ひとたび	*hito-tabi*
2 times	二度 / 再び	ふたたび	*futa-tabi*
3 times	三度	さんたび / みたび	*san-tabi* / *mi-tabi*
4 times	四度	よんたび / よたび	*yon-tabi* / *yo-tabi*
5 times	五度	ごたび	*go-tabi*
6 times	六度	ろくたび	*roku-tabi*
7 times	七度	ななたび	*nana-tabi*
8 times	八度	はったび / はちたび	*hat-tabi* / *hachi-tabi*
9 times	九度	きゅうたび	*kyuu-tabi*
10 times	十度	じゅったび / じったび	*jut-tabi* / *jit-tabi*

Irregularities or Special beyond Ten: none
Notes: none

玉—たま—*tama*

Japanese: たま
Romanized: *tama*
Pattern: 和 III-T or 和 I-T
Used with, or Means: bullets, ammunition; balls of udon, soba (饂飩一塊 *udon hito-katamari*); heads of lettuce; balls, round objects; units of paulownia wood

1 bullet	一玉	ひとたま	*hito-tama*
2 bullets	二玉	ふたたま	*futa-tama*
3 bullets	三玉	みたま / さんたま	*mi-tama* / *san-tama*
4 bullets	四玉	よたま / よんたま	*yo-tama* / *yon-tama*
5 bullets	五玉	ごたま	*go-tama*
6 bullets	六玉	ろくたま	*roku-tama*
7 bullets	七玉	ななたま	*nana-tama*
8 bullets	八玉	はったま / はちたま	*hat-tama* / *hachi-tama*
9 bullets	九玉	きゅうたま	*kyuu-tama*
10 bullets	十玉	じゅったま / じったま	*jut-tama* / *jit-tama*

Irregularities or Special beyond Ten: none
Notes: none

珠―たま―*tama*

Japanese: たま
Romanized: *tama*
Pattern: 和 III-T or 和 I-T
Used with, or Means: jewels

1 jewel	一珠	ひとたま	*hito-tama*
2 jewels	二珠	ふたたま	*futa-tama*
3 jewels	三珠	みたま さんたま	*mi-tama* *san-tama*
4 jewels	四珠	よたま よんたま	*yo-tama* *yon-tama*
5 jewels	五珠	ごたま	*go-tama*
6 jewels	六珠	ろくたま	*roku-tama*
7 jewels	七珠	ななたま	*nana-tama*
8 jewels	八珠	はったま はちたま	*hat-tama* *hachi-tama*
9 jewels	九珠	きゅうたま	*kyuu-tama*
10 jewels	十珠	じゅったま じったま	*jut-tama* *jit-tama*

Irregularities or Special beyond Ten: none
Notes: none

樽—たる—*taru*

Japanese: たる
Romanized: *taru*
Pattern: 和 I-T
Used with, or Means: casks, barrels, kegs, see also 駄 (*da*)

1 cask	一樽	ひとたる	*hito-taru*
2 casks	二樽	ふたたる	*futa-taru*
3 casks	三樽	さんたる	*san-taru*
4 casks	四樽	よんたる	*yon-taru*
5 casks	五樽	ごたる	*go-taru*
6 casks	六樽	ろくたる	*roku-taru*
7 casks	七樽	ななたる	*nana-taru*
8 casks	八樽	はったる / はちたる	*hat-taru* / *hachi-taru*
9 casks	九樽	きゅうたる	*kyuu-taru*
10 casks	十樽	じゅったる / じったる	*jut-taru* / *jit-taru*

Irregularities or Special beyond Ten: none
Notes: none

垂れ—たれ—*tare*

Japanese: たれ
Romanized: *tare*
Pattern: 和 I-T or 和 III-T
Used with, or Means: bamboo blinds, rattan blinds, curtains; sign curtain hung over restaurant doors; mosquito nets

1 blind	一垂れ	ひとたれ	*hito-tare*
2 blinds	二垂れ	ふたたれ	*futa-tare*
3 blinds	三垂れ	さんたれ みたれ	*san-tare* *mi-tare*
4 blinds	四垂れ	よんたれ よたれ	*yon-tare* *yo-tare*
5 blinds	五垂れ	ごたれ	*go-tare*
6 blinds	六垂れ	ろくたれ	*roku-tare*
7 blinds	七垂れ	ななたれ	*nana-tare*
8 blinds	八垂れ	はったれ はちたれ	*hat-tare* *hachi-tare*
9 blinds	九垂れ	きゅうたれ	*kyuu-tare*
10 blinds	十垂れ	じゅったれ じったれ	*jut-tare* *jit-tare*

Irregularities or Special beyond Ten: none
Notes: none

反・段—たん—*tan*

Japanese: たん
Romanized: *tan*
Pattern: 漢 T
Used with, or Means: *tan*, a unit of area, 300 坪 (*tsubo*), 1,537,193.15390 in² (10,674.95246 ft²)/991.73554 m²; a length of cloth, see also 端 (*tan*); professional/technical jargon) gill nets, boat sails

1 *tan*	一反・段	いったん	*it-tan*
2 *tan*	二反・段	にたん	*ni-tan*
3 *tan*	三反・段	さんたん	*san-tan*
4 *tan*	四反・段	よんたん	*yon-tan*
5 *tan*	五反・段	ごたん	*go-tan*
6 *tan*	六反・段	ろくたん	*roku-tan*
7 *tan*	七反・段	ななたん	*nana-tan*
8 *tan*	八反・段	はったん	*hat-tan*
9 *tan*	九反・段	きゅうたん	*kyuu-tan*
10 *tan*	十反・段	じゅったん / じったん	*jut-tan* / *jit-tan*

Irregularities or Special beyond Ten: none
Notes: none

担 — たん — *tan*

Japanese: たん
Romanized: *tan*
Pattern: 漢 T

Used with, or Means: the number of bags, suitcases one person is carrying; the Japanese word for *picul*, a unit of weight about 60 kg, see also ピクル (*pikuru*)

1 bag	一担	いったん	*it-tan*
2 bags	二担	にたん	*ni-tan*
3 bags	三担	さんたん	*san-tan*
4 bags	四担	よんたん	*yon-tan*
5 bags	五担	ごたん	*go-tan*
6 bags	六担	ろくたん	*roku-tan*
7 bags	七担	ななたん	*nana-tan*
8 bags	八担	はったん	*hat-tan*
9 bags	九担	きゅうたん	*kyuu-tan*
10 bags	十担	じゅったん / じったん	*jut-tan* / *jit-tan*

Irregularities or Special beyond Ten: none
Notes: none

端 — たん — *tan*

Japanese: たん
Romanized: *tan*
Pattern: 漢 T
Used with, or Means: scrolls; a length of cloth: 31.069 ft/9.470 m to 37.283 ft/11.364 m, see also 反 (*tan*)

1 scroll	一端	いったん	*it-tan*
2 scrolls	二端	にたん	*ni-tan*
3 scrolls	三端	さんたん	*san-tan*
4 scrolls	四端	よんたん	*yon-tan*
5 scrolls	五端	ごたん	*go-tan*
6 scrolls	六端	ろくたん	*roku-tan*
7 scrolls	七端	ななたん	*nana-tan*
8 scrolls	八端	はったん	*hat-tan*
9 scrolls	九端	きゅうたん	*kyuu-tan*
10 scrolls	十端	じゅったん じったん	*jut-tan* *jit-tan*

Irregularities or Special beyond Ten: none
Notes: none

団 — だん — dan

Japanese: だん
Romanized: dan
Pattern: 漢 ∅
Used with, or Means: groups, gangs, clubs, associations, see also グループ (guruupu), see also 群 (gun)

1 group	一団	いちだん	ichi-dan
2 groups	二団	にだん	ni-dan
3 groups	三団	さんだん	san-dan
4 groups	四団	よんだん	yon-dan
5 groups	五団	ごだん	go-dan
6 groups	六団	ろくだん	roku-dan
7 groups	七団	ななだん	nana-dan
8 groups	八団	はちだん	hachi-dan
9 groups	九団	きゅうだん	kyuu-dan
10 groups	十団	じゅうだん	juu-dan

Irregularities or Special beyond Ten: none
Notes: none

段―だん―dan

Japanese: だん
Romanized: dan
Pattern: 漢 ∅
Used with, or Means: a rank awarded in the martial arts, *Go*, or *Shougi* (2nd *dan* in *Karate*, for example), see also 級 (*kyuu*); the number of steps on a staircase; the number of things piled up (二段ベッド *ni-dan beddo* a bunk bed)

level 1	一段	いちだん	*ichi-dan*
	初段	しょだん	*shodan*
level 2	二段	にだん	*ni-dan*
level 3	三段	さんだん	*san-dan*
level 4	四段	よんだん	*yon-dan*
level 5	五段	ごだん	*go-dan*
level 6	六段	ろくだん	*roku-dan*
level 7	七段	ななだん	*nana-dan*
level 8	八段	はちだん	*hachi-dan*
level 9	九段	きゅうだん	*kyuu-dan*
level 10	十段	じゅうだん	*juu-dan*

Irregularities or Special beyond Ten: none
Notes: When speaking about rank or level, rather than 一段, one says 初段.

弾—だん—dan

Japanese: だん
Romanized: *dan*
Pattern: 漢 Ø
Used with, or Means: steps, measures, stages; shots, bullets, see also 発 (*hatsu*)

1 bullet	一弾	いちだん	*ichi-dan*
2 bullets	二弾	にだん	*ni-dan*
3 bullets	三弾	さんだん	*san-dan*
4 bullets	四弾	よんだん	*yon-dan*
5 bullets	五弾	ごだん	*go-dan*
6 bullets	六弾	ろくだん	*roku-dan*
7 bullets	七弾	ななだん	*nana-dan*
8 bullets	八弾	はちだん	*hachi-dan*
9 bullets	九弾	きゅうだん	*kyuu-dan*
10 bullets	十弾	じゅうだん	*juu-dan*

Irregularities or Special beyond Ten: none
Notes: none

単位—たんい—*tan'i*

Japanese: たんい
Romanized: *tan'i*
Pattern: 漢 T
Used with, or Means: units; credits

1 unit	一単位	いったんい いちたんい	*it-tan'i* *ichi-tan'i*
2 units	二単位	にたんい	*ni-tan'i*
3 units	三単位	さんたんい	*san-tan'i*
4 units	四単位	よんたんい	*yon-tan'i*
5 units	五単位	ごたんい	*go-tan'i*
6 units	六単位	ろくたんい	*roku-tan'i*
7 units	七単位	ななたんい	*nana-tan'i*
8 units	八単位	はったんい はちたんい	*hat-tan'i* *hachi-tan'i*
9 units	九単位	きゅうたんい	*kyuu-tan'i*
10 units	十単位	じゅったんい じったんい	*jut-tan'i* *jit-tan'i*

Irregularities or Special beyond Ten: none
Notes: none

段階—だんかい—dankai

Japanese: だんかい
Romanized: *dankai*
Pattern: 漢 ∅
Used with, or Means: Nth grade, level, order

1st grade	一段階	いちだんかい	*ichi-dankai*
2nd grade	二段階	にだんかい	*ni-dankai*
3rd grade	三段階	さんだんかい	*san-dankai*
4th grade	四段階	よんだんかい	*yon-dankai*
5th grade	五段階	ごだんかい	*go-dankai*
6th grade	六段階	ろくだんかい	*roku-dankai*
7th grade	七段階	ななだんかい	*nana-dankai*
8th grade	八段階	はちだんかい	*hachi-dankai*
9th grade	九段階	きゅうだんかい	*kyuu-dankai*
10th grade	十段階	じゅうだんかい	*juu-dankai*

Irregularities or Special beyond Ten: none
Notes: none

反歩・段歩—たんぶ—*tambu*

Japanese: たんぶ
Romanized: *tambu*
Pattern: 漢 T
Used with, or Means: decares/dekares (S. I. symbol: daa/dka), 1/10th of a hectare, 1,000 m², see also 歩 (*bu*)

1 daa/dka	一反歩・段歩	いったんぶ	*it-tambu*
2 daa/dka	二反歩・段歩	にたんぶ	*ni-tambu*
3 daa/dka	三反歩・段歩	さんたんぶ	*san-tambu*
4 daa/dka	四反歩・段歩	よんたんぶ	*yon-tambu*
5 daa/dka	五反歩・段歩	ごたんぶ	*go-tambu*
6 daa/dka	六反歩・段歩	ろくたんぶ	*roku-tambu*
7 daa/dka	七反歩・段歩	ななたんぶ	*nana-tambu*
8 daa/dka	八反歩・段歩	はったんぶ	*hat-tambu*
9 daa/dka	九反歩・段歩	きゅうたんぶ	*kyuu-tambu*
10 daa/dka	十反歩・段歩	じゅったんぶ じったんぶ	*jut-tambu* *jit-tambu*

Irregularities or Special beyond Ten: none
Notes: none

段落—だんらく—*danraku*

Japanese: だんらく
Romanized: *danraku*
Pattern: 漢 ∅
Used with, or Means: paragraphs

1 paragraph	一段落	いちだんらく	*ichi-danraku*
2 paragraphs	二段落	にだんらく	*ni-danraku*
3 paragraphs	三段落	さんだんらく	*san-danraku*
4 paragraphs	四段落	よんだんらく	*yon-danraku*
5 paragraphs	五段落	ごだんらく	*go-danraku*
6 paragraphs	六段落	ろくだんらく	*roku-danraku*
7 paragraphs	七段落	ななだんらく	*nana-danraku*
8 paragraphs	八段落	はちだんらく	*hachi-danraku*
9 paragraphs	九段落	きゅうだんらく	*kyuu-danraku*
10 paragraphs	十段落	じゅうだんらく	*juu-danraku*

Irregularities or Special beyond Ten: none
Notes: none

ち・ぢ—Chi/Ji
地区—ちく—chiku

Japanese: ちく
Romanized: *chiku*
Pattern: 漢 T
Used with, or Means: districts, sections, sectors

1 district	一地区	いっちく	*it-chiku*
2 districts	二地区	にちく	*ni-chiku*
3 districts	三地区	さんちく	*san-chiku*
4 districts	四地区	よんちく	*yon-chiku*
5 districts	五地区	ごちく	*go-chiku*
6 districts	六地区	ろくちく	*roku-chiku*
7 districts	七地区	ななちく	*nana-chiku*
8 districts	八地区	はっちく	*hat-chiku*
9 districts	九地区	きゅうちく	*kyuu-chiku*
10 districts	十地区	じゅっちく / じっちく	*jut-chiku* / *jit-chiku*

Irregularities or Special beyond Ten: none
Notes: none

帙―ちつ―*chitsu*

Japanese: ちつ
Romanized: *chitsu*
Pattern: 漢 T
Used with, or Means: Japanese-style books (和書 *washo*/和文 *wabun*)

1 Japanese-style book	一帙	いっちつ	*it-chitsu*
2 Japanese-style books	二帙	にちつ	*ni-chitsu*
3 Japanese-style books	三帙	さんちつ	*san-chitsu*
4 Japanese-style books	四帙	よんちつ	*yon-chitsu*
5 Japanese-style books	五帙	ごちつ	*go-chitsu*
6 Japanese-style books	六帙	ろくちつ	*roku-chitsu*
7 Japanese-style books	七帙	ななちつ	*nana-chitsu*
8 Japanese-style books	八帙	はっちつ	*hat-chitsu*
9 Japanese-style books	九帙	きゅうちつ	*kyuu-chitsu*
10 Japanese-style books	十帙	じゅっちつ / じっちつ	*jut-chitsu* / *jit-chitsu*

Irregularities or Special beyond Ten: none
Notes: none

地点 — ちてん — *chiten*

Japanese: ちてん
Romanized: *chiten*
Pattern: 漢 T
Used with, or Means: sites, points on a map

1 site	一地点	<u>いっちてん</u>	<u>*it-chiten*</u>
2 sites	二地点	にちてん	*ni-chiten*
3 sites	三地点	さんちてん	*san-chiten*
4 sites	四地点	よんちてん	*yon-chiten*
5 sites	五地点	ごちてん	*go-chiten*
6 sites	六地点	ろくちてん	*roku-chiten*
7 sites	七地点	ななちてん	*nana-chiten*
8 sites	八地点	<u>はっちてん</u>	<u>*hat-chiten*</u>
9 sites	九地点	きゅうちてん	*kyuu-chiten*
10 sites	十地点	じゅっちてん じっちてん	<u>*jut-chiten*</u> <u>*jit-chiten*</u>

Irregularities or Special beyond Ten: none
Notes: none

着 — ちゃく — *chaku*

Japanese: ちゃく
Romanized: *chaku*
Pattern: 漢 T
Used with, or Means: suits, dresses, trousers, see also 枚 (*mai*), see also 領 (*ryou*); finishing position (in a race), see also 手 (*te*)

1 suit	一着	いっちゃく	*it-chaku*
2 suits	二着	にちゃく	*ni-chaku*
3 suits	三着	さんちゃく	*san-chaku*
4 suits	四着	よんちゃく	*yon-chaku*
5 suits	五着	ごちゃく	*go-chaku*
6 suits	六着	ろくちゃく	*roku-chaku*
7 suits	七着	ななちゃく	*nana-chaku*
8 suits	八着	はっちゃく	*hat-chaku*
9 suits	九着	きゅうちゃく	*kyuu-chaku*
10 suits	十着	じゅっちゃく / じっちゃく	*jut-chaku* / *jit-chaku*

Irregularities or Special beyond Ten: none
Notes: none

丁 — ちょう — *chou*

Japanese: ちょう
Romanized: *chou*
Pattern: 漢 丁
Used with, or Means: handled objects: carpenters' tools, scissors, pistols, saws, baskets, candles, forks; *chou*, a unit of length, 360 尺 (*shaku*), 4,294.91768 in (357.90981 ft)/109.09091 m; cakes of tofu; servings, sheets bound Japanese-style; town blocks, see also 町 (*chou*), see also 挺 (*chou*), see also 挺 (*tei*)

1 *chou*	一丁	いっちょう	*it-chou*
2 *chou*	二丁	にちょう	*ni-chou*
3 *chou*	三丁	さんちょう	*san-chou*
4 *chou*	四丁	よんちょう	*yon-chou*
5 *chou*	五丁	ごちょう	*go-chou*
6 *chou*	六丁	ろくちょう	*roku-chou*
7 *chou*	七丁	ななちょう	*nana-chou*
8 *chou*	八丁	はっちょう	*hat-chou*
9 *chou*	九丁	きゅうちょう	*kyuu-chou*
10 *chou*	十丁	じゅっちょう / じっちょう	*jut-chou* / *jit-chou*

Irregularities or Special beyond Ten: none
Notes: none

町 — ちょう — chou

Japanese: ちょう
Romanized: chou
Pattern: 漢 T

Used with, or Means: *chou*, a unit of length, 360 尺 (*shaku*), 4,294.91768 in (357.90981 ft)/109.09091 m; *chou*, a unit of area, 3,000 坪 (*tsubo*), 15,371,931.53895 in² (106,749.52458 ft²)/9,917.35537 m²; town blocks, see also 丁 (*chou*), see also 挺 (*chou*), see also 挺 (*tei*)

1 *chou*	一町	いっちょう	*it-chou*
2 *chou*	二町	にちょう	*ni-chou*
3 *chou*	三町	さんちょう	*san-chou*
4 *chou*	四町	よんちょう	*yon-chou*
5 *chou*	五町	ごちょう	*go-chou*
6 *chou*	六町	ろくちょう	*roku-chou*
7 *chou*	七町	ななちょう	*nana-chou*
8 *chou*	八町	はっちょう	*hat-chou*
9 *chou*	九町	きゅうちょう	*kyuu-chou*
10 *chou*	十町	じゅっちょう / じっちょう	*jut-chou* / *jit-chou*

Irregularities or Special beyond Ten: none
Notes: none

丁目・町目—ちょうめ—*chou-me*

Japanese: ちょうめ
Romanized: *chou-me*
Pattern: 漢 T
Used with, or Means: N[th] block

1st block	一丁目・町目	<u>いっちょうめ</u>	<u>*it-chou-me*</u>
2nd block	二丁目・町目	にちょうめ	*ni-chou-me*
3rd block	三丁目・町目	さんちょうめ	*san-chou-me*
4th block	四丁目・町目	よんちょうめ	*yon-chou-me*
5th block	五丁目・町目	ごちょうめ	*go-chou-me*
6th block	六丁目・町目	ろくちょうめ	*roku-chou-me*
7th block	七丁目・町目	ななちょうめ	*nana-chou-me*
8th block	八丁目・町目	<u>はっちょうめ</u>	<u>*hat-chou-me*</u>
9th block	九丁目・町目	きゅうちょうめ	*kyuu-chou-me*
10th block	十丁目・町目	<u>じゅっちょうめ</u> <u>じっちょうめ</u>	<u>*jut-chou-me*</u> <u>*jit-chou-me*</u>

Irregularities or Special beyond Ten: none
Notes: none

兆—ちょう—*chou*

Japanese: ちょう
Romanized: *chou*
Pattern: 漢 ∅
Used with, or Means: 10,000 億 (*oku*), 1 trillion, 10^{12}

10^{12}	一兆	いちちょう	*ichi-chou*
2×10^{12}	二兆	にちょう	*ni-chou*
3×10^{12}	三兆	さんちょう	*san-chou*
4×10^{12}	四兆	よんちょう	*yon-chou*
5×10^{12}	五兆	ごちょう	*go-chou*
6×10^{12}	六兆	ろくちょう	*roku-chou*
7×10^{12}	七兆	ななちょう	*nana-chou*
8×10^{12}	八兆	はっちょう	*hat-chou*
9×10^{12}	九兆	きゅうちょう	*kyuu-chou*
10^{13}	十兆	じゅうちょう	*juu-chou*

Irregularities or Special beyond Ten:

10^{14}	百兆	ひゃくちょう	*hyaku-chou*
10^{15}	千兆	せんちょう	*sen-chou*

Notes: 10^{12} is 1 000 000 000 000

挺・丁—ちょう—*chou*

Japanese: ちょう
Romanized: *chou*
Pattern: 漢 T
Used with, or Means: long objects: guns (銃 *juu*), oars, guitars, palanquins, candles, cutlery, axes (斧 *ono*), sticks of ink, rickshaws, violins

1 long object	一挺・丁	いっちょう	*it-chou*
2 long objects	二挺・丁	にちょう	*ni-chou*
3 long objects	三挺・丁	さんちょう	*san-chou*
4 long objects	四挺・丁	よんちょう	*yon-chou*
5 long objects	五挺・丁	ごちょう	*go-chou*
6 long objects	六挺・丁	ろくちょう	*roku-chou*
7 long objects	七挺・丁	ななちょう	*nana-chou*
8 long objects	八挺・丁	はっちょう	*hat-chou*
9 long objects	九挺・丁	きゅうちょう	*kyuu-chou*
10 long objects	十挺・丁	じゅっちょう じっちょう	*jut-chou* *jit-chou*

Irregularities or Special beyond Ten: none
Notes: none

張—ちょう—chou

Japanese: ちょう
Romanized: *chou*
Pattern: 漢 T
Used with, or Means: bows, stringed instruments; curtains, screens, nets, mosquito nets, see also 張り (*hari*)

1 stringed instrument	一張	いっちょう	<u>*it-chou*</u>
2 stringed instruments	二張	にちょう	*ni-chou*
3 stringed instruments	三張	さんちょう	*san-chou*
4 stringed instruments	四張	よんちょう	*yon-chou*
5 stringed instruments	五張	ごちょう	*go-chou*
6 stringed instruments	六張	ろくちょう	*roku-chou*
7 stringed instruments	七張	ななちょう	*nana-chou*
8 stringed instruments	八張	はっちょう	<u>*hat-chou*</u>
9 stringed instruments	九張	きゅうちょう	*kyuu-chou*
10 stringed instruments	十張	<u>じゅっちょう</u> <u>じっちょう</u>	<u>*jut-chou*</u> <u>*jit-chou*</u>

Irregularities or Special beyond Ten: none
Notes: none

貼—ちょう—chou

Japanese: ちょう
Romanized: *chou*
Pattern: 漢 T
Used with, or Means: packets of powdered medicine (散剤 *sanzai*), see also 服 (*fuku*), see also 包 (*hou*)

1 packet	一貼	<u>いっちょう</u>	<u>*it-chou*</u>
2 packets	二貼	にちょう	*ni-chou*
3 packets	三貼	さんちょう	*san-chou*
4 packets	四貼	よんちょう	*yon-chou*
5 packets	五貼	ごちょう	*go-chou*
6 packets	六貼	ろくちょう	*roku-chou*
7 packets	七貼	ななちょう	*nana-chou*
8 packets	八貼	<u>はっちょう</u>	<u>*hat-chou*</u>
9 packets	九貼	きゅうちょう	*kyuu-chou*
10 packets	十貼	<u>じゅっちょう</u> <u>じっちょう</u>	<u>*jut-chou*</u> <u>*jit-chou*</u>

Irregularities or Special beyond Ten: none
Notes: none

提 — ちょう — chou

Japanese: ちょう
Romanized: *chou*
Pattern: 漢 T
Used with, or Means: liquor bottles, *sake* bottles (徳利 *tokkuri*, 銚子 *choushi*)

1 liquor bottle	一提	いっちょう	*it-chou*
2 liquor bottles	二提	にちょう	*ni-chou*
3 liquor bottles	三提	さんちょう	*san-chou*
4 liquor bottles	四提	よんちょう	*yon-chou*
5 liquor bottles	五提	ごちょう	*go-chou*
6 liquor bottles	六提	ろくちょう	*roku-chou*
7 liquor bottles	七提	ななちょう	*nana-chou*
8 liquor bottles	八提	はっちょう	*hat-chou*
9 liquor bottles	九提	きゅうちょう	*kyuu-chou*
10 liquor bottles	十提	じゅっちょう / じっちょう	*jut-chou* / *jit-chou*

Irregularities or Special beyond Ten: none
Notes: none

調 — ちょう — *chou*

Japanese: ちょう
Romanized: *chou*
Pattern: 漢 T
Used with, or Means: solos (guitar solo, drum solo, for example), musical parts

1 solo	一調	いっちょう	*it-chou*
2 solos	二調	にちょう	*ni-chou*
3 solos	三調	さんちょう	*san-chou*
4 solos	四調	よんちょう	*yon-chou*
5 solos	五調	ごちょう	*go-chou*
6 solos	六調	ろくちょう	*roku-chou*
7 solos	七調	ななちょう	*nana-chou*
8 solos	八調	はっちょう	*hat-chou*
9 solos	九調	きゅうちょう	*kyuu-chou*
10 solos	十調	じゅっちょう じっちょう	*jut-chou* *jit-chou*

Irregularities or Special beyond Ten: none
Notes: none

町歩—ちょうぶ—*choubu*

Japanese: ちょうぶ
Romanized: *choubu*
Pattern: 漢 T
Used with, or Means: hectares (S. I. symbol: ha), 10,000 m², see also 歩 (*bu*)

1 ha	一町歩	いっちょうぶ	*it-choubu*
2 ha	二町歩	にちょうぶ	*ni-choubu*
3 ha	三町歩	さんちょうぶ	*san-choubu*
4 ha	四町歩	よんちょうぶ	*yon-choubu*
5 ha	五町歩	ごちょうぶ	*go-choubu*
6 ha	六町歩	ろくちょうぶ	*roku-choubu*
7 ha	七町歩	ななちょうぶ	*nana-choubu*
8 ha	八町歩	はっちょうぶ	*hat-choubu*
9 ha	九町歩	きゅうちょうぶ	*kyuu-choubu*
10 ha	十町歩	じゅっちょうぶ じっちょうぶ	*jut-choubu* *jit-choubu*

Irregularities or Special beyond Ten: none
Notes: none

つ・づ—Tsu/Zu
つ—tsu

Japanese: つ
Romanized: *tsu*
Pattern: 漢 T
Used with, or Means: things; same as 個 (*ko*). First ten only (see Notes), see also 個 (*ko*), see also 歳 (*sai*)

1 thing	一つ	ひとつ	*hito-tsu*
2 things	二つ	ふたつ	*futa-tsu*
3 things	三つ	みっつ	*mit-tsu*
4 things	四つ	よっつ	*yot-tsu*
5 things	五つ	いつつ	*itsu-tsu*
6 things	六つ	むっつ	*mut-tsu*
7 things	七つ	ななつ	*nana-tsu*
8 things	八つ	やっつ	*yat-tsu*
9 things	九つ	ここのつ	*kokono-tsu*
10 things	十	とお	*too*

Irregularities or Special beyond Ten: none
Notes: This is only used for the first ten things, and can pretty much replace any non-living counter. Typically used in place of 個, for example: 二つの消しゴム (*futatsu no keshigomu* two erasers) versus 消しゴム二個 (*keshigomu niko* two erasers). Notice also that all four of the following sentences are perfectly okay and mean exactly the same thing:
1. 私は消しゴムを二つ持っています。 *Watashi wa keshigomu o futatsu motte imasu.* I have two erasers.
2. 私は二つの消しゴムを持っています。 *Watashi wa futatsu no keshigomu o motte imasu.* I have two erasers.
3. 私は消しゴムを二個持っています。 *Watashi wa keshigomu o niko motte imasu.* I have two erasers.
4. 私は二個の消しゴムを持っています。 *Watashi wa niko no keshigomu o motte imasu.* I have two erasers.

対 — つい — *tsui*

Japanese: つい
Romanized: *tsui*
Pattern: 漢 T
Used with, or Means: paired things; couples, married couples, see also 組 (*kumi*), see also 番 (*tsugai*); folding fans; *ikebana* (生け花)

1 pair	一対	いっつい	*it-tsui*
2 pairs	二対	につい	*ni-tsui*
3 pairs	三対	さんつい	*san-tsui*
4 pairs	四対	よんつい	*yon-tsui*
5 pairs	五対	ごつい	*go-tsui*
6 pairs	六対	ろくつい	*roku-tsui*
7 pairs	七対	ななつい	*nana-tsui*
8 pairs	八対	はっつい	*hat-tsui*
9 pairs	九対	きゅうつい	*kyuu-tsui*
10 pairs	十対	じゅっつい / じっつい	*jut-tsui* / *jit-tsui*

Irregularities or Special beyond Ten: none
Notes: none

通 — つう — *tsuu*

Japanese: つう
Romanized: *tsuu*
Pattern: 漢 T
Used with, or Means: communications: documents, messages, post cards (see also 葉 *you*), e-mails (see also 件 *ken*)

1 message	一通	いっつう	*it-tsuu*
2 messages	二通	につう	*ni-tsuu*
3 messages	三通	さんつう	*san-tsuu*
4 messages	四通	よんつう	*yon-tsuu*
5 messages	五通	ごつう	*go-tsuu*
6 messages	六通	ろくつう	*roku-tsuu*
7 messages	七通	ななつう	*nana-tsuu*
8 messages	八通	はっつう	*hat-tsuu*
9 messages	九通	きゅうつう	*kyuu-tsuu*
10 messages	十通	じゅっつう / じっつう	*jut-tsuu* / *jit-tsuu*

Irregularities or Special beyond Ten: none
Notes: none

通話——つうわ——*tsuuwa*

Japanese: つうわ
Romanized: *tsuuwa*
Pattern: 漢 T
Used with, or Means: telephone calls

1 call	一通話	いっつうわ	*it-tsuuwa*
2 calls	二通話	につうわ	*ni-tsuuwa*
3 calls	三通話	さんつうわ	*san-tsuuwa*
4 calls	四通話	よんつうわ	*yon-tsuuwa*
5 calls	五通話	ごつうわ	*go-tsuuwa*
6 calls	六通話	ろくつうわ	*roku-tsuuwa*
7 calls	七通話	ななつうわ	*nana-tsuuwa*
8 calls	八通話	はっつうわ	*hat-tsuuwa*
9 calls	九通話	きゅうつうわ	*kyuu-tsuuwa*
10 calls	十通話	じゅっつうわ / じっつうわ	*jut-tsuuwa* / *jit-tsuuwa*

Irregularities or Special beyond Ten: none
Notes: none

束 — つか — *tsuka*

Japanese: つか
Romanized: *tsuka*
Pattern: 和 II-T or 和 III-T (see Notes)
Used with, or Means: a unit of arrow length; former unit of weight of rice, see 束 (*soku*)

1 arrow length	一束	ひとつか	*hito-tsuka*
2 arrow lengths	二束	ふたつか	*futa-tsuka*
3 arrow lengths	三束	みつか	*mi-tsuka*
4 arrow lengths	四束	よんつか / よつか	*yon-tsuka* / *yo-tsuka*
5 arrow lengths	五束	ごつか	*go-tsuka*
6 arrow lengths	六束	ろくつか	*roku-tsuka*
7 arrow lengths	七束	ななつか	*nana-tsuka*
8 arrow lengths	八束	やつか / はちつか	*ya-tsuka* / *hachi-tsuka*
9 arrow lengths	九束	きゅうつか	*kyuu-tsuka*
10 arrow lengths	十束	とつか / じゅうつか	*to-tsuka* / *juu-tsuka*

Irregularities or Special beyond Ten: none
Notes: Notice that 8 and 10 are also different.

番——つがい——*tsugai*

Japanese: つがい
Romanized: *tsugai*
Pattern: 和 I-T
Used with, or Means: pairs of animals; couples, see also 組 (*kumi*), see also 対 (*tsui*)

1 pair	一番	ひとつがい	*hito-tsugai*
2 pairs	二番	ふたつがい	*futa-tsugai*
3 pairs	三番	さんつがい	*san-tsugai*
4 pairs	四番	よんつがい	*yon-tsugai*
5 pairs	五番	ごつがい	*go-tsugai*
6 pairs	六番	ろくつがい	*roku-tsugai*
7 pairs	七番	ななつがい	*nana-tsugai*
8 pairs	八番	はっつがい はちつがい	*hat-tsugai* *hachi-tsugai*
9 pairs	九番	きゅうつがい	*kyuu-tsugai*
10 pairs	十番	じゅっつがい じっつがい	*jut-tsugai* *jit-tsugai*

Irregularities or Special beyond Ten: none
Notes: none

月 — つき — *tsuki*

Japanese: つき
Romanized: *tsuki*
Pattern: 和 III-T
Used with, or Means: months, see also 月 (*getsu*), see also ヶ月 (*ka-getsu*)

1 month	一月	ひとつき	*hito-tsuki*
2 months	二月	ふたつき	*futa-tsuki*
3 months	三月	みつき	*mi-tsuki*
4 months	四月	よつき	*yo-tsuki*
5 months	五月	ごつき	*go-tsuki*
6 months	六月	ろくつき	*roku-tsuki*
7 months	七月	ななつき	*nana-tsuki*
8 months	八月	はっつき	*hat-tsuki*
9 months	九月	きゅうつき	*kyuu-tsuki*
10 months	十月	じゅっつき / じっつき	*jut-tsuki* / *jit-tsuki*

Irregularities or Special beyond Ten: none
Notes: none

次—つぎ—*tsugi*

Japanese: つぎ
Romanized: *tsugi*
Pattern: 漢 T
Used with, or Means: post stations of the Edo period highways, see Notes, see also 宿 (*shuku*)

1 station	一次	いっつぎ	*it-tsugi*
2 stations	二次	につぎ	*ni-tsugi*
3 stations	三次	さんつぎ	*san-tsugi*
4 stations	四次	よんつぎ	*yon-tsugi*
5 stations	五次	ごつぎ	*go-tsugi*
6 stations	六次	ろくつぎ	*roku-tsugi*
7 stations	七次	ななつぎ	*nana-tsugi*
8 stations	八次	はっつぎ	*hat-tsugi*
9 stations	九次	きゅうつぎ	*kyuu-tsugi*
10 stations	十次	じゅっつぎ / じっつぎ	*jut-tsugi* / *jit-tsugi*

Irregularities or Special beyond Ten: none

Notes: Ieyasu Tokugawa, after finally unifying Japan, ordered the construction of five main travel/trade routes, or highways connecting the rest of Japan to his capital, Edo (what is now Tokyo). Over time, so-called *post towns*, or *post stations*, grew around what were essentially the rest stops along these highway. The *Toukai* highway (東海道 *Toukaidou*) was one such route, which connected Edo to Kyoto.

In 1832, an *Ukiyo-e* artist, Utagawa Hiroshige (歌川広重, 1797 – October 12, 1858)[12] traveled along this highway. He then made a series of fifty-five woodblock prints for each of its fifty-three stations as well as the

---

[12] Utagawa Hiroshige was also known as Andō Hiroshige (安藤広重) as well as by his artist name of Ichiyūsai Hiroshige (一幽斎廣重).

beginning (*Leaving Edo: Nihombashi*) and end (*Arriving in Kyoto: Third-Avenue Bridge*).

Due to the success from the *Toukai* Highway series, he made another series depicting the sixty-nine stations of the *Kiso* Highway (*Kiso Kaidou*).

Figure 3: Utagawa Hiroshige—*Leaving Edo: Nihombashi*

筒—つつ—*tsutsu*

Japanese: つつ
Romanized: *tsutsu*
Pattern: 和 I-T
Used with, or Means: cylinders, cylindrical objects, see also 気筒 for engine cylinders

1 cylinder	一筒	ひとつつ	*hito-tsutsu*
2 cylinders	二筒	ふたつつ	*futa-tsutsu*
3 cylinders	三筒	さんつつ	*san-tsutsu*
4 cylinders	四筒	よんつつ	*yon-tsutsu*
5 cylinders	五筒	ごつつ	*go-tsutsu*
6 cylinders	六筒	ろくつつ	*roku-tsutsu*
7 cylinders	七筒	ななつつ	*nana-tsutsu*
8 cylinders	八筒	はっつつ	*hat-tsutsu*
9 cylinders	九筒	きゅうつつ	*kyuu-tsutsu*
10 cylinders	十筒	じゅっつつ じっつつ じゅうつつ	*jut-tsutsu* *jit-tsutsu* *juu-tsutsu*

Irregularities or Special beyond Ten: none
Notes: none

続き—つづき—*tsuzuki*

Japanese: つづき
Romanized: *tsuzuki*
Pattern: 和 I-T
Used with, or Means: series, parts of a series

1 series	一続き	ひとつづき	*hito-tsuzuki*
2 series	二続き	ふたつづき	*futa-tsuzuki*
3 series	三続き	さんつづき	*san-tsuzuki*
4 series	四続き	よんつづき	*yon-tsuzuki*
5 series	五続き	ごつづき	*go-tsuzuki*
6 series	六続き	ろくつづき	*roku-tsuzuki*
7 series	七続き	ななつづき	*nana-tsuzuki*
8 series	八続き	はっつづき / はちつづき	*hat-tsuzuki* / *hachi-tsuzuki*
9 series	九続き	きゅうつづき	*kyuu-tsuzuki*
10 series	十続き	じゅっつづき / じっつづき / じゅうつづき	*jut-tsuzuki* / *jit-tsuzuki* / *juu-tsuzuki*

Irregularities or Special beyond Ten: none
Notes: none

包み—つつみ—*tsutsumi*

Japanese: つつみ
Romanized: *tsutsumi*
Pattern: 和 III-T
Used with, or Means: doses of powdered medicine, see also 包 (*hou*)

1 dose	一包み	ひとつつみ	*hito-tsutsumi*
2 doses	二包み	ふたつつみ	*futa-tsutsumi*
3 doses	三包み	みつつみ	*mi-tsutsumi*
4 doses	四包み	よつつみ	*yo-tsutsumi*
5 doses	五包み	ごつつみ	*go-tsutsumi*
6 doses	六包み	ろくつつみ	*roku-tsutsumi*
7 doses	七包み	ななつつみ	*nana-tsutsumi*
8 doses	八包み	はっつつみ	*hat-tsutsumi*
		はちつつみ	*hachi-tsutsumi*
9 doses	九包み	きゅうつつみ	*kyuu-tsutsumi*
10 doses	十包み	じゅっつつみ	*jut-tsutsumi*
		じっつつみ	*jit-tsutsumi*
		じゅうつつみ	*juu-tsutsumi*

Irregularities or Special beyond Ten: none
Notes: none

綴り —つづり— *tsuzuri*

Japanese: つづり
Romanized: *tsuzuri*
Pattern: 和 I-T
Used with, or Means: papers

1 paper	一綴り	ひとつづり	*hito-tsuzuri*
2 papers	二綴り	ふたつづり	*futa-tsuzuri*
3 papers	三綴り	さんつづり	*san-tsuzuri*
4 papers	四綴り	よんつづり	*yon-tsuzuri*
5 papers	五綴り	ごつづり	*go-tsuzuri*
6 papers	六綴り	ろくつづり	*roku-tsuzuri*
7 papers	七綴り	ななつづり	*nana-tsuzuri*
8 papers	八綴り	はっつづり はちつづり	*hat-tsuzuri* *hachi-tsuzuri*
9 papers	九綴り	きゅうつづり	*kyuu-tsuzuri*
10 papers	十綴り	じゅっつづり じっつづり じゅうつづり	*jut-tsuzuri* *jit-tsuzuri* *juu-tsuzuri*

Irregularities or Special beyond Ten: none
Notes: none

粒 — つぶ — *tsubu*

Japanese: つぶ
Romanized: *tsubu*
Pattern: 和 III-T or 和 II-T
Used with, or Means: tiny particles, grains; drops, see also 滴 (*teki*); pills, see also 顆 (*ka*), see also 個 (*ko*), see also 錠 (*jou*)

1 particle	一粒	ひとつぶ	*hito-tsubu*
2 particles	二粒	ふたつぶ	*futa-tsubu*
3 particles	三粒	みつぶ	*mi-tsubu*
4 particles	四粒	よつぶ / よんつぶ	*yo-tsubu* / *yon-tsubu*
5 particles	五粒	ごつぶ	*go-tsubu*
6 particles	六粒	ろくつぶ	*roku-tsubu*
7 particles	七粒	ななつぶ	*nana-tsubu*
8 particles	八粒	はっつぶ / はちつぶ	*hat-tsubu* / *hachi-tsubu*
9 particles	九粒	きゅうつぶ	*kyuu-tsubu*
10 particles	十粒	じゅっつぶ / じっつぶ	*jut-tsubu* / *jit-tsubu*

Irregularities or Special beyond Ten: none
Notes: none

坪—つぼ—*tsubo*

Japanese: つぼ
Romanized: *tsubo*
Pattern: 和 III-T or 和 I-T
Used with, or Means: *tsubo*, a unit of area, 1 square 間 (*ken*), 5,123.97718 in² (35.58317 ft²)/3.30579 m², see also 歩 (*bu*); a unit of area for measuring graveyards; a unit of area for expensive fabrics, metal planks, tattoos, leather, photographs, printing plates; a unit of volume of earth, sand used in public works, also known as a 立坪 (*ryuutsubo*)

1 *tsubo*	一坪	ひとつぼ	*hito-tsubo*
2 *tsubo*	二坪	ふたつぼ	*futa-tsubo*
3 *tsubo*	三坪	みつぼ さんつぼ	*mi-tsubo* *san-tsubo*
4 *tsubo*	四坪	よつぼ よんつぼ	*yo-tsubo* *yon-tsubo*
5 *tsubo*	五坪	ごつぼ	*go-tsubo*
6 *tsubo*	六坪	ろくつぼ	*roku-tsubo*
7 *tsubo*	七坪	ななつぼ	*nana-tsubo*
8 *tsubo*	八坪	はっつぼ はちつぼ	*hat-tsubo* *hachi-tsubo*
9 *tsubo*	九坪	きゅうつぼ	*kyuu-tsubo*
10 *tsubo*	十坪	じゅっつぼ じっつぼ	*jut-tsubo* *jit-tsubo*

Irregularities or Special beyond Ten: none
Notes: none

壺—つぼ—*tsubo*

Japanese: つぼ
Romanized: *tsubo*
Pattern: 和 II-T, 和 I-T, or 和 III-T
Used with, or Means: pots, jars

1 jar	一壺	ひとつぼ	*hito-tsubo*
2 jars	二壺	ふたつぼ	*futa-tsubo*
3 jars	三壺	みつぼ / さんつぼ	*mi-tsubo* / *san-tsubo*
4 jars	四壺	よんつぼ / よつぼ	*yon-tsubo* / *yo-tsubo*
5 jars	五壺	ごつぼ	*go-tsubo*
6 jars	六壺	ろくつぼ	*roku-tsubo*
7 jars	七壺	ななつぼ	*nana-tsubo*
8 jars	八壺	はっつぼ	*hat-tsubo*
9 jars	九壺	きゅうつぼ	*kyuu-tsubo*
10 jars	十壺	じゅっつぼ / じっつぼ	*jut-tsubo* / *jit-tsubo*

Irregularities or Special beyond Ten: none
Notes: none

摘み・撮み—つまみ—*tsumami*

Japanese: つまみ
Romanized: *tsumami*
Pattern: 和 III-T or 和 I-T
Used with, or Means: pinches, dashes of salt, spices, bonito flakes

1 dash	一摘み・撮み	ひとつまみ	*hito-tsumami*
2 dashes	二摘み・撮み	ふたつまみ	*futa-tsumami*
3 dashes	三摘み・撮み	みつまみ さんつまみ	*mi-tsumami* *san-tsumami*
4 dashes	四摘み・撮み	よつまみ よんつまみ	*yo-tsumami* *yon-tsumami*
5 dashes	五摘み・撮み	ごつまみ	*go-tsumami*
6 dashes	六摘み・撮み	ろくつまみ	*roku-tsumami*
7 dashes	七摘み・撮み	ななつまみ	*nana-tsumami*
8 dashes	八摘み・撮み	はっつまみ	*hat-tsumami*
9 dashes	九摘み・撮み	きゅうつまみ	*kyuu-tsumami*
10 dashes	十摘み・撮み	じゅっつまみ じっつまみ	*jut-tsumami* *jit-tsumami*

Irregularities or Special beyond Ten: none
Notes: none

て・で—Te/De
dK—ディーケー—diikee

Japanese: ディーケー
Romanized: *diikee*
Pattern: 漢 T
Used with, or Means: deciKelvins (S. I. symbol: dK)

1 dK	1 ディーケー	いちでぃいけい	*ichi-diikee*
2 dK	2 ディーケー	にでぃいけい	*ni-diikee*
3 dK	3 ディーケー	さんでぃいけい	*san-diikee*
4 dK	4 ディーケー	よんでぃいけい	*yon-diikee*
5 dK	5 ディーケー	ごでぃいけい	*go-diikee*
6 dK	6 ディーケー	ろくでぃいけい	*roku-diikee*
7 dK	7 ディーケー	ななでぃいけい	*nana-diikee*
8 dK	8 ディーケー	はちでぃいけい	*hachi-diikee*
9 dK	9 ディーケー	きゅうでぃいけい	*kyuu-diikee*
10 dK	10 ディーケー	じゅうでぃいけい	*juu-diikee*

Irregularities or Special beyond Ten: none
Notes: Typically used in meteorology.

手 — て — te

Japanese: て
Romanized: te
Pattern: 和 I-T or 漢 T
Used with, or Means: a martial arts move; a Chess, Shougi, Go move; a dance move; a task; a pair of arrows (see Notes)

1 move	一手	ひとて / いって	<u>hito-te</u> / <u>it-te</u>
2 moves	二手	ふたて / にて	<u>futa-te</u> / <u>ni-te</u>
3 moves	三手	さんて	san-te
4 moves	四手	よんて	yon-te
5 moves	五手	ごて	go-te
6 moves	六手	ろくて	<u>roku</u>-te
7 moves	七手	ななて	nana-te
8 moves	八手	はって / はちて	<u>hat-te</u> / <u>hachi-te</u>
9 moves	九手	きゅうて	kyuu-te
10 moves	十手	じゅって / じって	<u>jut-te</u> / <u>jit-te</u>

Irregularities or Special beyond Ten: none

Notes: For arrows, this specifically refers to a practice in 弓術・弓道 (Kyuujutsu/Kyuudou Japanese Archery) of holding a pair of arrows and firing them in rapid succession. The first arrow is called the 甲矢・兄矢 (*haya*) and the second arrow is called the 乙矢・弟矢 (*otoya*).

邸 ― てい ― *tei*

Japanese: てい
Romanized: *tei*
Patteirn: 漢 T
Used with, or Means: splendid mansions, see also 戸 (*ko*), see also 軒 (*ken*)

1 mansion	一邸	いってい	*it-tei*
2 mansions	二邸	にてい	*ni-tei*
3 mansions	三邸	さんてい	*san-tei*
4 mansions	四邸	よんてい	*yon-tei*
5 mansions	五邸	ごてい	*go-tei*
6 mansions	六邸	ろくてい	*roku-tei*
7 mansions	七邸	ななてい	*nana-tei*
8 mansions	八邸	はってい / はちてい	*hat-tei* / *hachi-tei*
9 mansions	九邸	きゅうてい	*kyuu-tei*
10 mansions	十邸	じゅってい / じってい	*jut-tei* / *jit-tei*

Irregularities or Special beyond Ten: none
Notes: none

挺 — てい — *tei*

Japanese: てい
Romanized: *tei*
Patteirn: 漢 T
Used with, or Means: long objects: guns (銃 *juu*), oars, guitars, palanquins, candles, cutlery, axes (斧 *ono*), sticks of ink, rickshaws, violins; same as 挺・丁

1 long object	一挺	いってい	*it-tei*
2 long objects	二挺	にてい	*ni-tei*
3 long objects	三挺	さんてい	*san-tei*
4 long objects	四挺	よんてい	*yon-tei*
5 long objects	五挺	ごてい	*go-tei*
6 long objects	六挺	ろくてい	*roku-tei*
7 long objects	七挺	なpäてい	*nana-tei*
8 long objects	八挺	はってい / はちてい	*hat-tei* / *hachi-tei*
9 long objects	九挺	きゅうてい	*kyuu-tei*
10 long objects	十挺	じゅってい / じってい	*jut-tei* / *jit-tei*

Irregularities or Special beyond Ten: none
Notes: none

幀——てい——tei

Japanese: てい
Romanized: tei
Patteirn: 漢 T
Used with, or Means: hanging scrolls (掛け軸 *kakejiku*)

1 hanging scroll	一幀	いってい	it-tei
2 hanging scrolls	二幀	にてい	ni-tei
3 hanging scrolls	三幀	さんてい	san-tei
4 hanging scrolls	四幀	よんてい	yon-tei
5 hanging scrolls	五幀	ごてい	go-tei
6 hanging scrolls	六幀	ろくてい	roku-tei
7 hanging scrolls	七幀	ななてい	nana-tei
8 hanging scrolls	八幀	はってい / はちてい	hat-tei / hachi-tei
9 hanging scrolls	九幀	きゅうてい	kyuu-tei
10 hanging scrolls	十幀	じゅってい / じってい	jut-tei / jit-tei

Irregularities or Special beyond Ten: none
Notes: none

艇 —— てい —— *tei*

Japanese: てい
Romanized: *tei*
Patteirn: 漢 T
Used with, or Means: rowboats used in rowing competitions, yachts, see also 隻 (*seki*), see also 艘 (*sou*)

1 yacht	一艇	いってい	*it-tei*
2 yachts	二艇	にてい	*ni-tei*
3 yachts	三艇	さんてい	*san-tei*
4 yachts	四艇	よんてい	*yon-tei*
5 yachts	五艇	ごてい	*go-tei*
6 yachts	六艇	ろくてい	*roku-tei*
7 yachts	七艇	ななてい	*nana-tei*
8 yachts	八艇	はってい / はちてい	*hat-tei* / *hachi-tei*
9 yachts	九艇	きゅうてい	*kyuu-tei*
10 yachts	十艇	じゅってい / じってい	*jut-tei* / *jit-tei*

Irregularities or Special beyond Ten: none
Notes: none

蹄 —— てい —— *tei*

Japanese: てい
Romanized: *tei*
Patteirn: 漢 T
Used with, or Means: hooves, cows, horses, deer

1 hoof	一蹄	いってい	*it-tei*
2 hooves	二蹄	にてい	*ni-tei*
3 hooves	三蹄	さんてい	*san-tei*
4 hooves	四蹄	よんてい	*yon-tei*
5 hooves	五蹄	ごてい	*go-tei*
6 hooves	六蹄	ろくてい	*roku-tei*
7 hooves	七蹄	ななてい	*nana-tei*
8 hooves	八蹄	はってい / はちてい	*hat-tei* / *hachi-tei*
9 hooves	九蹄	きゅうてい	*kyuu-tei*
10 hooves	十蹄	じゅってい / じってい	*jut-tei* / *jit-tei*

Irregularities or Special beyond Ten: none
Notes: none

訂—てい—*tei*

Japanese: てい
Romanized: *tei*
Patteirn: 漢 T
Used with, or Means: revisions, corrections

1 revision	一訂	いってい	*it-tei*
2 revisions	二訂	にてい	*ni-tei*
3 revisions	三訂	さんてい	*san-tei*
4 revisions	四訂	よんてい	*yon-tei*
5 revisions	五訂	ごてい	*go-tei*
6 revisions	六訂	ろくてい	*roku-tei*
7 revisions	七訂	ななてい	*nana-tei*
8 revisions	八訂	はってい / はちてい	*hat-tei* / *hachi-tei*
9 revisions	九訂	きゅうてい	*kyuu-tei*
10 revisions	十訂	じゅってい / じってい	*jut-tei* / *jit-tei*

Irregularities or Special beyond Ten: none
Notes: none

daa/dka—デカール—*deka-aru*

Japanese: デカール
Romanized: *deka-aru*
Pattern: 漢 ∅
Used with, or Means: decares/dekares (S. I. symbol: daa/dka), a unit of area, 10 a, 1,000 m² (10,763.91040 ft²)

1 daa/dka	1デカール	いちでかある	*ichi-deka-aru*
2 daa/dka	2デカール	にでかある	*ni-deka-aru*
3 daa/dka	3デカール	さんでかある	*san-deka-aru*
4 daa/dka	4デカール	よんでかある	*yon-deka-aru*
5 daa/dka	5デカール	ごでかある	*go-deka-aru*
6 daa/dka	6デカール	ろくでかある	*roku-deka-aru*
7 daa/dka	7デカール	ななでかある	*nana-deka-aru*
8 daa/dka	8デカール	はちでかある	*hachi-deka-aru*
9 daa/dka	9デカール	きゅうでかある	*kyuu-deka-aru*
10 daa/dka	10デカール	じゅうでかある	*juu-deka-aru*

Irregularities or Special beyond Ten: none
Notes: none

デカグラム・瓧—でかぐらむ—*deka-guramu*

Japanese: でかぐらむ
Romanized: *deka-guramu*
Pattern: 漢 Ø
Used with, or Means: decagrams/dekagrams (S. I. symbol: dag/dkg), a unit of mass, 10 g (0.35274 oz)

1 dag/dkg	一デカグラム・瓧	いちでかぐらむ	*ichi-deka-guramu*
2 dag/dkg	二デカグラム・瓧	にでかぐらむ	*ni-deka-guramu*
3 dag/dkg	三デカグラム・瓧	さんでかぐらむ	*san-deka-guramu*
4 dag/dkg	四デカグラム・瓧	よんでかぐらむ	*yon-deka-guramu*
5 dag/dkg	五デカグラム・瓧	ごでかぐらむ	*go-deka-guramu*
6 dag/dkg	六デカグラム・瓧	ろくでかぐらむ	*roku-deka-guramu*
7 dag/dkg	七デカグラム・瓧	ななでかぐらむ	*nana-deka-guramu*
8 dag/dkg	八デカグラム・瓧	はちでかぐらむ	*hachi-deka-guramu*
9 dag/dkg	九デカグラム・瓧	きゅうでかぐらむ	*kyuu-deka-guramu*
10 dag/dkg	十デカグラム・瓧	じゅうでかぐらむ	*juu-deka-guramu*

Irregularities or Special beyond Ten: none
Notes: none

デカメートル・籵 — でかめえとる — *deka-meetoru*

Japanese: でかめえとる
Romanized: *deka-meetoru*
Pattern: 漢 ∅
Used with, or Means: decameters/dekameters (S. I. symbol: dam/dkm), a unit of length, 10 m (32.80840 ft)

1 dam/dkm	一デカメートル・籵	いちでかめえとる	*ichi-deka-meetoru*
2 dam/dkm	二デカメートル・籵	にでかめえとる	*ni-deka-meetoru*
3 dam/dkm	三デカメートル・籵	さんでかめえとる	*san-deka-meetoru*
4 dam/dkm	四デカメートル・籵	よんでかめえとる	*yon-deka-meetoru*
5 dam/dkm	五デカメートル・籵	ごでかめえとる	*go-deka-meetoru*
6 dam/dkm	六デカメートル・籵	ろくでかめえとる	*roku-deka-meetoru*
7 dam/dkm	七デカメートル・籵	ななでかめえとる	*nana-deka-meetoru*
8 dam/dkm	八デカメートル・籵	はちでかめえとる	*hachi-deka-meetoru*
9 dam/dkm	九デカメートル・籵	きゅうでかめえとる	*kyuu-deka-meetoru*
10 dam/dkm	十デカメートル・籵	じゅうでかめえとる	*juu-deka-meetoru*

Irregularities or Special beyond Ten: none
Notes: none

デカリットル・㍑—デカリットル—*deka-rittoru*

Japanese: デカリットル
Romanized: *deka-rittoru*
Pattern: 漢 ∅
Used with, or Means: decaliters/dekaliters (S. I. symbol: daL/dkL), a unit of volume, 10 L (338.14023 fl oz, 2.64172 gal)

1 daL/dkL	一デカリットル・㍑	いちデカリットル	*ichi-deka-rittoru*
2 daL/dkL	二デカリットル・㍑	にデカリットル	*ni-deka-rittoru*
3 daL/dkL	三デカリットル・㍑	さんデカリットル	*san-deka-rittoru*
4 daL/dkL	四デカリットル・㍑	よんデカリットル	*yon-deka-rittoru*
5 daL/dkL	五デカリットル・㍑	ごデカリットル	*go-deka-rittoru*
6 daL/dkL	六デカリットル・㍑	ろくデカリットル	*roku-deka-rittoru*
7 daL/dkL	七デカリットル・㍑	ななデカリットル	*nana-deka-rittoru*
8 daL/dkL	八デカリットル・㍑	はちデカリットル	*hachi-deka-rittoru*
9 daL/dkL	九デカリットル・㍑	きゅうデカリットル	*kyuu-deka-rittoru*
10 daL/dkL	十デカリットル・㍑	じゅうデカリットル	*juu-deka-rittoru*

Irregularities or Special beyond Ten: none
Notes: none

滴 — てき — *teki*

Japanese: てき
Romanized: *teki*
Pattern: 漢 T
Used with, or Means: drops, see also 滴 (*shizuku*)

1 drop	一滴	いってき	*it-teki*
2 drops	二滴	にてき	*ni-teki*
3 drops	三滴	さんてき	*san-teki*
4 drops	四滴	よんてき	*yon-teki*
5 drops	五滴	ごてき	*go-teki*
6 drops	六滴	ろくてき	*roku-teki*
7 drops	七滴	ななてき	*nana-teki*
8 drops	八滴	はってき / はちてき	*hat-teki* / *hachi-teki*
9 drops	九滴	きゅうてき	*kyuu-teki*
10 drops	十滴	じゅってき / じってき	*jut-teki* / *jit-teki*

Irregularities or Special beyond Ten: none
Notes: none

デシグラム・㎏—でしぐらむ—*deshi-guramu*

Japanese: でしぐらむ
Romanized: *deshi-guramu*
Pattern: 漢 Ø
Used with, or Means: decigrams (S. I. symbol: dg), a unit of mass, 0.1 g (0.00353 oz)

1 dg	一デシグラム・㎏	いちでしぐらむ	*ichi-deshi-guramu*
2 dg	二デシグラム・㎏	にでしぐらむ	*ni-deshi-guramu*
3 dg	三デシグラム・㎏	さんでしぐらむ	*san-deshi-guramu*
4 dg	四デシグラム・㎏	よんでしぐらむ	*yon-deshi-guramu*
5 dg	五デシグラム・㎏	ごでしぐらむ	*go-deshi-guramu*
6 dg	六デシグラム・㎏	ろくでしぐらむ	*roku-deshi-guramu*
7 dg	七デシグラム・㎏	ななでしぐらむ	*nana-deshi-guramu*
8 dg	八デシグラム・㎏	はちでしぐらむ	*hachi-deshi-guramu*
9 dg	九デシグラム・㎏	きゅうでしぐらむ	*kyuu-deshi-guramu*
10 dg	十デシグラム・㎏	じゅうでしぐらむ	*juu-deshi-guramu*

Irregularities or Special beyond Ten: none
Notes: none

デシメートル・粉 — でしめえとる — *deshi-meetoru*

Japanese: でしめえとる
Romanized: *deshi-meetoru*
Pattern: 漢 Ø
Used with, or Means: decimeters (S. I. symbol: dm), a unit of length, 0.1 m (3.93701 in)

1 dm	一デシメートル・粉	いちでしめえとる	*ichi-deshi-meetoru*
2 dm	二デシメートル・粉	にでしめえとる	*ni-deshi-meetoru*
3 dm	三デシメートル・粉	さんでしめえとる	*san-deshi-meetoru*
4 dm	四デシメートル・粉	よんでしめえとる	*yon-deshi-meetoru*
5 dm	五デシメートル・粉	ごでしめえとる	*go-deshi-meetoru*
6 dm	六デシメートル・粉	ろくでしめえとる	*roku-deshi-meetoru*
7 dm	七デシメートル・粉	ななでしめえとる	*nana-deshi-meetoru*
8 dm	八デシメートル・粉	はちでしめえとる	*hachi-deshi-meetoru*
9 dm	九デシメートル・粉	きゅうでしめえとる	*kyuu-deshi-meetoru*
10 dm	十デシメートル・粉	じゅうでしめえとる	*juu-deshi-meetoru*

Irregularities or Special beyond Ten: none
Notes: none

デシリットル・兊―でしりっとる―*deshi-rittoru*

Japanese: でしりっとる
Romanized: *deshi-rittoru*
Pattern: 漢 Ø
Used with, or Means: deciliters (S. I. symbol: dL), a unit of volume, 0.1 L (3.38140 fl oz)

1 dL	一デシリットル・兊	いちでしりっとる	*ichi-deshi-rittoru*
2 dL	二デシリットル・兊	にでしりっとる	*ni-deshi-rittoru*
3 dL	三デシリットル・兊	さんでしりっとる	*san-deshi-rittoru*
4 dL	四デシリットル・兊	よんでしりっとる	*yon-deshi-rittoru*
5 dL	五デシリットル・兊	ごでしりっとる	*go-deshi-rittoru*
6 dL	六デシリットル・兊	ろくでしりっとる	*roku-deshi-rittoru*
7 dL	七デシリットル・兊	ななでしりっとる	*nana-deshi-rittoru*
8 dL	八デシリットル・兊	はちでしりっとる	*hachi-deshi-rittoru*
9 dL	九デシリットル・兊	きゅうでしりっとる	*kyuu-deshi-rittoru*
10 dL	十デシリットル・兊	じゅうでしりっとる	*juu-deshi-rittoru*

Irregularities or Special beyond Ten: none
Notes: none

跌 — てつ — *tetsu*

Japanese: てつ
Romanized: *tetsu*
Pattern: 漢 T
Used with, or Means: bloopers, stumbles, mistakes, failures, blunders, slips

1 blooper	一跌	いってつ	*it-tetsu*
2 bloopers	二跌	にてつ	*ni-tetsu*
3 bloopers	三跌	さんてつ	*san-tetsu*
4 bloopers	四跌	よんてつ	*yon-tetsu*
5 bloopers	五跌	ごてつ	*go-tetsu*
6 bloopers	六跌	ろくてつ	*roku-tetsu*
7 bloopers	七跌	ななてつ	*nana-tetsu*
8 bloopers	八跌	はってつ / はちてつ	*hat-tetsu* / *hachi-tetsu*
9 bloopers	九跌	きゅうてつ	*kyuu-tetsu*
10 bloopers	十跌	じゅってつ / じってつ	*jut-tetsu* / *jit-tetsu*

Irregularities or Special beyond Ten: none
Notes: none

店 — てん — ten

Japanese: てん
Romanized: ten
Pattern: 漢 T
Used with, or Means: stores, shops; franchise, chain store, see also 軒 (ken), see also 店舗 (tempo)

1 store	一店	いってん	it-ten
2 stores	二店	にてん	ni-ten
3 stores	三店	さんてん	san-ten
4 stores	四店	よんてん	yon-ten
5 stores	五店	ごてん	go-ten
6 stores	六店	ろくてん	roku-ten
7 stores	七店	ななてん	nana-ten
8 stores	八店	はってん / はちてん	hat-ten / hachi-ten
9 stores	九店	きゅうてん	kyuu-ten
10 stores	十店	じゅってん / じってん	jut-ten / jit-ten

Irregularities or Special beyond Ten: none
Notes: none

点 — てん — *ten*

Japanese: てん
Romanized: *ten*
Pattern: 漢 T

Used with, or Means: 点数 (*tensuu*): marks, points, scores, runs, items, credits; 得点 (*tokuten*): points earned, points won, see also ポイント (*pointo*), see also 雫 (*shizuku*); spot, marks on a map, dots; commodities; stolen items 盗難品 (*tounanhin*); literary works 文学作品 (*bungaku sakuhin*), artistic works (*geijutsu sakuhin*), see 作 (*saku*), 作品 (*sakuhin*)

1 point	一点	いってん	*it-ten*
2 points	二点	にてん	*ni-ten*
3 points	三点	さんてん	*san-ten*
4 points	四点	よんてん	*yon-ten*
5 points	五点	ごてん	*go-ten*
6 points	六点	ろくてん	*roku-ten*
7 points	七点	ななてん	*nana-ten*
8 points	八点	はってん / はちてん	*hat-ten* / *hachi-ten*
9 points	九点	きゅうてん	*kyuu-ten*
10 points	十点	じゅってん / じってん	*jut-ten* / *jit-ten*

Irregularities or Special beyond Ten: none
Notes: Just as we say something like *one-point-five* in English, the Japanese say 一点五 (*it-ten go* one-point-five).

店舗——てんぽ——*tempo*

Japanese: てんぽ
Romanized: *tempo*
Pattern: 漢 T or 和 I-T
Used with, or Means: stores, shops, see also 店 (*ten*)

1 store	一店舗	いってんぽ ひとてんぽ いちてんぽ	*it-tempo* *hito-tempo* *ichi-tempo*
2 stores	二店舗	にてんぽ ふたてんぽ	*ni-tempo* *futa-tempo*
3 stores	三店舗	さんてんぽ	*san-tempo*
4 stores	四店舗	よんてんぽ	*yon-tempo*
5 stores	五店舗	ごてんぽ	*go-tempo*
6 stores	六店舗	ろくてんぽ	*roku-tempo*
7 stores	七店舗	ななてんぽ	*nana-tempo*
8 stores	八店舗	はってんぽ はちてんぽ	*hat-tempo* *hachi-tempo*
9 stores	九店舗	きゅうてんぽ	*kyuu-tempo*
10 stores	十店舗	じゅってんぽ じってんぽ	*jut-tempo* *jit-tempo*

Irregularities or Special beyond Tempo: none
Notes: none

と・ど—To/Do
斗—と—to

Japanese: と
Romanized: *to*
Pattern: 漢 T

Used with, or Means: *to*, a unit of volume, 10 升 (*shou*), 609.97347 fl oz (38.12334 pt, 4.76542 gal)/18.03907 L

1 *to*	一斗	いっと	*it-to*
2 *to*	二斗	にと	*ni-to*
3 *to*	三斗	さんと	*san-to*
4 *to*	四斗	よんと	*yon-to*
5 *to*	五斗	ごと	*go-to*
6 *to*	六斗	ろくと	*roku-to*
7 *to*	七斗	ななと	*nana-to*
8 *to*	八斗	はっと / はちと	*hat-to* / *hachi-to*
9 *to*	九斗	きゅうと	*kyuu-to*
10 *to*	十斗	じゅっと / じっと	*jut-to* / *jit-to*

Irregularities or Special beyond Ten: none
Notes: none

度 — ど — do

Japanese: ど
Romanized: do
Pattern: 漢 ∅
Used with, or Means: experiences, personal experiences, consecutive events, number of times, see also 回 (*kai*), see also 度 (*tabi*), see also 遍 (*hen*); degrees (temperature), degrees (angle), degrees (longitude), degrees (latitude) (symbol: °); alcohol concentration; water hardness; lens refraction (camera lens/telescope lens power); musical step

1°	一度	いちど	*ichi-do*
2°	二度	にど	*ni-do*
3°	三度	さんど	*san-do*
4°	四度	よんど	*yon-do*
5°	五度	ごど	*go-do*
6°	六度	ろくど	*roku-do*
7°	七度	ななど	*nana-do*
8°	八度	はちど	*hachi-do*
9°	九度	きゅうど / くど	*kyuu-do* / *ku-do*
10°	十度	じゅうど	*juu-do*

Irregularities or Special beyond Ten: none
Notes: For body temperature, rather than *kyuu-do*, use *ku-do*.

灯・燈 — とう — *tou*

Japanese: とう
Romanized: *tou*
Pattern: 漢 T
Used with, or Means: electric lights, flash lights, street lights, light bulbs, lamps, lights, see also 基 (*ki*); heaters, space heaters

1 light	一灯・燈	いっとう	*it-tou*
2 lights	二灯・燈	にとう	*ni-tou*
3 lights	三灯・燈	さんとう	*san-tou*
4 lights	四灯・燈	よんとう	*yon-tou*
5 lights	五灯・燈	ごとう	*go-tou*
6 lights	六灯・燈	ろくとう	*roku-tou*
7 lights	七灯・燈	ななとう	*nana-tou*
8 lights	八灯・燈	はっとう / はちとう	*hat-tou* / *hachi-tou*
9 lights	九灯・燈	きゅうとう	*kyuu-tou*
10 lights	十灯・燈	じゅっとう / じっとう	*jut-tou* / *jit-tou*

Irregularities or Special beyond Ten: none
Notes: none

投 — とう — *tou*

Japanese: とう
Romanized: *tou*
Pattern: 漢 T
Used with, or Means: number of shots, shells, bullets, cannon balls; number of times one casts one's fishing line into the water

1 shot	一投(目)	いっとう(め)	*it-tou-(me)*
2 shots	二投(目)	にとう(め)	*ni-tou-(me)*
3 shots	三投(目)	さんとう(め)	*san-tou-(me)*
4 shots	四投(目)	よんとう(め)	*yon-tou-(me)*
5 shots	五投(目)	ごとう(め)	*go-tou-(me)*
6 shots	六投(目)	ろくとう(め)	*roku-tou-(me)*
7 shots	七投(目)	ななとう(め)	*nana-tou-(me)*
8 shots	八投(目)	はっとう(め)	*hat-tou-(me)*
9 shots	九投(目)	きゅうとう(め)	*kyuu-tou-(me)*
10 shots	十投(目)	じゅっとう(め) じっとう(め)	*jut-tou-(me)* *jit-tou-(me)*

Irregularities or Special beyond Ten: none
Notes: Typically accompanied by 目 (*me*).

套 — とう — *tou*

Japanese: とう
Romanized: *tou*
Pattern: 漢 T
Used with, or Means: Japanese books (帙 *chitsu*) wrapped in a shroud; stacks of Japanese books

1 Japanese book	一套	いっとう	*it-tou*
2 Japanese books	二套	にとう	*ni-tou*
3 Japanese books	三套	さんとう	*san-tou*
4 Japanese books	四套	よんとう	*yon-tou*
5 Japanese books	五套	ごとう	*go-tou*
6 Japanese books	六套	ろくとう	*roku-tou*
7 Japanese books	七套	ななとう	*nana-tou*
8 Japanese books	八套	はっとう / はちとう	*hat-tou* / *hachi-tou*
9 Japanese books	九套	きゅうとう	*kyuu-tou*
10 Japanese books	十套	じゅっとう / じっとう	*jut-tou* / *jit-tou*

Irregularities or Special beyond Ten: none
Notes: none

刀 — とう — tou

Japanese: とう
Romanized: *tou*
Pattern: 漢 T
Used with, or Means: *katana* (Japanese swords)

1 *katana*	一刀	いっとう	*it-tou*
2 *katana*	二刀	にとう	*ni-tou*
3 *katana*	三刀	さんとう	*san-tou*
4 *katana*	四刀	よんとう	*yon-tou*
5 *katana*	五刀	ごとう	*go-tou*
6 *katana*	六刀	ろくとう	*roku-tou*
7 *katana*	七刀	ななとう	*nana-tou*
8 *katana*	八刀	はっとう はちとう	*hat-tou* *hachi-tou*
9 *katana*	九刀	きゅうとう	*kyuu-tou*
10 *katana*	十刀	じゅっとう じっとう	*jut-tou* *jit-tou*

Irregularities or Special beyond Ten: none
Notes: none

島 — とう — *tou*

Japanese: とう
Romanized: *tou*
Pattern: 漢 T
Used with, or Means: (literary language) islands

1 island	一島	いっとう	*it-tou*
2 islands	二島	にとう	*ni-tou*
3 islands	三島	さんとう	*san-tou*
4 islands	四島	よんとう	*yon-tou*
5 islands	五島	ごとう	*go-tou*
6 islands	六島	ろくとう	*roku-tou*
7 islands	七島	ななとう	*nana-tou*
8 islands	八島	はっとう	*hat-tou*
9 islands	九島	きゅうとう	*kyuu-tou*
10 islands	十島	じゅっとう / じっとう	*jut-tou* / *jit-tou*

Irregularities or Special beyond Ten: none
Notes: none

盗 — とう — *tou*

Japanese: とう
Romanized: *tou*
Pattern: 漢 T
Used with, or Means: (literary language) steals in baseball

1 steal	一盗	いっとう	*it-tou*
2 steals	二盗	にとう	*ni-tou*
3 steals	三盗	さんとう	*san-tou*
4 steals	四盗	よんとう	*yon-tou*
5 steals	五盗	ごとう	*go-tou*
6 steals	六盗	ろくとう	*roku-tou*
7 steals	七盗	ななとう	*nana-tou*
8 steals	八盗	はっとう / はちとう	*hat-tou* / *hachi-tou*
9 steals	九盗	きゅうとう	*kyuu-tou*
10 steals	十盗	じゅっとう / じっとう	*jut-tou* / *jit-tou*

Irregularities or Special beyond Ten: none
Notes: none

塔 — とう — *tou*

Japanese: とう
Romanized: *tou*
Pattern: 漢 T
Used with, or Means: (literary language) towers, *pagoda*, steeples

1 tower	一塔	いっとう	*it-tou*
2 towers	二塔	にとう	*ni-tou*
3 towers	三塔	さんとう	*san-tou*
4 towers	四塔	よんとう	*yon-tou*
5 towers	五塔	ごとう	*go-tou*
6 towers	六塔	ろくとう	*roku-tou*
7 towers	七塔	ななとう	*nana-tou*
8 towers	八塔	はっとう / はちとう	*hat-tou* / *hachi-tou*
9 towers	九塔	きゅうとう	*kyuu-tou*
10 towers	十塔	じゅっとう / じっとう	*jut-tou* / *jit-tou*

Irregularities or Special beyond Ten: none
Notes: none

棟 — とう — *tou*

Japanese: とう
Romanized: *tou*
Pattern: 漢 T
Used with, or Means: buildings, huts, cabins, sheds, animal pens, see also 棟 (*mune*), see also 軒 (*ken*); speculative-built houses on a block; households on a block; condominiums; apartments in an apartment building

1 house	一棟	いっとう	*it-tou*
2 houses	二棟	にとう	*ni-tou*
3 houses	三棟	さんとう	*san-tou*
4 houses	四棟	よんとう	*yon-tou*
5 houses	五棟	ごとう	*go-tou*
6 houses	六棟	ろくとう	*roku-tou*
7 houses	七棟	ななとう	*nana-tou*
8 houses	八棟	はっとう / はちとう	*hat-tou* / *hachi-tou*
9 houses	九棟	きゅうとう	*kyuu-tou*
10 houses	十棟	じゅっとう / じっとう	*jut-tou* / *jit-tou*

Irregularities or Special beyond Ten: none
Notes: none

湯 — とう — *tou*

Japanese: とう
Romanized: *tou*
Pattern: 漢 T
Used with, or Means: spas, hot springs, *onsen*, health resorts, see also 湯 (*yu*)

1 hot spring	一湯	いっとう	*it-tou*
2 hot springs	二湯	にとう	*ni-tou*
3 hot springs	三湯	さんとう	*san-tou*
4 hot springs	四湯	よんとう	*yon-tou*
5 hot springs	五湯	ごとう	*go-tou*
6 hot springs	六湯	ろくとう	*roku-tou*
7 hot springs	七湯	ななとう	*nana-tou*
8 hot springs	八湯	はっとう / はちとう	*hat-tou* / *hachi-tou*
9 hot springs	九湯	きゅうとう	*kyuu-tou*
10 hot springs	十湯	じゅっとう / じっとう	*jut-tou* / *jit-tou*

Irregularities or Special beyond Ten: none
Notes: none

等 — とう — *tou*

Japanese: とう
Romanized: *tou*
Pattern: 漢 T
Used with, or Means: placement in a race, order, rank, precedence; grade, class

1st place	一等	いっとう	*it-tou*
2nd place	二等	にとう	*ni-tou*
3rd place	三等	さんとう	*san-tou*
4th place	四等	よんとう	*yon-tou*
5th place	五等	ごとう	*go-tou*
6th place	六等	ろくとう	*roku-tou*
7th place	七等	ななとう	*nana-tou*
8th place	八等	はっとう / はちとう	*hat-tou* / *hachi-tou*
9th place	九等	きゅうとう	*kyuu-tou*
10th place	十等	じゅっとう / じっとう	*jut-tou* / *jit-tou*

Irregularities or Special beyond Ten: none
Notes: none

筒 — とう — *tou*

Japanese: とう
Romanized: *tou*
Pattern: 漢 T
Used with, or Means: formerly a unit of capacity for injections; currently the number of injections regardless of capacity (which is measured in mL); ampoules[13]

1 ampoule	一筒	いっとう	*it-tou*
2 ampoules	二筒	にとう	*ni-tou*
3 ampoules	三筒	さんとう	*san-tou*
4 ampoules	四筒	よんとう	*yon-tou*
5 ampoules	五筒	ごとう	*go-tou*
6 ampoules	六筒	ろくとう	*roku-tou*
7 ampoules	七筒	ななとう	*nana-tou*
8 ampoules	八筒	はっとう / はちとう	*hat-tou* / *hachi-tou*
9 ampoules	九筒	きゅうとう	*kyuu-tou*
10 ampoules	十筒	じゅっとう / じっとう	*jut-tou* / *jit-tou*

Irregularities or Special beyond Ten: none
Notes: none

---

[13] An ampoule ('æmpyul, -pul) is a glass phial or vial that is hermetically sealed by melting the top once it is filled. When one needs the contents of the ampoule, one snaps off the top and pours it out. They are made in such a way that when one snaps off the top, there are no glass shards and the phial itself does not break.

統 —とう— *tou*

Japanese: とう
Romanized: *tou*
Pattern: 漢 T
Used with, or Means: (professional/technical jargon) anchored fishnets

1 anchored fishnet	一統	いっとう	*it-tou*
2 anchored fishnets	二統	にとう	*ni-tou*
3 anchored fishnets	三統	さんとう	*san-tou*
4 anchored fishnets	四統	よんとう	*yon-tou*
5 anchored fishnets	五統	ごとう	*go-tou*
6 anchored fishnets	六統	ろくとう	*roku-tou*
7 anchored fishnets	七統	ななとう	*nana-tou*
8 anchored fishnets	八統	はっとう / はちとう	*hat-tou* / *hachi-tou*
9 anchored fishnets	九統	きゅうとう	*kyuu-tou*
10 anchored fishnets	十統	じゅっとう / じっとう	*jut-tou* / *jit-tou*

Irregularities or Special beyond Ten: none
Notes: none

頭 — とう — *tou*

Japanese: とう
Romanized: *tou*
Pattern: 漢 T
Used with, or Means: large animals, see also 匹 (*hiki*); sometimes used to count ostriches and other large birds, see 羽 (*wa*); (professional/technical jargon) animals (in general)

1 large animal	一頭	いっとう	*it-tou*
2 large animals	二頭	にとう	*ni-tou*
3 large animals	三頭	さんとう	*san-tou*
4 large animals	四頭	よんとう	*yon-tou*
5 large animals	五頭	ごとう	*go-tou*
6 large animals	六頭	ろくとう	*roku-tou*
7 large animals	七頭	ななとう	*nana-tou*
8 large animals	八頭	はっとう / はちとう	*hat-tou* / *hachi-tou*
9 large animals	九頭	きゅうとう	*kyuu-tou*
10 large animals	十頭	じゅっとう / じっとう	*jut-tou* / *jit-tou*

Irregularities or Special beyond Ten: none
Notes: none

党 — とう — *tou*

Japanese: とう
Romanized: *tou*
Pattern: 漢 T
Used with, or Means: political parties, cliques, factions, see also 派 (*ha*)

1 political party	一党	いっとう	*it-tou*
2 political parties	二党	にとう	*ni-tou*
3 political parties	三党	さんとう	*san-tou*
4 political parties	四党	よんとう	*yon-tou*
5 political parties	五党	ごとう	*go-tou*
6 political parties	六党	ろくとう	*roku-tou*
7 political parties	七党	ななとう	*nana-tou*
8 political parties	八党	はっとう / はちとう	*hat-tou* / *hachi-tou*
9 political parties	九党	きゅうとう	*kyuu-tou*
10 political parties	十党	じゅっとう / じっとう	*jut-tou* / *jit-tou*

Irregularities or Special beyond Ten: none
Notes: none

洞 — どう — *dou*

Japanese: どう
Romanized: *dou*
Pattern: 漢 Ø
Used with, or Means: (literary language) caves, limestone caves

1 cave	一洞	いちどう	*ichi-dou*
2 caves	二洞	にどう	*ni-dou*
3 caves	三洞	さんどう	*san-dou*
4 caves	四洞	よんどう	*yon-dou*
5 caves	五洞	ごどう	*go-dou*
6 caves	六洞	ろくどう	*roku-dou*
7 caves	七洞	ななどう	*nana-dou*
8 caves	八洞	はちどう	*hachi-dou*
9 caves	九洞	きゅうどう	*kyuu-dou*
10 caves	十洞	じゅうどう	*juu-dou*

Irregularities or Special beyond Ten: none
Notes: none

堂 — どう — *dou*

Japanese: どう
Romanized: *dou*
Pattern: 漢 ∅
Used with, or Means: (literary language) temples, churches, sanctuaries, worship halls; auditoriums, halls

1 temple	一堂	いちどう	*ichi-dou*
2 temples	二堂	にどう	*ni-dou*
3 temples	三堂	さんどう	*san-dou*
4 temples	四堂	よんどう	*yon-dou*
5 temples	五堂	ごどう	*go-dou*
6 temples	六堂	ろくどう	*roku-dou*
7 temples	七堂	ななどう	*nana-dou*
8 temples	八堂	はちどう	*hachi-dou*
9 temples	九堂	きゅうどう	*kyuu-dou*
10 temples	十堂	じゅうどう	*juu-dou*

Irregularities or Special beyond Ten: none
Notes: none

道 — どう — dou

Japanese: どう
Romanized: *dou*
Pattern: 漢 ∅
Used with, or Means: (literary language) rays of light

1 ray	一道	いちどう	*ichi-dou*
2 rays	二道	にどう	*ni-dou*
3 rays	三道	さんどう	*san-dou*
4 rays	四道	よんどう	*yon-dou*
5 rays	五道	ごどう	*go-dou*
6 rays	六道	ろくどう	*roku-dou*
7 rays	七道	ななどう	*nana-dou*
8 rays	八道	はちどう	*hachi-dou*
9 rays	九道	きゅうどう	*kyuu-dou*
10 rays	十道	じゅうどう	*juu-dou*

Irregularities or Special beyond Ten: none
Notes: For *ichi-dou* only, it can also mean the road, path, or way to which one should devote oneself, such as a career path, or academic path, or maybe a religious devotion.

銅 — どう — dou

Japanese: どう
Romanized: *dou*
Pattern: 漢 ∅
Used with, or Means: formerly used for counting copper coins (銅貨 *douka*)

1 coin	一銅	いちどう	*ichi-dou*
2 coins	二銅	にどう	*ni-dou*
3 coins	三銅	さんどう	*san-dou*
4 coins	四銅	よんどう	*yon-dou*
5 coins	五銅	ごどう	*go-dou*
6 coins	六銅	ろくどう	*roku-dou*
7 coins	七銅	ななどう	*nana-dou*
8 coins	八銅	はちどう	*hachi-dou*
9 coins	九銅	きゅうどう	*kyuu-dou*
10 coins	十銅	じゅうどう	*juu-dou*

Irregularities or Special beyond Ten: none
Notes: none

等分―とうぶん―*toubun*

Japanese: とうぶん
Romanized: *toubun*
Pattern: 和 I-T or 漢 T
Used with, or Means: divisions into equal parts

1 division	一等分	ひととうぶん いっとうぶん	*hito-toubun* *it-toubun*
2 divisions	二等分	ふたとうぶん にとうぶん	*futa-toubun* *ni-toubun*
3 divisions	三等分	さんとうぶん	*san-toubun*
4 divisions	四等分	よんとうぶん	*yon-toubun*
5 divisions	五等分	ごとうぶん	*go-toubun*
6 divisions	六等分	ろくとうぶん	*roku-toubun*
7 divisions	七等分	ななとうぶん	*nana-toubun*
8 divisions	八等分	はっとうぶん はちとうぶん	*hat-toubun* *hachi-toubun*
9 divisions	九等分	きゅうとうぶん	*kyuu-toubun*
10 divisions	十等分	じゅっとうぶん じっとうぶん	*jut-toubun* *jit-toubun*

Irregularities or Special beyond Ten: none
Notes: none

通し—とおし—*tooshi*

Japanese: とおし
Romanized: *tooshi*
Pattern: 和 I-T
Used with, or Means: the number of times paper is passed through a printing press

1 time	一通し	ひととおし	*hito-tooshi*
2 times	二通し	ふたとおし	*futa-tooshi*
3 times	三通し	さんとおし	*san-tooshi*
4 times	四通し	よんとおし	*yon-tooshi*
5 times	五通し	ごとおし	*go-tooshi*
6 times	六通し	ろくとおし	*roku-tooshi*
7 times	七通し	ななとおし	*nana-tooshi*
8 times	八通し	はっとおし / はちとおし	*hat-tooshi* / *hachi-tooshi*
9 times	九通し	きゅうとおし	*kyuu-tooshi*
10 times	十通し	じゅっとおし / じっとおし	*jut-tooshi* / *jit-tooshi*

Irregularities or Special beyond Ten: none
Notes: none

通り —とおり— *toori*

Japanese: とおり
Romanized: *toori*
Pattern: 和 I-T or 漢 T
Used with, or Means: methods, manners, ways, means, techniques, styles, forms, patterns; combinations, puzzle solutions

1 way	一通り	いっとおり	*it-toori*
		ひととおり	*hito-toori*
2 ways	二通り	にとおり	*ni-toori*
		ふたとおり	*futa-toori*
3 ways	三通り	さんとおり	*san-toori*
4 ways	四通り	よんとおり	*yon-toori*
5 ways	五通り	ごとおり	*go-toori*
6 ways	六通り	ろくとおり	*roku-toori*
7 ways	七通り	ななとおり	*nana-toori*
8 ways	八通り	はっとおり	*hat-toori*
		はちとおり	*hachi-toori*
9 ways	九通り	きゅうとおり	*kyuu-toori*
10 ways	十通り	じゅっとおり	*jut-toori*
		じっとおり	*jit-toori*

Irregularities or Special beyond Ten: none
Notes: One can use the 和 I-T or the 漢 T patterns: both mean the same thing and are interchangeable.

時 — とき — *toki*

Japanese: とき
Romanized: *toki*
Pattern: 和 I-T or 漢 T
Used with, or Means: two-hour periods in ancient times

1 two-hour period	一時	いっとき ひととき	*it-toki* *hito-toki*
2 two-hour periods	二時	にとき ふたとき	*ni-toki* *futa-toki*
3 two-hour periods	三時	さんとき	*san-toki*
4 two-hour periods	四時	よんとき	*yon-toki*
5 two-hour periods	五時	ごとき	*go-toki*
6 two-hour periods	六時	ろくとき	*roku-toki*
7 two-hour periods	七時	ななとき	*nana-toki*
8 two-hour periods	八時	はっとき はちとき	*hat-toki* *hachi-toki*
9 two-hour periods	九時	きゅうとき	*kyuu-toki*
10 two-hour periods	十時	じゅっとき じっとき	*jut-toki* *jit-toki*

Irregularities or Special beyond Ten: none
Notes: One can use the 和 I-T or the 漢 T patterns: both mean the same thing and are interchangeable.

床 — とこ — *toko*

Japanese: とこ
Romanized: *toko*
Pattern: 和 I-T
Used with, or Means: beds, see also 床 (*shou*); rafts (筏 *ikada*)

1 bed	一床	<u>ひととこ</u>	<u>*hito-toko*</u>
2 beds	二床	<u>ふたとこ</u>	<u>*futa-toko*</u>
3 beds	三床	さんとこ	*san-toko*
4 beds	四床	よんとこ	*yon-toko*
5 beds	五床	ごとこ	*go-toko*
6 beds	六床	ろくとこ	*roku-toko*
7 beds	七床	ななとこ	*nana-toko*
8 beds	八床	はっとこ / はちとこ	*hat-toko* / *hachi-toko*
9 beds	九床	きゅうとこ	*kyuu-toko*
10 beds	十床	<u>じゅっとこ</u> / <u>じっとこ</u>	<u>*jut-toko*</u> / <u>*jit-toko*</u>

Irregularities or Special beyond Ten: none
Notes: none

所・処 — ところ — *tokoro*

Japanese: ところ
Romanized: *tokoro*
Pattern: 和 I-T
Used with, or Means: places, see also 箇所・ヶ所 (*kasho*); gods, Buddhas, honored persons, see also 方 (*kata*)

1 place	一所・処	<u>ひとところ</u>	<u>*hito-tokoro*</u>
2 places	二所・処	<u>ふたところ</u>	<u>*futa-tokoro*</u>
3 places	三所・処	さんところ	*san-tokoro*
4 places	四所・処	よんところ	*yon-tokoro*
5 places	五所・処	ごところ	*go-tokoro*
6 places	六所・処	ろくところ	*roku-tokoro*
7 places	七所・処	ななところ	*nana-tokoro*
8 places	八所・処	<u>はっところ</u> <u>はちところ</u>	<u>*hat-tokoro*</u> <u>*hachi-tokoro*</u>
9 places	九所・処	きゅうところ	*kyuu-tokoro*
10 places	十所・処	<u>じゅっところ</u> <u>じっところ</u>	<u>*jut-tokoro*</u> <u>*jit-tokoro*</u>

Irregularities or Special beyond Ten: none
Notes: none

度数—どすう—*dosuu*

Japanese: どすう
Romanized: *dosuu*
Pattern: 漢 ∅
Used with, or Means: experiences, personal experiences, consecutive events, number of times, see also 回 (*kai*), see also 度 (*tabi*), see also 遍 (*hen*); degrees (temperature), degrees (angle), degrees (longitude), degrees (latitude) (symbol: °); alcohol concentration; water hardness; lens refraction (camera lens/telescope lens power); musical step; the number of times one may use a telephone card

1°	一度数	いちどすう	*ichi-dosuu*
2°	二度数	にどすう	*ni-dosuu*
3°	三度数	さんどすう	*san-dosuu*
4°	四度数	よんどすう	*yon-dosuu*
5°	五度数	ごどすう	*go-dosuu*
6°	六度数	ろくどすう	*roku-dosuu*
7°	七度数	ななどすう	*nana-dosuu*
8°	八度数	はちどすう	*hachi-dosuu*
9°	九度数	きゅうどすう / くどすう	*kyuu-dosuu* / *ku-dosuu*
10°	十度数	じゅうどすう	*juu-dosuu*

Irregularities or Special beyond Ten: none
Notes: For body temperature, rather than *kyuu-dosuu*, use *ku-dosuu*.

年・歳 —— とせ —— *tose*

Japanese: とせ
Romanized: *tose*
Pattern: 和 I-T
Used with, or Means: (polite) age, years, see also 歳 (*sai*), see also 年 (*nen*)

1 year	一年・歳	ひととせ	*hito-tose*
2 years	二年・歳	ふたとせ	*futa-tose*
3 years	三年・歳	みとせ	*mi-tose*
4 years	四年・歳	よとせ	*yo-tose*
5 years	五年・歳	いつとせ	*itsu-tose*
6 years	六年・歳	むとせ	*mu-tose*
7 years	七年・歳	ななとせ	*nana-tose*
8 years	八年・歳	やとせ	*ya-tose*
9 years	九年・歳	ここのとせ	*kokono-tose*
10 years	十年・歳	とおとせ	*too-tose*

Irregularities or Special beyond Ten:

100 years	百年・歳	ももとせ	*momo-tose*
1,000 years	千年・歳	ちとせ	*chi-tose*
10,000 years	万年・歳	よろずとせ	*yorozu-tose*
How many years?	何年・歳	なにとせ	*nani-tose*

Notes: none

戸前——とまえ——*tomae*

Japanese: とまえ
Romanized: *tomae*
Pattern: 漢 T
Used with, or Means: cellars, warehouses, godowns, store houses

1 cellar	一戸前	ひととまえ	*hito-tomae*
2 cellars	二戸前	ふたとまえ	*futa-tomae*
3 cellars	三戸前	さんとまえ	*san-tomae*
4 cellars	四戸前	よんとまえ	*yon-tomae*
5 cellars	五戸前	ごとまえ	*go-tomae*
6 cellars	六戸前	ろくとまえ	*roku-tomae*
7 cellars	七戸前	ななとまえ	*nana-tomae*
8 cellars	八戸前	はっとまえ / はちとまえ	*hat-tomae* / *hachi-tomae*
9 cellars	九戸前	きゅうとまえ	*kyuu-tomae*
10 cellars	十戸前	じゅっとまえ / じっとまえ	*jut-tomae* / *jit-tomae*

Irregularities or Special beyond Ten: none
Notes: none

度目 — どめ — *do-me*

Japanese: どめ
Romanized: *dome*
Pattern: 漢 Ø
Used with, or Means: experiences, personal experiences, consecutive events, number of times, see also 回 (*kai*), see also 度 (*tabi*), see also 遍 (*hen*); degrees (temperature), degrees (angle), degrees (longitude), degrees (latitude) (symbol: °); alcohol concentration; water hardness; lens refraction (camera lens/telescope lens power); musical step; the number of times one may use a telephone card

1st degree	一度目	いちどめ	*ichi-do-me*
2nd degree	二度目	にどめ	*ni-do-me*
3rd degree	三度目	さんどめ	*san-do-me*
4th degree	四度目	よんどめ	*yon-do-me*
5th degree	五度目	ごどめ	*go-do-me*
6th degree	六度目	ろくどめ	*roku-do-me*
7th degree	七度目	ななどめ	*nana-do-me*
8th degree	八度目	はちどめ	*hachi-do-me*
9th degree	九度目	きゅうどめ	*kyuu-do-me*
10th degree	十度目	じゅうどめ	*juu-do-me*

Irregularities or Special beyond Ten: none
Notes: none

撮り —どり— *dori*

Japanese: どり
Romanized: *dori*
Pattern: 漢 ∅
Used with, or Means: the number of available shots in a roll of film

1 shot	一撮り	いちどり	*ichi-dori*
2 shots	二撮り	にどり	*ni-dori*
3 shots	三撮り	さんどり	*san-dori*
4 shots	四撮り	よんどり	*yon-dori*
5 shots	五撮り	ごどり	*go-dori*
6 shots	六撮り	ろくどり	*roku-dori*
7 shots	七撮り	ななどり	*nana-dori*
8 shots	八撮り	はちどり	*hachi-dori*
9 shots	九撮り	きゅうどり	*kyuu-dori*
10 shots	十撮り	じゅうどり	*juu-dori*

Irregularities or Special beyond Ten: none
Notes: none

ドル・弗—どる—doru

Japanese: どる
Romanized: *doru*
Pattern: 漢 ∅
Used with, or Means: dollars

$1.00	1 ドル・弗	いちどる	*ichi-doru*
$2.00	2 ドル・弗	にどる	*ni-doru*
$3.00	3 ドル・弗	さんどる	*san-doru*
$4.00	4 ドル・弗	よんどる	*yon-doru*
$5.00	5 ドル・弗	ごどる	*go-doru*
$6.00	6 ドル・弗	ろくどる	*roku-doru*
$7.00	7 ドル・弗	ななどる	*nana-doru*
$8.00	8 ドル・弗	はちどる	*hachi-doru*
$9.00	9 ドル・弗	きゅうどる	*kyuu-doru*
$10.00	10 ドル・弗	じゅうどる	*juu-doru*

Irregularities or Special beyond Ten: none
Notes: none

トン・屯・瓲・噸—とん—*ton*

Japanese: とん
Romanized: *ton*
Pattern: 漢 T
Used with, or Means: tons (symbol: ton), a unit of weight, 2,000 lbs/907,184.74000 g; tonnes (metric) (S. I. symbol: t), a unit of mass, 1,000 kg (35,273.96190 oz, 2,204.62260 lb)

1 ton(ne)	1 トン・屯・瓲・噸	いっとん	*it-ton*
2 ton(ne)s	2 トン・屯・瓲・噸	にとん	*ni-ton*
3 ton(ne)s	3 トン・屯・瓲・噸	さんとん	*san-ton*
4 ton(ne)s	4 トン・屯・瓲・噸	よんとん	*yon-ton*
5 ton(ne)s	5 トン・屯・瓲・噸	ごとん	*go-ton*
6 ton(ne)s	6 トン・屯・瓲・噸	ろくとん	*roku-ton*
7 ton(ne)s	7 トン・屯・瓲・噸	ななとん	*nana-ton*
8 ton(ne)s	8 トン・屯・瓲・噸	はっとん / はちとん	*hat-ton* / *hachi-ton*
9 ton(ne)s	9 トン・屯・瓲・噸	きゅうとん	*kyuu-ton*
10 ton(ne)s	10 トン・屯・瓲・噸	じゅっとん / じっとん	*jut-ton* / *jit-ton*

Irregularities or Special beyond Ten: none
Notes: none

な—Na
流れ—ながれ—nagare

Japanese: ながれ
Romanized: nagare
Pattern: 和 III
Used with, or Means: flags, banners, standards, streamers, see also 旒 (*ryuu*); a string of characters (文字 *moji*) lined up in a row (or vertically, in a column), see also 行 (*kudari*); water flows, rivers, streams, see also 河 (*ga*), see also 河川 (*kasen*)

1 flag	一流れ	ひとながれ	*hito-nagare*
2 flags	二流れ	ふたながれ	*futa-nagare*
3 flags	三流れ	みながれ	*mi-nagare*
4 flags	四流れ	よながれ	*yo-nagare*
5 flags	五流れ	ごながれ	*go-nagare*
6 flags	六流れ	ろくながれ	*roku-nagare*
7 flags	七流れ	ななながれ	*nana-nagare*
8 flags	八流れ	はちながれ	*hachi-nagare*
9 flags	九流れ	きゅうながれ	*kyuu-nagare*
10 flags	十流れ	じゅうながれ	*juu-nagare*

Irregularities or Special beyond Ten: none
Notes: none

七日—なぬか・なのか—*nanuka/nanoka*

Japanese: なぬか・なのか
Romanized: *nanuka/nanoka*
Pattern: 漢 Ø
Used with, or Means: death anniversaries, see also 回忌 (*kaiki*); weeks, see also 週 (*shuu*), see also 週間 (*shuukan*)

1st week	初七日	しょなぬか・なのか	*sho-nanuka/nanoka*
2nd week	二七日	になぬか・なのか	*ni-nanuka/nanoka*
3rd week	三七日	さんなぬか・なのか	*san-nanuka/nanoka*
4th week	四七日	よんなぬか・なのか	*yon-nanuka/nanoka*
5th week	五七日	ごなぬか・なのか	*go-nanuka/nanoka*
6th week	六七日	ろくなぬか・なのか	*roku-nanuka/nanoka*
7th week	七七日	ななゃぬか・なのか	*nana-nanuka/nanoka*
8th week	八七日	はちなぬか・なのか	*hachi-nanuka/nanoka*
9th week	九七日	きゅうなぬか・なのか	*kyuu-nanuka/nanoka*
10th week	十七日	じゅうなぬか・なのか	*juu-nanuka/nanoka*

Irregularities or Special beyond Ten: none
Notes: These are not so much a death *anniversary*, so much as seven-day-periods that follow a persons death. One should probably avoid using this counter for any other week-long periods of time.

Notice also the irregular *first seven days*, *sho-nanoka* rather than *ichi-nanoka*.

鍋—なべ—*nabe*

Japanese: なべ
Romanized: *nabe*
Pattern: 和 I
Used with, or Means: pots, saucepans, see also 釜 (*kama*), see also 口 (*ku*), see also 口 (*kou*), see also 壺 (*tsubo*)

1 pot	一鍋	ひとなべ	*hito-nabe*
2 pots	二鍋	ふたなべ	*futa-nabe*
3 pots	三鍋	さんなべ	*san-nabe*
4 pots	四鍋	よんなべ	*yon-nabe*
5 pots	五鍋	ごなべ	*go-nabe*
6 pots	六鍋	ろくなべ	*roku-nabe*
7 pots	七鍋	ななべ	*nana-nabe*
8 pots	八鍋	はちなべ	*hachi-nabe*
9 pots	九鍋	きゅうなべ	*kyuu-nabe*
10 pots	十鍋	じゅうなべ	*juu-nabe*

Irregularities or Special beyond Ten: none
Notes: none

男 — なん — *nan*

Japanese: なん
Romanized: *nan*
Pattern: 漢 ∅
Used with, or Means: sons (see Notes); boys; brothers

1 son	一男	いちなん	*ichi-nan*
1st son	長男	ちょうなん	*chou-nan*
2 sons	二男	になん	*ni-nan*
2nd son	次男	じなん	*ji-nan*
3 sons	三男	さんなん	*san-nan*
3rd son			
4 sons	四男	よんなん	*yon-nan*
4th son			
5 sons	五男	ごなん	*go-nan*
5th son			
6 sons	六男	ろくなん	*roku-nan*
6th son			
7 sons	七男	しちなん	*shichi-nan*
7th son			
8 sons	八男	はちなん	*hachi-nan*
8th son			
9 sons	九男	きゅうなん	*kyuu-nan*
9th son			
10 sons	十男	じゅうなん	*juu-nan*
10th son			

Irregularities or Special beyond Ten: none
Notes: When counting sons, your first son is your *chou-nan*, and second is *ji-nan*, rather than *ichi-nan* and *ni-nan*.

に—Ni
握り—にぎり—*nigiri*

Japanese: にぎり
Romanized: *nigiri*
Pattern: 和 I
Used with, or Means: objects grasped in the hand, see also 握 (*aku*), see also 掴み (*tsukami*); small, hand-sized balls of rice used for making *nigiri-zushi*

1 grasped object	一握り	ひとにぎり	*hito-nigiri*
2 grasped objects	二握り	ふたにぎり	*futa-nigiri*
3 grasped objects	三握り	さんにぎり	*san-nigiri*
4 grasped objects	四握り	よんにぎり	*yon-nigiri*
5 grasped objects	五握り	ごにぎり	*go-nigiri*
6 grasped objects	六握り	ろくにぎり	*roku-nigiri*
7 grasped objects	七握り	ななにぎり	*nana-nigiri*
8 grasped objects	八握り	はちにぎり	*hachi-nigiri*
9 grasped objects	九握り	きゅうにぎり	*kyuu-nigiri*
10 grasped objects	十握り	じゅうにぎり	*juu-nigiri*

Irregularities or Special beyond Ten: none
Notes: none

人—にん・たり・り—*nin/tari/ri*

Japanese: にん
Romanized: *nin/tari/ri*
Pattern: 漢 ∅ (see Notes)
Used with, or Means: people, persons, human beings, see also 方 (*kata*), see also 名 (*mei*)

1 person	一人	ひとり	*hito-ri*
2 people	二人	ふたり	*futa-ri*
3 people	三人	さんにん みたり	*san-nin* *mi-tari*
4 people	四人	よにん よたり よったり	*yo-nin* *yo-tari* *yot-tari*
5 people	五人	ごにん	*go-nin*
6 people	六人	ろくにん	*roku-nin*
7 people	七人	ななにん	*nana-nin*
8 people	八人	はちにん	*hachi-nin*
9 people	九人	きゅうにん	*kyuu-nin*
10 people	十人	じゅうにん	*juu-nin*

Irregularities or Special beyond Ten: none
Notes: The first two are always *hitori* and *futari*, but beyond ten, they return to *nin*. In several dialects, *yotari* or *yottari* is standard rather than *yo-nin*. *Mitari* is almost never used anymore, but exists, nonetheless.

人組—にんぐみ—*nin-gumi*

Japanese: にんぐみ
Romanized: *nin-gumi*
Pattern: 漢 ∅ (see Notes)
Used with, or Means: N-person group

1-person group	一人組	ひとりぐみ	*hitori-gumi*
2-person group	二人組	ふたりぐみ	*futari-gumi*
3-person group	三人組	さんにんぐみ	*san-nin-gumi*
4-person group	四人組	よにんぐみ	*yo-nin-gumi*
5-person group	五人組	ごにんぐみ	*go-nin-gumi*
6-person group	六人組	ろくにんぐみ	*roku-nin-gumi*
7-person group	七人組	ななにんぐみ	*nana-nin-gumi*
8-person group	八人組	はちにんぐみ	*hachi-nin-gumi*
9-person group	九人組	きゅうにんぐみ	*kyuu-nin-gumi*
10-person group	十人組	じゅうにんぐみ	*juu-nin-gumi*

Irregularities or Special beyond Ten: none

Notes: This counter falls under the same patterns as 人 (*nin*). Incidentally, one *can* have a one-person group. This would come about by dividing a larger group into smaller sub-groups and having a single remaining person. Of course, that person would likely be inserted into one of the others rather than be left by him or herself.

人工 — にんく — *ninku*

Japanese: にんく
Romanized: *ninku*
Pattern: 漢 ∅
Used with, or Means: man-hours (the number of hours someone or a group of people works)

1 man-hour	一人工	いちにんく	*ichi-ninku*
2 man-hours	二人工	ににんく	*ni-ninku*
3 man-hours	三人工	さんにんく	*san-ninku*
4 man-hours	四人工	<u>よにんく</u>	<u>*yo-ninku*</u>
5 man-hours	五人工	ごにんく	*go-ninku*
6 man-hours	六人工	ろくにんく	*roku-ninku*
7 man-hours	七人工	ななにんく	*nana-ninku*
8 man-hours	八人工	はちにんく	*hachi-ninku*
9 man-hours	九人工	きゅうにんく	*kyuu-ninku*
10 man-hours	十人工	じゅうにんく	*juu-ninku*

Irregularities or Special beyond Ten: none
Notes: Notice that it is *ichi-ninku* and *ni-ninku*, NOT *hitoriku* or *futariku*.

人時—にんじ—*ninji*

Japanese: にんじ
Romanized: *ninji*
Pattern: 漢 ∅
Used with, or Means: man-hours (the number of hours someone or a group of people works)

1 man-hour	一人時	いちにんじ	*ichi-ninji*
2 man-hours	二人時	ににんじ	*ni-ninji*
3 man-hours	三人時	さんにんじ	*san-ninji*
4 man-hours	四人時	よにんじ	*yo-ninji*
5 man-hours	五人時	ごにんじ	*go-ninji*
6 man-hours	六人時	ろくにんじ	*roku-ninji*
7 man-hours	七人時	ななにんじ	*nana-ninji*
8 man-hours	八人時	はちにんじ	*hachi-ninji*
9 man-hours	九人時	きゅうにんじ	*kyuu-ninji*
10 man-hours	十人時	じゅうにんじ	*juu-ninji*

Irregularities or Special beyond Ten: none
Notes: Notice that it is *ichi-ninji* and *ni-ninji*, NOT *hitoji* or *futariji*.

人月 — にんげつ — *ningetsu*

Japanese: にんげつ
Romanized: *ningetsu*
Pattern: 漢 ∅
Used with, or Means: man-months (the number of months someone or a group of people works)

1 man-month	一人月	いちにんげつ	*ichi-ningetsu*
2 man-months	二人月	ににんげつ	*ni-ningetsu*
3 man-months	三人月	さんにんげつ	*san-ningetsu*
4 man-months	四人月	よんにんげつ よにんげつ	*yon-ningetsu* <u>*yo-ningetsu*</u>
5 man-months	五人月	ごにんげつ	*go-ningetsu*
6 man-months	六人月	ろくにんげつ	*roku-ningetsu*
7 man-months	七人月	ななにんげつ	*nana-ningetsu*
8 man-months	八人月	はちにんげつ	*hachi-ningetsu*
9 man-months	九人月	きゅうにんげつ	*kyuu-ningetsu*
10 man-months	十人月	じゅうにんげつ	*juu-ningetsu*

Irregularities or Special beyond Ten: none
Notes: Notice that it is *ichi-ningetsu* and *ni-ningetsu*, NOT *hitorigetsu* or *futarigetsu*.

人前—にんまえ—*ninmae*

Japanese: にんまえ
Romanized: *ninmae*
Pattern: 漢 ∅
Used with, or Means: food portions

1 food portion	一人前	いちにんまえ	*ichi-ninmae*
2 food portions	二人前	ににんまえ	*ni-ninmae*
3 food portions	三人前	さんにんまえ	*san-ninmae*
4 food portions	四人前	よんにんまえ よにんまえ	*yon-ninmae* *yo-ninmae*
5 food portions	五人前	ごにんまえ	*go-ninmae*
6 food portions	六人前	ろくにんまえ	*roku-ninmae*
7 food portions	七人前	ななにんまえ	*nana-ninmae*
8 food portions	八人前	はちにんまえ	*hachi-ninmae*
9 food portions	九人前	きゅうにんまえ	*kyuu-ninmae*
10 food portions	十人前	じゅうにんまえ	*juu-ninmae*

Irregularities or Special beyond Ten: none
Notes: Notice that it is *ichi-ninmae* and *ni-ninmae*, NOT *hitorimae* or *futarimae*. 一人前になる (*ichi-ninmae ni naru*) means *to become an adult, succeed,* or *to qualify for a job.* 半人前 (*han-ninmae*) means both *half a food portion* as well as *still a child* or *not fully qualified.*

ぬ—*Nu*
貫き—ぬき—*nuki*

Japanese: ぬき
Romanized: *nuki*
Pattern: 和 I
Used with, or Means: rosary beads, prayer beads (数珠 *juzu*)

1 prayer bead	一貫き	ひとぬき	*hito-nuki*
2 prayer beads	二貫き	ふたぬき	*futa-nuki*
3 prayer beads	三貫き	さんぬき	*san-nuki*
4 prayer beads	四貫き	よんぬき	*yon-nuki*
5 prayer beads	五貫き	ごぬき	*go-nuki*
6 prayer beads	六貫き	ろくぬき	*roku-nuki*
7 prayer beads	七貫き	ななぬき	*nana-nuki*
8 prayer beads	八貫き	はちぬき	*hachi-nuki*
9 prayer beads	九貫き	きゅうぬき	*kyuu-nuki*
10 prayer beads	十貫き	じゅうぬき	*juu-nuki*

Irregularities or Special beyond Ten: none
Notes: none

ね—Ne
ネット—netto

Japanese: ねっと
Romanized: *netto*
Pattern: 和 I or 漢 ∅
Used with, or Means: the number of commodities in a net

1 commodity	1 ネット	ひとねっと いちねっと	*hito-netto* *ichi-netto*
2 commodities	2 ネット	ふたねっと にねっと	*futa-netto* *ni-netto*
3 commodities	3 ネット	さんねっと	*san-netto*
4 commodities	4 ネット	よんねっと	*yon-netto*
5 commodities	5 ネット	ごねっと	*go-netto*
6 commodities	6 ネット	ろくねっと	*roku-netto*
7 commodities	7 ネット	ななねっと	*nana-netto*
8 commodities	8 ネット	はちねっと	*hachi-netto*
9 commodities	9 ネット	きゅうねっと	*kyuu-netto*
10 commodities	10 ネット	じゅうねっと	*juu-netto*

Irregularities or Special beyond Ten: none
Notes: none

年 — ねん — *nen*

Japanese: ねん
Romanized: *nen*
Pattern: 漢 ∅
Used with, or Means: the year

the year 1	一年 元年	いちねん がんねん	*ichi-nen* *gan-nen*
the year 2	二年	にねん	*ni-nen*
the year 3	三年	さんねん	*san-nen*
the year 4	四年	よねん よんねん	*yo-nen* *yon-nen*
the year 5	五年	ごねん	*go-nen*
the year 6	六年	ろくねん	*roku-nen*
the year 7	七年	ななねん しちねん	*nana-nen* *shichi-nen*
the year 8	八年	はちねん	*hachi-nen*
the year 9	九年	きゅうねん	*kyuu-nen*
the year 10	十年	じゅうねん	*juu-nen*

Irregularities or Special beyond Ten: none

Notes: This counter by itself is used to indicate the exact year just as 日 indicates the eact day and 月 (*gatsu*) indicates the exact month, and so forth. What we could call B. C. (*before Christ*) or B. C. E. (*before common era*) is 紀元前 (*kigenzen*); and, A. D. (*anno Domini*) is 西暦 (*seireki*) but C. E. (*common era*) is 紀元 (*kigen*).

The current year (as of writing this book) is 2011 年 (*ni-sen-juu-ichi-nen*).

Japanese Years *vs.* the Gregorian Calendar

The Japanese have two methods for indicating a year: the emperor's reign system and the Gregorian system. Under the first system, each new emperor's reign constitutes a new period or era. The current era, 平成 (*Heisei*) began on January 8, 1986, whilst the previous era, 昭和 (*Shouwa*) ended on January 7, 1986 with Hirohito's death. This means that 1986 corresponds to both *Shouwa* 64 *and Heisei* 1.

When writing a year in Japanese, simply place the 年 (*nen*) character after the year number. Thus, 2010 年 (*ni-sen-juu-nen*) means *the year 2010*. Typically, Gregorian years are written with Arabic numerals in stead of *kanji*. However, if you are going to use the Japanese system, you must precede it with the era name as well: 平成二十四年 (*Heisei ni-juu-yon-nen*) means *the 24th year of Heisei*.

The Modern Era for Japan began in 1868, which saw the Meiji Restoration during the *Meiji* (明治) period. The *Meiji* period ended July 30, 1912. Japan's next modern period, beginning on July 31, 1912 was the *Taishou* (大正) period. The *Taishou* period ended on December 25, 1926. The *Shouwa* period began on December 26, 1926. Traditionally, the first year of a period is not *ichi-nen* but 元年 (*gan-nen*). Thus:

- 明治元年〜明治 45 年—October 23, 1868 〜 July 30, 1912
- 大正元年〜大正 15 年—July 31, 1912 〜 December 25, 1926
- 昭和元年〜昭和 64 年—December 26, 1926 〜 January 7, 1986
- 平成元年〜Present—January 8, 1986 〜 Present

When you fill out official forms in Japanese, you will often see something like this to indicate your year of birth:

| 明 大 | 年 |
| 昭 平 | |

Thus, you would circle the *kanji* corresponding to the period in which you were born; and, in the second box, you put the number of the year. As you can see here, 明 (*mei*) stands for 明治 (*Meiji*), 大 (*tai*) stands for 大正 (*Taishou*), 昭 (*shou*) stands for 昭和 (*Shouwa*), and 平 (*hei*) stands for 平成 (*Heisei*). For example, one might write . . .

| 明 大 | 55 年 |
| (昭) 平 | |

. . . indicating that one was born in the 55th year of *Shouwa*.

年間—ねんかん—nen-kan

Japanese: ねんかん
Romanized: *nen-kan*
Pattern: 漢 ∅
Used with, or Means: years

1 year	一年間	いちねんかん	*ichi-nen-kan*
2 years	二年間	にねんかん	*ni-nen-kan*
3 years	三年間	さんねんかん	*san-nen-kan*
4 years	四年間	よねんかん よんねんかん	*yo-nen-kan* *yon-nen-kan*
5 years	五年間	ごねんかん	*go-nen-kan*
6 years	六年間	ろくねんかん	*roku-nen-kan*
7 years	七年間	ななねんかん しちねんかん	*nana-nen-kan* *shichi-nen-kan*
8 years	八年間	はちねんかん	*hachi-nen-kan*
9 years	九年間	きゅうねんかん	*kyuu-nen-kan*
10 years	十年間	じゅうねんかん	*juu-nen-kan*

Irregularities or Special beyond Ten: none
Notes: none

年生—ねんせい—*nensei*

Japanese: ねんせい
Romanized: *nensei*
Pattern: 漢 ∅
Used with, or Means: N^(th)-grader, N^(th)-grade student, N^(th)-year student

1st grader	一年生	いちねんせい	*ichi-nensei*
2nd grader	二年生	にねんせい	*ni-nensei*
3rd grader	三年生	さんねんせい	*san-nensei*
4th grader	四年生	よねんせい よんねんせい	*yo-nensei* *yon-nensei*
5th grader	五年生	ごねんせい	*go-nensei*
6th grader	六年生	ろくねんせい	*roku-nensei*
7th grader	七年生	ななねんせい しちねんせい	*nana-nensei* *shichi-nensei*
8th grader	八年生	はちねんせい	*hachi-nensei*
9th grader	九年生	きゅうねんせい	*kyuu-nensei*
10th grader	十年生	じゅうねんせい	*juu-nensei*

Irregularities or Special beyond Ten: none
Notes: none

年代—ねんだい—*nendai*

Japanese: ねんだい
Romanized: *nendai*
Pattern: 漢 ∅
Used with, or Means: N-year-long period

1-year-long period	一年代	いちねんだい	*ichi-nendai*
2-year-long period	二年代	にねんだい	*ni-nendai*
3-year-long period	三年代	さんねんだい	*san-nendai*
4-year-long period	四年代	よねんだい よんねんだい	*yo-nendai* *yon-nendai*
5-year-long period	五年代	ごねんだい	*go-nendai*
6-year-long period	六年代	ろくねんだい	*roku-nendai*
7-year-long period	七年代	ななねんだい しちねんだい	*nana-nendai* *shichi-nendai*
8-year-long period	八年代	はちねんだい	*hachi-nendai*
9-year-long period	九年代	きゅうねんだい	*kyuu-nendai*
10-year-long period	十年代	じゅうねんだい	*juu-nendai*

Irregularities or Special beyond Ten: none
Notes: none

の —— No
幅・布 —— の —— no

Japanese: の
Romanized: *no*
Pattern: 和 I
Used with, or Means: *no*, a unit of area for cloth

1 *no*	一幅・布	ひとの	*hito-no*
2 *no*	二幅・布	ふたの	*futa-no*
3 *no*	三幅・布	さんの	*san-no*
4 *no*	四幅・布	よんの	*yon-no*
5 *no*	五幅・布	ごの	*go-no*
6 *no*	六幅・布	ろくの	*roku-no*
7 *no*	七幅・布	ななの	*nana-no*
8 *no*	八幅・布	はちの	*hachi-no*
9 *no*	九幅・布	きゅうの	*kyuu-no*
10 *no*	十幅・布	じゅうの	*juu-no*

Irregularities or Special beyond Ten: none
Notes: none

能 — のう — *nou*

Japanese: のう
Romanized: *nou*
Pattern: 漢 ∅
Used with, or Means: (polite) technical skills, abilities, capacities, talents, see also 芸 (*gei*)

1 talent	一能	いちのう	*ichi-nou*
2 talents	二能	にのう	*ni-nou*
3 talents	三能	さんのう	*san-nou*
4 talents	四能	よんのう	*yon-nou*
5 talents	五能	ごのう	*go-nou*
6 talents	六能	ろくのう	*roku-nou*
7 talents	七能	ななのう	*nana-nou*
8 talents	八能	はちのう	*hachi-nou*
9 talents	九能	きゅうのう	*kyuu-nou*
10 talents	十能	じゅうのう	*juu-nou*

Irregularities or Special beyond Ten: none
Notes: none

kn—ノット—*notto*

Japanese: ノット
Romanized: *notto*
Pattern: 漢 ∅
Used with, or Means: knots, (symbol: kn), nautical miles, a unit of length, 6,076.116 ft/1,852 m

1 kn	1ノット	いちのっと	*ichi-notto*
2 kn	2ノット	にのっと	*ni-notto*
3 kn	3ノット	さんのっと	*san-notto*
4 kn	4ノット	よんのっと	*yon-notto*
5 kn	5ノット	ごのっと	*go-notto*
6 kn	6ノット	ろくのっと	*roku-notto*
7 kn	7ノット	ななのっと	*nana-notto*
8 kn	8ノット	はちのっと	*hachi-notto*
9 kn	9ノット	きゅうのっと	*kyuu-notto*
10 kn	10ノット	じゅうのっと	*juu-notto*

Irregularities or Special beyond Ten: none
Notes: none

は・ば・ぱ—Ha/Ba/Pa
波—は—ha

Japanese: は
Romanized: ha
Pattern: 漢 H
Used with, or Means: waves, ripples, *tsunami*, tidal waves; air-raids, parades, events occurring in waves

1 wave	一波	いっぱ	ip-pa
2 waves	二波	には	ni-ha
3 waves	三波	さんば	sam-pa
4 waves	四波	よんは / よんば	yon-ha / yom-pa
5 waves	五波	ごは	go-ha
6 waves	六波	ろっぱ / ろくは	rop-pa / roku-ha
7 waves	七波	ななは	nana-ha
8 waves	八波	はっぱ / はちは	hap-pa / hachi-ha
9 waves	九波	きゅうは	kyuu-ha
10 waves	十波	じゅっぱ / じっぱ	jup-pa / jip-pa

Irregularities or Special beyond Ten:

100 waves	百波	ひゃっぱ	hyap-pa
1,000 waves	千波	せんば	sem-pa
10,000 waves	万波	まんば	mam-pa
how many waves?	何波	なんば	nam-pa

Notes: none

派 — は — ha

Japanese: は
Romanized: *ha*
Pattern: 漢 H
Used with, or Means: schools of thought; political factions, political party; sect; group

1 faction	一派	いっぱ	*ip-pa*
2 factions	二派	には	*ni-ha*
3 factions	三派	さんぱ	*sam-pa*
4 factions	四派	よんは / よんぱ	*yon-ha* / *yom-pa*
5 factions	五派	ごは	*go-ha*
6 factions	六派	ろっぱ / ろくは	*rop-pa* / *roku-ha*
7 factions	七派	ななは	*nana-ha*
8 factions	八派	はっぱ / はちは	*hap-pa* / *hachi-ha*
9 factions	九派	きゅうは	*kyuu-ha*
10 factions	十派	じゅっぱ / じっぱ	*jup-pa* / *jip-pa*

Irregularities or Special beyond Ten:

100 factions	百派	ひゃっぱ	*hyap-pa*
1,000 factions	千派	せんぱ	*sem-pa*
10,000 factions	万派	まんぱ	*mam-pa*
how many factions?	何派	なんぱ	*nam-pa*

Notes: none

場—ば—ba

Jabanese: ば
Romanized: *ba*
Battern: 漢 ∅
Used with, or Means: scenes, acts of a play, see also 齣 (*koma*), see also 幕 (*maku*)

1 scene	一場	いちば	*ichi-ba*
2 scenes	二場	にば	*ni-ba*
3 scenes	三場	さんば	*sam-ba*
4 scenes	四場	よんば	*yom-ba*
5 scenes	五場	ごば	*go-ba*
6 scenes	六場	ろくば	*roku-ba*
7 scenes	七場	ななば	*nana-ba*
8 scenes	八場	はちば	*hachi-ba*
9 scenes	九場	きゅうば	*kyuu-ba*
10 scenes	十場	じゅうば	*juu-ba*

Irregularities or Special beyond Ten: none
Notes: none

％ — パーセント — *paasento*

Japanese: パーセント
Romanized: *paasento*
Pattern: 漢 ∅ or 漢 P
Used with, or Means: *per cent* (symbol: %)

1%	1パーセント	いちぱあせんと いっぱあせんと	*ichi-paasento* *ip-paasento*
2%	2パーセント	にぱあせんと	*ni-paasento*
3%	3パーセント	さんぱあせんと	*sam-paasento*
4%	4パーセント	よんぱあせんと	*yom-paasento*
5%	5パーセント	ごぱあせんと	*go-paasento*
6%	6パーセント	ろくぱあせんと ろっぱあせんと	*roku-paasento* *rop-paasento*
7%	7パーセント	ななぱあせんと	*nana-paasento*
8%	8パーセント	はちぱあせんと はっぱあせんと	*hachi-paasento* *hap-paasento*
9%	9パーセント	きゅうぱあせんと	*kyuu-paasento*
10%	10パーセント	じゅうぱあせんと	*juu-paasento*

Irregularities or Special beyond Ten:

100%	100パーセント	ひゃくぱあせんと ひゃっぱあせんと	*hyaku-paasento* *hyap-paasento*

Notes: none

฿ —バーツ— *baatsu*

Japanese: バーツ
Romanized: *baatsu*
Pattern: 漢 ∅
Used with, or Means: *Baht*, Thai monetary unit (symbol: ฿)

1 ฿	1 バーツ	いちばあつ	*ichi-baatsu*
2 ฿	2 バーツ	にばあつ	*ni-baatsu*
3 ฿	3 バーツ	さんばあつ	*sam-baatsu*
4 ฿	4 バーツ	よんばあつ	*yom-baatsu*
5 ฿	5 バーツ	ごばあつ	*go-baatsu*
6 ฿	6 バーツ	ろくばあつ	*roku-baatsu*
7 ฿	7 バーツ	ななばあつ	*nana-baatsu*
8 ฿	8 バーツ	はちばあつ	*hachi-baatsu*
9 ฿	9 バーツ	きゅうばあつ	*kyuu-baatsu*
10 ฿	10 バーツ	じゅうばあつ	*juu-baatsu*

Irregularities or Special beyond Ten: none
Notes: none

杯・盃—はい—*hai*

Japanese: はい
Romanized: *hai*
Pattern: 漢 H
Used with, or Means: glassfuls, cupfuls, bowlfuls, spoonfuls, containersful, drinks, see also 掬 (*kiku*), see also 掬い (*sukui*); squid, octopi, cuttlefish, see also 匹 (*hiki*); ships

1 glassful	一杯・盃	いっぱい	*ip-pai*
2 glassfuls	二杯・盃	にはい	*ni-hai*
3 glassfuls	三杯・盃	さんばい / さんぱい	*sam-bai* / *sam-pai*
4 glassfuls	四杯・盃	よんはい / よんぱい	*yon-hai* / *yom-pai*
5 glassfuls	五杯・盃	ごはい	*go-hai*
6 glassfuls	六杯・盃	ろっぱい	*rop-pai*
7 glassfuls	七杯・盃	ななはい	*nana-hai*
8 glassfuls	八杯・盃	はっぱい	*hap-pai*
9 glassfuls	九杯・盃	きゅうはい	*kyuu-hai*
10 glassfuls	十杯・盃	じゅっぱい / じっぱい	*jup-pai* / *jip-pai*

Irregularities or Special beyond Ten:

100 glassfuls	百杯・盃	ひゃっぱい	*hyap-pai*
1,000 glassfuls	千杯・盃	せんばい / せんぱい	*sem-bai* / *sem-pai*
10,000 glassfuls	万杯・盃	まんばい / まんぱい	*mam-bai* / *mam-pai*
how many glassfuls?	何杯・盃	なんばい / なんぱい	*nam-bai* / *nam-pai*

Notes: none

敗 — はい — *hai*

Japanese: はい
Romanized: *hai*
Pattern: 漢 H
Used with, or Means: defeats, failures

1 defeat	一敗	いっぱい	*ip-pai*
2 defeats	二敗	にはい	*ni-hai*
3 defeats	三敗	さんぱい	*sam-pai*
4 defeats	四敗	よんはい よんぱい	*yon-hai* *yom-pai*
5 defeats	五敗	ごはい	*go-hai*
6 defeats	六敗	ろっぱい ろくはい	*rop-pai* *roku-hai*
7 defeats	七敗	ななはい	*nana-hai*
8 defeats	八敗	はっぱい はちはい	*hap-pai* *hachi-hai*
9 defeats	九敗	きゅうはい	*kyuu-hai*
10 defeats	十敗	じゅっぱい じっぱい	*jup-pai* *jip-pai*

Irregularities or Special beyond Ten:

100 defeats	百敗	ひゃっぱい	*hyap-pai*
1,000 defeats	千敗	せんぱい	*sem-pai*
10,000 defeats	万敗	まんぱい	*mam-pai*
how many defeats?	何敗	なんぱい	*nam-pai*

Notes: none

貝—ばい—*bai*

Japanese: ばい
Romanized: *bai*
Pattern: 漢 ∅
Used with, or Means: doses of ointment, same as 貝 (*kai*)

1 dose	一貝	いちばい	*ichi-bai*
2 doses	二貝	にばい	*ni-bai*
3 doses	三貝	さんばい	*sam-bai*
4 doses	四貝	よんばい	*yom-bai*
5 doses	五貝	ごばい	*go-bai*
6 doses	六貝	ろくばい	*roku-bai*
7 doses	七貝	ななばい	*nana-bai*
8 doses	八貝	はちばい	*hachi-bai*
9 doses	九貝	きゅうばい	*kyuu-bai*
10 doses	十貝	じゅうばい	*juu-bai*

Irregularities or Special beyond Ten: none
Notes: none

倍—ばい—*bai*

Japanese: ばい
Romanized: *bai*
Pattern: 漢 ∅
Used with, or Means: multiples of N, N times as much/many, N-fold

1-fold	一倍	いちばい	*ichi-bai*
2-fold	二倍	にばい	*ni-bai*
3-fold	三倍	さんばい	*sam-bai*
4-fold	四倍	よんばい	*yom-bai*
5-fold	五倍	ごばい	*go-bai*
6-fold	六倍	ろくばい	*roku-bai*
7-fold	七倍	ななばい	*nana-bai*
8-fold	八倍	はちばい	*hachi-bai*
9-fold	九倍	きゅうばい	*kyuu-bai*
10-fold	十倍	じゅうばい	*juu-bai*

Irregularities or Special beyond Ten: none
Notes: none

バイト—*baito*

Japanese: ばいと
Romanized: *baito*
Pattern: 漢 ∅
Used with, or Means: bytes (symbol: B), 8 bits

1 bytes	1バイト	いちばいと	*ichi-baito*
2 bytes	2バイト	にばいと	*ni-baito*
3 bytes	3バイト	さんばいと	*sam-baito*
4 bytes	4バイト	よんばいと	*yom-baito*
5 bytes	5バイト	ごばいと	*go-baito*
6 bytes	6バイト	ろくばいと	*roku-baito*
7 bytes	7バイト	ななばいと	*nana-baito*
8 bytes	8バイト	はちばいと	*hachi-baito*
9 bytes	9バイト	きゅうばいと	*kyuu-baito*
10 bytes	10バイト	じゅうばいと	*juu-baito*

Irregularities or Special beyond Ten: none
Notes: none

拍 — はく — *haku*

Japanese: はく
Romanized: *haku*
Pattern: 漢 H
Used with, or Means: musical beats; syllables in a word, *morae*[14]

1 syllable	一拍	いっぱく	*ip-paku*
2 syllables	二拍	にはく	*ni-haku*
3 syllables	三拍	さんぱく	*sam-paku*
4 syllables	四拍	よんはく / よんぱく	*yon-haku* / *yom-paku*
5 syllables	五拍	ごはく	*go-haku*
6 syllables	六拍	ろっぱく / ろくはく	*rop-paku* / *roku-haku*
7 syllables	七拍	ななはく	*nana-haku*
8 syllables	八拍	はっぱく / はちはく	*hap-paku* / *hachi-haku*
9 syllables	九拍	きゅうはく	*kyuu-haku*
10 syllables	十拍	じゅっぱく / じっぱく	*jup-paku* / *jip-paku*

Irregularities or Special beyond Ten:

100 syllables	百拍	ひゃっぱく	*hyap-paku*
1,000 syllables	千拍	せんぱく	*sem-paku*
10,000 syllables	万拍	まんぱく	*mam-paku*
how many syllables?	何拍	なんぱく	*nam-paku*

Notes: none

---

[14] A *mora* (plural: *morae*), from the Latin word for *linger* or *delay*, is, according to linguist James D. McCawley, *Something of which a long syllable consists of two and a short syllable consists of one.*

泊 — はく — *haku*

Japanese: はく
Romanized: *haku*
Pattern: 漢 H
Used with, or Means: night's stays, see also 宿 (*shuku*)

1 night's stay	一泊	いっぱく	*ip-paku*
2 nights' stay	二泊	にはく	*ni-haku*
3 nights' stay	三泊	さんぱく	*sam-paku*
4 nights' stay	四泊	よんはく / よんぱく	*yon-haku* / *yom-paku*
5 nights' stay	五泊	ごはく	*go-haku*
6 nights' stay	六泊	ろっぱく / ろくはく	*rop-paku* / *roku-haku*
7 nights' stay	七泊	ななはく	*nana-haku*
8 nights' stay	八泊	はっぱく / はちはく	*hap-paku* / *hachi-haku*
9 nights' stay	九泊	きゅうはく	*kyuu-haku*
10 nights' stay	十泊	じゅっぱく / じっぱく	*jup-paku* / *jip-paku*

Irregularities or Special beyond Ten:

100 nights' stay	百泊	ひゃっぱく	*hyap-paku*
1,000 nights' stay	千泊	せんぱく	*sem-paku*
10,000 nights' stay	万泊	まんぱく	*mam-paku*
how many nights' stay?	何泊	なんぱく	*nam-paku*

Notes: none

刷毛—はけ—*hake*

Japanese: はけ
Romanized: *hake*
Pattern: 和 II or 和 I
Used with, or Means: coats of paint

1 coat of paint	一刷毛	ひとはけ	*hito-hake*
2 coats of paint	二刷毛	ふたはけ	*futa-hake*
3 coats of paint	三刷毛	みはけ さんはけ	*mi-hake* *san-hake*
4 coats of paint	四刷毛	よはけ よんはけ	*yo-hake* *yon-hake*
5 coats of paint	五刷毛	ごはけ	*go-hake*
6 coats of paint	六刷毛	ろくぱけ ろくはけ	*rop-hake* *roku-hake*
7 coats of paint	七刷毛	ななはけ	*nana-hake*
8 coats of paint	八刷毛	はっぱけ はちはけ	*hap-pake* *hachi-hake*
9 coats of paint	九刷毛	きゅうはけ	*kyuu-hake*
10 coats of paint	十刷毛	じゅっぱけ じっぱけ じゅうはけ	*jup-pake* *jip-pake* *juu-hake*

Irregularities or Special beyond Ten:

100 coats of paint	百泊	ひゃっぱけ ひゃくはけ	*hyap-pake* *hyaku-hake*
1,000 coats of paint	千泊	せんはけ	*sen-hake*
10,000 coats of paint	万泊	まんはけ	*man-hake*
how many coats of paint?	何泊	なんぱけ なんはけ	*nam-pake* *nan-hake*

Notes: none

箱―はこ―*hako*

Japanese: はこ
Romanized: *hako*
Pattern: 和 III-H
Used with, or Means: boxes, boxfuls, see also 折り (*ori*) for catered boxed lunches (仕出し弁当 *shidashi bentou*)

1 box	一箱	ひとはこ	*hito-hako*
2 boxes	二箱	ふたはこ	*futa-hako*
3 boxes	三箱	みはこ さんぱこ or さんはこ	*mi-hako* *sam-pako* or *san-hako*
4 boxes	四箱	よんはこ よはこ or よんぱこ	*yon-hako* *yo-hako* or *yom-pako*
5 boxes	五箱	ごはこ	*go-hako*
6 boxes	六箱	ろっぱこ or ろくはこ	*rop-pako* or *roku-hako*
7 boxes	七箱	ななはこ	*nana-hako*
8 boxes	八箱	はっぱこ or はちはこ	*hap-pako* or *hachi-hako*
9 boxes	九箱	きゅうはこ	*kyuu-hako*
10 boxes	十箱	じゅっぱこ or じっぱこ じゅうはこ or とおはこ	*jup-pako* or *jip-pako* *juu-hako* or *too-hako*

Irregularities or Special beyond Ten:

100 boxes	百箱	ひゃっぱこ or ひゃくはこ	*hyap-pako* or *hyaku-hako*
1,000 boxes	千箱	せんぱこ	*sem-pako*
10,000 boxes	万箱	まんぱこ	*man-hako*
how many boxes?	何箱	なんぱこ or なんはこ	*nam-bako* or *nan-hako*

Notes: none

箸 — はし — *hashi*

Japanese: はし
Romanized: *hashi*
Pattern: 和 I-H
Used with, or Means: bites of food, mouthfuls of food

1 mouthful	一箸	ひとはし	*hito-hashi*
2 mouthfuls	二箸	ふたはし	*futa-hashi*
3 mouthfuls	三箸	さんばし	*sam-bashi*
4 mouthfuls	四箸	よんはし よんばし	*yon-hashi* *yom-bashi*
5 mouthfuls	五箸	ごはし	*go-hashi*
6 mouthfuls	六箸	ろっぱし ろくはし	*rop-pashi* *roku-hashi*
7 mouthfuls	七箸	ななはし	*nana-hashi*
8 mouthfuls	八箸	はっぱし はちはし	*hap-pashi* *hachi-hashi*
9 mouthfuls	九箸	きゅうはし	*kyuu-hashi*
10 mouthfuls	十箸	じゅっぱし じっぱし じゅうはし	*jup-pashi* *jip-pashi* *juu-hashi*

Irregularities or Special beyond Ten:

100 mouthfuls	百箸	ひゃっぱし ひゃくはし	*hyap-pashi* *hyaku-hashi*
1,000 mouthfuls	千箸	せんばし せんばし	*sem-bashi* *sem-pashi*
10,000 mouthfuls	万箸	まんばし	*mam-bashi*
how many mouthfuls?	何箸	なんばし	*nam-bashi*

Notes: none

場所—ばしょ—*basho*

Japanese: ばしょ
Romanized: *basho*
Pattern: 和 I
Used with, or Means: places, locations, see also ヶ所 (*kasho*)

1 place	一場所	ひとばしょ	*hito-basho*
2 places	二場所	ふたばしょ	*futa-basho*
3 places	三場所	さんばしょ	*sam-basho*
4 places	四場所	よんばしょ	*yom-basho*
5 places	五場所	ごばしょ	*go-basho*
6 places	六場所	ろくばしょ	*roku-basho*
7 places	七場所	ななばしょ	*nana-basho*
8 places	八場所	はちばしょ	*hachi-basho*
9 places	九場所	きゅうばしょ	*kyuu-basho*
10 places	十場所	じゅうばしょ	*juu-basho*

Irregularities or Special beyond Ten: none
Notes: none

柱 — はしら — *hashira*

Japanese: はしら
Romanized: *hashira*
Pattern: 和 ∅
Used with, or Means: gods, god-bodies (神体 *shintai*), statues of gods, images of gods; Buddhist mortuary tablets, ashes, remains of the deceased; spirits of the war dead (英霊 *eirei*), great men (英霊 *eirei*), high-class people

1 god	一柱	ひとはしら	*hito-hashira*
2 gods	二柱	ふたはしら	*futa-hashira*
3 gods	三柱	さんはしら さんばしら	*san-hashira* *sam-bashira*
4 gods	四柱	よんはしら よんばしら	*yon-hashira* *yom-bashira*
5 gods	五柱	ごはしら	*go-hashira*
6 gods	六柱	ろくはしら	*roku-hashira*
7 gods	七柱	ななはしら	*nana-hashira*
8 gods	八柱	はちはしら	*hachi-hashira*
9 gods	九柱	きゅうはしら	*kyuu-hashira*
10 gods	十柱	じゅうはしら	*juu-hashira*

Irregularities or Special beyond Ten: none
Notes: none

馬身―ばしん―*bashin*

Japanese: ばしん
Romanized: *bashin*
Pattern: 漢 ∅
Used with, or Means: the difference in a horse's size, horse lengths in horse racing

1 length	一馬身	いちばしん	*ichi-bashin*
2 lengths	二馬身	にばしん	*ni-bashin*
3 lengths	三馬身	さんばしん	*sam-bashin*
4 lengths	四馬身	よんばしん	*yom-bashin*
5 lengths	五馬身	ごばしん	*go-bashin*
6 lengths	六馬身	ろくばしん	*roku-bashin*
7 lengths	七馬身	ななばしん	*nana-bashin*
8 lengths	八馬身	はちばしん	*hachi-bashin*
9 lengths	九馬身	きゅうばしん	*kyuu-bashin*
10 lengths	十馬身	じゅうばしん	*juu-bashin*

Irregularities or Special beyond Ten: none
Notes: none

鉢 — はち — *hachi*

Japanese: はち
Romanized: *hachi*
Pattern: 和 I-H
Used with, or Means: potted plants, *bonsai* trees; bowls

1 *bonsai* tree	一鉢	ひとはち	*hito-hachi*
2 *bonsai* trees	二鉢	ふたはち	*futa-hachi*
3 *bonsai* trees	三鉢	さんばち	*sam-bachi*
4 *bonsai* trees	四鉢	よんはち / よんばち	*yon-hachi* / *yom-bachi*
5 *bonsai* trees	五鉢	ごはち	*go-hachi*
6 *bonsai* trees	六鉢	ろっぱち / ろくはち	*rop-pachi* / *roku-hachi*
7 *bonsai* trees	七鉢	ななはち	*nana-hachi*
8 *bonsai* trees	八鉢	はっぱち / はちはち	*hap-pachi* / *hachi-hachi*
9 *bonsai* trees	九鉢	きゅうはち	*kyuu-hachi*
10 *bonsai* trees	十鉢	じゅっぱち / じっぱち / じゅうはち	*jup-pachi* / *jip-pachi* / *juu-hachi*

Irregularities or Special beyond Ten:

100 *bonsai* trees	100 鉢	ひゃっぱち / ひゃくはち	*hyap-pachi* / *hyaku-hachi*
1,000 *bonsai* trees	1,000 鉢	せんばち or せんはち	*sem-bachi* or *sen-hachi*
10,000 *bonsai* trees	10,000 鉢	まんばち or まんはち	*mam-bachi* or *man-hachi*
how many *bonsai* trees?	何鉢	なんばち or なんはち	*nam-bachi* or *nan-hachi*

Notes: none

発—はつ—*hatsu*

Japanese: はつ
Romanized: *hatsu*
Pattern: 漢 H
Used with, or Means: arrows loosed, shots fired, explosions, fireworks explosions; strikes in decisive games; orgasms, ejaculations, sex acts

1 shot	一発	いっぱつ	*ip-patsu*
2 shots	二発	にはつ	*ni-hatsu*
3 shots	三発	さんぱつ	*sam-patsu*
4 shots	四発	よんはつ / よんぱつ	*yon-hatsu* / *yom-patsu*
5 shots	五発	ごはつ	*go-hatsu*
6 shots	六発	ろっぱつ / ろくはつ	*rop-patsu* / *roku-hatsu*
7 shots	七発	ななはつ	*nana-hatsu*
8 shots	八発	はっぱつ / はちはつ	*hap-patsu* / *hachi-hatsu*
9 shots	九発	きゅうはつ	*kyuu-hatsu*
10 shots	十発	じゅっぱつ / じっぱつ	*jup-patsu* / *jip-patsu*

Irregularities or Special beyond Ten:

100 shots	百発	ひゃっぱつ	*hyap-patsu*
1,000 shots	千発	せんぱつ	*sem-patsu*
10,000 shots	万発	まんばつ	*mam-batsu*
how many shots?	何発	なんばつ	*nam-patsu*

Notes: none

パック —*pakku*

Japanese: ぱっく
Romanized: *pakku*
Pattern: 和 I-P or 漢 P
Used with, or Means: commodities sealed in plastic packs, see also 袋 (*fukuro*), see also 枚 (*mai*); a unit of commodities being sold (for example, a pack of playing cards), see also 個 (*ko*)

1 pack	1 パック	ひとぱっく / いっぱっく / いちぱっく	*hito-pakku* / *ip-pakku* / *ichi-pakku*
2 packs	2 パック	にぱっく	*ni-pakku*
3 packs	3 パック	さんぱっく	*sam-pakku*
4 packs	4 パック	よんぱっく	*yom-pakku*
5 packs	5 パック	ごぱっく	*go-pakku*
6 packs	6 パック	ろっぱっく / ろくぱっく	*rop-pakku* / *roku-pakku*
7 packs	7 パック	ななぱっく	*nana-pakku*
8 packs	8 パック	はっぱっく / はちぱっく	*hap-pakku* / *hachi-pakku*
9 packs	9 パック	きゅうぱっく	*kyuu-pakku*
10 packs	10 パック	じゅっぱっく / じっぱっく	*jup-pakku* / *jip-pakku*

Irregularities or Special beyond Ten:

100 packs	100 パック	ひゃっぱっく / ひゃくぱっく	*hyap-pakku* / *hyaku-pakku*

Notes: none

刎——はね——*hane*

Japanese: はね
Romanized: *hane*
Pattern: 和 I-H
Used with, or Means: formerly used for counting enemy helmets (兜 *kabuto*)

1 helmet	一刎	ひとはね	*hito-hane*
2 helmets	二刎	ふたはね	*futa-hane*
3 helmets	三刎	さんばね	*sam-bane*
4 helmets	四刎	よんはね or よんばね	*yon-hane* or *yom-bane*
5 helmets	五刎	ごはね	*go-hane*
6 helmets	六刎	ろっぱね or ろくはね	*rop-pane* or *roku-hane*
7 helmets	七刎	ななはね	*nana-hane*
8 helmets	八刎	はっぱね or はちはね	*hap-pane* or *hachi-hane*
9 helmets	九刎	きゅうはね	*kyuu-hane*
10 helmets	十刎	じゅっぱね じっぱね	*jup-pane* *jip-pane*

Irregularities or Special beyond Ten:

100 helmets	百刎	ひゃっぱね or ひゃくはね	*hyap-pane* or *hyaku-hane*
1,000 helmets	千刎	せんばね or せんはね	*sem-bane* or *sen-hane*
10,000 helmets	万刎	まんばね or まんはね	*mam-bane* or *man-hane*
how many helmets?	何刎	なんばね or なんはね	*nam-bane* or *nan-hane*

Notes: none

腹・肚——はら——*hara*

Japarase: はら
Romanized: *hara*
Pattern: 和 I-H
Used with, or Means: pots, jars, jugs, vats, urns, vases; one fish-belly's worth of codfish roe (鱈子 *tarako*), caviar; a single instance of a bird's or reptile's egg-laying (鰐の一腹で16個の卵を産卵する *wani no hito-hara de juu-rok-ko no tamago o sanran suru* an alligator lays 16 eggs at a time)

1 jar	一腹・肚	ひとはら		*hito-hara*
2 jars	二腹・肚	ふたはら		*futa-hara*
3 jars	三腹・肚	さんばら or さんはら		*sam-bara* or *san-hara*
4 jars	四腹・肚	よんはら or よんばら		*yon-hara* or *yom-bara*
5 jars	五腹・肚	ごはら		*go-hara*
6 jars	六腹・肚	ろっぱら or ろくはら		*rop-para* or *roku-hara*
7 jars	七腹・肚	ななはら		*nana-hara*
8 jars	八腹・肚	はっぱら or はちはら		*hap-para* or *hachi-hara*
9 jars	九腹・肚	きゅうはら		*kyuu-hara*
10 jars	十腹・肚	じゅっぱら or じっぱら じゅうはら or じゅうばら		*jup-para* or *jip-para* *juu-hara* or *juu-bara*

Irregularities or Special beyond Ten:

100 jars	百腹・肚	ひゃっぱら or ひゃくはら		*hyap-para* or *hyaku-hara*
1,000 jars	千腹・肚	せんばら or せんはら		*sem-bara* or *sen-hara*
10,000 jars	万腹・肚	まんばら or まんはら		*mam-bara* or *man-hara*
how many jars?	何腹・肚	なんばら or なんはら		*nam-bara* or *nan-hara*

Notes: none

針 — はり — *hari*

Japanese: はり
Romanized: *hari*
Pattern: 和 I-H
Used with, or Means: stitches, seams, surgical stitches; net meshes, see also 針 (*shin*) for professional/technical usage

1 stitch	一針	ひとはり	*hito-hari*
2 stitches	二針	ふたはり	*futa-hari*
3 stitches	三針	さんばり or さんはり	*sam-bari* or *san-hari*
4 stitches	四針	よんはり or よんばり	*yon-hari* or *yom-bari*
5 stitches	五針	ごはり	*go-hari*
6 stitches	六針	ろっぱり or ろくはり	*rop-pari* or *roku-hari*
7 stitches	七針	ななはり	*nana-hari*
8 stitches	八針	はっぱり or はちはり	*hap-pari* or *hachi-hari*
9 stitches	九針	きゅうはり	*kyuu-hari*
10 stitches	十針	じゅっぱり or じっぱり じゅうはり or じゅうばり	*jup-pari* or *jip-pari* *juu-hari* or *juu-bari*

Irregularities or Special beyond Ten:

100 stitches	百針	ひゃっぱり or ひゃくはり	*hyap-pari* or *hyaku-hari*
1,000 stitches	千針	せんばり or せんはり	*sem-bari* or *sen-hari*
10,000 stitches	万針	まんばり or まんはり	*mam-bari* or *man-hari*
how many stitches?	何針	なんばり or なんはり	*nam-bari* or *nan-hari*

Notes: none

張り —はり— *hari*

Japanese: はり
Romanized: *hari*
Pattern: 和 I-H
Used with, or Means: coverings draped, stretched over a frame: tents, mosquito nets, paper lanterns, umbrellas; (violin) bows, (guitar) strings, stringed instruments, see also 本 (*hon*); (archery) bows, see also 張 (*chou*), see also 挺・丁 (*chou*); *koto* (Chinese, seven-stringed zither), see also 張 (*chou*), see also 面 (*men*)

1 bow	一張り	ひとはり	*hito-hari*
2 bows	二張り	ふたはり	*futa-hari*
3 bows	三張り	さんばり or さんはり	*sam-bari* or *san-hari*
4 bows	四張り	よんはり or よんばり	*yon-hari* or *yom-bari*
5 bows	五張り	ごはり	*go-hari*
6 bows	六張り	ろっぱり or ろくはり	*rop-pari* or *roku-hari*
7 bows	七張り	ななはり	*nana-hari*
8 bows	八張り	はっぱり or はちはり	*hap-pari* or *hachi-hari*
9 bows	九張り	きゅうはり	*kyuu-hari*
10 bows	十張り	じゅっぱり or じっぱり / じゅうはり or じゅうばり	*jup-pari* / *jip-pari*

Irregularities or Special beyond Ten:

100 bows	百張り	ひゃっぱり or ひゃくはり	*hyap-pari* or *hyaku-hari*
1,000 bows	千張り	せんばり or せんはり	*sem-bari* or *sen-hari*
10,000 bows	万張り	まんばり or まんはり	*mam-bari* or *man-hari*
how many bows?	何張り	なんばり or なんはり	*nam-bari* or *nan-hari*

Notes: none

bbl—バレル—*bareru*

Japanese: ばれる
Romanized: *bareru*
Pattern: 漢 ∅
Used with, or Means: barrels (symbol: bbl), a unit of volume, 4,032 fl oz (31.5 gal)/119.240471 L; a unit of volume for oil, 5,376 fl oz (42 gal)/158.987295 L

1 barrel	1バレル	いちばれる	*ichi-bareru*
2 barrels	2バレル	にばれる	*ni-bareru*
3 barrels	3バレル	さんばれる	*sam-bareru*
4 barrels	4バレル	よんばれる	*yom-bareru*
5 barrels	5バレル	ごばれる	*go-bareru*
6 barrels	6バレル	ろくばれる	*roku-bareru*
7 barrels	7バレル	ななばれる	*nana-bareru*
8 barrels	8バレル	はちばれる	*hachi-bareru*
9 barrels	9バレル	きゅうばれる	*kyuu-bareru*
10 barrels	10バレル	じゅうばれる	*juu-bareru*

Irregularities or Special beyond Ten: none
Notes: none

furlongs—ハロン—haron

Japanese: はろん
Romanized: *haron*
Pattern: 漢 ∅
Used with, or Means: furlongs (symbol: fur), a unit of length, 7,920 in (660 ft)/201.16800 m

1 furlong	1 ハロン	いちはろん	*ichi-haron*
2 furlongs	2 ハロン	にはろん	*ni-haron*
3 furlongs	3 ハロン	さんはろん	*sam-haron*
4 furlongs	4 ハロン	よんはろん	*yon-haron*
5 furlongs	5 ハロン	ごはろん	*go-haron*
6 furlongs	6 ハロン	ろくはろん	*roku-haron*
7 furlongs	7 ハロン	ななはろん	*nana-haron*
8 furlongs	8 ハロン	はちはろん	*hachi-haron*
9 furlongs	9 ハロン	きゅうはろん	*kyuu-haron*
10 furlongs	10 ハロン	じゅうはろん	*juu-haron*

Irregularities or Special beyond Ten: none
Notes: none

犯 — はん — *han*

Japanese: はん
Romanized: *han*
Pattern: 漢 H
Used with, or Means: judgments received, prior offenses

1 prior offense	一犯	いっぱん	*ip-pan*
2 prior offenses	二犯	にはん	*ni-han*
3 prior offenses	三犯	さんぱん	*sam-pan*
4 prior offenses	四犯	よんはん / よんぱん	*yon-han* / *yom-pan*
5 prior offenses	五犯	ごはん	*go-han*
6 prior offenses	六犯	ろっぱん / ろくはん	*rop-pan* / *roku-han*
7 prior offenses	七犯	ななはん	*nana-han*
8 prior offenses	八犯	はっぱん / はちはん	*hap-pan* / *hachi-han*
9 prior offenses	九犯	きゅうはん	*kyuu-han*
10 prior offenses	十犯	じゅっぱん / じっぱん	*jup-pan* / *jip-pan*

Irregularities or Special beyond Ten:

100 prior offenses	百犯	ひゃっぱん / ひゃくはん	*hyap-pan* / *hyaku-han*
1,000 prior offenses	千犯	せんぱん	*sem-pan*
10,000 prior offenses	万犯	まんぱん	*mam-pan*
how many prior offenses?	何犯	なんぱん / なんはん	*nam-pan* / *nan-han*

Notes: none

判—はん—han

Japanese: はん
Romanized: *han*
Pattern: 漢 H
Used with, or Means: standard paper sizes, such as A4 判 (210 mm × 297 mm)

size A(B)0	A(B)0 判	A(B)ぜろはん	A(B)*zero-han*
		A(B)零判 A(B)れいはん	A(B)*rei-han*
size A(B)1	A(B)1 判	A(B)いっぱん	A(B)*ip-pan*
size A(B)2	A(B)2 判	A(B)にはん	A(B)*ni-han*
size A(B)3	A(B)3 判	A(B)さんばん	A(B)*sam-ban*
size A(B)4	A(B)4 判	A(B)よんはん	A(B)*yon-han*
		A(B)よんばん	A(B)*yom-ban*
size A(B)5	A(B)5 判	A(B)ごはん	A(B)*go-han*
size A(B)6	A(B)6 判	A(B)ろっぱん	A(B)*rop-pan*
		A(B)ろくはん	A(B)*roku-han*
size A(B)7	A(B)7 判	A(B)ななはん	A(B)*nana-han*
size A(B)8	A(B)8 判	A(B)はっぱん	A(B)*hap-pan*
		A(B)はちはん	A(B)*hachi-han*

Irregularities or Special beyond Ten: none

Notes: *Letter*, *U. S. Letter*, or *Letter Size* paper (8.5 in × 11 in) is called 国際判 (*kokusaihan*) in Japanese.

The two paper sizes used in Japan are ISO[15] A and a non-ISO B, where A0 and B0 are the largest and as each successive number is reached by cutting the previous number in half through its long-side, parallel to its short side. The A series has a ratio of $1:\sqrt{2}$, whilst the Japanese B series has a ratio of $1:\sqrt{1.5}$. There is an ISO B as well as an ISO C series, but Japan does not use them.

There are only 9 of each of the A and B series: A0 through A8 and B0 through B8. The largest of the A series, A0, is 841 mm × 1189 mm. The smallest in the A series, A8, is 52 mm × 74 mm.

---

[15] International Organization for Standardization

版 — はん — han

Japanese: はん
Romanized: *han*
Pattern: 漢 H
Used with, or Means: editions; see 刷り (*suri*) for revisions (where the content does *not* change)

1st edition	一版	いっぱん	*ip-pan*
	初版	しょはん	*sho-han*
2nd edition	二版	にはん	*ni-han*
3rd edition	三版	さんばん or さんはん	*sam-ban* or *san-han*
4th edition	四版	よんはん or よんばん	*yon-han* or *yom-ban*
5th edition	五版	ごはん	*go-han*
6th edition	六版	ろっぱん or ろくはん	*rop-pan* or *roku-han*
7th edition	七版	ななはん	*nana-han*
8th edition	八版	はっぱん or はちはん	*hap-pan* or *hachi-han*
9th edition	九版	きゅうはん	*kyuu-han*
10th edition	十版	じゅっぱん	*jup-pan*
		じっぱん	*jip-pan*

Irregularities or Special beyond Ten:

100th edition	百版	ひゃっぱん	*hyap-pan*
1,000th edition	千版	せんばん	*sem-ban*
10,000th edition	万版	まんばん	*mam-ban*
which edition?	何版	なんばん or なんはん	*nam-ban* or *nan-han*

Notes: *Han* is used for editions of books, as opposed to revisions or successive printings. In this case, the content itself changes, such as when advances change what we actually know, or new chapters are added.

斑 — はん — *han*

Japanese: はん
Romanized: *han*
Pattern: 漢 H
Used with, or Means: (literary language) animal spots

1 spot	一斑	いっぱん	*ip-pan*
2 spots	二斑	にはん	*ni-han*
3 spots	三斑	さんばん or さんはん	*sam-ban* or *san-han*
4 spots	四斑	よんはん or よんばん	*yon-han* or *yom-ban*
5 spots	五斑	ごはん	*go-han*
6 spots	六斑	ろっぱん or ろくはん	*rop-pan* or *roku-han*
7 spots	七斑	ななはん	*nana-han*
8 spots	八斑	はっぱん or はちはん	*hap-pan* or *hachi-han*
9 spots	九斑	きゅうはん	*kyuu-han*
10 spots	十斑	じゅっぱん / じっぱん	*jup-pan* / *jip-pan*

Irregularities or Special beyond Ten:

100 spots	百斑	ひゃっぱん or ひゃくはん	*hyap-pan* or *hyaku-han*
1,000 spots	千斑	せんばん	*sem-ban*
10,000 spots	万斑	まんばん	*mam-ban*
which spot?	何斑	なんばん or なんはん	*nam-ban* or *nan-han*

Notes: There is an expression, 一斑を見て全豹を卜す (*ip-pan o mite zenpyou o bokusu*), which roughly translates to, *you may know the lion by its claw*. It literally means, *if you see one spot, you may predict an entire leopard.*

飯 — はん — *han*

Japanese: はん
Romanized: *han*
Pattern: 漢 H
Used with, or Means: meals; bowls of rice, see also 食 (*shoku*), see also 膳 (*zen*)

1 meal	一飯	いっぱん	*ip-pan*
2 meals	二飯	にはん	*ni-han*
3 meals	三飯	さんばん or さんはん	*sam-ban* or *san-han*
4 meals	四飯	よんはん or よんばん	*yon-han* or *yom-ban*
5 meals	五飯	ごはん	*go-han*
6 meals	六飯	ろっぱん or ろくはん	*rop-pan* or *roku-han*
7 meals	七飯	ななはん	*nana-han*
8 meals	八飯	はっぱん or はちはん	*hap-pan* or *hachi-han*
9 meals	九飯	きゅうはん	*kyuu-han*
10 meals	十飯	じゅっぱん / じっぱん	*jup-pan* / *jip-pan*

Irregularities or Special beyond Ten:

100 meals	百飯	ひゃっぱん or ひゃくはん	*hyap-pan* or *hyaku-han*
1,000 meals	千飯	せんばん	*sem-ban*
10,000 meals	万飯	まんばん	*mam-ban*
which meal?	何飯	なんばん or なんはん	*nam-ban* or *nan-han*

Notes: none

晩 — ばん — ban

Japanese: ばん
Romanized: ban
Pattern: 和 I
Used with, or Means: evenings, nights, see also 夜 (ya), see also 泊 (haku)

1 night	一晩	ひとばん	hito-ban
2 nights	二晩	ふたばん	futa-ban
3 nights	三晩	さんばん	sam-ban
4 nights	四晩	よんばん	yom-ban
5 nights	五晩	ごばん	go-ban
6 nights	六晩	ろくばん	roku-ban
7 nights	七晩	ななばん	nana-ban
8 nights	八晩	はちばん	hachi-ban
9 nights	九晩	きゅうばん	kyuu-ban
10 nights	十晩	じゅうばん	juu-ban

Irregularities or Special beyond Ten: none
Notes: none

番—ばん—ban

Japanese: ばん
Romanized: *ban*
Pattern: 漢 ∅

Used with, or Means: the order in which things occur, numerical order, see also 第 (*dai*); rank, see also 位 (*i*); successive matches in Go, *Shougi*, or *Sumo*; a musical piece or tune; thread, wire, or needle width, see also 番手 (*bante*); sheet steel, steel wire, or cellophane thickness; gun caliber (such as a .44 caliber)

No. 1	一番	いちばん	*ichi-ban*
No. 2	二番	にばん	*ni-ban*
No. 3	三番	さんばん	*sam-ban*
No. 4	四番	よんばん	*yom-ban*
No. 5	五番	ごばん	*go-ban*
No. 6	六番	ろくばん	*roku-ban*
No. 7	七番	ななばん	*nana-ban*
No. 8	八番	はちばん	*hachi-ban*
No. 9	九番	きゅうばん	*kyuu-ban*
No. 10	十番	じゅうばん	*juu-ban*

Irregularities or Special beyond Ten: none

Notes: 一番 (*ichi-ban*) also means *the best* or *the most* or *~est*. When used to mean *the most* it is used grammatically, such as in the sentence: 世界中でエベレスト(エヴェレスト)は一番高い山です (*Sekaijuu de Eberesuto (Everesuto) wa ichiban takai yama desu*), which means, *Mount Everest is the highest mountain in the world.*

第○番—だい○ばん—dai-○-ban

Japanese: だい○ばん
Romanized: *dai-○-ban*
Pattern: 漢 ∅
Used with, or Means: the Nth in line; Nth place, see also 番目 (*bam-me*)

1st place	第一番	だいいちばん	*dai-ichi-ban*
2nd place	第二番	だいにばん	*dai-ni-ban*
3rd place	第三番	だいさんばん	*dai-sam-ban*
4th place	第四番	だいよんばん	*dai-yom-ban*
5th place	第五番	だいごばん	*dai-go-ban*
6th place	第六番	だいろくばん	*dai-roku-ban*
7th place	第七番	だいななばん	*dai-nana-ban*
8th place	第八番	だいはちばん	*dai-hachi-ban*
9th place	第九番	だいきゅうばん	*dai-kyuu-ban*
10th place	第十番	だいじゅうばん	*dai-juu-ban*

Irregularities or Special beyond Ten: none
Notes: Ludwig van Beethoven's 9th symphony (the famous *Ode to Joy*) is, in Japanese: 交響曲第九番 (*dai-ku-ban*), rather than the expected *dai-kyuu-ban*. Just as we simply call it *Beethoven's 9th*, most Japanese just call it ベートーヴェンの第9 *Beetoovuen no dai-ku*.

番線 — ばんせん — *bansen*

Japanese: ばんせん
Romanized: *bansen*
Pattern: 漢 ∅
Used with, or Means: track number

track 1	一番線	いちばんせん	*ichi-bansen*
track 2	二番線	にばんせん	*ni-bansen*
track 3	三番線	さんばんせん	*sam-bansen*
track 4	四番線	よんばんせん	*yom-bansen*
track 5	五番線	ごばんせん	*go-bansen*
track 6	六番線	ろくばんせん	*roku-bansen*
track 7	七番線	ななばんせん	*nana-bansen*
track 8	八番線	はちばんせん	*hachi-bansen*
track 9	九番線	きゅうばんせん	*kyuu-bansen*
track 10	十番線	じゅうばんせん	*juu-bansen*

Irregularities or Special beyond Ten: none
Notes: none

番地—ばんち—*banchi*

Japanese: ばんち
Romanized: *banchi*
Pattern: 漢 ∅
Used with, or Means: (used in addresses) lot number, plot number

lot 1	一番地	いちばんち	*ichi-banchi*
lot 2	二番地	にばんち	*ni-banchi*
lot 3	三番地	さんばんち	*sam-banchi*
lot 4	四番地	よんばんち	*yom-banchi*
lot 5	五番地	ごばんち	*go-banchi*
lot 6	六番地	ろくばんち	*roku-banchi*
lot 7	七番地	ななばんち	*nana-banchi*
lot 8	八番地	はちばんち	*hachi-banchi*
lot 9	九番地	きゅうばんち	*kyuu-banchi*
lot 10	十番地	じゅうばんち	*juu-banchi*

Irregularities or Special beyond Ten: none
Notes: none

番手—ばんて—*bante*

Japanese: ばんて
Romanized: *bante*
Pattern: 漢 ∅
Used with, or Means: yarn, thread width: a unit of width (see Notes); thread count, yarn count; the number of soldiers guarding a castle; the order in which things occur

1 count yarn	一番手	いちばんて	*ichi-bante*
2 count yarn	二番手	にばんて	*ni-bante*
3 count yarn	三番手	さんばんて	*sam-bante*
4 count yarn	四番手	よんばんて	*yom-bante*
5 count yarn	五番手	ごばんて	*go-bante*
6 count yarn	六番手	ろくばんて	*roku-bante*
7 count yarn	七番手	ななばんて	*nana-bante*
8 count yarn	八番手	はちばんて	*hachi-bante*
9 count yarn	九番手	きゅうばんて	*kyuu-bante*
10 count yarn	十番手	じゅうばんて	*juu-bante*

Irregularities or Special beyond Ten: none

Notes: One *bante* is the width or thickness of yarn wherein 840 yd (768 m) of that yarn weighs exactly 1 lb (453.6 g); or, 1 km of that yarn weighs exactly 1 kg. For hemp or flaxen yarn, one *bante* is when 300 yd (274 m) weighs exactly 1 lb.

There are other units for other materials as well, such as the denier (symbol: D; 9,000 m *per* 1 g) and tex. One 9,000 m silk strand weighs 1 g, which is where they formed the basis of the denier. The tex (S. I. symbol: tex; 1,000 m *per* 1 g). The most commonly used version of the tex is the decitex or dtex (10,000 m *per* 1 g).

番目—ばんめ—bam-me

Japanese: ばんめ
Romanized: *bam-me*
Pattern: 漢 ∅
Used with, or Means: same as 第○番

1st	一番目	いちばんめ	*ichi-bam-me*
2nd	二番目	にばんめ	*ni-bam-me*
3rd	三番目	さんばんめ	*sam-bam-me*
4th	四番目	よんばんめ	*yom-bam-me*
5th	五番目	ごばんめ	*go-bam-me*
6th	六番目	ろくばんめ	*roku-bam-me*
7th	七番目	ななばんめ	*nana-bam-me*
8th	八番目	はちばんめ	*hachi-bam-me*
9th	九番目	きゅうばんめ	*kyuu-bam-me*
10th	十番目	じゅうばんめ	*juu-bam-me*

Irregularities or Special beyond Ten: none
Notes: none

ひ・び・ぴ—Hi/Bi/Pi
ヒ—ひ—hi

Japanese: ひ
Romanized: hi
Pattern: 漢 H
Used with, or Means: daggers (短刀 *tantou*), *kaiken* (懐剣); doses of medicine

1 dagger	一ヒ	いっぴ	*ip-pi*
2 daggers	二ヒ	にひ	*ni-hi*
3 daggers	三ヒ	さんび	*sam-bi*
4 daggers	四ヒ	よんひ / よんび	*yon-hi* / *yom-bi*
5 daggers	五ヒ	ごひ	*go-hi*
6 daggers	六ヒ	ろっぴ	*rop-pi*
7 daggers	七ヒ	ななひ	*nana-hi*
8 daggers	八ヒ	はっぴ	*hap-pi*
9 daggers	九ヒ	きゅうひ	*kyuu-hi*
10 daggers	十ヒ	じゅっぴ / じっぴ	*jup-pi* / *jip-pi*

Irregularities or Special beyond Ten:

100 daggers	百ヒ	ひゃっぴ	*hyap-pi*
1,000 daggers	千ヒ	せんび	*sem-bi*
10,000 daggers	万ヒ	まんび	*mam-bi*
how many daggers?	何ヒ	なんび	*nam-bi*

Notes: A *kaiken* is a special, small dagger that women in the Edo period would conceal for self-defense.

日 — ひ — hi

Japanese: ひ
Romanized: hi
Pattern: 漢 H
Used with, or Means: number of days, see also 日間 (*ka-kan/ nichi-kan*), see also 日 (*ka*), see also 日 (*nichi*)

1 day	一日	いっぴ	*ip-pi*
2 days	二日	にひ	*ni-hi*
3 days	三日	さんび	*sam-bi*
4 days	四日	よんひ よんび	*yon-hi* *yom-bi*
5 days	五日	ごひ	*go-hi*
6 days	六日	ろっぴ	*rop-pi*
7 days	七日	ななひ	*nana-hi*
8 days	八日	はっぴ	*hap-pi*
9 days	九日	きゅうひ	*kyuu-hi*
10 days	十日	じゅっぴ じっぴ	*jup-pi* *jip-pi*

Irregularities or Special beyond Ten:

100 days	百日	ひゃっぴ	*hyap-pi*
1,000 days	千日	せんび	*sem-bi*
10,000 days	万日	まんび	*mam-bi*
how many days?	何日	なんび	*nam-bi*

Notes: none

尾 — び — bi

Japanese: び
Romanized: bi
Pattern: 漢 Ø
Used with, or Means: shrimp, small fish, fish with their tails still attached (尾鰭の付いた魚 *obire no tsuita sakana*), see also 匹 (*hiki*)

1 shrimp	一尾	いちび	*ichi-bi*
2 shrimp	二尾	にび	*ni-bi*
3 shrimp	三尾	さんび	*sam-bi*
4 shrimp	四尾	よんび	*yom-bi*
5 shrimp	五尾	ごび	*go-bi*
6 shrimp	六尾	ろくび	*roku-bi*
7 shrimp	七尾	ななび	*nana-bi*
8 shrimp	八尾	はちび	*hachi-bi*
9 shrimp	九尾	きゅうび	*kyuu-bi*
10 shrimp	十尾	じゅうび	*juu-bi*

Irregularities or Special beyond Ten: none
Notes: Typically used by the shrimping and fishing industry to count large quantities of fish and shrimp. Also used by petshops to count the number of fish one buys.

尾 literally means *tail*, which is why the name for the mythical 9-tailed fox is *kyuubi* (九尾). 尾鰭を付ける (*obire o tsukeru*) means *to exaggerate, to stretch the truth*, or *to embellish a story*. 尾鰭の付いた噂 (*obire no tsuita uwasa*) is an *exaggerated rumor*.

微 — び — *bi*

Japanese: び
Romanized: *bi*
Pattern: 漢 S
Used with, or Means: 1/1,000,000th, 10⁻⁶

10⁻⁶	一微	いっび	*is-bi*
2×10⁻⁶	二微	にび	*ni-bi*
3×10⁻⁶	三微	さんび	*sam-bi*
4×10⁻⁶	四微	よんび	*yom-bi*
5×10⁻⁶	五微	ごび	*go-bi*
6×10⁻⁶	六微	ろくび	*roku-bi*
7×10⁻⁶	七微	ななび	*nana-bi*
8×10⁻⁶	八微	はっび	*has-bi*
9×10⁻⁶	九微	きゅうび	*kyuu-bi*
10⁻⁵	十微	じゅうび	*juu-bi*

Irregularities or Special beyond Ten:

10⁻⁴	百微	ひゃくび	*hyaku-bi*
10⁻³	千微	せんび	*sem-bi*

Notes: none

ピース—*piisu*

Japanese: ぴいす
Romanized: *piisu*
Pattern: 漢 P
Used with, or Means: pieces; clothing pieces (three-piece suit), see Notes

1 piece	1 ピース	いっぴいす / ワンぴいす / いちぴいす	*ip-piisu* / *wam-piisu* / *ichi-piisu*
2 pieces	2 ピース	にぴいす / ツーぴいす	*ni-piisu* / *tsuu-piisu*
3 pieces	3 ピース	さんぴいす / スリーぴいす	*sam-piisu* / *surii-piisu*
4 pieces	4 ピース	よんぴいす	*yom-piisu*
5 pieces	5 ピース	ごぴいす	*go-piisu*
6 pieces	6 ピース	ろっぴいす / ろくぴいす	*rop-piisu* / *roku-piisu*
7 pieces	7 ピース	ななぴいす	*nana-piisu*
8 pieces	8 ピース	はっぴいす / はちぴいす	*hap-piisu* / *hachi-piisu*
9 pieces	9 ピース	きゅうぴいす	*kyuu-piisu*
10 pieces	10 ピース	じゅっぴいす / じっぴいす	*jup-piisu* / *jip-piisu*

Irregularities or Special beyond Ten:

100 pieces	100 ピース	ひゃっぴいす / ひゃくぴいす	*hyap-piisu* / *hyaku-piisu*

Notes: When talking about the number of parts that make up an article of clothing, such as a one-piece swimsuit or a three-piece suit, use the Japanese pronunciations of English numerals: ワンピース (*wam-piisu*), ツーピース (*tsuu-piisu*), and スリーピース (*surii-piisu*), and so on.

ppm—ピーピーエム—*piipiiemu*

Japanese: ピーピーエム
Romanized: *piipiiemu*
Pattern: 漢 ∅
Used with, or Means: parts *per* million, (symbol: ppm)

1 ppm	1 ピーピーエム	いちぴいぴいえむ	*ichi-piipiiemu*
2 ppm	2 ピーピーエム	にぴいぴいえむ	*ni-piipiiemu*
3 ppm	3 ピーピーエム	さんぴいぴいえむ	*sam-piipiiemu*
4 ppm	4 ピーピーエム	よんぴいぴいえむ	*yom-piipiiemu*
5 ppm	5 ピーピーエム	ごぴいぴいえむ	*go-piipiiemu*
6 ppm	6 ピーピーエム	ろくぴいぴいえむ	*roku-piipiiemu*
7 ppm	7 ピーピーエム	ななぴいぴいえむ	*nana-piipiiemu*
8 ppm	8 ピーピーエム	はちぴいぴいえむ	*hachi-piipiiemu*
9 ppm	9 ピーピーエム	きゅうぴいぴいえむ	*kyuu-piipiiemu*
10 ppm	10 ピーピーエム	じゅうぴいぴいえむ	*juu-piipiiemu*

Irregularities or Special beyond Ten: none
Notes: Used in chemistry to measure the amount of very small quantities of chemicals in proportion to very large amounts of their medium (such as water or blood). For example, only six to nine parts per million of a hormone is needed in the blood stream to affect the changes that occur in puberty, so even minor changes in that proportion can have massive effects on a person.

匹 — ひき — *hiki*

Japanese: ひき
Romanized: *hiki*
Pattern: 漢 H
Used with, or Means: animals, see also 頭 (*tou*); fish, see also 尾 (*bi*); insects; brutish persons; robots, computer viruses

1 animal	一匹	いっぴき	*ip-piki*
2 animals	二匹	にひき	*ni-hiki*
3 animals	三匹	さんびき	*sam-biki*
4 animals	四匹	よんひき / よんびき	*yon-hiki* / *yom-biki*
5 animals	五匹	ごひき	*go-hiki*
6 animals	六匹	ろっぴき	*rop-piki*
7 animals	七匹	ななひき	*nana-hiki*
8 animals	八匹	はっぴき / はちひき	*hap-piki* / *hachi-hiki*
9 animals	九匹	きゅうひき	*kyuu-hiki*
10 animals	十匹	じゅっぴき / じっぴき	*jup-piki* / *jip-piki*

Irregularities or Special beyond Ten:

100 animals	百匹	ひゃっぴき	*hyap-piki*
1,000 animals	千匹	せんびき	*sem-biki*
10,000 animals	万匹	まんびき	*mam-biki*
how many animals?	何匹	なんびき	*nam-biki*

Notes: Large animas are counted with 頭 (*tou*). Cutsomarily, birds and rabbits are counted with 羽 (*wa*).

疋 — ひき — *hiki*

Japanese: ひき
Romanized: *hiki*
Pattern: 漢 H
Used with, or Means: animals; *hiki*, former monetary unit, 10 (later 25) 文 (*mon*); lengths of cloth, 2 反, 62.138 ft/18.940 m to 74.565 ft/22.727 m

1 *hiki*	一疋	いっぴき	*ip-piki*
2 *hiki*	二疋	にひき	*ni-hiki*
3 *hiki*	三疋	さんびき	*sam-biki*
4 *hiki*	四疋	よんひき よんびき	*yon-hiki* *yom-biki*
5 *hiki*	五疋	ごひき	*go-hiki*
6 *hiki*	六疋	ろっぴき	*rop-piki*
7 *hiki*	七疋	ななひき	*nana-hiki*
8 *hiki*	八疋	はっぴき はちひき	*hap-piki* *hachi-hiki*
9 *hiki*	九疋	きゅうひき	*kyuu-hiki*
10 *hiki*	十疋	じゅっぴき じっぴき	*jup-piki* *jip-piki*

Irregularities or Special beyond Ten:

100 *hiki*	百疋	ひゃっぴき	*hyap-piki*
1,000 *hiki*	千疋	せんびき	*sem-biki*
10,000 *hiki*	万疋	まんびき	*mam-biki*
how many *hiki*?	何疋	なんびき	*nam-biki*

Notes: none

ピクセル—*pikuseru*

Japanese: ぴくせる
Romanized: *pikuseru*
Pattern: 漢 Ø
Used with, or Means: pixels, see also 画素 (*gaso*)

1 pixel	1 ピクセル	いちぴくせる	*ichi-pikuseru*
2 pixels	2 ピクセル	にぴくせる	*ni-pikuseru*
3 pixels	3 ピクセル	さんぴくせる	*sam-pikuseru*
4 pixels	4 ピクセル	よんぴくせる	*yom-pikuseru*
5 pixels	5 ピクセル	ごぴくせる	*go-pikuseru*
6 pixels	6 ピクセル	ろくぴくせる	*roku-pikuseru*
7 pixels	7 ピクセル	ななぴくせる	*nana-pikuseru*
8 pixels	8 ピクセル	はちぴくせる	*hachi-pikuseru*
9 pixels	9 ピクセル	きゅうぴくせる	*kyuu-pikuseru*
10 pixels	10 ピクセル	じゅうぴくせる	*juu-pikuseru*

Irregularities or Special beyond Ten: none
Notes: none

ピクル・担 — ぴくる — *pikuru*

Japanese: ぴくる
Romanized: *pikuru*
Pattern: 漢 P
Used with, or Means: piculs: a unit of weight, about 2,116.43772 oz (132.27736 lb)/600 g

1 picul	一ピクル・担	いっぴくる / いちぴくる	*ip-pikuru* / *ichi-pikuru*
2 piculs	二ピクル・担	にぴくる	*ni-pikuru*
3 piculs	三ピクル・担	さんぴくる	*sam-pikuru*
4 piculs	四ピクル・担	よんぴくる	*yom-pikuru*
5 piculs	五ピクル・担	ごぴくる	*go-pikuru*
6 piculs	六ピクル・担	ろっぴくる / ろくぴくる	*rop-pikuru* / *roku-pikuru*
7 piculs	七ピクル・担	ななぴくる	*nana-pikuru*
8 piculs	八ピクル・担	はっぴくる / はちぴくる	*hap-pikuru* / *hachi-pikuru*
9 piculs	九ピクル・担	きゅうぴくる	*kyuu-pikuru*
10 piculs	十ピクル・担	じゅっぴくる / じっぴくる / じゅうぴくる	*jup-pikuru* / *jip-pikuru* / *juu-pikuru*

Irregularities or Special beyond Ten:

100 piculs	百ピクル・担	ひゃっぴくる / ひゃくぴくる	*hyap-pikuru* / *hyaku-pikuru*

Notes: Originally a Javanese unit of measure based on the average load a person could carry, the Dutch were responsible for its ubiquitous use for a very long time. In Hong Kong, one picul is defined as 60.478982 kg, and in Ordinance 22: 1884, one picul was defined as 133 1/3rd lb *avoirdupois*. In Taiwan, it is defined as an even 60 kg.

筆—ひつ—*hitsu*

Japanese: ひつ
Romanized: *hitsu*
Pattern: 漢 H
Used with, or Means: documents, papers, see Notes; (polite) publications; number of strokes, see also 画 (*kaku*), see also 筆 (*fude*); land registrations; rice fields

1 document	一筆	いっぴつ	*ip-pitsu*
2 documents	二筆	にひつ	*ni-hitsu*
3 documents	三筆	さんぴつ	*sam-pitsu*
4 documents	四筆	よんひつ よんぴつ	*yon-hitsu* *yom-pitsu*
5 documents	五筆	ごひつ	*go-hitsu*
6 documents	六筆	ろっぴつ	*rop-pitsu*
7 documents	七筆	ななひつ	*nana-hitsu*
8 documents	八筆	はっぴつ	*hap-pitsu*
9 documents	九筆	きゅうひつ	*kyuu-hitsu*
10 documents	十筆	じゅっぴつ じっぴつ	*jup-pitsu* *jip-pitsu*

Irregularities or Special beyond Ten:

100 documents	百筆	ひゃっぴつ ひゃくひつ	*hyap-pitsu* *hyaku-hitsu*
1,000 documents	千筆	せんぴつ せんひつ	*sem-bitsu* *sen-hitsu*
10,000 documents	万筆	まんぴつ まんひつ	*mam-bitsu* *man-hitsu*
how many documents?	何筆	なんぴつ なんひつ	*nam-bitsu* *nan-hitsu*

Notes: *Ippitsu* can mean *a few lines* or *a signature*.

bits—ビット—*bitto*

Japanese: びっと
Romanized: *bitto*
Pattern: 漢 ∅
Used with, or Means: bits, the smallest unit of information in computing (either a 1 or a 0)

1 bit	1 ビット	いちびっと	*ichi-bitto*
2 bits	2 ビット	にびっと	*ni-bitto*
3 bits	3 ビット	さんびっと	*sam-bitto*
4 bits	4 ビット	よんびっと	*yom-bitto*
5 bits	5 ビット	ごびっと	*go-bitto*
6 bits	6 ビット	ろくびっと	*roku-bitto*
7 bits	7 ビット	ななびっと	*nana-bitto*
8 bits	8 ビット	はちびっと	*hachi-bitto*
9 bits	9 ビット	きゅうびっと	*kyuu-bitto*
10 bits	10 ビット	じゅうびっと	*juu-bitto*

Irregularities or Special beyond Ten: none
Notes: 8 bits make 1 byte.

百 — ひゃく — *hyaku*

Japanese: ひゃく
Romanized: *hyaku*
Pattern: 漢 ∅
Used with, or Means: 100, hundred, 10^2

100	百	ひゃく	*hyaku*
200	二百	にひゃく	*ni-hyaku*
300	三百	さんびゃく	*sam-byaku*
400	四百	よんひゃく	*yon-hyaku*
500	五百	ごひゃく	*go-hyaku*
600	六百	ろっぴゃく	*rop-pyaku*
700	七百	ななひゃく	*nana-hyaku*
800	八百	はっぴゃく	*hap-pyaku*
900	九百	きゅうひゃく	*kyuu-hyaku*

Irregularities or Special beyond Ten: none

Notes: 十百 (*jup-pyaku/jip-pyaku*) does not exist because that would be 千 (*sen*).

百目—ひゃくめ—*hyakume*

Japanese: ひゃくめ
Romanized: *hyakume*
Pattern: 漢 K
Used with, or Means: *hyakume*, a former unit of weight, 100 匁 (*monme*), 13.22774 oz/375 g

1 *hyakume*	一百目	いっぴゃくめ	*ip-pyakume*
2 *hyakume*	二百目	にひゃくめ	*ni-hyakume*
3 *hyakume*	三百目	さんびゃくめ	*sam-byakume*
4 *hyakume*	四百目	よんひゃくめ よんびゃくめ	*yon-hyakume* *yom-byakume*
5 *hyakume*	五百目	ごひゃくめ	*go-hyakume*
6 *hyakume*	六百目	ろっぴゃくめ	*rop-pyakume*
7 *hyakume*	七百目	ななひゃくめ	*nana-hyakume*
8 *hyakume*	八百目	はっぴゃくめ	*hap-pyakume*
9 *hyakume*	九百目	きゅうひゃくめ	*kyuu-hyakume*
10 *hyakume*	十百目	じゅっぴゃくめ じっぴゃくめ	*jup-pyakume* *jip-pyakume*

Irregularities or Special beyond Ten:

100 *hyakume*	百百目	ひゃっぴゃくめ	*hyap-pyakume*
1,000 *hyakume*	千百目	せんびゃくめ	*sem-byakume*
10,000 *hyakume*	万百目	まんびゃくめ	*mam-byakume*
how many *hyakume*?	何百目	なんびゃくめ	*nam-byakume*

Notes: none

俵—ひょう—*hyou*

Japanese: ひょう
Romanized: *hyou*
Pattern: 漢 H
Used with, or Means: bags of rice (俵 *tawara*), grain, cereal; sackfuls

1 sackful	一俵	いっぴょう	ip-pyou
2 sackfuls	二俵	にひょう	ni-hyou
3 sackfuls	三俵	さんびょう さんびょう or さんひょう	sam-byou sam-pyou or san-hyou
4 sackfuls	四俵	よんひょう よんびょう or よんぴょう	yon-hyou yom-byou or yom-pyou
5 sackfuls	五俵	ごひょう	go-hyou
6 sackfuls	六俵	ろっぴょう or ろくひょう	rop-pyou or roku-hyou
7 sackfuls	七俵	ななひょう	nana-hyou
8 sackfuls	八俵	はっぴょう or はちひょう	hap-pyou or hachi-hyou
9 sackfuls	九俵	きゅうひょう	kyuu-hyou
10 sackfuls	十俵	じゅっぴょう or じっぴょう	jup-pyou or jip-pyou

Irregularities or Special beyond Ten:

100 sackfuls	百俵	ひゃっぴょう or ひゃくひょう	hyap-pyou or hyaku-hyou
1,000 sackfuls	千俵	せんびょう せんびょう or せんひょう	sem-byou sem-pyou or sen-hyou
10,000 sackfuls	万俵	まんびょう まんびょう or まんひょう	mam-byou mam-pyou or man-hyou
how many sackfuls?	何俵	なんびょう なんびょう or なんひょう	nam-byou nam-pyou or nan-hyou

Notes: none

票 — ひょう — *hyou*

Japanese: ひょう
Romanized: *hyou*
Pattern: 漢 H
Used with, or Means: ballots, votes in an election, an answer to a poll question, raised hands in a show-of-hands vote

1 vote	一票	いっぴょう	*ip-pyou*
2 votes	二票	にひょう	*ni-hyou*
3 votes	三票	さんびょう さんぴょう or さんひょう	*sam-byou* *sam-pyou* or *san-hyou*
4 votes	四票	よんひょう よんびょう or よんぴょう	*yon-hyou* *yom-byou* or *yom-pyou*
5 votes	五票	ごひょう	*go-hyou*
6 votes	六票	ろっぴょう or ろくひょう	*rop-pyou* or *roku-hyou*
7 votes	七票	ななひょう	*nana-hyou*
8 votes	八票	はっぴょう or はちひょう	*hap-pyou* or *hachi-hyou*
9 votes	九票	きゅうひょう	*kyuu-hyou*
10 votes	十票	じゅっぴょう or じっぴょう	*jup-pyou* or *jip-pyou*

Irregularities or Special beyond Ten:

100 votes	百票	ひゃっぴょう or ひゃくひょう	*hyap-pyou* or *hyaku-hyou*
1,000 votes	千票	せんびょう せんぴょう or せんひょう	*sem-byou* *sem-pyou* or *sen-hyou*
10,000 votes	万票	まんびょう まんぴょう or まんひょう	*mam-byou* *mam-pyou* or *man-hyou*
how many votes?	何票	なんびょう なんぴょう or なんひょう	*nam-byou* *nam-pyou* or *nan-hyou*

Notes: none

瓢 — ひょう — *hyou*

Japanese: ひょう
Romanized: *hyou*
Pattern: 漢 H
Used with, or Means: (literary language) hollowed-out gourds

1 gourd	一瓢	いっぴょう	*ip-pyou*
2 gourds	二瓢	にひょう	*ni-hyou*
3 gourds	三瓢	さんびょう さんぴょう or さんひょう	*sam-byou* *sam-pyou* or *san-hyou*
4 gourds	四瓢	よんひょう よんびょう or よんぴょう	*yon-hyou* *yom-byou* or *yom-pyou*
5 gourds	五瓢	ごひょう	*go-hyou*
6 gourds	六瓢	ろっぴょう or ろくひょう	*rop-pyou* or *roku-hyou*
7 gourds	七瓢	ななひょう	*nana-hyou*
8 gourds	八瓢	はっぴょう or はちひょう	*hap-pyou* or *hachi-hyou*
9 gourds	九瓢	きゅうひょう	*kyuu-hyou*
10 gourds	十瓢	じゅっぴょう or じっぴょう	*jup-pyou* or *jip-pyou*

Irregularities or Special beyond Ten:

100 gourds	百瓢	ひゃっぴょう or ひゃくひょう	*hyap-pyou* or *hyaku-hyou*
1,000 gourds	千瓢	せんびょう せんぴょう or せんひょう	*sem-byou* *sem-pyou* or *sen-hyou*
10,000 gourds	万瓢	まんびょう まんぴょう or まんひょう	*mam-byou* *mam-pyou* or *man-hyou*
how many gourds?	何瓢	なんびょう なんぴょう or なんひょう	*nam-byou* *nam-pyou* or *nan-hyou*

Notes: none

秒 — びょう — byou

Japanese: びょう
Romanized: *byou*
Pattern: 漢 ∅
Used with, or Means: the second of the minute; number of seconds

second 1	一秒	いちびょう	*ichi-byou*
second 2	二秒	にびょう	*ni-byou*
second 3	三秒	さんびょう	*sam-byou*
second 4	四秒	よんびょう	*yom-byou*
second 5	五秒	ごびょう	*go-byou*
second 6	六秒	ろくびょう	*roku-byou*
second 7	七秒	ななびょう	*nana-byou*
second 8	八秒	はちびょう	*hachi-byou*
second 9	九秒	きゅうびょう	*kyuu-byou*
second 10	十秒	じゅうびょう	*juu-byou*

Irregularities or Special beyond Ten: none

Notes: Although the *number of seconds* is properly 秒間 (*byoukan*), one can simply omit the ~*kan*, as one sees on the countdown timers at walk lights in Japan.

拍子—ひょうし—*hyoushi*

Japanese: ひょうし
Romanized: *hyoushi*
Pattern: 漢 H
Used with, or Means: beats (tempo), syllables in Japanese words

1 beat	一拍子	いっぴょうし	ip-byoushi
2 beats	二拍子	にびょうし	ni-byoushi
3 beats	三拍子	さんびょうし	sam-byoushi
4 beats	四拍子	よんひょうし or よんびょうし	yon-hyoushi or yom-byoushi
5 beats	五拍子	ごひょうし	go-hyoushi
6 beats	六拍子	ろっぴょう or ろくひょう	rop-pyou or roku-hyou
7 beats	七拍子	ななひょう	nana-hyou
8 beats	八拍子	はっぴょう or はちひょう	hap-pyou or hachi-hyou
9 beats	九拍子	きゅうひょう	kyuu-hyou
10 beats	十拍子	じゅっぴょう or じっぴょう	jup-pyou or jip-pyou

Irregularities or Special beyond Ten:

100 beats	百拍子	ひゃっぴょうし / ひゃくひょうし	hyap-pyoushi / hyaku-hyoushi
1,000 beats	千拍子	せんびょうし / せんびょうし or せんひょうし	sem-byoushi / sem-pyoushi or sen-hyoushi
10,000 beats	万拍子	まんびょうし / まんびょうし or まんひょうし	mam-byoushi / mam-pyoushi or man-hyoushi
how many beats?	何拍子	なんびょうし / なんびょうし or なんひょうし	nam-byoushi / nam-pyoushi or nan-hyoushi

Notes: none

片 — ひら — *hira*

Japanese: ひら
Romanized: *hira*
Pattern: 和 I
Used with, or Means: snowflakes, flower petals, see also 片 (*hen*), see also 弁 (*ben*); formerly used to count sheets of paper, leaves, straw mats

1 petal	一片	ひとひら	*hito-hira*
2 petals	二片	ふたひら	*futa-hira*
3 petals	三片	さんひら	*san-hira*
4 petals	四片	よんひら	*yon-hira*
5 petals	五片	ごひら	*go-hira*
6 petals	六片	ろくひら	*roku-hira*
7 petals	七片	ななひら	*nana-hira*
8 petals	八片	はちひら	*hachi-hira*
9 petals	九片	きゅうひら	*kyuu-hira*
10 petals	十片	じゅうひら	*juu-hira*

Irregularities or Special beyond Ten: none
Notes: none

尋 — ひろ — *hiro*

Japanese: ひろ
Romanized: *hiro*
Pattern: 和 I
Used with, or Means: Japanese fathoms, *hiro*, a unit of length, 6 尺 (*shaku*), 71.58196 in (5.96516 ft)/1.81818 m/0.99419 fathoms, same as 尋 (*jin*)

1 fathom	一尋	ひとひろ	*hito-hiro*
2 fathoms	二尋	ふたひろ	*futa-hiro*
3 fathoms	三尋	さんひろ	*san-hiro*
4 fathoms	四尋	よんひろ	*yon-hiro*
5 fathoms	五尋	ごひろ	*go-hiro*
6 fathoms	六尋	ろくひろ	*roku-hiro*
7 fathoms	七尋	ななひろ	*nana-hiro*
8 fathoms	八尋	はちひろ	*hachi-hiro*
9 fathoms	九尋	きゅうひろ	*kyuu-hiro*
10 fathoms	十尋	じゅうひろ	*juu-hiro*

Irregularities or Special beyond Ten: none
Notes: none

品—ひん—*hin*

Japanese: ひん
Romanized: *hin*
Pattern: 漢 H
Used with, or Means: items, commodities, see also 品 (*shina*), varieties of food: a variety platter with three kinds of *hors d'oeuvres* (前菜 3 品盛り合わせ *zenzai sambin moriawase*); meal courses

1 item	一品	いっぴん	*ip-pin*
2 items	二品	にひん	*ni-hin*
3 items	三品	さんびん さんぴん or さんひん	*sam-bin* *sam-pin* or *san-hin*
4 items	四品	よんひん よんぴん or よんびん	*yon-hin* *yom-bin* or *yom-pin*
5 items	五品	ごひん	*go-hin*
6 items	六品	ろっぴん or ろくひん	*rop-pin* or *roku-hin*
7 items	七品	ななひん	*nana-hin*
8 items	八品	はっぴん or はちひん	*hap-pin* or *hachi-hin*
9 items	九品	きゅうひん	*kyuu-hin*
10 items	十品	じゅっぴん or じっぴん	*jup-pin* or *jip-pin*

Irregularities or Special beyond Ten:

100 items	百品	ひゃっぴん or ひゃくひん	*hyap-pin* or *hyaku-hin*
1,000 items	千品	せんびん せんぴん or せんひん	*sem-bin* *sem-pin* or *sen-hin*
10,000 items	万品	まんびん まんぴん or まんひん	*mam-bin* *mam-pin* or *man-hin*
how many items?	何品	なんびん なんぴん or なんひん	*nam-bin* *nam-pin* or *nan-hin*

Notes: none

便 — びん — bin

Japanese: びん
Romanized: *bin*
Pattern: 和 I
Used with, or Means: flights, trips, transports

1 flight	一便	ひとびん	*hito-bin*
2 flights	二便	ふたびん	*futa-bin*
3 flights	三便	さんびん	*sam-bin*
4 flights	四便	よんびん	*yom-bin*
5 flights	五便	ごびん	*go-bin*
6 flights	六便	ろくびん	*roku-bin*
7 flights	七便	ななびん	*nana-bin*
8 flights	八便	はちびん	*hachi-bin*
9 flights	九便	きゅうびん	*kyuu-bin*
10 flights	十便	じゅうびん	*juu-bin*

Irregularities or Special beyond Ten: none
Notes: none

瓶 — びん — *bin*

Japanese: びん
Romanized: *bin*
Pattern: 和 I
Used with, or Means: bottles, vases

1 bottle	一瓶	<u>ひとびん</u>	<u>*hito-bin*</u>
2 bottles	二瓶	<u>ふたびん</u>	<u>*futa-bin*</u>
3 bottles	三瓶	さんびん	*sam-bin*
4 bottles	四瓶	よんびん	*yom-bin*
5 bottles	五瓶	ごびん	*go-bin*
6 bottles	六瓶	ろくびん	*roku-bin*
7 bottles	七瓶	ななびん	*nana-bin*
8 bottles	八瓶	はちびん	*hachi-bin*
9 bottles	九瓶	きゅうびん	*kyuu-bin*
10 bottles	十瓶	じゅうびん	*juu-bin*

Irregularities or Special beyond Ten: none
Notes: none

品目—ひんもく—*hinmoku*

Japanese: ひんもく
Romanized: *hinmoku*
Pattern: 漢 ∅
Used with, or Means: items of business

1 item of business	一品目	いちひんもく	*ichi-hinmoku*
2 items of business	二品目	にひんもく	*ni-hinmoku*
3 items of business	三品目	さんひんもく	*sam-hinmoku*
4 items of business	四品目	よんひんもく	*yom-hinmoku*
5 items of business	五品目	ごひんもく	*go-hinmoku*
6 items of business	六品目	ろくひんもく	*roku-hinmoku*
7 items of business	七品目	ななひんもく	*nana-hinmoku*
8 items of business	八品目	はちひんもく	*hachi-hinmoku*
9 items of business	九品目	きゅうひんもく	*kyuu-hinmoku*
10 items of business	十品目	じゅうひんもく	*juu-hinmoku*

Irregularities or Special beyond Ten: none
Notes: none

ふ・ぶ・ぷ—Fu/Bu/Pu
節・編—ふ—fu

Japanese: ふ
Romanized: fu
Pattern: 和 I-Fu
Used with, or Means: stitches, knots on in a straw mat, tatami mat, see also 節 (setsu)

1 stitch	一節・編	ひとふ	hito-fu
2 stitches	二節・編	ふたふ	futa-fu
3 stitches	三節・編	さんぷ	sam-pu
4 stitches	四節・編	よんふ / よんぷ	yon-fu / yom-pu
5 stitches	五節・編	ごふ	go-fu
6 stitches	六節・編	ろっぷ	rop-pu
7 stitches	七節・編	ななふ	nana-fu
8 stitches	八節・編	はっぷ	hap-pu
9 stitches	九節・編	きゅうふ	kyuu-fu
10 stitches	十節・編	じゅっぷ / じっぷ	jup-pu / jip-pu

Irregularities or Special beyond Ten:

100 stitches	百節・編	ひゃっぷ	hyap-pu
1,000 stitches	千節・編	せんぶ	sem-pu
10,000 stitches	万節・編	まんぶ	mam-pu
how many stitches?	何節・編	なんぶ	nam-pu

Notes: none

分 — ぶ — bu

Japanese: ぶ
Romanized: bu
Pattern: 漢 Ø

Used with, or Means: *bu*, a unit of length, 1/100th of a 尺 (*shaku*), 0.1193032688 in/0.0030303030 m; *bu*, a unit of weight, 1/10th of a 匁 (*momme*), 0.01323 oz/0.37500 g; *bu*, *bu*, former monetary unit, ¼th of a 両 (*ryou*); shoe size; 1/10th of an equally divided whole, later 1/100th

1 *bu*	一分	いちぶ	ichi-bu
2 *bu*	二分	にぶ	ni-bu
3 *bu*	三分	さんぶ	sam-bu
4 *bu*	四分	しぶ / よぶ / よんぶ	<u>shi-bu</u> / <u>yo-bu</u> / <u>yom-bu</u>
5 *bu*	五分	ごぶ	go-bu
6 *bu*	六分	ろくぶ	roku-bu
7 *bu*	七分	しちぶ / ななぶ	<u>shichi-bu</u> / <u>nana-bu</u>
8 *bu*	八分	はちぶ	hachi-bu
9 *bu*	九分	きゅうぶ	kyuu-bu
10 *bu*	十分	じゅうぶ	juu-bu

Irregularities or Special beyond Ten: none
Notes: none

歩 — ぶ — *bu*

Japanese: ぶ
Romanized: *bu*
Pattern: 漢 Ø
Used with, or Means: *bu*, a unit of area, 1 坪 (*tsubo*), 5,123.97718 in^2 (35.58317 ft^2)/3.30579 m^2, see also 町歩 (*choubu*), see also 反歩・段歩 (*tambu*)

1 *bu*	一歩	いちぶ	*ichi-bu*
2 *bu*	二歩	にぶ	*ni-bu*
3 *bu*	三歩	さんぶ	*sam-bu*
4 *bu*	四歩	よんぶ	*yom-bu*
5 *bu*	五歩	ごぶ	*go-bu*
6 *bu*	六歩	ろくぶ	*roku-bu*
7 *bu*	七歩	ななぶ / しちぶ	*nana-bu* / *shichi-bu*
8 *bu*	八歩	はちぶ	*hachi-bu*
9 *bu*	九歩	きゅうぶ	*kyuu-bu*
10 *bu*	十歩	じゅうぶ	*juu-bu*

Irregularities or Special beyond Ten: none
Notes: none

部 — ぶ — bu

Japanese: ぶ
Romanized: *bu*
Pattern: 漢 ∅
Used with, or Means: books, publications, newspapers, magazines, sets of books, see also 冊 (*satsu*), see also 紙 (*shi*), see also 誌 (*shi*); verses of a poem, scripture; sections of a dictionary

1 publication	一部	いちぶ	*ichi-bu*
2 publications	二部	にぶ	*ni-bu*
3 publications	三部	さんぶ	*sam-bu*
4 publications	四部	よんぶ	*yom-bu*
5 publications	五部	ごぶ	*go-bu*
6 publications	六部	ろくぶ	*roku-bu*
7 publications	七部	ななぶ / しちぶ	*nana-bu* / *shichi-bu*
8 publications	八部	はちぶ	*hachi-bu*
9 publications	九部	きゅうぶ	*kyuu-bu*
10 publications	十部	じゅうぶ	*juu-bu*

Irregularities or Special beyond Ten: none
Notes: none

フィート・呎 — ふぃいと — *fuiito*

Japanese: ふぃいと
Romanized: *fuiito*
Pattern: 漢 Ø
Used with, or Means: feet (symbol: ft), a unit of length, 12 in/0.30480 m

1 ft	1フィート・呎	いちふぃいと	*ichi-fuiito*
2 ft	2フィート・呎	にふぃいと	*ni-fuiito*
3 ft	3フィート・呎	さんふぃいと	*san-fuiito*
4 ft	4フィート・呎	よんふぃいと	*yon-fuiito*
5 ft	5フィート・呎	ごふぃいと	*go-fuiito*
6 ft	6フィート・呎	ろくふぃいと	*roku-fuiito*
7 ft	7フィート・呎	ななふぃいと	*nana-fuiito*
8 ft	8フィート・呎	はちふぃいと	*hachi-fuiito*
9 ft	9フィート・呎	きゅうふぃいと	*kyuu-fuiito*
10 ft	10フィート・呎	じゅうふぃいと	*juu-fuiito*

Irregularities or Special beyond Ten:
Notes: none

封 — ふう — *fuu*

Japanese: ふう
Romanized: *fuu*
Pattern: 漢 Fu
Used with, or Means: letters, correspondence; sealed documents; wrapped cash, gifts, offereings

1 letter	一封	いっぷう	*ip-puu*
2 letters	二封	にふう	*ni-fuu*
3 letters	三封	さんぷう	*sam-puu*
4 letters	四封	よんふう or よんぷう	*yon-fuu* or *yom-puu*
5 letters	五封	ごふう	*go-fuu*
6 letters	六封	ろっぷう or ろくふう	*rop-puu* or *roku-fuu*
7 letters	七封	ななふう	*nana-fuu*
8 letters	八封	はっぷう or はちふう	*hap-puu* or *hachi-fuu*
9 letters	九封	きゅうふう	*kyuu-fuu*
10 letters	十封	じゅっぷう じっぷう	*jup-puu* *jip-puu*

Irregularities or Special beyond Ten:

100 letters	百封	ひゃっぷく ひゃくふく	*hyap-puku* *hyaku-fuku*
1,000 letters	千封	せんぷく or せんふく	*sem-puku* or *sen-fuku*
10,000 letters	万封	まんぷく or まんふく	*mam-puku* or *man-fuku*
how many letters?	何封	なんぷく	*nam-puku*

Notes: none

服 — ふく — *fuku*

Japanese: ふく
Romanized: *fuku*
Pattern: 漢 Fu
Used with, or Means: doses of powdered medicine, see also 包 (*hou*), see also 貼 (*chou*); puffs of a cigarette, sips of tea; a rest, see Notes

1 dose	一服	いっぷく	*ip-puku*
2 doses	二服	にふく	*ni-fuku*
3 doses	三服	さんぷく or さんふく	*sam-puku* or *san-fuku*
4 doses	四服	よんふく or よんぷく	*yon-fuku* or *yom-puku*
5 doses	五服	ごふく	*go-fuku*
6 doses	六服	ろっぷく or ろくふく	*rop-puku* or *roku-fuku*
7 doses	七服	ななふく	*nana-fuku*
8 doses	八服	はっぷく or はちふく	*hap-puku* or *hachi-fuku*
9 doses	九服	きゅうふく	*kyuu-fuku*
10 doses	十服	じゅっぷく じっぷく or じゅうふく	*jup-puku* *jip-puku* or *juu-fuku*

Irregularities or Special beyond Ten:

100 doses	百服	ひゃっぷく ひゃくふく	*hyap-puku* *hyaku-fuku*
1,000 doses	千服	せんぷく or せんふく	*sem-puku* or *sen-fuku*
10,000 doses	万服	まんぷく or まんふく	*mam-puku* or *man-fuku*
how many doses?	何服	なんぷく or なんふく	*nam-puku* or *nan-fuku*

Notes: 一服する (*ippuku suru*) means *to take a rest/break*. It can also mean *to smoke a cigarette*, combining the idea of an entire cigarette as a *one, single dose*, with the idea of taking a break to smoke.

幅 — ふく — *fuku*

Japanese: ふく
Romanized: *fuku*
Pattern: 漢 Fu
Used with, or Means: hanging pictures, scrolls, see also 軸 (*jiku*); (polite) firelight, shadows, forms moving in firelight, see also 幅 (*ho*)

1 scroll	一幅	いっぷく	*ip-puku*
2 scrolls	二幅	にふく	*ni-fuku*
3 scrolls	三幅	さんぷく or さんふく	*sam-puku* or *san-fuku*
4 scrolls	四幅	よんふく or よんぷく	*yon-fuku* or *yom-puku*
5 scrolls	五幅	ごふく	*go-fuku*
6 scrolls	六幅	ろっぷく or ろくふく	*rop-puku* or *roku-fuku*
7 scrolls	七幅	ななふく	*nana-fuku*
8 scrolls	八幅	はっぷく or はちふく	*hap-puku* or *hachi-fuku*
9 scrolls	九幅	きゅうふく	*kyuu-fuku*
10 scrolls	十幅	じゅっぷく / じっぷく or じゅうふく	*jup-puku* / *jip-puku* or *juu-fuku*

Irregularities or Special beyond Ten:

100 scrolls	百幅	ひゃっぷく / ひゃくふく	*hyap-puku* / *hyaku-fuku*
1,000 scrolls	千幅	せんぷく or せんふく	*sem-puku* or *sen-fuku*
10,000 scrolls	万幅	まんぷく or まんふく	*mam-puku* or *man-fuku*
how many scrolls?	何幅	なんぷく or なんふく	*nam-puku* or *nan-fuku*

Notes: A 二幅対 (*nifuku-tsui*) is a 対幅 (*tsuifuku*), also known as a 双幅 (*soufuku*), 対軸 (*tsuijiku*), or 独幅 (*dokufuku*). A 三幅対 (*sampuku-tsui*) is *a triad; a three-piece set.* See also 三つ揃い (*mitsu zoroi*), *a three-piece suit.*

袋 —ふくろ— *fukuro*

Japanese: ふくろ
Romanized: *fukuro*
Pattern: 和 I
Used with, or Means: bags, bagfuls, see also 叺 (*kamasu*), see also 袋 (*tai*), see Notes

1 bagful	一袋	ひとふくろ	*hito-fukuro*
2 bagfuls	二袋	ふたふくろ	*futa-fukuro*
3 bagfuls	三袋	さんぶくろ or さんふくろ	*sam-pukuro* or *san-fukuro*
4 bagfuls	四袋	よんふくろ or よんぶくろ	*yon-fukuro* or *yom-pukuro*
5 bagfuls	五袋	ごふくろ	*go-fukuro*
6 bagfuls	六袋	ろっぷくろ or ろくふくろ	*rop-pukuro* or *roku-fukuro*
7 bagfuls	七袋	ななふくろ	*nana-fukuro*
8 bagfuls	八袋	はっぷくろ or はちふくろ	*hap-pukuro* or *hachi-fukuro*
9 bagfuls	九袋	きゅうふくろ	*kyuu-fukuro*
10 bagfuls	十袋	じゅっぷくろ / じっぷくろ or じゅうふくろ	*jup-pukuro* / *jip-pukuro* or *juu-fukuro*

Irregularities or Special beyond Ten:

100 bagfuls	百袋	ひゃっぷくろ / ひゃくふくろ	*hyap-pukuro* / *hyaku-fukuro*
1,000 bagfuls	千袋	せんぶくろ or せんふくろ	*sem-pukuro* or *sen-fukuro*
10,000 bagfuls	万袋	まんぶくろ or まんふくろ	*mam-pukuro* or *man-fukuro*
how many bagfuls?	何袋	なんぶくろ or なんふくろ	*nam-pukuro* or *nan-fukuro*

Notes: In general, sacks with nothing in them are counted with 枚 (*mai*), however handbags and backpacks are still counted with 袋 (*fukuro*) whether or not they have anything in them. Bunches of fruit are also counted with 房 (*fusa*).

房 — ふさ — *fusa*

Japanese: ふさ
Romanized: *fusa*
Pattern: 和 I
Used with, or Means: bunches of fruit, flowers, strands of hair, strings

1 bunch	一房	<u>ひとふさ</u>	<u>*hito-fusa*</u>
2 bunches	二房	<u>ふたふさ</u>	<u>*futa-fusa*</u>
3 bunches	三房	さんふさ	*mi-fusa*
4 bunches	四房	よんふさ よんぶさ	*yon-fusa* *yom-busa*
5 bunches	五房	ごふさ	*itsu-fusa*
6 bunches	六房	ろくふさ	*mu-fusa*
7 bunches	七房	ななふさ	*nana-fusa*
8 bunches	八房	はちふさ	*ya-fusa*
9 bunches	九房	きゅうふさ	*kokono-fusa*
10 bunches	十房	じゅうふさ	*too-fusa*

Irregularities or Special beyond Ten: none
Notes: none

節 — ふし — *fushi*

Japanese: ふし
Romanized: *fushi*
Pattern: 和 I
Used with, or Means: the number of knobs in a stalk of bamboo, reeds; connection points in a series; songs, tunes, melodies; scenes in a ballad, drama; slices of fish, flakes of *katsuobushi*; nodes

1 node	一節	ひとふし	*hito-fushi*
2 nodes	二節	ふたふし	*futa-fushi*
3 nodes	三節	さんぶし or さんふし	*san-fushi* or *sam-bushi*
4 nodes	四節	よんふし or よんぶし	*yon-fushi* or *yom-bushi*
5 nodes	五節	ごふし	*go-fushi*
6 nodes	六節	ろくふし or ろくぶし	*roku-fushi* or *roku-bushi*
7 nodes	七節	ななふし	*nana-fushi*
8 nodes	八節	はちふし or はちぶし	*hachi-fushi* or *hachi-bushi*
9 nodes	九節	きゅうふし	*kyuu-fushi*
10 nodes	十節	じゅうふし	*juu-fushi*

Irregularities or Special beyond Ten:

100 nodes	百節	ひゃくふし / ひゃくぶし	*hyaku-fushi* / *hyaku-bushi*
1,000 nodes	千節	せんふし or せんぶし	*sen-fushi* or *sem-bushi*
10,000 nodes	万節	まんふし or まんぶし	*man-fushi* or *mam-bushi*
how many nodes?	何節	なんふし	*nan-fushi*

Notes: *Katsuobushi* are flakes of dried bonito fish that appear to dance when heated.

伏せ—ぶせ—*buse*

Japanese: ぶせ
Romanized: *buse*
Pattern: 和 I
Used with, or Means: arrow lengths

1 arrow length	一伏せ	ひとぶせ ひとふせ	*hito-buse* *hito-fuse*
2 arrow lengths	二伏せ	ふたぶせ	*futa-buse*
3 arrow lengths	三伏せ	さんぶせ	*sam-buse*
4 arrow lengths	四伏せ	よんぶせ	*yom-buse*
5 arrow lengths	五伏せ	ごぶせ	*go-buse*
6 arrow lengths	六伏せ	ろくぶせ	*roku-buse*
7 arrow lengths	七伏せ	ななぶせ	*nana-buse*
8 arrow lengths	八伏せ	はちぶせ	*hachi-buse*
9 arrow lengths	九伏せ	きゅうぶせ	*kyuu-buse*
10 arrow lengths	十伏せ	じゅうぶせ	*juu-buse*

Irregularities or Special beyond Ten: none
Notes: none

仏—ぶつ—*butsu*

Japanese: ぶつ
Romanized: *butsu*
Pattern: 漢 ∅
Used with, or Means: (literary language) statues of the Buddha, see also 体 (*tai*)

1 Buddha statue	一仏	いちぶつ	*ichi-butsu*
2 Buddha statues	二仏	にぶつ	*ni-butsu*
3 Buddha statues	三仏	さんぶつ	*sam-butsu*
4 Buddha statues	四仏	よんぶつ	*yom-butsu*
5 Buddha statues	五仏	ごぶつ	*go-butsu*
6 Buddha statues	六仏	ろくぶつ	*roku-butsu*
7 Buddha statues	七仏	ななぶつ	*nana-butsu*
8 Buddha statues	八仏	はちぶつ	*hachi-butsu*
9 Buddha statues	九仏	きゅうぶつ	*kyuu-butsu*
10 Buddha statues	十仏	じゅうぶつ	*juu-butsu*

Irregularities or Special beyond Ten: none
Notes: none

筆——ふで——*fude*

Japanese: ふで
Romanized: *fude*
Pattern: 和 III
Used with, or Means: number of brush strokes, pen-strokes without taking one's pen, brush off the page, canvas

1 stroke	一筆	ひとふで	*hito-fude*
2 strokes	二筆	ふたふで	*futa-fude*
3 strokes	三筆	みふで / さんふで	*mi-fude* / *san-fude*
4 strokes	四筆	よふで / よんふで	*yo-fude* / *yon-fude*
5 strokes	五筆	ごふで	*go-fude*
6 strokes	六筆	ろくふで	*roku-fude*
7 strokes	七筆	ななふで	*nana-fude*
8 strokes	八筆	はちふで	*hachi-fude*
9 strokes	九筆	きゅうふで	*kyuu-fude*
10 strokes	十筆	じゅうふで	*juu-fude*

Irregularities or Special beyond Ten: none
Notes: No relation to 筆 (*hitsu*), which has to do with documents and land registrations.

舟—ふね—*fune*

Japanese: ふね
Romanized: *fune*
Pattern: 和 IV
Used with, or Means: boat-shaped food container used for fancy presentation (usually *sashimi*)

1 food boat	一舟	ひとふね	*hito-fune*
2 food boats	二舟	ふたふね	*futa-fune*
3 food boats	三舟	みふね / さんふね	*mi-fune* / *san-fune*
4 food boats	四舟	よふね / よんふね	*yo-fune* / *yon-fune*
5 food boats	五舟	ごふね	*go-fune*
6 food boats	六舟	ろくふね	*roku-fune*
7 food boats	七舟	ななふね	*nana-fune*
8 food boats	八舟	はちふね	*hachi-fune*
9 food boats	九舟	きゅうふね	*kyuu-fune*
10 food boats	十舟	じゅうふね	*juu-fune*

Irregularities or Special beyond Ten: none
Notes: none

F—フラン—*furan*

Japanese: フラン
Romanized: *furan*
Pattern: 漢 ∅
Used with, or Means: *francs*, former French monetary unit

1 F	1 フラン	いちふらん	*ichi-furan*
2 F	2 フラン	にふらん	*ni-furan*
3 F	3 フラン	さんふらん	*san-furan*
4 F	4 フラン	よんふらん	*yon-furan*
5 F	5 フラン	ごふらん	*go-furan*
6 F	6 フラン	ろくふらん	*roku-furan*
7 F	7 フラン	ななふらん	*nana-furan*
8 F	8 フラン	はちふらん	*hachi-furan*
9 F	9 フラン	きゅうふらん	*kyuu-furan*
10 F	10 フラン	じゅうふらん	*juu-furan*

Irregularities or Special beyond Ten: none
Notes: none

振り —ふり— *furi*

Japanese: ふり
Romanized: *furi*
Pattern: 和 III
Used with, or Means: downward swings, chops with a sword or bamboo practice sword (竹刀 *shinai*, 木刀 *bokutou*, 木剣 *bokken*); swords, *naginata* (Japanese halberds) see also 口 (*ku, kuchi, kou, furi*), see also 剣 (*ken*); tennis racket, baseball bat swings

1 swing	一振り	ひとふり	*hito-furi*
2 swings	二振り	ふたふり	*futa-furi*
3 swings	三振り	みふり / さんふり	*mi-furi* / *san-furi*
4 swings	四振り	よふり / よんふり	*yo-furi* / *yon-furi*
5 swings	五振り	ごふり	*go-furi*
6 swings	六振り	ろくふり	*roku-furi*
7 swings	七振り	ななふり	*nana-furi*
8 swings	八振り	はちふり	*hachi-furi*
9 swings	九振り	きゅうふり	*kyuu-furi*
10 swings	十振り	じゅうふり	*juu-furi*

Irregularities or Special beyond Ten: none
Notes: none

降り —ふり— *furi*

Japanese: ふり
Romanized: *furi*
Pattern: 和 IV
Used with, or Means: rain events

1 rain event	一降り	ひとふり	*hito-furi*
2 rain events	二降り	ふたふり	*futa-furi*
3 rain events	三降り	みふり / さんふり	*mi-furi* / *san-furi*
4 rain events	四降り	よふり / よんふり	*yo-furi* / *yon-furi*
5 rain events	五降り	ごふり	*go-furi*
6 rain events	六降り	ろくふり	*roku-furi*
7 rain events	七降り	ななふり	*nana-furi*
8 rain events	八降り	はちふり	*hachi-furi*
9 rain events	九降り	きゅうふり	*kyuu-furi*
10 rain events	十降り	じゅうふり	*juu-furi*

Irregularities or Special beyond Ten: none
Notes: none

口 —ふり —*furi*

Japanese: ふり
Romanized: *furi*
Pattern: 和 IV
Used with, or Means: downward swings, chops with a sword or bamboo practice sword, same as 振り (*furi*)

1 swing	一口	ひとふり	*hito-furi*
2 swings	二口	ふたふり	*futa-furi*
3 swings	三口	みふり さんふり	*mi-furi* *san-furi*
4 swings	四口	よふり よんふり	*yo-furi* *yon-furi*
5 swings	五口	ごふり	*go-furi*
6 swings	六口	ろくふり	*roku-furi*
7 swings	七口	ななふり	*nana-furi*
8 swings	八口	はちふり	*hachi-furi*
9 swings	九口	きゅうふり	*kyuu-furi*
10 swings	十口	じゅうふり	*juu-furi*

Irregularities or Special beyond Ten: none
Notes: none

ブロック—*burokku*

Japanese: ぶろっく
Romanized: *burokku*
Pattern: 漢 ∅
Used with, or Means: toy blocks, play blocks

1 block	1 ブロック	いちぶろっく	*ichi-burokku*
2 blocks	2 ブロック	にぶろっく	*ni-burokku*
3 blocks	3 ブロック	さんぶろっく	*sam-burokku*
4 blocks	4 ブロック	よんぶろっく	*yom-burokku*
5 blocks	5 ブロック	ごぶろっく	*go-burokku*
6 blocks	6 ブロック	ろくぶろっく	*roku-burokku*
7 blocks	7 ブロック	ななぶろっく	*nana-burokku*
8 blocks	8 ブロック	はちぶろっく	*hachi-burokku*
9 blocks	9 ブロック	きゅうぶろっく	*kyuu-burokku*
10 blocks	10 ブロック	じゅうぶろっく	*juu-burokku*

Irregularities or Special beyond Ten: none
Notes: none

分(間)—ふん(かん)—fun(kan)

Japanese: ふん(かん)
Romanized: *fun(kan)*
Pattern: 漢 Fu
Used with, or Means: minutes; 1/10th of a 匁 (*monme*); degrees

1 minute	一分(間)	いっぷん(かん)	*ip-pun(kan)*
2 minutes	二分(間)	にふん(かん)	*ni-fun(kan)*
3 minutes	三分(間)	さんぷん(かん)	*sam-pun(kan)*
4 minutes	四分(間)	よんふん(かん) or よんぷん(かん)	*yon-fun(kan)* or *yom-pun(kan)*
5 minutes	五分(間)	ごふん(かん)	*go-fun(kan)*
6 minutes	六分(間)	ろっぷん(かん) or ろくふん(かん)	*rop-pun(kan)* or *roku-fun(kan)*
7 minutes	七分(間)	ななふん(かん)	*nana-fun(kan)*
8 minutes	八分(間)	はっぷん(かん) or はちふん(かん)	*hap-pun(kan)* or *hachi-fun(kan)*
9 minutes	九分(間)	きゅうふん(かん)	*kyun(kan)-fun(kan)*
10 minutes	十分(間)	じゅっぷん(かん) or じっぷん(かん)	*jup-pun(kan)* or *jip-pun(kan)*

Irregularities or Special beyond Ten:

100 minutes	百分(間)	ひゃっぷん(かん) ひゃくふん(かん)	*hyap-pun(kan)* *hyaku-fun(kan)*
1,000 minutes	千分(間)	せんぷん(かん) or せんふん(かん)	*sem-pun(kan)* or *sen-fun(kan)*
10,000 minutes	万分(間)	まんぷん(かん) or まんふん(かん)	*mam-pun(kan)* or *man-fun(kan)*
how many minutes?	何分(間)	なんぷん(かん) or なんふん(かん)	*nam-pun(kan)* or *nan-fun(kan)*

Notes: Without 間 (*kan*), 分 (*fun*) means *minutes of the hour*, but with 間, 分 means *number of minutes*.

分 — ぶん — bun

Japanese: ぶん
Romanized: bun
Pattern: 漢 Ø
Used with, or Means: parts, portions, fraction denominators, see Notes

one whole	一分	いちぶん	ichi-bun
halves	二分	にぶん	ni-bun
thirds	三分	さんぶん	sam-bun
fourths	四分	よんぶん	yom-bun
fifths	五分	ごぶん	go-bun
sixths	六分	ろくぶん	roku-bun
sevenths	七分	ななぶん	nana-bun
eighths	八分	はちぶん	hachi-bun
ninths	九分	きゅうぶん	kyuu-bun
tenths	十分	じゅうぶん	juu-bun

Irregularities or Special beyond Ten: none

Notes: In order to express fractions in Japanese, $\frac{2}{3}$ for example, one must say the denominator first in the form given above, followed by の (*no*), and then the numerator. Thus, $\frac{2}{3}$ is 三分の二 (*sam-bun no ni*). $\frac{1}{2}$ is 二分の一 (*ni-bun no ichi*). Remember: denominator *first*, numerator *second*, or just reverse the way we say it: 9 tenths = 十分の九 (*juu-bun no kyuu*).

An eighth of a pizza, for example, would be ピザの八分の一 (*piza no hachi-bun no ichi*). Remember to add the の一 (*no ichi*) part, as it shows that you are talking about a fraction of something. Otherwise, it would mean *eight pieces of a pizza*.

文 —ぶん— *bun*

Japanese: ぶん
Romanized: *bun*
Pattern: 漢 ∅
Used with, or Means: sentences, novels

1 sentence	一文	いちぶん	*ichi-bun*
2 sentences	二文	にぶん	*ni-bun*
3 sentences	三文	さんぶん	*sam-bun*
4 sentences	四文	よんぶん	*yom-bun*
5 sentences	五文	ごぶん	*go-bun*
6 sentences	六文	ろくぶん	*roku-bun*
7 sentences	七文	ななぶん	*nana-bun*
8 sentences	八文	はちぶん	*hachi-bun*
9 sentences	九文	きゅうぶん	*kyuu-bun*
10 sentences	十文	じゅうぶん	*juu-bun*

Irregularities or Special beyond Ten: none
Notes: none

文節—ぶんせつ—*bunsetsu*

Japanese: ぶんせつ
Romanized: *bunsetsu*
Pattern: 漢 ∅
Used with, or Means: phrases, paragraphs

1 phrase	一文節	いちぶんせつ	*ichi-bunsetsu*
2 phrases	二文節	にぶんせつ	*ni-bunsetsu*
3 phrases	三文節	さんぶんせつ	*sam-bunsetsu*
4 phrases	四文節	よんぶんせつ	*yom-bunsetsu*
5 phrases	五文節	ごぶんせつ	*go-bunsetsu*
6 phrases	六文節	ろくぶんせつ	*roku-bunsetsu*
7 phrases	七文節	ななぶんせつ	*nana-bunsetsu*
8 phrases	八文節	はちぶんせつ	*hachi-bunsetsu*
9 phrases	九文節	きゅうぶんせつ	*kyuu-bunsetsu*
10 phrases	十文節	じゅうぶんせつ	*juu-bunsetsu*

Irregularities or Special beyond Ten: none
Notes: none

へ・べ・ぺ—He/Be/Pe

瓶—へい—*hei*

Japanese: へい
Romanized: *hei*
Pattern: 漢 H
Used with, or Means: flower pots, bottles, vials, jars, jugs, vats, urns

1 flower pot	一瓶	いっぺい	*ip-pei*
2 flower pots	二瓶	にへい	*ni-hei*
3 flower pots	三瓶	さんべい	*sam-bei*
4 flower pots	四瓶	よんへい / よんべい	*yon-hei* / *yom-bei*
5 flower pots	五瓶	ごへい	*go-hei*
6 flower pots	六瓶	ろっぺい	*rop-pei*
7 flower pots	七瓶	ななへい	*nana-hei*
8 flower pots	八瓶	はっぺい	*hap-pei*
9 flower pots	九瓶	きゅうへい	*kyuu-hei*
10 flower pots	十瓶	じゅっぺい / じっぺい	*jup-pei* / *jip-pei*

Irregularities or Special beyond Ten:

100 flower pots	百瓶	ひゃっぺい	*hyap-pei*
1,000 flower pots	千瓶	せんべい	*sem-bei*
10,000 flower pots	万瓶	まんべい	*mam-bei*
how many flower pots?	何瓶	なんべい	*nam-bei*

Notes: none

平方○—へいほう○—heihou ○

Japanese: へいほう○
Romanized: *heihou* ○
Pattern: 漢 ∅
Used with, or Means: square ○s, see Notes

1 square ○	一平方○	いちへいほう○	*ichi-heihou* ○
2 square ○s	二平方○	にへいほう○	*ni-heihou* ○
3 square ○s	三平方○	さんへいほう○	*san-heihou* ○
4 square ○s	四平方○	よんへいほう○	*yon-heihou* ○
5 square ○s	五平方○	ごへいほう○	*go-heihou* ○
6 square ○s	六平方○	ろくへいほう○	*roku-heihou* ○
7 square ○s	七平方○	ななへいほう○	*nana-heihou* ○
8 square ○s	八平方○	はちへいほう○	*hachi-heihou* ○
9 square ○s	九平方○	きゅうへいほう○	*kyuu-heihou* ○
10 square ○s	十平方○	じゅうへいほう○	*juu-heihou* ○

Irregularities or Special beyond Ten: none
Notes: One can replace ○ with whatever measure of length is needed, such that using メートル (*meetoru* meters) yields 平方メートル (*heihou meetoru* square meters). 平方フィート (*heihou fuiito*) would be *square feet*.

Notice, though, that 平方 (*heihou*) does not interact phonologically with numbers, so rather than the expected *ip-peihou*, it is *ichi-heihou*.

ページ・頁—ぺえじ—*peeji*

Japanese: ぺえじ
Romanized: *peeji*
Pattern: 漢 P
Used with, or Means: page number, pages

page 1	一ページ・頁	いちぺえじ	*ichi-peeji*
page 2	二ページ・頁	にぺえじ	*ni-peeji*
page 3	三ページ・頁	さんぺえじ	*sam-peeji*
page 4	四ページ・頁	よんぺえじ	*yom-peeji*
page 5	五ページ・頁	ごぺえじ	*go-peeji*
page 6	六ページ・頁	ろくぺえじ	*roku-peeji*
page 7	七ページ・頁	ななぺえじ	*nana-peeji*
page 8	八ページ・頁	はちぺえじ	*hachi-peeji*
page 9	九ページ・頁	きゅうぺえじ	*kyuu-peeji*
page 10	十ページ・頁	じゅうぺえじ	*juu-peeji*

Irregularities or Special beyond Ten: none
Notes: none

ベース—*beesu*

Jabeesunese: べえす
Romanized: *beesu*
Beesuttern: 漢 Ø
Used with, or Means: baseball bases, see also 塁 (*rui*)

1 base	1ベース	いちべえす	*ichi-beesu*
2 bases	2ベース	にべえす	*ni-beesu*
3 bases	3ベース	さんべえす	*sam-beesu*
4 bases	4ベース	よんべえす	*yom-beesu*

Irregularities or Special beyond Ten: none
Notes: none

ha—ヘクタール—*hekutaaru*

Japanese: へくたある
Romanized: *hekutaaru*
Pattern: 漢 H
Used with, or Means: hectares(S. I. symbol: ha), a unit of area, 100 m² (15,500,031.00000 in², 107,639.10400 ft²)

1 ha	1ヘクタール	いちへくたある	*ichi-hekutaaru*
2 ha	2ヘクタール	にへくたある	*ni-hekutaaru*
3 ha	3ヘクタール	さんへくたある	*san-hekutaaru*
4 ha	4ヘクタール	よんへくたある	*yon-hekutaaru*
5 ha	5ヘクタール	ごへくたある	*go-hekutaaru*
6 ha	6ヘクタール	ろくへくたある	*ruku-hekutaaru*
7 ha	7ヘクタール	ななへくたある	*nana-hekutaaru*
8 ha	8ヘクタール	はちへくたある	*hachi-hekutaaru*
9 ha	9ヘクタール	きゅうへくたある	*kyuu-hekutaaru*
10 ha	10ヘクタール	じゅうへくたある	*juu-hekutaaru*

Irregularities or Special beyond Ten: none
Notes: none

ヘクトグラム・瓱—へくとぐらむ—*hekuto-guramu*

Japanese: へくとぐらむ
Romanized: *hekuto-guramu*
Pattern: 漢 H
Used with, or Means: hectograms (S. I. symbol: hg), a unit of mass, 100 g (3.52740 oz)

1 hg	一ヘクトグラム・瓱	いちへくとぐらむ	*ichi-hekuto-guramu*
2 hg	二ヘクトグラム・瓱	にへくとぐらむ	*ni-hekuto-guramu*
3 hg	三ヘクトグラム・瓱	さんへくとぐらむ	*san-hekuto-guramu*
4 hg	四ヘクトグラム・瓱	よんへくとぐらむ	*yon-hekuto-guramu*
5 hg	五ヘクトグラム・瓱	ごへくとぐらむ	*go-hekuto-guramu*
6 hg	六ヘクトグラム・瓱	ろくへくとぐらむ	*roku-hekuto-guramu*
7 hg	七ヘクトグラム・瓱	ななへくとぐらむ	*nana-hekuto-guramu*
8 hg	八ヘクトグラム・瓱	はちへくとぐらむ	*hachi-hekuto-guramu*
9 hg	九ヘクトグラム・瓱	きゅうへくとぐらむ	*kyuu-hekuto-guramu*
10 hg	十ヘクトグラム・瓱	じゅうへくとぐらむ	*juu-hekuto-guramu*

Irregularities or Special beyond Ten: none
Notes: none

ヘクトメートル・粨—へくとめえとる—*hekuto-meetoru*

Japanese: へくとめえとる
Romanized: *hekuto-meetoru*
Pattern: 漢 H
Used with, or Means: hectometers (S. I. symbol: hm), a unit of length, 100 m (3,937.00787in, 328.08399 ft)

1 hm	一ヘクトメートル・粨	いちへくとめえとる	*ichi-hekuto-meetoru*
2 hm	二ヘクトメートル・粨	にへくとめえとる	*ni-hekuto-meetoru*
3 hm	三ヘクトメートル・粨	さんへくとめえとる	*san-hekuto-meetoru*
4 hm	四ヘクトメートル・粨	よんへくとめえとる	*yon-hekuto-meetoru*
5 hm	五ヘクトメートル・粨	ごへくとめえとる	*go-hekuto-meetoru*
6 hm	六ヘクトメートル・粨	ろくへくとめえとる	*roku-hekuto-meetoru*
7 hm	七ヘクトメートル・粨	ななへくとめえとる	*nana-hekuto-meetoru*
8 hm	八ヘクトメートル・粨	はちへくとめえとる	*hachi-hekuto-meetoru*
9 hm	九ヘクトメートル・粨	きゅうへくとめえとる	*kyuu-hekuto-meetoru*
10 hm	十ヘクトメートル・粨	じゅうへくとめえとる	*juu-hekuto-meetoru*

Irregularities or Special beyond Ten: none
Notes: none

ヘクトリットル・竓—へくとりっとる—*hekuto-rittoru*

Japanese: へくとりっとる
Romanized: *hekuto-rittoru*
Pattern: 漢 H
Used with, or Means: hectoliters (S. I. symbol: hL), a unit of volume, 100 L (3,381.40227 fl oz, 26.41721 gal)

1 hL	一ヘクトリットル・竓	いちへくとりっとる	*ichi-hekuto-rittoru*
2 hL	二ヘクトリットル・竓	にへくとりっとる	*ni-hekuto-rittoru*
3 hL	三ヘクトリットル・竓	さんへくとりっとる	*san-hekuto-rittoru*
4 hL	四ヘクトリットル・竓	よんへくとりっとる	*yon-hekuto-rittoru*
5 hL	五ヘクトリットル・竓	ごへくとりっとる	*go-hekuto-rittoru*
6 hL	六ヘクトリットル・竓	ろくへくとりっとる	*roku-hekuto-rittoru*
7 hL	七ヘクトリットル・竓	ななへくとりっとる	*nana-hekuto-rittoru*
8 hL	八ヘクトリットル・竓	はちへくとりっとる	*hachi-hekuto-rittoru*
9 hL	九ヘクトリットル・竓	きゅうへくとりっとる	*kyuu-hekuto-rittoru*
10 hL	十ヘクトリットル・竓	じゅうへくとりっとる	*juu-hekuto-rittoru*

Irregularities or Special beyond Ten: none
Notes: none

ペセタ—*peseta*

Japanese: ぺせた
Romanized: *peseta*
Pattern: 漢 ∅
Used with, or Means: *peseta*, former Spanish monetary unit

1 peseta	1ペセタ	いちぺせた	*ichi-peseta*
2 pesetas	2ペセタ	にぺせた	*ni-peseta*
3 pesetas	3ペセタ	さんぺせた	*sam-peseta*
4 pesetas	4ペセタ	よんぺせた	*yom-peseta*
5 pesetas	5ペセタ	ごぺせた	*go-peseta*
6 pesetas	6ペセタ	ろくぺせた	*roku-peseta*
7 pesetas	7ペセタ	ななぺせた	*nana-peseta*
8 pesetas	8ペセタ	はちぺせた	*hachi-peseta*
9 pesetas	9ペセタ	きゅうぺせた	*kyuu-peseta*
10 pesetas	10ペセタ	じゅうぺせた	*juu-peseta*

Irregularities or Special beyond Ten: none
Notes: none

ペソ — ぺそ — *peso*

Japanese: ぺそ
Romanized: *peso*
Pattern: 漢 ∅
Used with, or Means: Peso, unit of currency in a variety of Spanish-speaking countries

1 peso	1ペソ	いちぺそ	*ichi-peso*
2 pesos	2ペソ	にぺそ	*ni-peso*
3 pesos	3ペソ	さんぺそ	*sam-peso*
4 pesos	4ペソ	よんぺそ	*yom-peso*
5 pesos	5ペソ	ごぺそ	*go-peso*
6 pesos	6ペソ	ろくぺそ	*roku-peso*
7 pesos	7ペソ	ななぺそ	*nana-peso*
8 pesos	8ペソ	はちぺそ	*hachi-peso*
9 pesos	9ペソ	きゅうぺそ	*kyuu-peso*
10 pesos	10ペソ	じゅうぺそ	*juu-peso*

Irregularities or Special beyond Ten: none
Notes: none

部屋 — へや — *heya*

Japanese: へや
Romanized: *heya*
Pattern: 和 III or 漢 Ø
Used with, or Means: rooms

1 room	一部屋	ひとへや	*hito-heya*
2 rooms	二部屋	ふたへや / にへや	*futa-heya* / *ni-heya*
3 rooms	三部屋	みへや / さんへや	*mi-heya* / *san-heya*
4 rooms	四部屋	よへや / よんへや	*yo-heya* / *yon-heya*
5 rooms	五部屋	ごへや	*go-heya*
6 rooms	六部屋	ろくへや	*roku-heya*
7 rooms	七部屋	ななへや	*nana-heya*
8 rooms	八部屋	はちへや	*hachi-heya*
9 rooms	九部屋	きゅうへや	*kyuu-heya*
10 rooms	十部屋	じゅうへや	*juu-heya*

Irregularities or Special beyond Ten: none
Notes: none

Hz—ヘルツ—*herutsu*

Japanese: ヘルツ
Romanized: *herutsu*
Pattern: 漢 ∅
Used with, or Means: Hertz (S. I. symbol: Hz), $1 \frac{cycle}{second}$

1 Hz	1ヘルツ	いちへるつ	*ichi-herutsu*
2 Hz	2ヘルツ	にへるつ	*ni-herutsu*
3 Hz	3ヘルツ	さんへるつ	*san-herutsu*
4 Hz	4ヘルツ	よんへるつ	*yon-herutsu*
5 Hz	5ヘルツ	ごへるつ	*go-herutsu*
6 Hz	6ヘルツ	ろくへるつ	*roku-herutsu*
7 Hz	7ヘルツ	ななへるつ	*nana-herutsu*
8 Hz	8ヘルツ	はちへるつ	*hachi-herutsu*
9 Hz	9ヘルツ	きゅうへるつ	*kyuu-herutsu*
10 Hz	10ヘルツ	じゅうへるつ	*juu-herutsu*

Irregularities or Special beyond Ten: none
Notes: none

片 — へん — hen

Japanese: へん
Romanized: *hen*
Pattern: 漢 H
Used with, or Means: second-hand stamps, tickets; flower petals; fragments, flakes, see also 片 (*hira*)

1 flower petal	一片	いっぺん	*ip-pen*
2 flower petals	二片	にへん	*ni-hen*
3 flower petals	三片	さんぺん さんべん さんへん	*sam-pen* *sam-ben* *san-hen*
4 flower petals	四片	よんへん or よんべん	*yon-hen* or *yom-ben*
5 flower petals	五片	ごへん	*go-hen*
6 flower petals	六片	ろっぺん or ろくへん	*rop-pen* or *roku-hen*
7 flower petals	七片	ななへん	*nana-hen*
8 flower petals	八片	はっぺん or はちへん	*hap-pen* or *hachi-hen*
9 flower petals	九片	きゅうへん	*kyuu-hen*
10 flower petals	十片	じゅっぺん じっぺん	*jup-pen* *jip-pen*

Irregularities or Special beyond Ten:

100 flower petals	百片	ひゃっぺん ひゃくへん	*hyap-pen* *hyaku-hen*
1,000 flower petals	千片	せんべん or せんへん	*sem-ben* or *sen-hen*
10,000 flower petals	万片	まんべん or まんへん	*mam-ben* or *man-hen*
how many flower petals?	何片	なんべん or なんへん	*nam-ben* or *nan-hen*

Notes: none

遍・辺—へん—*hen*

Japanese: へん
Romanized: *hen*
Pattern: 漢 H
Used with, or Means: number of times, see also 回 (*kai*), see also 度 (*do*)

once	一遍・辺	いっぺん	<u>*ip-pen*</u>
twice	二遍・辺	にへん	*ni-hen*
thrice / three times	三遍・辺	さんぺん / さんべん / さんへん	*sam-pen* / *sam-ben* / *san-hen*
4 times	四遍・辺	よんへん or よんべん	*yon-hen* or <u>*yom-ben*</u>
5 times	五遍・辺	ごへん	*go-hen*
6 times	六遍・辺	<u>ろっぺん</u> or <u>ろくへん</u>	<u>*rop-pen*</u> or <u>*roku-hen*</u>
7 times	七遍・辺	ななへん	*nana-hen*
8 times	八遍・辺	<u>はっぺん</u> or <u>はちへん</u>	<u>*hap-pen*</u> or <u>*hachi-hen*</u>
9 times	九遍・辺	きゅうへん	*kyuu-hen*
10 times	十遍・辺	<u>じゅっぺん</u> / <u>じっぺん</u>	<u>*jup-pen*</u> / <u>*jip-pen*</u>

Irregularities or Special beyond Ten:

100 times	百遍・辺	<u>ひゃっぺん</u> / <u>ひゃくへん</u>	<u>*hyap-pen*</u> / <u>*hyaku-hen*</u>
1,000 times	千遍・辺	<u>せんべん</u> or <u>せんへん</u>	<u>*sem-ben*</u> or <u>*sen-hen*</u>
10,000 times	万遍・辺	<u>まんべん</u> or <u>まんへん</u>	<u>*mam-ben*</u> or <u>*man-hen*</u>
how many times?	何遍・辺	<u>なんべん</u> or <u>なんへん</u>	<u>*nam-ben*</u> or <u>*nan-hen*</u>

Notes: none

編・篇 — へん — *hen*

Japanese: へん
Romanized: *hen*
Pattern: 漢 H
Used with, or Means: parts of a book, story arcs, chapters; Chinese poems

1 story arc	一編・篇	いっぺん	*ip-pen*
2 story arcs	二編・篇	にへん	*ni-hen*
3 story arcs	三編・篇	さんぺん / さんべん / さんへん	*sam-pen* / *sam-ben* / *san-hen*
4 story arcs	四編・篇	よんへん or よんべん	*yon-hen* or *yom-ben*
5 story arcs	五編・篇	ごへん	*go-hen*
6 story arcs	六編・篇	ろっぺん or ろくへん	*rop-pen* or *roku-hen*
7 story arcs	七編・篇	ななへん	*nana-hen*
8 story arcs	八編・篇	はっぺん or はちへん	*hap-pen* or *hachi-hen*
9 story arcs	九編・篇	きゅうへん	*kyuu-hen*
10 story arcs	十編・篇	じゅっぺん / じっぺん	*jup-pen* / *jip-pen*

Irregularities or Special beyond Ten:

100 story arcs	百編・篇	ひゃっぺん / ひゃくへん	*hyap-pen* / *hyaku-hen*
1,000 story arcs	千編・篇	せんべん or せんへん	*sem-ben* or *sen-hen*
10,000 story arcs	万編・篇	まんべん or まんへん	*mam-ben* or *man-hen*
how many story arcs?	何編・篇	なんべん or なんへん	*nam-ben* or *nan-hen*

Notes: none

弁—べん—ben

Jabennese: べん
Romanized: ben
Benttern: 漢 Ø
Used with, or Means: (literary language) flower petals, see also 片 (hira), see also 片 (hen)

1 flower petal	一弁	いちべん	ichi-ben
2 flower petals	二弁	にべん	ni-ben
3 flower petals	三弁	さんべん	sam-ben
4 flower petals	四弁	よんべん	yom-ben
5 flower petals	五弁	ごべん	go-ben
6 flower petals	六弁	ろくべん	roku-ben
7 flower petals	七弁	ななべん	nana-ben
8 flower petals	八弁	はちべん	hachi-ben
9 flower petals	九弁	きゅうべん	kyuu-ben
10 flower petals	十弁	じゅうべん	juu-ben

Irregularities or Special beyond Ten: none
Notes: none

ほ・ぼ・ぽ—Ho/Bo/Po
歩—ほ—ho

Japanese: ほ
Romanized: *ho*
Pattern: 漢 H
Used with, or Means: steps, footsteps

1 footstep	一歩	いっぽ	ip-po
2 footsteps	二歩	にほ	ni-ho
3 footsteps	三歩	さんぽ さんぼ or さんほ	sam-po sam-bo or san-ho
4 footsteps	四歩	よんほ よんぽ or よんぼ	yon-ho yom-po or yom-bo
5 footsteps	五歩	ごほ	go-ho
6 footsteps	六歩	ろっぽ or ろくほ	rop-po or roku-ho
7 footsteps	七歩	ななほ	nana-ho
8 footsteps	八歩	はっぽ or はちほ	hap-po or hachi-ho
9 footsteps	九歩	きゅうほ	kyuu-ho
10 footsteps	十歩	じゅっぽ じっぽ	jup-po jip-po

Irregularities or Special beyond Ten:

100 footsteps	百歩	ひゃっぽ ひゃくほ	hyap-po hyaku-ho
1,000 footsteps	千歩	せんぼ or せんぽ	sem-bo or sem-po
10,000 footsteps	万歩	まんぼ or まんぽ	mam-bo or mam-po
how many footsteps?	何歩	なんぽ or なんほ	nam-po or nan-ho

Notes: none

畝 — ほ — *ho*

Japanese: ほ
Romanized: *ho*
Pattern: 漢 H
Used with, or Means: *ho*, a unit of area, 30 坪 (*tsubo*), 153,720 in² (1067.5 ft²)/99.17399 m², see also 畝 (*se*)

1 *ho*	一畝	いっぽ		*ip-po*
2 *ho*	二畝	にほ		*ni-ho*
3 *ho*	三畝	さんぽ さんぽ or さんほ		*sam-po* *sam-bo* or *san-ho*
4 *ho*	四畝	よんほ よんぽ or よんぼ		*yon-ho* *yom-po* or *yom-bo*
5 *ho*	五畝	ごほ		*go-ho*
6 *ho*	六畝	ろっぽ or ろくほ		*rop-po* or *roku-ho*
7 *ho*	七畝	ななほ		*nana-ho*
8 *ho*	八畝	はっぽ or はちほ		*hap-po* or *hachi-ho*
9 *ho*	九畝	きゅうほ		*kyuu-ho*
10 *ho*	十畝	じゅっぽ じっぽ		*jup-po* *jip-po*

Irregularities or Special beyond Ten:

100 *ho*	百畝	ひゃっぽ ひゃくほ		*hyap-po* *hyaku-ho*
1,000 *ho*	千畝	せんぽ or せんぼ		*sem-bo* or *sem-po*
10,000 *ho*	万畝	まんぽ or まんぼ		*mam-bo* or *mam-po*
how many *ho*?	何畝	なんぽ or なんほ		*nam-po* or *nam-ho*

Notes: none

舗・鋪——ほ——*ho*

Japanese: ほ
Romanized: *ho*
Pattern: 漢 H
Used with, or Means: (literary language) maps

1 map	一舗・鋪	いっぽ	*ip-po*
2 maps	二舗・鋪	にほ	*ni-ho*
3 maps	三舗・鋪	さんぽ さんぽ or さんほ	*sam-po* *sam-bo* or *san-ho*
4 maps	四舗・鋪	よんほ よんぽ or よんぼ	*yon-ho* *yom-po* or *yom-bo*
5 maps	五舗・鋪	ごほ	*go-ho*
6 maps	六舗・鋪	ろっぽ or ろくほ	*rop-po* or *roku-ho*
7 maps	七舗・鋪	ななほ	*nana-ho*
8 maps	八舗・鋪	はっぽ or はちほ	*hap-po* or *hachi-ho*
9 maps	九舗・鋪	きゅうほ	*kyuu-ho*
10 maps	十舗・鋪	じゅっぽ じっぽ	*jup-po* *jip-po*

Irregularities or Special beyond Ten:

100 maps	百舗・鋪	ひゃっぽ ひゃくほ	*hyap-po* *hyaku-ho*
1,000 maps	千舗・鋪	せんぼ or せんぽ	*sem-bo* or *sem-po*
10,000 maps	万舗・鋪	まんぼ or まんぽ	*mam-bo* or *mam-po*
how many maps?	何舗・鋪	なんぼ or なんほ	*nam-po* or *nam-ho*

Notes: none

幅—ほ—*ho*

Japanese: ほ
Romanized: *ho*
Pattern: 漢 H
Used with, or Means: (polite) firelight, shadows, forms moving in firelight, see also 幅 (*fuku*)

1 shadow	一幅	いっぽ	ip-po
2 shadows	二幅	にほ	ni-ho
3 shadows	三幅	さんぽ さんぼ or さんほ	sam-po sam-bo or san-ho
4 shadows	四幅	よんほ よんぽ or よんぼ	yon-ho yom-po or yom-bo
5 shadows	五幅	ごほ	go-ho
6 shadows	六幅	ろっぽ or ろくほ	rop-po or roku-ho
7 shadows	七幅	ななほ	nana-ho
8 shadows	八幅	はっぽ or はちほ	hap-po or hachi-ho
9 shadows	九幅	きゅうほ	kyuu-ho
10 shadows	十幅	じゅっぽ じっぽ	jup-po jip-po

Irregularities or Special beyond Ten:

100 shadows	百幅	ひゃっぽ ひゃくほ	hyap-po hyaku-ho
1,000 shadows	千幅	せんぼ or せんぽ	sem-bo or sem-po
10,000 shadows	万幅	まんぼ or まんぽ	mam-bo or mam-po
how many shadows?	何幅	なんぽ or なんほ	nam-po or nam-ho

Notes: none

ポイント—*pointo*

Japanese: ぽいんと
Romanized: *pointo*
Pattern: 漢 P

Used with, or Means: particular parts, sections, places; marks, points, points made, score, runs, number of items, credits, marks obtained, see Notes, see also 点 (*ten*); font size in word processing (as in 12-point type), see Notes, see also 号 (*gou*), see also 級 (*kyuu*); a fluctuation in percentage points (as in, his approval rating dropped 3 points)

1 point	1 ポイント	いちぽいんと	*ichi-pointo*
2 points	2 ポイント	にぽいんと	*ni-pointo*
3 points	3 ポイント	さんぽいんと	*sam-pointo*
4 points	4 ポイント	よんぽいんと	*yom-pointo*
5 points	5 ポイント	ごぽいんと	*go-pointo*
6 points	6 ポイント	ろくぽいんと	*roku-pointo*
7 points	7 ポイント	ななぽいんと	*nana-pointo*
8 points	8 ポイント	はちぽいんと	*hachi-pointo*
9 points	9 ポイント	きゅうぽいんと	*kyuu-pointo*
10 points	10 ポイント	じゅうぽいんと	*juu-pointo*

Irregularities or Special beyond Ten: none

Notes: In sports, one can also use Japanized English numbers with ポイント: ワンポイント (1 point), ツーポイント (2 points), and so on. For font size, rather than ポイント (*pointo*), the size is often abbreviated to ポ (*po*), instead.

包 — ほう — *hou*

Japanese: ほう
Romanized: *hou*
Pattern: 漢 H
Used with, or Means: pills, tablets; packets of powdered medicine, tea, see also 包み (*tsutsumi*)

1 packet	一包	いっぽう	*ip-pou*
2 packets	二包	にほう	*ni-hou*
3 packets	三包	さんぽう さんぼう or さんほう	*sam-pou* *sam-bou* or *san-hou*
4 packets	四包	よんほう よんぽう or よんぼう	*yon-hou* *yom-pou* or *yom-bou*
5 packets	五包	ごほう	*go-hou*
6 packets	六包	ろっぽう or ろくほう	*rop-pou* or *roku-hou*
7 packets	七包	ななほう	*nana-hou*
8 packets	八包	はっぽう or はちほう	*hap-pou* or *hachi-hou*
9 packets	九包	きゅうほう	*kyuu-hou*
10 packets	十包	じゅっぽう じっぽう	*jup-pou* *jip-pou*

Irregularities or Special beyond Ten:

100 packets	百包	ひゃっぽう ひゃくほう	*hyap-pou* *hyaku-hou*
1,000 packets	千包	せんぼう or せんぽう	*sem-bou* or *sem-pou*
10,000 packets	万包	まんぼう or まんぽう	*mam-bou* or *mam-pou*
how many packets?	何包	なんぼう or なんほう	*nam-pou* or *nan-hou*

Notes: none

報 — ほう — hou

Japanese: ほう
Romanized: hou
Pattern: 漢 H
Used with, or Means: notices, announcements, pieces of information, intelligence reports, reports, written reports, papers

1 report	一報	いっぽう	ip-pou
2 reports	二報	にほう	ni-hou
3 reports	三報	さんぽう or さんほう	sam-pou / sam-bou or san-hou
4 reports	四報	よんほう / よんぽう or よんぼう	yon-hou / yom-pou or yom-bou
5 reports	五報	ごほう	go-hou
6 reports	六報	ろっぽう or ろくほう	rop-pou or roku-hou
7 reports	七報	ななほう	nana-hou
8 reports	八報	はっぽう or はちほう	hap-pou or hachi-hou
9 reports	九報	きゅうほう	kyuu-hou
10 reports	十報	じゅっぽう / じっぽう	jup-pou / jip-pou

Irregularities or Special beyond Ten:

100 reports	百報	ひゃっぽう / ひゃくほう	hyap-pou / hyaku-hou
1,000 reports	千報	せんぼう or せんぽう	sem-bou or sem-pou
10,000 reports	万報	まんぼう or まんぽう	mam-bou or mam-pou
how many reports?	何報	なんぼう or なんほう	nam-pou or nan-hou

Notes: none

峰 — ほう — hou

Japanese: ほう
Romanized: *hou*
Pattern: 漢 H
Used with, or Means: sharp, pointed mountains; summits, spires, see also 嶺 (*rei*)

1 summit	一峰	いっぽう	*ip-pou*
2 summits	二峰	にほう	*ni-hou*
3 summits	三峰	さんぽう	*sam-bou*
4 summits	四峰	よんほう よんぽう	*yon-hou* *yom-bou*
5 summits	五峰	ごほう	*go-hou*
6 summits	六峰	ろっぽう	*rop-pou*
7 summits	七峰	ななほう	*nana-hou*
8 summits	八峰	はっぽう	*hap-pou*
9 summits	九峰	きゅうほう	*kyuu-hou*
10 summits	十峰	じゅっぽう じっぽう	*jup-pou* *jip-pou*

Irregularities or Special beyond Ten:

100 summits	百峰	ひゃっぽう	*hyap-pou*
1,000 summits	千峰	せんぼう	*sem-bou*
10,000 summits	万峰	まんぼう	*mam-bou*
how many summits?	何峰	なんぼう	*nam-bou*

Notes: none

法 — ほう — hou

Japanese: ほう
Romanized: hou
Pattern: 漢 H
Used with, or Means: methods, manners, ways, means, techniques, ways of doing something

1 method	一法	いっぽう	ip-pou
2 methods	二法	にほう	ni-hou
3 methods	三法	さんぽう	sam-bou
4 methods	四法	よんほう / よんぼう	yon-hou / yom-bou
5 methods	五法	ごほう	go-hou
6 methods	六法	ろっぽう	rop-pou
7 methods	七法	ななほう	nana-hou
8 methods	八法	はっぽう	hap-pou
9 methods	九法	きゅうほう	kyuu-hou
10 methods	十法	じゅっぽう / じっぽう	jup-pou / jip-pou

Irregularities or Special beyond Ten:

100 methods	百法	ひゃっぽう	hyap-pou
1,000 methods	千法	せんぼう	sem-bou
10,000 methods	万法	まんぼう	mam-bou
how many methods?	何法	なんぼう	nam-bou

Notes: none

木 — ぼく — *boku*

Japanese: ぼく
Romanized: *boku*
Pattern: 漢 ∅
Used with, or Means: pieces of lumber

1 piece of lumber	一木	いちぼく	*ichi-boku*
2 pieces of lumber	二木	にぼく	*ni-boku*
3 pieces of lumber	三木	さんぼく	*sam-boku*
4 pieces of lumber	四木	よんぼく	*yom-boku*
5 pieces of lumber	五木	ごぼく	*go-boku*
6 pieces of lumber	六木	ろくぼく	*roku-boku*
7 pieces of lumber	七木	ななぼく	*nana-boku*
8 pieces of lumber	八木	はちぼく	*hachi-boku*
9 pieces of lumber	九木	きゅくぼく	*kyuu-boku*
10 pieces of lumber	十木	じゅうぼく	*juu-boku*

Irregularities or Special beyond Ten: none
Notes: none

V —ぼると— *boruto*

Japanese: ぼると
Romanized: *boruto*
Pattern: 漢 ∅

Used with, or Means: volts (symbol: V), $V = \frac{W}{A} = \sqrt{W \cdot \Omega} = \frac{J}{A \cdot s} = \frac{N \cdot m}{A \cdot s} = \frac{kg \cdot m^2}{A \cdot s^3} = \frac{kg \cdot m^2}{C \cdot s^2} = \frac{N \cdot m}{C} = \frac{J}{C}$

1 volt	1 ボルト	いちぼると	*ichi-boruto*
2 volts	2 ボルト	にぼると	*ni-boruto*
3 volts	3 ボルト	さんぼると	*sam-boruto*
4 volts	4 ボルト	よんぼると	*yom-boruto*
5 volts	5 ボルト	ごぼると	*go-boruto*
6 volts	6 ボルト	ろくぼると	*roku-boruto*
7 volts	7 ボルト	ななぼると	*nana-boruto*
8 volts	8 ボルト	はちぼると	*hachi-boruto*
9 volts	9 ボルト	きゅくぼると	*kyuu-boruto*
10 volts	10 ボルト	じゅうぼると	*juu-boruto*

Irregularities or Special beyond Ten: none
Notes: none

本—ほん—*hon*

Japanese: ほん
Romanized: *hon*
Pattern: 漢 H
Used with, or Means: long, cylindrical objects: pencils, bottles, rivers, roads, train tracks, ties, guitars; rounds or points of a competition (karate); baseball safe hits; movies; letters; telephone calls (see also 通話 *tsuuwa*); train or bus routes

1 bottle	一本	いっぽん	*ip-pon*
2 bottles	二本	にほん	*ni-hon*
3 bottles	三本	さんぼん	*sam-bon*
4 bottles	四本	よんほん or よんぼん	*yon-hon* or *yom-bon*
5 bottles	五本	ごほん	*go-hon*
6 bottles	六本	ろっぽん or ろくほん	*rop-pon* or *roku-hon*
7 bottles	七本	ななほん	*nana-hon*
8 bottles	八本	はっぽん or はちほん	*hap-pon* or *hachi-hon*
9 bottles	九本	きゅうほん	*kyuu-hon*
10 bottles	十本	じゅっぽん or じっぽん	*jup-pon* or *jip-pon*

Irregularities or Special beyond Ten:

100 bottles	百本	ひゃっぽん or ひゃくほん	*hyap-pon* or *hyaku-hon*
1,000 bottles	千本	せんぼん or せんほん	*sem-bon* or *sen-hon*
10,000 bottles	万本	まんぼん or まんほん	*mam-bon* or *man-hon*
how many bottles?	何本	なんぼん or なんほん	*nam-bon* or *nan-hon*

Notes: none

ポンド・听—ぽんど—*pondo*

Japanese: ぽんど
Romanized: *pondo*
Pattern: 漢 P
Used with, or Means: Pounds Sterling, £, British monetary unit

1 Pound	1 ポンド・听	いちぽんど	*ichi-pondo*
2 Pounds	2 ポンド・听	にぽんど	*ni-pondo*
3 Pounds	3 ポンド・听	さんぽんど	*sam-pondo*
4 Pounds	4 ポンド・听	よんぽんど	*yom-pondo*
5 Pounds	5 ポンド・听	ごぽんど	*go-pondo*
6 Pounds	6 ポンド・听	ろくぽんど	*roku-pondo*
7 Pounds	7 ポンド・听	ななぽんど	*nana-pondo*
8 Pounds	8 ポンド・听	はちぽんど	*hachi-pondo*
9 Pounds	9 ポンド・听	きゅうぽんど	*kyuu-pondo*
10 Pounds	10 ポンド・听	じゅうぽんど	*juu-pondo*

Irregularities or Special beyond Ten: none
Notes: none

ポンド・封・磅―ぽんど―*pondo*

Japanese: ぽんど
Romanized: *pondo*
Pattern: 漢 P
Used with, or Means: pounds (symbol: lb), a unit of weight, about 453.59237 g

1 pound	1 ポンド・封・磅	いちぽんど	*ichi-pondo*
2 pounds	2 ポンド・封・磅	にぽんど	*ni-pondo*
3 pounds	3 ポンド・封・磅	さんぽんど	*sam-pondo*
4 pounds	4 ポンド・封・磅	よんぽんど	*yom-pondo*
5 pounds	5 ポンド・封・磅	ごぽんど	*go-pondo*
6 pounds	6 ポンド・封・磅	ろくぽんど	*roku-pondo*
7 pounds	7 ポンド・封・磅	ななぽんど	*nana-pondo*
8 pounds	8 ポンド・封・磅	はちぽんど	*hachi-pondo*
9 pounds	9 ポンド・封・磅	きゅうぽんど	*kyuu-pondo*
10 pounds	10 ポンド・封・磅	じゅうぽんど	*juu-pondo*

Irregularities or Special beyond Ten: none
Notes: none

ま—Ma
間—ま—ma

Japanese: ま
Romanized: *ma*
Pattern: 和 I
Used with, or Means: rooms

1 room	一間	ひとま	*hito-ma*
2 rooms	二間	ふたま	*futa-ma*
3 rooms	三間	さんま	*sam-ma*
4 rooms	四間	よんま	*yom-ma*
5 rooms	五間	ごま	*go-ma*
6 rooms	六間	ろくま	*roku-ma*
7 rooms	七間	ななま	*nana-ma*
8 rooms	八間	はちま	*hachi-ma*
9 rooms	九間	きゅうま	*kyuu-ma*
10 rooms	十間	じゅうま	*juu-ma*

Irregularities or Special beyond Ten: none
Notes: none

枚—まい—*mai*

Japanese: まい
Romanized: *mai*
Pattern: 漢 ∅
Used with, or Means: thin, flat objects, planes, sheets of paper, mats, see also 個 (*ko*), see also 片 (*hen*), see also 葉 (*you*); the position or ranking of a person (especially in Sumo); slices (of *sashimi*); food and drink orders (by the plate); sets of clothing, see also 着 (*chaku*)

1 sheet	一枚	いちまい	*ichi-mai*
2 sheets	二枚	にまい	*ni-mai*
3 sheets	三枚	さんまい	*sam-mai*
4 sheets	四枚	よんまい	*yom-mai*
5 sheets	五枚	ごまい	*go-mai*
6 sheets	六枚	ろくまい	*roku-mai*
7 sheets	七枚	ななまい	*nana-mai*
8 sheets	八枚	はちまい	*hachi-mai*
9 sheets	九枚	きゅうまい	*kyuu-mai*
10 sheets	十枚	じゅうまい	*juu-mai*

Irregularities or Special beyond Ten: none
Notes: none

マイル・哩—まいる—*mairu*

Japanese: まいる
Romanized: *mairu*
Pattern: 漢 ∅
Used with, or Means: miles (symbol: mi), a unit of length, 63,360 in (5,280 ft)/1,609.34400 m

1 mile	一マイル・哩	いちまいる	*ichi-mairu*
2 miles	二マイル・哩	にまいる	*ni-mairu*
3 miles	三マイル・哩	さんまいる	*sam-mairu*
4 miles	四マイル・哩	よんまいる	*yom-mairu*
5 miles	五マイル・哩	ごまいる	*go-mairu*
6 miles	六マイル・哩	ろくまいる	*roku-mairu*
7 miles	七マイル・哩	ななまいる	*nana-mairu*
8 miles	八マイル・哩	はちまいる	*hachi-mairu*
9 miles	九マイル・哩	きゅうまいる	*kyuu-mairu*
10 miles	十マイル・哩	じゅうまいる	*juu-mairu*

Irregularities or Special beyond Ten: none
Notes: none

巻き—まき—*maki*

Japanese: まき
Romanized: *maki*
Pattern: 和 I
Used with, or Means: rolls of silk, cloth, scrolls, windings, scriptures, sacred books

1 scroll	一巻き	ひとまき	*hito-maki*
2 scrolls	二巻き	ふたまき	*futa-maki*
3 scrolls	三巻き	さんまき	*sam-maki*
4 scrolls	四巻き	よんまき	*yom-maki*
5 scrolls	五巻き	ごまき	*go-maki*
6 scrolls	六巻き	ろくまき	*roku-maki*
7 scrolls	七巻き	ななまき	*nana-maki*
8 scrolls	八巻き	はちまき	*hachi-maki*
9 scrolls	九巻き	きゅうまき	*kyuu-maki*
10 scrolls	十巻き	じゅうまき	*juu-maki*

Irregularities or Special beyond Ten: none
Notes: none

幕—まく—*maku*

Japanese: まく
Romanized: *maku*
Pattern: 漢 ∅ or 和 I
Used with, or Means: acts, performances, shows, sections of a play

1 act	一幕	いちまく / ひとまく	*ichi-maku* / *hito-maku*
2 acts	二幕	にまく / ふたまく	*ni-maku* / *futa-maku*
3 acts	三幕	さんまく	*sam-maku*
4 acts	四幕	よんまく	*yom-maku*
5 acts	五幕	ごまく	*go-maku*
6 acts	六幕	ろくまく	*roku-maku*
7 acts	七幕	ななまく	*nana-maku*
8 acts	八幕	はちまく	*hachi-maku*
9 acts	九幕	きゅうまく	*kyuu-maku*
10 acts	十幕	じゅうまく	*juu-maku*

Irregularities or Special beyond Ten: none
Notes: none

第〇幕 ― だい〇まく ― *dai-*〇*-maku*

Japanese: だい〇まく
Romanized: *dai-*〇*-maku*
Pattern: 漢 ∅
Used with, or Means: the Nth act (of a play)

the 1st act	第一幕 序幕	だいいちまく じょまく	*dai-ichi-maku* *jomaku*
the 2nd act	第二幕	だいにまく	*dai-ni-maku*
the 3rd act	第三幕	だいさんまく	*dai-sam-maku*
the 4th act	第四幕	だいよんまく	*dai-yom-maku*
the 5th act	第五幕	だいごまく	*dai-go-maku*
the 6th act	第六幕	だいろくまく	*dai-roku-maku*
the 7th act	第七幕	だいななまく	*dai-nana-maku*
the 8th act	第八幕	だいはちまく	*dai-hachi-maku*
the 9th act	第九幕	だいきゅうまく	*dai-kyuu-maku*
the 10th act	第十幕	だいじゅうまく	*dai-juu-maku*

Irregularities or Special beyond Ten: none
Notes: none

幕目—まくめ—*maku-me*

Japanese: まくめ
Romanized: *maku-me*
Pattern: 漢 ∅ or 和 I
Used with, or Means: the Nth act (of a Classical *Kabuki* play)

the 1st act	一幕目 　 序幕	いちまくめ ひとまくめ じょまく	*ichi-maku-me* *hito-maku-me* *jomaku*
the 2nd act	二幕目	にまくめ ふたまくめ	*ni-maku-me* *futa-maku-me*
the 3rd act	三幕目	さんまくめ	*sam-maku-me*
the 4th act	四幕目	よんまくめ	*yom-maku-me*
the 5th act	五幕目	ごまくめ	*go-maku-me*
the 6th act	六幕目	ろくまくめ	*roku-maku-me*
the 7th act	七幕目	ななまくめ	*nana-maku-me*
the 8th act	八幕目	はちまくめ	*hachi-maku-me*
the 9th act	九幕目	きゅうまくめ	*kyuu-maku-me*
the 10th act	十幕目	じゅうまくめ	*juu-maku-me*

Irregularities or Special beyond Ten: none
Notes: none

升 — ます — *masu*

Japanese: ます
Romanized: *masu*
Pattern: 和 III or 和 I
Used with, or Means: *masu*, a unit of volume, 60.99735 fl oz (3.81233 pt)/1.80391 L, see also 升 (*shou*)

1 *masu*	一升	ひとます	*hito-masu*
2 *masu*	二升	ふたます	*futa-masu*
3 *masu*	三升	みます / さんます	*mi-masu* / *sam-masu*
4 *masu*	四升	よます / よんます	*yo-masu* / *yom-masu*
5 *masu*	五升	ごます	*go-masu*
6 *masu*	六升	ろくます	*roku-masu*
7 *masu*	七升	ななます	*nana-masu*
8 *masu*	八升	はちます	*hachi-masu*
9 *masu*	九升	きゅうます	*kyuu-masu*
10 *masu*	十升	じゅうます	*juu-masu*

Irregularities or Special beyond Ten: none
Notes: none

曲げ—まげ—*mage*

Japanese: まげ
Romanized: *mage*
Pattern: 和 IV or 和 I
Used with, or Means: servings of *tsukudani* (佃煮), seaweed preserved by boiling it down in soysauce (about one tablespoon per bowl of rice)

1 serving	一曲げ	ひとまげ	*hito-mage*
2 servings	二曲げ	ふたまげ	*futa-mage*
3 servings	三曲げ	みまげ / さんまげ	*mi-mage* / *sam-mage*
4 servings	四曲げ	よまげ / よんまげ	*yo-mage* / *yom-mage*
5 servings	五曲げ	ごまげ	*go-mage*
6 servings	六曲げ	ろくまげ	*roku-mage*
7 servings	七曲げ	ななまげ	*nana-mage*
8 servings	八曲げ	はちまげ	*hachi-mage*
9 servings	九曲げ	きゅうまげ	*kyuu-mage*
10 servings	十曲げ	とおまげ	*juu-mage*

Irregularities or Special beyond Ten: none
Notes: none

マルク—まるく—*maruku*

Japanese: まるく
Romanized: *maruku*
Pattern: 漢 ∅
Used with, or Means: *Deutsche Mark*, German monetary unit (symbol: DM)

1 DM	1マルク	いちまるく	*ichi-maruku*
2 DM	2マルク	にまるく	*ni-maruku*
3 DM	3マルク	さんまるく	*sam-maruku*
4 DM	4マルク	よんまるく	*yom-maruku*
5 DM	5マルク	ごまるく	*go-maruku*
6 DM	6マルク	ろくまるく	*roku-maruku*
7 DM	7マルク	ななまるく	*nana-maruku*
8 DM	8マルク	はちまるく	*hachi-maruku*
9 DM	9マルク	きゅうまるく	*kyuu-maruku*
10 DM	10マルク	じゅうまるく	*juu-maruku*

Irregularities or Special beyond Ten: none
Notes: none

回り・廻り・周り — まわり — *mawari*

Japanese: まわり
Romanized: *mawari*
Pattern: 和 III or 和 I
Used with, or Means: number of times around a course, revolutions of revolving objects or rotating objects, the circumference of a rotation, revolution

1 rotation	一回り・廻り・周り	ひとまわり	*hito-mawari*
2 rotations	二回り・廻り・周り	ふたまわり	*futa-mawari*
3 rotations	三回り・廻り・周り	みまわり さんまわり	*mi-mawari* *sam-mawari*
4 rotations	四回り・廻り・周り	よまわり よんまわり	*yo-mawari* *yom-mawari*
5 rotations	五回り・廻り・周り	ごまわり	*itsu-mawari*
6 rotations	六回り・廻り・周り	ろくまわり	*roku-mawari*
7 rotations	七回り・廻り・周り	ななまわり	*nana-mawari*
8 rotations	八回り・廻り・周り	はちまわり	*hachi-mawari*
9 rotations	九回り・廻り・周り	きゅうまわり	*kyuu-mawari*
10 rotations	十回り・廻り・周り	じゅうまわり	*juu-mawari*

Irregularities or Special beyond Ten: none
Notes: none

万・萬 — まん — *man*

Japanese: まん
Romanized: *man*
Pattern: 漢 ∅
Used with, or Means: 10,000, 10 thousand, 10⁴

10,000	一万・萬	いちまん	*ichi-man*
20,000	二万・萬	にまん	*ni-man*
30,000	三万・萬	さんまん	*sam-man*
40,000	四万・萬	よんまん	*yom-man*
50,000	五万・萬	ごまん	*go-man*
60,000	六万・萬	ろくまん	*roku-man*
70,000	七万・萬	ななまん	*nana-man*
80,000	八万・萬	はちまん	*hachi-man*
90,000	九万・萬	きゅうまん	*kyuu-man*
100,000	十万・萬	じゅうまん	*juu-man*

Irregularities or Special beyond Ten:

1,000,000	百万・萬	ひゃくまん	*hyaku-man*
10,000,000	千万・萬	せんまん	*sem-man*

Notes: Unlike 十 (*juu*), 百 (*hyaku*), and 千 (*sen*), 万 (*man*), by itself, requires 一 (*ichi*) to precede it: 一万 (*ichi-man*). In this volume, in the interest of space, as well as sparing the reader undue confusion, I do *not* precede instances of 万〇 (*man-*〇) with 一 (*ichi*).

み—Mi
味—み—mi

Japanese: み
Romanized: *mi*
Pattern: 漢 ∅
Used with, or Means: condiments, flavors, ingredients

1 flavor	一味	いちみ	*ichi-mi*
2 flavors	二味	にみ	*ni-mi*
3 flavors	三味	さんみ	*sam-mi*
4 flavors	四味	よんみ	*yom-mi*
5 flavors	五味	ごみ	*go-mi*
6 flavors	六味	ろくみ	*roku-mi*
7 flavors	七味	ななみ / しちみ	*nana-mi* / *shichi-mi*
8 flavors	八味	はちみ	*hachi-mi*
9 flavors	九味	きゅうみ	*kyuu-mi*
10 flavors	十味	じゅうみ	*juu-mi*

Irregularities or Special beyond Ten: none
Notes: 一味 also means *a gang*, see also 一党 (*ittou*).

ミリグラム・瓱—ミリグラム—*miri-guramu*

Japanese: ミリグラム
Romanized: *miri-guramu*
Pattern: 漢 Ø
Used with, or Means: milligrams (S. I. symbol: mg), a unit of mass, 0.001 g (0.0000352740 oz)

1 mg	一ミリグラム・瓱	いちミリグラム	*ichi-miri-guramu*
2 mg	二ミリグラム・瓱	にミリグラム	*ni-miri-guramu*
3 mg	三ミリグラム・瓱	さんミリグラム	*sam-miri-guramu*
4 mg	四ミリグラム・瓱	よんミリグラム	*yom-miri-guramu*
5 mg	五ミリグラム・瓱	ごミリグラム	*go-miri-guramu*
6 mg	六ミリグラム・瓱	ろくミリグラム	*roku-miri-guramu*
7 mg	七ミリグラム・瓱	ななミリグラム	*nana-miri-guramu*
8 mg	八ミリグラム・瓱	はちミリグラム	*hachi-miri-guramu*
9 mg	九ミリグラム・瓱	きゅうミリグラム	*kyuu-miri-guramu*
10 mg	十ミリグラム・瓱	じゅうミリグラム	*juu-miri-guramu*

Irregularities or Special beyond Ten: none
Notes: none

ミリバール—みりばある—*miri-baaru*

Japanese: みりばある
Romanized: *miri-baaru*
Pattern: 漢 ∅
Used with, or Means: millibars (S. I. symbol: mbar/mb), 100 Pascals

1 mbar/mb	1 ミリバール	いちみりばある	*ichi-miri-baaru*
2 mbar/mb	2 ミリバール	にみりばある	*ni-miri-baaru*
3 mbar/mb	3 ミリバール	さんみりばある	*sam-miri-baaru*
4 mbar/mb	4 ミリバール	よんみりばある	*yom-miri-baaru*
5 mbar/mb	5 ミリバール	ごみりばある	*go-miri-baaru*
6 mbar/mb	6 ミリバール	ろくみりばある	*roku-miri-baaru*
7 mbar/mb	7 ミリバール	ななみりばある	*nana-miri-baaru*
8 mbar/mb	8 ミリバール	はちみりばある	*hachi-miri-baaru*
9 mbar/mb	9 ミリバール	きゅうみりばある	*kyuu-miri-baaru*
10 mbar/mb	10 ミリバール	じゅうみりばある	*juu-miri-baaru*

Irregularities or Special beyond Ten: none
Notes: none

ミリメートル・粍—みりめえとる—*miri-meetoru*

Japanese: みりめえとる
Romanized: *miri-meetoru*
Pattern: 漢 Ø
Used with, or Means: millimeters (S. I. symbol: mm), a unit of length, 0.001 m (0.0393700787 in)

1 mm	一ミリメートル・粍	いちみりめえとる	*ichi-miri-meetoru*
2 mm	二ミリメートル・粍	にみりめえとる	*ni-miri-meetoru*
3 mm	三ミリメートル・粍	さんみりめえとる	*sam-miri-meetoru*
4 mm	四ミリメートル・粍	よんみりめえとる	*yom-miri-meetoru*
5 mm	五ミリメートル・粍	ごみりめえとる	*go-miri-meetoru*
6 mm	六ミリメートル・粍	ろくみりめえとる	*roku-miri-meetoru*
7 mm	七ミリメートル・粍	ななみりめえとる	*nana-miri-meetoru*
8 mm	八ミリメートル・粍	はちみりめえとる	*hachi-miri-meetoru*
9 mm	九ミリメートル・粍	きゅうみりめえとる	*kyuu-miri-meetoru*
10 mm	十ミリメートル・粍	じゅうみりめえとる	*juu-miri-meetoru*

Irregularities or Special beyond Ten: none
Notes: none

ミリリットル・竓—みりりっとる—*miri-rittoru*

Japanese: みりりっとる
Romanized: *miri-rittoru*
Pattern: 漢 Ø
Used with, or Means: milliliters (S. I. symbol: mL), a unit of volume, 0.001 L (0.0338140227 fl oz)

1 mL	一ミリリットル・竓	いちみりりっとる	*ichi-miri-rittoru*
2 mL	二ミリリットル・竓	にみりりっとる	*ni-miri-rittoru*
3 mL	三ミリリットル・竓	さんみりりっとる	*sam-miri-rittoru*
4 mL	四ミリリットル・竓	よんみりりっとる	*yom-miri-rittoru*
5 mL	五ミリリットル・竓	ごみりりっとる	*go-miri-rittoru*
6 mL	六ミリリットル・竓	ろくみりりっとる	*roku-miri-rittoru*
7 mL	七ミリリットル・竓	ななみりりっとる	*nana-miri-rittoru*
8 mL	八ミリリットル・竓	はちみりりっとる	*hachi-miri-rittoru*
9 mL	九ミリリットル・竓	きゅうみりりっとる	*kyuu-miri-rittoru*
10 mL	十ミリリットル・竓	じゅうみりりっとる	*juu-miri-rittoru*

Irregularities or Special beyond Ten: none
Notes: none

む—Mu
棟—むね—mune

Japanese: むね
Romanized: *mune*
Pattern: 和 III or 和 I
Used with, or Means: buildings, houses, see also 棟 (*tou*)

1 building	一棟	ひとむね	*hito-mune*
2 buildings	二棟	ふたむね	*futa-mune*
3 buildings	三棟	みむね / さんむね	*mi-mune* / *sam-mune*
4 buildings	四棟	よむね / よんむね	*yo-mune* / *yom-mune*
5 buildings	五棟	ごむね	*go-mune*
6 buildings	六棟	ろくむね	*roku-mune*
7 buildings	七棟	ななむね	*nana-mune*
8 buildings	八棟	はちむね	*hachi-mune*
9 buildings	九棟	きゅうむね	*kyuu-mune*
10 buildings	十棟	じゅうむね	*juu-mune*

Irregularities or Special beyond Ten: none
Notes: none

匹・疋—むら—*mura*

Japanese: むら
Romanized: *mura*
Pattern: 和 III or 和 I
Used with, or Means: rolls of fabric

1 roll	一匹・疋	ひとむら	*hito-mura*
2 rolls	二匹・疋	ふたむら	*futa-mura*
3 rolls	三匹・疋	みむら / さんむら	*mi-mura* / *sam-mura*
4 rolls	四匹・疋	よむら / よんむら	*yo-mura* / *yom-mura*
5 rolls	五匹・疋	ごむら	*go-mura*
6 rolls	六匹・疋	ろくむら	*roku-mura*
7 rolls	七匹・疋	ななむら	*nana-mura*
8 rolls	八匹・疋	はちむら	*hachi-mura*
9 rolls	九匹・疋	きゅうむら	*kyuu-mura*
10 rolls	十匹・疋	じゅうむら	*juu-mura*

Irregularities or Special beyond Ten: none
Notes: none

群・叢・簇—むら—*mura*

Japanese: むら
Romanized: *mura*
Pattern: 和 III or 和 I
Used with, or Means: groves, thickets, bunches of flowers, bouquets; (social) groups, crowds, throngs, mobs, multitudes, see also 群 (*gun*), see also 団 (*dan*)

1 bouquet	一群・叢・簇	ひとむら	*hito-mura*
2 bouquets	二群・叢・簇	ふたむら	*futa-mura*
3 bouquets	三群・叢・簇	みむら / さんむら	*mi-mura* / *sam-mura*
4 bouquets	四群・叢・簇	よむら / よんむら	*yo-mura* / *yom-mura*
5 bouquets	五群・叢・簇	ごむら	*go-mura*
6 bouquets	六群・叢・簇	ろくむら	*roku-mura*
7 bouquets	七群・叢・簇	ななむら	*nana-mura*
8 bouquets	八群・叢・簇	はちむら	*hachi-mura*
9 bouquets	九群・叢・簇	きゅうむら	*kyuu-mura*
10 bouquets	十群・叢・簇	じゅうむら	*juu-mura*

Irregularities or Special beyond Ten: none
Notes: none

群れ—むれ—*mure*

Japanese: むれ
Romanized: *mure*
Pattern: 和 III or 和 I
Used with, or Means: groups, flocks, see also 群 (*gun*), see also 団 (*dan*)

1 flock	一群れ	ひとむれ	*hito-mure*
2 flocks	二群れ	ふたむれ	*futa-mure*
3 flocks	三群れ	みむれ / さんむれ	*mi-mure* / *sam-mure*
4 flocks	四群れ	よむれ / よんむれ	*yo-mure* / *yom-mure*
5 flocks	五群れ	ごむれ	*go-mure*
6 flocks	六群れ	ろくむれ	*roku-mure*
7 flocks	七群れ	ななむれ	*nana-mure*
8 flocks	八群れ	はちむれ	*hachi-mure*
9 flocks	九群れ	きゅうむれ	*kyuu-mure*
10 flocks	十群れ	じゅうむれ	*juu-mure*

Irregularities or Special beyond Ten: none
Notes: none

め — Me
目 — め — me

Japanese: め
Romanized: *me*
Pattern: 和 I
Used with, or Means: *me*; a unit of weight: 1 匁 (*monme*), 0.1323 oz/3.75 g; stitches, net meshes

1 *me*	一目	一目	*hito-me*
2 *me*	二目	二目	*futa-me*
3 *me*	三目	さんめ	*sam-me*
4 *me*	四目	よんめ	*yom-me*
5 *me*	五目	ごめ	*go-me*
6 *me*	六目	ろくめ	*roku-me*
7 *me*	七目	ななめ	*nana-me*
8 *me*	八目	はちめ	*hachi-me*
9 *me*	九目	きゅうめ	*kyuu-me*
10 *me*	十目	じゅうめ	*juu-me*

Irregularities or Special beyond Ten: none
Notes: By adding 目 to another counter, you make it ordidnal:
  三本のビール (*sam-bon no biiru*) is *three bottles of beer.*
  三本目のビール (*sam-bom-me no biiru*) is *the third bottle of beer.*

名——めい——*mei*

Japanese: めい
Romanized: *mei*
Pattern: 漢 ∅
Used with, or Means: (polite) people; members

1 person	一名	いちめい	*ichi-mei*
2 people	二名	にめい	*ni-mei*
3 people	三名	さんめい	*sam-mei*
4 people	四名	よんめい	*yom-mei*
5 people	五名	ごめい	*go-mei*
6 people	六名	ろくめい	*roku-mei*
7 people	七名	ななめい	*nana-mei*
8 people	八名	はちめい	*hachi-mei*
9 people	九名	きゅうめい	*kyuu-mei*
10 people	十名	じゅうめい	*juu-mei*

Irregularities or Special beyond Ten: none

Notes: You will often hear this used by restaurant hosts/hostesses or theater ticket booth attendants asking how many people there are in your party:

　　　Clerk: 何名様ですか。 (*Nam-mei-sama desu ka?*): How many in your party?

　　　Customer: 三人です。 (*San-nin desu.*): Three people.

　　　Clerk: ああ、三名様ですか。畏まりました。 (*Aa, sam-mei-sama desu ka? Kashikomarimashita.*): Ah, a party of three. Certainly, sir/ma'am!

メートル・米 — めえとる — *meetoru*

Japanese: めえとる
Romanized: *meetoru*
Pattern: 漢 ∅
Used with, or Means: meters (S. I. symbol: m), a unit of length, 1 m (39.37008 in, 3.28084 ft)

1 m	一メートル・米	いちめえとる	*ichi-meetoru*
2 m	二メートル・米	にめえとる	*ni-meetoru*
3 m	三メートル・米	さんめえとる	*sam-meetoru*
4 m	四メートル・米	よんめえとる	*yom-meetoru*
5 m	五メートル・米	ごめえとる	*go-meetoru*
6 m	六メートル・米	ろくめえとる	*roku-meetoru*
7 m	七メートル・米	ななめえとる	*nana-meetoru*
8 m	八メートル・米	はちめえとる	*hachi-meetoru*
9 m	九メートル・米	きゅうめえとる	*kyuu-meetoru*
10 m	十メートル・米	じゅうめえとる	*juu-meetoru*

Irregularities or Special beyond Ten: none
Notes: none

面 — めん — men

Japanese: めん
Romanized: *men*
Pattern: 漢 ∅
Used with, or Means: *Noh* masks, facemasks, binoculars, field glasses, opera glasses; instruments with flat surfaces: drums, *biwa*, *koto*; mirrors, inkstones, large-screen televisions, newspaper pages; *Go* boards, *Shougi* boards, tennis courts, ground pools; fields, paddy fields (水田 *suiden*), see also 枚 (*mai*)

1 flat surface	一面	いちめん	*ichi-men*
2 flat surfaces	二面	にめん	*ni-men*
3 flat surfaces	三面	さんめん	*sam-men*
4 flat surfaces	四面	よんめん	*yom-men*
5 flat surfaces	五面	ごめん	*go-men*
6 flat surfaces	六面	ろくめん	*roku-men*
7 flat surfaces	七面	ななめん	*nana-men*
8 flat surfaces	八面	はちめん	*hachi-men*
9 flat surfaces	九面	きゅうめん	*kyuu-men*
10 flat surfaces	十面	じゅうめん	*juu-men*

Irregularities or Special beyond Ten: none
Notes: none

も—Mo
毛・毫—もう—mou

Japanese: もう
Romanized: *mou*
Pattern: 漢 ∅
Used with, or Means: *mou*, former monetary unit, 0.0001 円 (*en*); *mou*, former unit of length, 0.0001 尺 (*shaku*), 0.0011930327 in/0.0000303030 m; *mou*, former unit of weight, 0.001 匁 (*monme*), 0.0001322774 oz/0.00375 g; 1/1,000th of an equally divided whole, later 1/10,000th; the number harvests in a year; (literary language) the hairs on one's head

1 *mou*	一毛・毫	いちもう	*ichi-mou*
2 *mou*	二毛・毫	にもう	*ni-mou*
3 *mou*	三毛・毫	さんもう	*sam-mou*
4 *mou*	四毛・毫	よんもう	*yom-mou*
5 *mou*	五毛・毫	ごもう	*go-mou*
6 *mou*	六毛・毫	ろくもう	*roku-mou*
7 *mou*	七毛・毫	ななもう	*nana-mou*
8 *mou*	八毛・毫	はちもう	*hachi-mou*
9 *mou*	九毛・毫	きゅうもう	*kyuu-mou*
10 *mou*	十毛・毫	じゅうもう	*juu-mou*

Irregularities or Special beyond Ten: none
Notes: none

目 — もく — *moku*

Japanese: もく
Romanized: *moku*
Pattern: 漢 ∅
Used with, or Means: items, *Go* board intersections

1 item	一目	いちもく	*ichi-moku*
2 items	二目	にもく	*ni-moku*
3 items	三目	さんもく	*sam-moku*
4 items	四目	よんもく	*yom-moku*
5 items	五目	ごもく	*go-moku*
6 items	六目	ろくもく	*roku-moku*
7 items	七目	ななもく	*nana-moku*
8 items	八目	はちもく	*hachi-moku*
9 items	九目	きゅうもく	*kyuu-moku*
10 items	十目	じゅうもく	*juu-moku*

Irregularities or Special beyond Ten: none
Notes: none

文字—もじ—*moji*

Japanese: もじ
Romanized: *moji*
Pattern: 漢 Ø/和 IV
Used with, or Means: characters, letters, symbols, numerals

1 character	一文字	いちもじ / ひともじ	*ichi-moji* / *hito-moji*
2 characters	二文字	にもじ / ふたもじ	*ni-moji* / *futa-moji*
3 characters	三文字	さんもじ	*sam-moji*
4 characters	四文字	よんもじ	*yom-moji*
5 characters	五文字	ごもじ	*go-moji*
6 characters	六文字	ろくもじ	*roku-moji*
7 characters	七文字	ななもじ	*nana-moji*
8 characters	八文字	はちもじ	*hachi-moji*
9 characters	九文字	きゅうもじ	*kyuu-moji*
10 characters	十文字	じゅうもじ	*juu-moji*

Irregularities or Special beyond Ten: none

Notes: 文字 (*moji*) is a generic word that simply means a *written character*. However, often people will specify what kind of character it is by replacing the 文 (*mo*) with a qualifier: ローマ字 (*roomaji*) are *Roman letters*, 数字 (*suuji*) are *numerals*, 漢字 (*kanji*) are *Chinese characters*, and so on.

本・連 — もと — *moto*

Japanese: もと
Romanized: *moto*
Pattern: 和 I
Used with, or Means: same as 本 (*hon*); (polite) plants, vegetation; formerly, hunting hawks (鷹狩り *taka-kari*), see also 本 (*hon*), see also 連 (*ren*)

1 plant	一本・連	ひともと	*hito-moto*
2 plants	二本・連	ふたもと	*futa-moto*
3 plants	三本・連	さんもと	*sam-moto*
4 plants	四本・連	よんもと	*yom-moto*
5 plants	五本・連	ごもと	*go-moto*
6 plants	六本・連	ろくもと	*roku-moto*
7 plants	七本・連	ななもと	*nana-moto*
8 plants	八本・連	はちもと	*hachi-moto*
9 plants	九本・連	きゅうもと	*kyuu-moto*
10 plants	十本・連	じゅうもと	*juu-moto*

Irregularities or Special beyond Ten: none
Notes: none

盛 — も り — *mori*

Japanese: もり
Romanized: *mori*
Pattern: 和 I
Used with, or Means: medicine doses; piles of food, fruits, rice, see also 山 (*yama*)

1 dose	一盛	ひともり	*hito-mori*
2 doses	二盛	ふたもり	*futa-mori*
3 doses	三盛	さんもり	*sam-mori*
4 doses	四盛	よんもり	*yom-mori*
5 doses	五盛	ごもり	*go-mori*
6 doses	六盛	ろくもり	*roku-mori*
7 doses	七盛	ななもり	*nana-mori*
8 doses	八盛	はちもり	*hachi-mori*
9 doses	九盛	きゅうもり	*kyuu-mori*
10 doses	十盛	じゅうもり	*juu-mori*

Irregularities or Special beyond Ten: none

Notes: 大盛 (*oomori* – large pile) and 小盛 (*komori* – small pile) are terms used to indicate a large or small amount of rice in your bowl or pile of food on your plate.

文—もん—*mon*

Japanese: もん
Romanized: *mon*
Pattern: 漢 ∅

Used with, or Means: *mon*, former monetary unit, 0.001 貫 (*kan*); a unit of footware size for *tabi* socks (足袋 *tabi*) and shoes, 0.94488 in/0.02400 m

1 *mon*	一文	いちもん	*ichi-mon*
2 *mon*	二文	にもん	*ni-mon*
3 *mon*	三文	さんもん	*sam-mon*
4 *mon*	四文	よんもん	*yom-mon*
5 *mon*	五文	ごもん	*go-mon*
6 *mon*	六文	ろくもん	*roku-mon*
7 *mon*	七文	ななもん	*nana-mon*
8 *mon*	八文	はちもん	*hachi-mon*
9 *mon*	九文	きゅうもん	*kyuu-mon*
10 *mon*	十文	じゅうもん	*juu-mon*

Irregularities or Special beyond Ten: none
Notes: none

門 — もん — *mon*

Japanese: もん
Romanized: *mon*
Pattern: 漢 ∅
Used with, or Means: gates, two-story tower gates (楼門 *roumon*); gate pines (門松 *kadomatsu*, 松飾り *matsukazari*); cannons, artillery

1 cannon	一門	いちもん	*ichi-mon*
2 cannons	二門	にもん	*ni-mon*
3 cannons	三門	さんもん	*sam-mon*
4 cannons	四門	よんもん	*yom-mon*
5 cannons	五門	ごもん	*go-mon*
6 cannons	六門	ろくもん	*roku-mon*
7 cannons	七門	ななもん	*nana-mon*
8 cannons	八門	はちもん	*hachi-mon*
9 cannons	九門	きゅうもん	*kyuu-mon*
10 cannons	十門	じゅうもん	*juu-mon*

Irregularities or Special beyond Ten: none
Notes: none

問 — もん — *mon*

Japanese: もん
Romanized: *mon*
Pattern: 漢 ∅
Used with, or Means: questions

1 question	一問	いちもん	*ichi-mon*
2 questions	二問	にもん	*ni-mon*
3 questions	三問	さんもん	*sam-mon*
4 questions	四問	よんもん	*yom-mon*
5 questions	五問	ごもん	*go-mon*
6 questions	六問	ろくもん	*roku-mon*
7 questions	七問	ななもん	*nana-mon*
8 questions	八問	はちもん	*hachi-mon*
9 questions	九問	きゅうもん	*kyuu-mon*
10 questions	十問	じゅうもん	*juu-mon*

Irregularities or Special beyond Ten: none
Notes: none

匁—もんめ—*monme*

Japanese: もんめ
Romanized: *monme*
Pattern: 漢 Ø
Used with, or Means: *monme*, former monetary unit, 1/60th of a 両 (*ryou*); *monme*, former unit of weight, 0.13228 oz/3.75 g

1 *monme*	一匁	いちもんめ	*ichi-monme*
2 *monme*	二匁	にもんめ	*ni-monme*
3 *monme*	三匁	さんもんめ	*sam-monme*
4 *monme*	四匁	よんもんめ	*yom-monme*
5 *monme*	五匁	ごもんめ	*go-monme*
6 *monme*	六匁	ろくもんめ	*roku-monme*
7 *monme*	七匁	ななもんめ	*nana-monme*
8 *monme*	八匁	はちもんめ	*hachi-monme*
9 *monme*	九匁	きゅうもんめ	*kyuu-monme*
10 *monme*	十匁	じゅうもんめ	*juu-monme*

Irregularities or Special beyond Ten: none
Notes: none

や—Ya
夜—や—ya

Japanese: や
Romanized: ya
Pattern: 漢 ∅
Used with, or Means: evenings, nights, see also 夜 (yo)

1 night	一夜	いちや	ichi-ya
2 nights	二夜	にや	ni-ya
3 nights	三夜	さんや	san-ya
4 nights	四夜	よんや	yon-ya
5 nights	五夜	ごや	go-ya
6 nights	六夜	ろくや	roku-ya
7 nights	七夜	ななや	nana-ya
8 nights	八夜	はちや	hachi-ya
9 nights	九夜	きゅうや	kyuu-ya
10 nights	十夜	じゅうや	juu-ya

Irregularities or Special beyond Ten: none

Notes: 十六夜 (*izayoi*) is the night after the full moon. However, in ancient times, it was pronounced *isayoi*, which coincidentally sounded like the conjunctive form (otherwise known as the *masu*-form) of the verb 猶予う (*isayou* to hesitate). Both terms evolved over time into *izayoi* and *izayou*, respectively. Thus, *izayoi* has been used for a long time to also mean *hesitant*. 十六夜 (*Izayoi*) is also a girl's name in Japan.

ヤード・碼―やあど―*yaado*

Japanese: やあど
Romanized: *yaado*
Pattern: 漢 ∅
Used with, or Means: yards (symbol: yd), a unit of length, 36 in (3 ft)/0.91440 m

1 yd	一ヤード・碼	いちやあど	*ichi-yaado*
2 yd	二ヤード・碼	にやあど	*ni-yaado*
3 yd	三ヤード・碼	さんやあど	*san-yaado*
4 yd	四ヤード・碼	よんやあど	*yon-yaado*
5 yd	五ヤード・碼	ごやあど	*go-yaado*
6 yd	六ヤード・碼	ろくやあど	*roku-yaado*
7 yd	七ヤード・碼	ななやあど	*nana-yaado*
8 yd	八ヤード・碼	はちやあど	*hachi-yaado*
9 yd	九ヤード・碼	きゅうやあど	*kyuu-yaado*
10 yd	十ヤード・碼	じゅうやあど	*juu-yaado*

Irregularities or Special beyond Ten: none
Notes: none

役 — やく — *yaku*

Japanese: やく
Romanized: *yaku*
Pattern: 和 I
Used with, or Means: roles, parts in a play or movie, the number of roles an actor or actress plays in a movie or play

1 role	一役	ひとやく	*hito-yaku*
2 roles	二役	ふたやく	*futa-yaku*
3 roles	三役	さんやく	*san-yaku*
4 roles	四役	よんやく	*yon-yaku*
5 roles	五役	ごやく	*go-yaku*
6 roles	六役	ろくやく	*roku-yaku*
7 roles	七役	ななやく	*nana-yaku*
8 roles	八役	はちやく	*hachi-yaku*
9 roles	九役	きゅうやく	*kyuu-yaku*
10 roles	十役	じゅうやく	*juu-yaku*

Irregularities or Special beyond Ten:
Notes: 一役 (*ichi-yaku*) is *an (important) office, a high office*.
　二役 (*futa-yaku*) also means *a double role*, as in, the same actor playing more than one role.
　三役 (*san-yaku*) are the three highest ranks in an organization or in a sport.

社—やしろ—*yashiro*

Japanese: やく
Romanized: *yaku*
Pattern: 和 I
Used with, or Means: Shinto shrines, see also 社 (*sha*)

1 shrine	一社	ひとやしろ	*hito-yashiro*
2 shrines	二社	ふたやしろ	*futa-yashiro*
3 shrines	三社	さんやしろ	*san-yashiro*
4 shrines	四社	よんやしろ	*yon-yashiro*
5 shrines	五社	ごやしろ	*go-yashiro*
6 shrines	六社	ろくやしろ	*roku-yashiro*
7 shrines	七社	ななやしろ	*nana-yashiro*
8 shrines	八社	はちやしろ	*hachi-yashiro*
9 shrines	九社	きゅうやしろ	*kyuu-yashiro*
10 shrines	十社	じゅうやしろ	*juu-yashiro*

Irregularities or Special beyond Ten: none
Notes: none

山 — やま — *yama*

Japanese: やま
Romanized: *yama*
Pattern: 和 I
Used with, or Means: mountains; mountains of fruit, see also 盛 (*mori*)

1 mountain	一山	ひとやま	*hito-yama*
2 mountains	二山	ふたやま	*futa-yama*
3 mountains	三山	さんやま	*san-yama*
4 mountains	四山	よんやま	*yon-yama*
5 mountains	五山	ごやま	*go-yama*
6 mountains	六山	ろくやま	*roku-yama*
7 mountains	七山	ななやま	*nana-yama*
8 mountains	八山	はちやま	*hachi-yama*
9 mountains	九山	きゅうやま	*kyuu-yama*
10 mountains	十山	じゅうやま	*juu-yama*

Irregularities or Special beyond Ten: none
Notes: none

ゆ—Yu
湯—ゆ—yu

Japanese: ゆ
Romanized: yu
Pattern: 和 I
Used with, or Means: spas, hot springs, *onsen*, health resorts, see also 湯 (*tou*)

1 spa	一湯	ひとゆ	*hito-yu*
2 spas	二湯	ふたゆ	*futa-yu*
3 spas	三湯	さんゆ	*san-yu*
4 spas	四湯	よんゆ	*yon-yu*
5 spas	五湯	ごゆ	*go-yu*
6 spas	六湯	ろくゆ	*roku-yu*
7 spas	七湯	ななゆ	*nana-yu*
8 spas	八湯	はちゆ	*hachi-yu*
9 spas	九湯	きゅうゆ	*kyuu-yu*
10 spas	十湯	じゅうゆ	*juu-yu*

Irregularities or Special beyond Ten: none
Notes: none

ユアン・元 — ゆあん — *yuan*

Japanese: ゆあん
Romanized: *yuan*
Pattern: 漢 ∅
Used with, or Means: *yuan*, Chinese monetary unit

1 *yuan*	一ユアン・元	いちゆあん	*ichi-yuan*
2 *yuan*	二ユアン・元	にゆあん	*ni-yuan*
3 *yuan*	三ユアン・元	さんゆあん	*san-yuan*
4 *yuan*	四ユアン・元	よんゆあん	*yon-yuan*
5 *yuan*	五ユアン・元	ごゆあん	*go-yuan*
6 *yuan*	六ユアン・元	ろくゆあん	*roku-yuan*
7 *yuan*	七ユアン・元	ななゆあん	*nana-yuan*
8 *yuan*	八ユアン・元	はちゆあん	*hachi-yuan*
9 *yuan*	九ユアン・元	きゅうゆあん	*kyuu-yuan*
10 *yuan*	十ユアン・元	じゅうゆあん	*juu-yuan*

Irregularities or Special beyond Ten: none
Notes: none

結い—ゆい—*yui*

Japanese: ゆい
Romanized: *yui*
Pattern: 和 IV
Used with, or Means: coins, money, 銭 (*zeni*)

1 coin	一結い	ひとゆい	*hito-yui*
2 coins	二結い	ふたゆい	*futa-yui*
3 coins	三結い	みゆい	*mi-yui*
4 coins	四結い	よゆい	*yo-yui*
5 coins	五結い	いつゆい	*itsu-yui*
6 coins	六結い	むゆい	*mu-yui*
7 coins	七結い	ななゆい	*nana-yui*
8 coins	八結い	やゆい	*ya-yui*
9 coins	九結い	ここのゆい	*kokono-yui*
10 coins	十結い	とおゆい	*too-yui*

Irregularities or Special beyond Ten:

100 coins	百結い	ひゃくゆい	*hyaku-yui*
1,000 coins	千結い	ちゆい	*chi-yui*
10,000 coins	万結い	まんゆい	*man-yui*
how many coins?	何結い	なんゆい	*nan-yui*

Notes: none

桁 — ゆき — *yuki*

Japanese: ゆき
Romanized: *yuki*
Pattern: 和 IV
Used with, or Means: *hakama* (袴)

1 *hakama*	一桁	ひとゆき	hito-yuki
2 *hakama*	二桁	ふたゆき	futa-yuki
3 *hakama*	三桁	みゆき	mi-yuki
4 *hakama*	四桁	よゆき	yo-yuki
5 *hakama*	五桁	いつゆき	itsu-yuki
6 *hakama*	六桁	むゆき	mu-yuki
7 *hakama*	七桁	ななゆき	nana-yuki
8 *hakama*	八桁	やゆき	ya-yuki
9 *hakama*	九桁	ここのゆき	kokono-yuki
10 *hakama*	十桁	とおゆき	too-yuki

Irregularities or Special beyond Ten: none
Notes: *Hakama* are a set of pleated pants or skirt. One wears it over a kimono called a *hakui* (白衣). There are two types: 馬乗り (*umanori* horse-riding) and 行灯袴 (*andom-bakama* lantern-carrying *hakama*). The *umanori* style are divided like pants. The *andom-bakama* style is undivided like a skirt. Shrine Maidens (巫女 *miko*) wear red *hakama*. Shrine priests (神主 *kannushi*) wear sky-blue *hakama*. Martial artists wear black *hakama*.

ユニット—ゆにっと—*yunitto*

Japanese: ゆにっと
Romanized: *yunitto*
Pattern: 漢 ∅
Used with, or Means: units

1 unit	1ユニット	いちゆにっと	*ichi-yunitto*
2 units	2ユニット	にゆにっと	*ni-yunitto*
3 units	3ユニット	さんゆにっと	*san-yunitto*
4 units	4ユニット	よんゆにっと	*yon-yunitto*
5 units	5ユニット	ごゆにっと	*go-yunitto*
6 units	6ユニット	ろくゆにっと	*roku-yunitto*
7 units	7ユニット	ななゆにっと	*nana-yunitto*
8 units	8ユニット	はちゆにっと	*hachi-yunitto*
9 units	9ユニット	きゅうゆにっと	*kyuu-yunitto*
10 units	10ユニット	じゅうゆにっと	*juu-yunitto*

Irregularities or Special beyond Ten: none
Notes: The Japanese also use the English counting system for this counter as well: ワンユニット (*wan-yunitto* one unit)、ツーユニット (*tsuu-yunitto* two units)、スリーユニット (*surii-yunitto* three units)、etc...

よ — Yo
夜 — よ — yo

Japanese: よ
Romanized: *yo*
Pattern: 和 IV
Used with, or Means: nights, see also 夜 (*ya*)

1 night	一夜	ひとよ	*hito-yo*
2 nights	二夜	ふたよ	*futa-yo*
3 nights	三夜	さんよ	*san-yo*
4 nights	四夜	よんよ	*yon-yo*
5 nights	五夜	ごよ	*go-yo*
6 nights	六夜	ろくよ	*roku-yo*
7 nights	七夜	ななよ	*nana-yo*
8 nights	八夜	はちよ	*hachi-yo*
9 nights	九夜	きゅうよ	*kyuu-yo*
10 nights	十夜	じゅうよ	*juu-yo*

Irregularities or Special beyond Ten: none
Notes: none

余 — よ — yo

Japanese: よ
Romanized: yo
Pattern: 漢 Ø
Used with, or Means: N-some odd..., some...more than N

1-some odd...	一余	いちよ	*ichi-yo*
2-some odd...	二余	によ	*ni-yo*
3-some odd...	三余	さんよ	*san-yo*
4-some odd...	四余	よんよ	*yon-yo*
5-some odd...	五余	ごよ	*go-yo*
6-some odd...	六余	ろくよ	*roku-yo*
7-some odd...	七余	ななよ	*nana-yo*
8-some odd...	八余	はちよ	*hachi-yo*
9-some odd...	九余	きゅうよ	*kyuu-yo*
10-some odd...	十余	じゅうよ	*juu-yo*

Irregularities or Special beyond Ten: none

Notes: This is not technically a counter in itself, but a counter-modifier, so to speak. For example, to say, *30-some odd dogs*, you would write 犬 30 余匹 (*inu san-juu-yo-hiki*).

葉 — よう — you

Japanese: よう
Romanized: you
Pattern: 漢 ∅

Used with, or Means: leaves, postcards, bookmarks (栞・枝折 *shiori*), sheets of paper, pages, see also 枚 (*mai*), see also 頁 (*peeji*); (polite) dirt, dust; (polite) small boats

1 leaf	一葉	いちよう	*ichi-you*
2 leaves	二葉	によう	*ni-you*
3 leaves	三葉	さんよう	*san-you*
4 leaves	四葉	ようんよう	*youn-you*
5 leaves	五葉	ごよう	*go-you*
6 leaves	六葉	ろくよう	*roku-you*
7 leaves	七葉	ななよう	*nana-you*
8 leaves	八葉	はちよう	*hachi-you*
9 leaves	九葉	きゅうよう	*kyuu-you*
10 leaves	十葉	じゅうよう	*juu-you*

Irregularities or Special beyound Ten: none

Notes: When counting sheets of paper or pages, one can use the kanji 頁, but still pronounce it as *you*.

腰 — よう — *you*

Japanese: よう
Romanized: *you*
Pattern: 漢 ∅
Used with, or Means: *hakama*, see also 腰 (*koshi*), see also 裄 (*yuki*)

1 *hakama*	一腰	いちよう	*ichi-you*
2 *hakama*	二腰	によう	*ni-you*
3 *hakama*	三腰	さんよう	*san-you*
4 *hakama*	四腰	ようんよう	*youn-you*
5 *hakama*	五腰	ごよう	*go-you*
6 *hakama*	六腰	ろくよう	*roku-you*
7 *hakama*	七腰	ななよう	*nana-you*
8 *hakama*	八腰	はちよう	*hachi-you*
9 *hakama*	九腰	きゅうよう	*kyuu-you*
10 *hakama*	十腰	じゅうよう	*juu-you*

Irregularities or Special beyound Ten: none
Notes: none

翼—よく—*yoku*

Japanese: よく
Romanized: *yoku*
Pattern: 漢 Ø

Used with, or Means: (literary language) birds, see also 羽 (*wa*); one's job, station, position, post, route, part, role, duties

1 bird	一翼	いちよく	*ichi-yoku*
2 birds	二翼	によく	*ni-yoku*
3 birds	三翼	さんよく	*san-yoku*
4 birds	四翼	よんよく	*yon-yoku*
5 birds	五翼	ごよく	*go-yoku*
6 birds	六翼	ろくよく	*roku-yoku*
7 birds	七翼	ななよく	*nana-yoku*
8 birds	八翼	はちよく	*hachi-yoku*
9 birds	九翼	きゅうよく	*kyuu-yoku*
10 birds	十翼	じゅうよく	*juu-yoku*

Irregularities or Special beyond Ten: none

Notes: 一翼を担う (*ichi-yoku o ninau*) means *to shoulder a burden*.

装い—よそい—*yosoi*

Japanese: よそい
Romanized: *yosoi*
Pattern: 和 I
Used with, or Means: uniform sets of clothing and supplies, see also 具 (*yoroi*); servings of food and drink, see also 杯 (*hai*)

1 serving	一装い	ひとよそい	*hito-yosoi*
2 servings	二装い	ふたよそい	*futa-yosoi*
3 servings	三装い	さんよそい	*san-yosoi*
4 servings	四装い	よんよそい	*yon-yosoi*
5 servings	五装い	ごよそい	*go-yosoi*
6 servings	六装い	ろくよそい	*roku-yosoi*
7 servings	七装い	ななよそい	*nana-yosoi*
8 servings	八装い	はちよそい	*hachi-yosoi*
9 servings	九装い	きゅうよそい	*kyuu-yosoi*
10 servings	十装い	じゅうよそい	*juu-yosoi*

Irregularities or Special beyond Ten: none
Notes: none

度—より—*yori*

Japanese: より
Romanized: *yori*
Pattern: 和 IV
Used with, or Means: movements, actions, see also 度 (*do*)

1 action	一度	ひとより	*hito-yori*
2 actions	二度	ふたより	*futa-yori*
3 actions	三度	さんより	*san-yori*
4 actions	四度	よんより	*yon-yori*
5 actions	五度	ごより	*go-yori*
6 actions	六度	ろくより	*roku-yori*
7 actions	七度	ななより	*nana-yori*
8 actions	八度	はちより	*hachi-yori*
9 actions	九度	きゅうより	*kyuu-yori*
10 actions	十度	じゅうより	*juu-yori*

Irregularities or Special beyond Ten: none
Notes: none

具—よろい—*yoroi*

Japanese: よろい
Romanized: *yoroi*
Pattern: 和 IV
Used with, or Means: sets of gathered supplies for performing a task, such as a bow-and-arrows set, or a set of inkstone, brushes and paper for calligraphy, see also 具 (*gu*), see also 装い (*yosoi*)

1 set	一具	ひとよろり	*hito-yoroi*
2 sets	二具	ふたよろり	*futa-yoroi*
3 sets	三具	さんよろり	*san-yoroi*
4 sets	四具	よんよろり	*yon-yoroi*
5 sets	五具	ごよろり	*go-yoroi*
6 sets	六具	ろくよろり	*roku-yoroi*
7 sets	七具	ななよろり	*nana-yoroi*
8 sets	八具	はちよろり	*hachi-yoroi*
9 sets	九具	きゅうよろり	*kyuu-yoroi*
10 sets	十具	じゅうよろり	*juu-yoroi*

Irregularities or Special beyond Ten: none
Notes: none

ら—Ra
ラウンド—raundo

Japanese: らうんど
Romanized: *raundo*
Pattern: 漢 ∅
Used with, or Means: rounds

1 round	1ラウンド	いちらうんど	*ichi-raundo*
2 rounds	2ラウンド	にらうんど	*ni-raundo*
3 rounds	3ラウンド	さんらうんど	*san-raundo*
4 rounds	4ラウンド	よんらうんど	*yon-raundo*
5 rounds	5ラウンド	ごらうんど	*go-raundo*
6 rounds	6ラウンド	ろくらうんど	*roku-raundo*
7 rounds	7ラウンド	なならうんど	*nana-raundo*
8 rounds	8ラウンド	はちらうんど	*hachi-raundo*
9 rounds	9ラウンド	きゅうらうんど	*kyuu-raundo*
10 rounds	10ラウンド	じゅうらうんど	*juu-raundo*

Irregularities or Special beyond Ten: none
Notes: Rounds may also be counted using English numbers:
　　ワンラウンド (*wan-raundo*),
　　ツーラウンド (*tsuu-raundo*),
　　スリーラウンド (*surii-raundo*), etc . . .

り — R*i*
里 — り — *ri*

Japanese: り
Romanized: *ri*
Pattern: 漢 ∅

Used with, or Means: *ri*, a unit of length, 12,960 尺 (*shaku*), 36 丁・町 (*chou*), 154,617.03635 in (12,884.75303 ft, 2.44029 mi)/3,927.27273 m

1 *ri*	一里	いちり	*ichi-ri*
2 *ri*	二里	にり	*ni-ri*
3 *ri*	三里	さんり	*san-ri*
4 *ri*	四里	よんり	*yon-ri*
5 *ri*	五里	ごり	*go-ri*
6 *ri*	六里	ろくり	*roku-ri*
7 *ri*	七里	ななり	*nana-ri*
8 *ri*	八里	はちり	*hachi-ri*
9 *ri*	九里	きゅうり	*kyuu-ri*
10 *ri*	十里	じゅうり	*juu-ri*

Irregularities or Special beyond Ten: none
Notes: none

リットル・立—りっとる—*rittoru*

Japanese: りっとる
Romanized: *rittoru*
Pattern: 漢 K
Used with, or Means: liters (S. I. symbol: L), a unit of volume, (33.81402 fl oz, 2.11338 pt)

1 L	一リットル・立	いちりっとる	*ichi-rittoru*
2 L	二リットル・立	にりっとる	*ni-rittoru*
3 L	三リットル・立	さんりっとる	*san-rittoru*
4 L	四リットル・立	よんりっとる	*yon-rittoru*
5 L	五リットル・立	ごりっとる	*go-rittoru*
6 L	六リットル・立	ろくりっとる	*roku-rittoru*
7 L	七リットル・立	ななりっとる	*nana-rittoru*
8 L	八リットル・立	はちりっとる	*hachi-rittoru*
9 L	九リットル・立	きゅうりっとる	*kyuu-rittoru*
10 L	十リットル・立	じゅうりっとる	*juu-rittoru*

Irregularities or Special beyond Ten: none
Notes: Technically, the symbol for liters is simply "l," but in the United States, "L" is more typical. In some countries, such as Japan, "ℓ" is also seen.

立方〇 — りっぽう〇 — rippou-〇

Japanese: りっぽう〇
Romanized: *rippou-*〇
Pattern: 漢 ∅
Used with, or Means: cubic 〇s: 立方センチメートル (*rippou-senchi-meetoru* cubic centimeters)

1 cubic 〇	一立方〇	いちりっぽう〇	*ichi-rippou-*〇
2 cubic 〇s	二立方〇	にりっぽう〇	*ni-rippou-*〇
3 cubic 〇s	三立方〇	さんりっぽう〇	*san-rippou-*〇
4 cubic 〇s	四立方〇	よんりっぽう〇	*yon-rippou-*〇
5 cubic 〇s	五立方〇	ごりっぽう〇	*go-rippou-*〇
6 cubic 〇s	六立方〇	ろくりっぽう〇	*roku-rippou-*〇
7 cubic 〇s	七立方〇	ななりっぽう〇	*nana-rippou-*〇
8 cubic 〇s	八立方〇	はちりっぽう〇	*hachi-rippou-*〇
9 cubic 〇s	九立方〇	きゅうりっぽう〇	*kyuu-rippou-*〇
10 cubic 〇s	十立方〇	じゅうりっぽう〇	*juu-rippou-*〇

Irregularities or Special beyond Ten: none
Notes: none

旒・流 — りゅう — *ryuu*

Japanese: りゅう
Romanized: *ryuu*
Pattern: 漢 Ø
Used with, or Means: flags; schools (of thought, types of art)

1 flag	一旒・流	いちりゅう	*ichi-ryuu*
2 flags	二旒・流	にりゅう	*ni-ryuu*
3 flags	三旒・流	さんりゅう	*san-ryuu*
4 flags	四旒・流	よんりゅう	*yon-ryuu*
5 flags	五旒・流	ごりゅう	*go-ryuu*
6 flags	六旒・流	ろくりゅう	*roku-ryuu*
7 flags	七旒・流	ななりゅう	*nana-ryuu*
8 flags	八旒・流	はちりゅう	*hachi-ryuu*
9 flags	九旒・流	きゅうりゅう	*kyuu-ryuu*
10 flags	十旒・流	じゅうりゅう	*juu-ryuu*

Irregularities or Special beyond Ten: none
Notes: none

笠 — りゅう — *ryuu*

Japanese: りゅう
Romanized: *ryuu*
Pattern: 漢 Ø
Used with, or Means: bamboo hats (笠 *kasa*)

1 bamboo hat	一笠	いちりゅう	*ichi-ryuu*
2 bamboo hats	二笠	にりゅう	*ni-ryuu*
3 bamboo hats	三笠	さんりゅう	*san-ryuu*
4 bamboo hats	四笠	よんりゅう	*yon-ryuu*
5 bamboo hats	五笠	ごりゅう	*go-ryuu*
6 bamboo hats	六笠	ろくりゅう	*roku-ryuu*
7 bamboo hats	七笠	ななりゅう	*nana-ryuu*
8 bamboo hats	八笠	はちりゅう	*hachi-ryuu*
9 bamboo hats	九笠	きゅうりゅう	*kyuu-ryuu*
10 bamboo hats	十笠	じゅうりゅう	*juu-ryuu*

Irregularities or Special beyond Ten: none
Notes: none

粒 — りゅう — *ryuu*

Japanese: りゅう
Romanized: *ryuu*
Pattern: 漢 ∅
Used with, or Means: grains, tiny particles, see also 粒 (*tsubu*)

1 grain	一粒	いちりゅう	*ichi-ryuu*
2 grains	二粒	にりゅう	*ni-ryuu*
3 grains	三粒	さんりゅう	*san-ryuu*
4 grains	四粒	よんりゅう	*yon-ryuu*
5 grains	五粒	ごりゅう	*go-ryuu*
6 grains	六粒	ろくりゅう	*roku-ryuu*
7 grains	七粒	ななりゅう	*nana-ryuu*
8 grains	八粒	はちりゅう	*hachi-ryuu*
9 grains	九粒	きゅうりゅう	*kyuu-ryuu*
10 grains	十粒	じゅうりゅう	*juu-ryuu*

Irregularities or Special beyond Ten: none
Notes: none

両 — りょう — *ryou*

Japanese: りょう
Romanized: *ryou*
Pattern: 漢 ∅
Used with, or Means: railway cars, cars, see also 台 (*dai*); *ryou*, a former unit of weight, 10 匁 (*monme*), 1.32277 oz/37.5 g; *ryou*, former monetary unit, 4 分 (*bu*); formerly, pairs of clothing items:錦の襪 5 両 (*nishiki no shitouzu go-ryou* five pairs of brocade socks)

1 car	一両	いちりょう	*ichi-ryou*
2 cars	二両	にりょう	*ni-ryou*
3 cars	三両	さんりょう	*san-ryou*
4 cars	四両	よんりょう	*yon-ryou*
5 cars	五両	ごりょう	*go-ryou*
6 cars	六両	ろくりょう	*roku-ryou*
7 cars	七両	ななりょう	*nana-ryou*
8 cars	八両	はちりょう	*hachi-ryou*
9 cars	九両	きゅうりょう	*kyuu-ryou*
10 cars	十両	じゅうりょう	*juu-ryou*

Irregularities or Special beyond Ten: none
Notes: none

嶺 — りょう — *ryou*

Japanese: りょう
Romanized: *ryou*
Pattern: 漢 ∅
Used with, or Means: tall peaks, mountain ridges, see also 峰 (*hou*)

1 mountain ridge	一嶺	いちりょう	*ichi-ryou*
2 mountain ridges	二嶺	にりょう	*ni-ryou*
3 mountain ridges	三嶺	さんりょう	*san-ryou*
4 mountain ridges	四嶺	よんりょう	*yon-ryou*
5 mountain ridges	五嶺	ごりょう	*go-ryou*
6 mountain ridges	六嶺	ろくりょう	*roku-ryou*
7 mountain ridges	七嶺	ななりょう	*nana-ryou*
8 mountain ridges	八嶺	はちりょう	*hachi-ryou*
9 mountain ridges	九嶺	きゅうりょう	*kyuu-ryou*
10 mountain ridges	十嶺	じゅうりょう	*juu-ryou*

Irregularities or Special beyond Ten: none
Notes: none

輌 — りょう — *ryou*

Japanese: りょう
Romanized: *ryou*
Pattern: 漢 ∅
Used with, or Means: railway cars, vehicles, rolling stock cars

1 car	一輌	いちりょう	*ichi-ryou*
2 cars	二輌	にりょう	*ni-ryou*
3 cars	三輌	さんりょう	*san-ryou*
4 cars	四輌	よんりょう	*yon-ryou*
5 cars	五輌	ごりょう	*go-ryou*
6 cars	六輌	ろくりょう	*roku-ryou*
7 cars	七輌	ななりょう	*nana-ryou*
8 cars	八輌	はちりょう	*hachi-ryou*
9 cars	九輌	きゅうりょう	*kyuu-ryou*
10 cars	十輌	じゅうりょう	*juu-ryou*

Irregularities or Special beyond Ten: none
Notes: none

領 — りょう — *ryou*

Japanese: りょう
Romanized: *ryou*
Pattern: 漢 ∅
Used with, or Means: suits of armor, sets of Japanese clothing, quilts (衾 *fusuma*), surplices (袈裟 *kesa*)

1 suit of armor	一領	いちりょう	*ichi-ryou*
2 suits of armor	二領	にりょう	*ni-ryou*
3 suits of armor	三領	さんりょう	*san-ryou*
4 suits of armor	四領	よんりょう	*yon-ryou*
5 suits of armor	五領	ごりょう	*go-ryou*
6 suits of armor	六領	ろくりょう	*roku-ryou*
7 suits of armor	七領	ななりょう	*nana-ryou*
8 suits of armor	八領	はちりょう	*hachi-ryou*
9 suits of armor	九領	きゅうりょう	*kyuu-ryou*
10 suits of armor	十領	じゅうりょう	*juu-ryou*

Irregularities or Special beyond Ten: none
Notes: none

リラ—りら—rira

Japanese: りら
Romanized: *rira*
Pattern: 漢 Ø
Used with, or Means: *Lira*, a former Italian monetary unit, still used in Turkey, and other Middle Eastern countries.

1 Lira	1 リラ	いちりら	*ichi-rira*
2 Lira	2 リラ	にりら	*ni-rira*
3 Lira	3 リラ	さんりら	*san-rira*
4 Lira	4 リラ	よんりら	*yon-rira*
5 Lira	5 リラ	ごりら	*go-rira*
6 Lira	6 リラ	ろくりら	*roku-rira*
7 Lira	7 リラ	ななりら	*nana-rira*
8 Lira	8 リラ	はちりら	*hachi-rira*
9 Lira	9 リラ	きゅうりら	*kyuu-rira*
10 Lira	10 リラ	じゅうりら	*juu-rira*

Irregularities or Special beyond Ten: none
Notes: none

厘 — りん — *rin*

Japanese: りん
Romanized: *rin*
Pattern: 漢 ∅

Used with, or Means: *rin*, former monetary unit, 1/1,000th of a 円 (*yen*); *rin*, a unit of length, 1/1,000th of a 尺 (*shaku*), 0.0119303269 in/0.0003030303 m; *rin*, a unit of weight, 1/100th of a 匁 (*momme*), 0.0013227736 oz/ 0.0375 g

1 *rin*	一厘	いちりん	*ichi-rin*
2 *rin*	二厘	にりん	*ni-rin*
3 *rin*	三厘	さんりん	*san-rin*
4 *rin*	四厘	よんりん	*yon-rin*
5 *rin*	五厘	ごりん	*go-rin*
6 *rin*	六厘	ろくりん	*roku-rin*
7 *rin*	七厘	ななりん	*nana-rin*
8 *rin*	八厘	はちりん	*hachi-rin*
9 *rin*	九厘	きゅうりん	*kyuu-rin*
10 *rin*	十厘	じゅうりん	*juu-rin*

Irregularities or Special beyond Ten: none
Notes: none

輪 — りん — rin

Japanese: りん
Romanized: *rin*
Pattern: 漢 ∅
Used with, or Means: wheels; flowers

1 wheel	一輪	いちりん	*ichi-rin*
2 wheels	二輪	にりん	*ni-rin*
3 wheels	三輪	さんりん	*san-rin*
4 wheels	四輪	よんりん	*yon-rin*
5 wheels	五輪	ごりん	*go-rin*
6 wheels	六輪	ろくりん	*roku-rin*
7 wheels	七輪	ななりん	*nana-rin*
8 wheels	八輪	はちりん	*hachi-rin*
9 wheels	九輪	きゅうりん	*kyuu-rin*
10 wheels	十輪	じゅうりん	*juu-rin*

Irregularities or Special beyond Ten: none
Notes: none

鱗 — りん — *rin*

Japanese: りん
Romanized: *rin*
Pattern: 漢 ∅
Used with, or Means: fish scales; (polite) fish

1 fish scale	一鱗	いちりん	*ichi-rin*
2 fish scales	二鱗	にりん	*ni-rin*
3 fish scales	三鱗	さんりん	*san-rin*
4 fish scales	四鱗	よんりん	*yon-rin*
5 fish scales	五鱗	ごりん	*go-rin*
6 fish scales	六鱗	ろくりん	*roku-rin*
7 fish scales	七鱗	ななりん	*nana-rin*
8 fish scales	八鱗	はちりん	*hachi-rin*
9 fish scales	九鱗	きゅうりん	*kyuu-rin*
10 fish scales	十鱗	じゅうりん	*juu-rin*

Irregularities or Special beyond Ten: none
Notes: none

る—Ru
塁—るい—*rui*

Japanese: るい
Romanized: *rui*
Pattern: 漢 ∅
Used with, or Means: baseball bases, see also ベース (*beesu*)

1 base	一塁	いちるい	*ichi-rui*
2 bases	二塁	にるい	*ni-rui*
3 bases	三塁	さんるい	*san-rui*
4 bases	四塁	よんるい	*yon-rui*

Irregularities or Special beyond Ten: none
Notes: 四塁 (*yon-rui*) is home plate.

類 — るい — *rui*

Japanese: るい
Romanized: *rui*
Pattern: 漢 ∅
Used with, or Means: types, kinds

1 type	一類	いちるい	*ichi-rui*
2 types	二類	にるい	*ni-rui*
3 types	三類	さんるい	*san-rui*
4 types	四類	よんるい	*yon-rui*
5 types	五類	ごるい	*go-rui*
6 types	六類	ろくるい	*roku-rui*
7 types	七類	ななるい	*nana-rui*
8 types	八類	はちるい	*hachi-rui*
9 types	九類	きゅうるい	*kyuu-rui*
10 types	十類	じゅうるい	*juu-rui*

Irregularities or Special beyond Ten: none
Notes: none

ルーブル・руб—るうぶる—*ruuburu*

Japanese: るうぶる
Romanized: *ruuburu*
Pattern: 漢 ∅
Used with, or Means: *rubles*, monetary unit in Russia, Belarus, and Transnistria

1 ruble	1 ルーブル・руб	いちるうぶる	*ichi-ruuburu*
2 rubles	2 ルーブル・руб	にるうぶる	*ni-ruuburu*
3 rubles	3 ルーブル・руб	さんるうぶる	*san-ruuburu*
4 rubles	4 ルーブル・руб	よんるうぶる	*yon-ruuburu*
5 rubles	5 ルーブル・руб	ごるうぶる	*go-ruuburu*
6 rubles	6 ルーブル・руб	ろくるうぶる	*roku-ruuburu*
7 rubles	7 ルーブル・руб	ななるうぶる	*nana-ruuburu*
8 rubles	8 ルーブル・руб	はちるうぶる	*hachi-ruuburu*
9 rubles	9 ルーブル・руб	きゅうるうぶる	*kyuu-ruuburu*
10 rubles	10 ルーブル・руб	じゅうるうぶる	*juu-ruuburu*

Irregularities or Special beyond Ten: none
Notes: none

ルクス・lx—ルクス—*rukusu*

Japanese: るくす
Romanized: *rukusu*
Pattern: 漢 ∅
Used with, or Means: lux (S. I. symbol: lx), a unit of of illuminance and luminous emittance, $1 \text{ lx} = \frac{1 lm}{m^2}$

1 lx	1 ルクス・lx	いちるくす	*ichi-rukusu*
2 lx	2 ルクス・lx	にるくす	*ni-rukusu*
3 lx	3 ルクス・lx	さんるくす	*san-rukusu*
4 lx	4 ルクス・lx	よんるくす	*yon-rukusu*
5 lx	5 ルクス・lx	ごるくす	*go-rukusu*
6 lx	6 ルクス・lx	ろくるくす	*roku-rukusu*
7 lx	7 ルクス・lx	ななるくす	*nana-rukusu*
8 lx	8 ルクス・lx	はちるくす	*hachi-rukusu*
9 lx	9 ルクス・lx	きゅうるくす	*kyuu-rukusu*
10 lx	10 ルクス・lx	じゅうるくす	*juu-rukusu*

Irregularities or Special beyond Ten: none
Notes: none

ルピー・Rs—るぴい—*rupii*

Japanese: るぴい
Romanized: *rupii*
Pattern: 漢 ∅
Used with, or Means: *Rupees*, monetary unit in India, Sri Lanka, Nepal, Pakistan, Mauritius, Seychelles, Indonesia, Maldives and formerly in Burma, and Afghanistan

1 *Rupee*	1 ルピー・Rs	いちるぴい	*ichi-rupii*
2 *Rupees*	2 ルピー・Rs	にるぴい	*ni-rupii*
3 *Rupees*	3 ルピー・Rs	さんるぴい	*san-rupii*
4 *Rupees*	4 ルピー・Rs	よんるぴい	*yon-rupii*
5 *Rupees*	5 ルピー・Rs	ごるぴい	*go-rupii*
6 *Rupees*	6 ルピー・Rs	ろくるぴい	*roku-rupii*
7 *Rupees*	7 ルピー・Rs	ななるぴい	*nana-rupii*
8 *Rupees*	8 ルピー・Rs	はちるぴい	*hachi-rupii*
9 *Rupees*	9 ルピー・Rs	きゅうるぴい	*kyuu-rupii*
10 *Rupees*	10 ルピー・Rs	じゅうるぴい	*juu-rupii*

Irregularities or Special beyond Ten: none
Notes: none

れ—Re
礼—れい—rei

Japanese: れい
Romanized: rei
Pattern: 漢 ∅
Used with, or Means: bows at a shrine, bows during worship at a shrine

1 bow	一礼	いちれい	ichi-rei
2 bows	二礼	にれい	ni-rei
3 bows	三礼	さんれい	san-rei
4 bows	四礼	よんれい	yon-rei
5 bows	五礼	ごれい	go-rei
6 bows	六礼	ろくれい	roku-rei
7 bows	七礼	ななれい	nana-rei
8 bows	八礼	はちれい	hachi-rei
9 bows	九礼	きゅうれい	kyuu-rei
10 bows	十礼	じゅうれい	juu-rei

Irregularities or Special beyond Ten: none
Notes: none

嶺 — れい — rei

Japanese: れい
Romanized: rei
Pattern: 漢 Ø
Used with, or Means: tall peaks, mountain ridges, see also 峰 (*hou*), see also 嶺 (*ryou*)

1 mountain ridge	一嶺	いちれい	*ichi-rei*
2 mountain ridges	二嶺	にれい	*ni-rei*
3 mountain ridges	三嶺	さんれい	*san-rei*
4 mountain ridges	四嶺	よんれい	*yon-rei*
5 mountain ridges	五嶺	ごれい	*go-rei*
6 mountain ridges	六嶺	ろくれい	*roku-rei*
7 mountain ridges	七嶺	ななれい	*nana-rei*
8 mountain ridges	八嶺	はちれい	*hachi-rei*
9 mountain ridges	九嶺	きゅうれい	*kyuu-rei*
10 mountain ridges	十嶺	じゅうれい	*juu-rei*

Irregularities or Special beyond Ten: none
Notes: none

レース—*reesu*

Japanese: れえす
Romanized: *reesu*
Pattern: 漢 ∅
Used with, or Means: competitive races

1 race	1 レース	いちれえす	*ichi-reesu*
2 races	2 レース	にれえす	*ni-reesu*
3 races	3 レース	さんれえす	*san-reesu*
4 races	4 レース	よんれえす	*yon-reesu*
5 races	5 レース	ごれえす	*go-reesu*
6 races	6 レース	ろくれえす	*roku-reesu*
7 races	7 レース	ななれえす	*nana-reesu*
8 races	8 レース	はちれえす	*hachi-reesu*
9 races	9 レース	きゅうれえす	*kyuu-reesu*
10 races	10 レース	じゅうれえす	*juu-reesu*

Irregularities or Special beyond Ten: none
Notes: none

レーン —— *reen*

Japanese: れえん
Romanized: *reen*
Pattern: 漢 Ø
Used with, or Means: bowling lanes, road lanes, highway lanes

1 lane	1 レーン	いちれえん	*ichi-reen*
2 lanes	2 レーン	にれえん	*ni-reen*
3 lanes	3 レーン	さんれえん	*san-reen*
4 lanes	4 レーン	よんれえん	*yon-reen*
5 lanes	5 レーン	ごれえん	*go-reen*
6 lanes	6 レーン	ろくれえん	*roku-reen*
7 lanes	7 レーン	ななれえん	*nana-reen*
8 lanes	8 レーン	はちれえん	*hachi-reen*
9 lanes	9 レーン	きゅうれえん	*kyuu-reen*
10 lanes	10 レーン	じゅうれえん	*juu-reen*

Irregularities or Special beyond Ten: none
Notes: none

列—れつ—*retsu*

Japanese: れつ
Romanized: *retsu*
Pattern: 漢 Ø
Used with, or Means: rows, lines, queues, ranks, columns

1 row	一列	いちれつ	*ichi-retsu*
2 rows	二列	にれつ	*ni-retsu*
3 rows	三列	さんれつ	*san-retsu*
4 rows	四列	よんれつ	*yon-retsu*
5 rows	五列	ごれつ	*go-retsu*
6 rows	六列	ろくれつ	*roku-retsu*
7 rows	七列	ななれつ	*nana-retsu*
8 rows	八列	はちれつ	*hachi-retsu*
9 rows	九列	きゅうれつ	*kyuu-retsu*
10 rows	十列	じゅうれつ	*juu-retsu*

Irregularities or Special beyond Ten: none
Notes: none

列車—れっしゃ—*ressha*

Japanese: れっしゃ
Romanized: *ressha*
Pattern: 漢 ∅
Used with, or Means: trains

1 train	一列車	いちれっしゃ	*ichi-ressha*
2 trains	二列車	にれっしゃ	*ni-ressha*
3 trains	三列車	さんれっしゃ	*san-ressha*
4 trains	四列車	よんれっしゃ	*yon-ressha*
5 trains	五列車	ごれっしゃ	*go-ressha*
6 trains	六列車	ろくれっしゃ	*roku-ressha*
7 trains	七列車	ななれっしゃ	*nana-ressha*
8 trains	八列車	はちれっしゃ	*hachi-ressha*
9 trains	九列車	きゅうれっしゃ	*kyuu-ressha*
10 trains	十列車	じゅうれっしゃ	*juu-ressha*

Irregularities or Special beyond Ten: none
Notes: none

聯・聯 — れん — *ren*

Japanese: れん
Romanized: *ren*
Pattern: 漢 ∅
Used with, or Means: verses, stanzas, see also 連 (*ren*)

1 stanza	一聯・聯	いちれん	*ichi-ren*
2 stanzas	二聯・聯	にれん	*ni-ren*
3 stanzas	三聯・聯	さんれん	*san-ren*
4 stanzas	四聯・聯	よんれん	*yon-ren*
5 stanzas	五聯・聯	ごれん	*go-ren*
6 stanzas	六聯・聯	ろくれん	*roku-ren*
7 stanzas	七聯・聯	ななれん	*nana-ren*
8 stanzas	八聯・聯	はちれん	*hachi-ren*
9 stanzas	九聯・聯	きゅうれん	*kyuu-ren*
10 stanzas	十聯・聯	じゅうれん	*juu-ren*

Irregularities or Special beyond Ten: none
Notes: none

連 — れん — *ren*

Japanese: れん
Romanized: *ren*
Pattern: 漢 ∅
Used with, or Means: strings of pearls, rosaries, linked objects, chains, see also 聯 (*ren*); knit, stacked objects such as bamboo screens (簾 *sudare*); formerly, hunting hawks (鷹狩り *taka-kari*), see also 本 (*moto*); reams of paper; Chinese poems

1 chain	一連	いちれん	*ichi-ren*
2 chains	二連	にれん	*ni-ren*
3 chains	三連	さんれん	*san-ren*
4 chains	四連	よんれん	*yon-ren*
5 chains	五連	ごれん	*go-ren*
6 chains	六連	ろくれん	*roku-ren*
7 chains	七連	ななれん	*nana-ren*
8 chains	八連	はちれん	*hachi-ren*
9 chains	九連	きゅうれん	*kyuu-ren*
10 chains	十連	じゅうれん	*juu-ren*

Irregularities or Special beyond Ten: none
Notes: none

ろ—Ro
浪—ろう—*rou*

Japanese: ろう
Romanized: *rou*
Pattern: 漢 ∅
Used with, or Means: waves, years of exam preparation, 予備校 (*yobikou*)

1 wave	一浪	いちろう	*ichi-rou*
2 waves	二浪	にろう	*ni-rou*
3 waves	三浪	さんろう	*san-rou*
4 waves	四浪	よんろう	*yon-rou*
5 waves	五浪	ごろう	*go-rou*
6 waves	六浪	ろくろう	*roku-rou*
7 waves	七浪	ななろう	*nana-rou*
8 waves	八浪	はちろう	*hachi-rou*
9 waves	九浪	きゅうろう	*kyuu-rou*
10 waves	十浪	じゅうろう	*juu-rou*

Irregularities or Special beyond Ten: none
Notes: none

ロール—*rooru*

Japanese: ろおる
Romanized: *rooru*
Pattern: 漢 ∅
Used with, or Means: rolls of paper, rolls of cloth, see also 巻き (*maki*)

1 roll	1 ロール	いちろおる	*ichi-rooru*
2 rolls	2 ロール	にろおる	*ni-rooru*
3 rolls	3 ロール	さんろおる	*san-rooru*
4 rolls	4 ロール	よんろおる	*yon-rooru*
5 rolls	5 ロール	ごろおる	*go-rooru*
6 rolls	6 ロール	ろくろおる	*roku-rooru*
7 rolls	7 ロール	ななろおる	*nana-rooru*
8 rolls	8 ロール	はちろおる	*hachi-rooru*
9 rolls	9 ロール	きゅうろおる	*kyuu-rooru*
10 rolls	10 ロール	じゅうろおる	*juu-rooru*

Irregularities or Special beyond Ten: none
Notes: Rolls may also be counted using English numbers:
　　　ワンロール (*wan- rooru*),
　　　ツーロール (*tsuu- rooru*),
　　　スリーロール (*surii- rooru*), etc . . .

路線—ろせん—*rosen*

Japanese: ろせん
Romanized: *rosen*
Pattern: 漢 Ø
Used with, or Means: train routes, bus routes, see also 本 (*hon*)

1 route	一路線	いちろせん	*ichi-rosen*
2 routes	二路線	にろせん	*ni-rosen*
3 routes	三路線	さんろせん	*san-rosen*
4 routes	四路線	よんろせん	*yon-rosen*
5 routes	五路線	ごろせん	*go-rosen*
6 routes	六路線	ろくろせん	*roku-rosen*
7 routes	七路線	ななろせん	*nana-rosen*
8 routes	八路線	はちろせん	*hachi-rosen*
9 routes	九路線	きゅうろせん	*kyuu-rosen*
10 routes	十路線	じゅうろせん	*juu-rosen*

Irregularities or Special beyond Ten: none
Notes: none

わ — Wa
把 — わ — wa

Japanese: わ
Romanized: wa
Pattern: 漢 Wa
Used with, or Means: bundles, bunches, sheaves; postal letters, envelopes

1 bundle	一把	いちわ	ichi-wa
2 bundles	二把	にわ	ni-wa
3 bundles	三把	さんば さんぱ さんわ	sam-ba sam-pa sam-wa
4 bundles	四把	よんわ よんば	yom-wa yom-ba
5 bundles	五把	ごわ	go-wa
6 bundles	六把	ろっぱ ろくわ	rop-pa roku-wa
7 bundles	七把	ななわ しちわ	nana-wa shichi-wa
8 bundles	八把	はちわ はっぱ	hachi-wa hap-pa
9 bundles	九把	きゅうわ	kyuu-wa
10 bundles	十把	じゅっぱ じっぱ じゅうわ	jup-pa jip-pa juu-wa

Irregularities or Special beyond Ten:

100 bundles	百羽	ひゃくわ ひゃっぱ	hyaku-wa hyap-pa

Notes: none

羽 — わ — *wa*

Japanese: わ
Romanized: *wa*
Pattern: 漢 Wa
Used with, or Means: birds; rabbits, hares

1 bird	一羽	いちわ	*ichi-wa*
2 birds	二羽	にわ	*ni-wa*
3 birds	三羽	さんば or さんぱ さんわ	*sam-ba* or *sam-pa* *sam-wa*
4 birds	四羽	よんわ or よんば	*yom-wa* or *yom-ba*
5 birds	五羽	ごわ	*go-wa*
6 birds	六羽	ろっぱ or ろくわ	*rop-pa* or *roku-wa*
7 birds	七羽	ななわ or しちわ	*nana-wa* or *shichi-wa*
8 birds	八羽	はちわ or はっぱ	*hachi-wa* or *hap-pa*
9 birds	九羽	きゅうわ	*kyuu-wa*
10 birds	十羽	じゅうわ or じっぱ じゅっぱ	*juu-wa* or *jip-pa*, *jup-pa*

Irregularities or Special beyond Ten:

100 birds	百羽	ひゃくわ or ひゃっぱ	*hyaku-wa* or *hyap-pa*
1,000 birds	千羽	せんわ or せんば	*sem-wa* or *sem-ba*

Notes: Although this is a general counter for birds (羽 literally means *feather, plume,* or *wing*), there is an amusing story for why rabbits, too, get counted using this counter. Supposedly, because Buddhist monks cannot eat meat (but they can eat fish and birds), they started claiming that the rabbit ears were wings, so the monks could eat the rabbits without violating their prohibition against eating meat.

話—わ—*wa*

Japanese: わ
Romanized: *wa*
Pattern: 漢 Wa
Used with, or Means: tales, stories, legends, myths, fairytales, folktales, traditions

1 tale	一話	いちわ	*ichi-wa*
2 tales	二話	にわ	*ni-wa*
3 tales	三話	さんわ	*sam-wa*
4 tales	四話	よんわ	*yom-wa*
5 tales	五話	ごわ	*go-wa*
6 tales	六話	ろくわ	*roku-wa*
7 tales	七話	ななわ	*nana-wa*
8 tales	八話	はちわ	*hachi-wa*
9 tales	九話	きゅうわ	*kyuu-wa*
10 tales	十話	じゅうわ	*juu-wa*

Irregularities or Special beyond Ten: none
Notes: none

ワード—わあど—*waado*

Japanese: わあど
Romanized: *waado*
Pattern: 漢 ∅
Used with, or Means: words, see also 語 (*go*)

1 word	1 ワード	いちわあど	*ichi-waado*
2 words	2 ワード	にわあど	*ni-waado*
3 words	3 ワード	さんわあど	*sam-waado*
4 words	4 ワード	よんわあど	*yom-waado*
5 words	5 ワード	ごわあど	*go-waado*
6 words	6 ワード	ろくわあど	*roku-waado*
7 words	7 ワード	ななわあど	*nana-waado*
8 words	8 ワード	はちわあど	*hachi-waado*
9 words	9 ワード	きゅうわあど	*kyuu-waado*
10 words	10 ワード	じゅうわあど	*juu-waado*

Irregularities or Special beyond Ten: none
Notes: Words may also be counted using English numbers:
　　ワンワード (*wam-waado*),
　　ツーワード (*tsuu-waado*),
　　スリーワード (*surii-waado*), etc . . .

盃・沸 —わかし— *wakashi*

Japanese: わかし
Romanized: *wakashi*
Pattern: 和 I
Used with, or Means: the portion of raw material for shochu (焼酎 *shouchuu* distilled spirits, liquor), mash (醪 *moromi*)

1 portion	一盃・沸	ひとわかし	<u>*hito-wakashi*</u>
2 portions	二盃・沸	ふたわかし	<u>*futa-wakashi*</u>
3 portions	三盃・沸	さんわかし	*sam-wakashi*
4 portions	四盃・沸	よんわかし	*yom-wakashi*
5 portions	五盃・沸	ごわかし	*go-wakashi*
6 portions	六盃・沸	ろくわかし	*roku-wakashi*
7 portions	七盃・沸	ななわかし	*nana-wakashi*
8 portions	八盃・沸	はちわかし	*hachi-wakashi*
9 portions	九盃・沸	きゅうわかし	*kyuu-wakashi*
10 portions	十盃・沸	じゅうわかし	*juu-wakashi*

Irregularities or Special beyond Ten: none
Notes: none

枠 — わく — *waku*

Japanese: わく
Romanized: *waku*
Pattern: 和 I
Used with, or Means: frames, slides; the order of horses out the gate in a horse race

1 frame	一枠	ひとわく	*hito-waku*
2 frames	二枠	ふたわく	*futa-waku*
3 frames	三枠	さんわく	*sam-waku*
4 frames	四枠	よんわく	*yom-waku*
5 frames	五枠	ごわく	*go-waku*
6 frames	六枠	ろくわく	*roku-waku*
7 frames	七枠	ななわく	*nana-waku*
8 frames	八枠	はちわく	*hachi-waku*
9 frames	九枠	きゅうわく	*kyuu-waku*
10 frames	十枠	じゅうわく	*juu-waku*

Irregularities or Special beyond Ten: none
Notes: none

ワット・W —わっと— *watto*

Japanese: わっと
Romanized: *watto*
Pattern: 漢 ∅
Used with, or Means: Watts (symbol: W),

$$W = \frac{J}{s} = \frac{N \cdot m}{s} = \frac{kg \cdot m^2}{s^3} = V \cdot A = \frac{V^2}{\Omega} = A^2 \cdot \Omega$$

1 Watt	1 ワット・W	いちわっと	*ichi-watto*
2 Watts	2 ワット・W	にわっと	*ni-watto*
3 Watts	3 ワット・W	さんわっと	*sam-watto*
4 Watts	4 ワット・W	よんわっと	*yom-watto*
5 Watts	5 ワット・W	ごわっと	*go-watto*
6 Watts	6 ワット・W	ろくわっと	*roku-watto*
7 Watts	7 ワット・W	ななわっと	*nana-watto*
8 Watts	8 ワット・W	はちわっと	*hachi-watto*
9 Watts	9 ワット・W	きゅうわっと	*kyuu-watto*
10 Watts	10 ワット・W	じゅうわっと	*juu-watto*

Irregularities or Special beyond Ten: none
Notes: none

割 — わり — *wari*

Japanese: わり
Romanized: *wari*
Pattern: 漢 ∅
Used with, or Means: 1/10th of an equally divided whole, tenths

1 tenth	一割	いちわり	*ichi-wari*
2 tenths	二割	にわり	*ni-wari*
3 tenths	三割	さんわり	*sam-wari*
4 tenths	四割	よんわり	*yom-wari*
5 tenths	五割	ごわり	*go-wari*
6 tenths	六割	ろくわり	*roku-wari*
7 tenths	七割	ななわり	*nana-wari*
8 tenths	八割	はちわり	*hachi-wari*
9 tenths	九割	きゅうわり	*kyuu-wari*
10 tenths	十割	じゅうわり	*juu-wari*

Irregularities or Special beyond Ten: none

Notes: 割 is also a span of 10%. A 割引き (*waribiki*) is a discount of 10% off the original price of an item; therefore, 三割引き (*sam-waribiki*) is 30% off the price.

碗・椀——わん——*wan*

Japanese: わん
Romanized: *wan*
Pattern: 和 I
Used with, or Means: helpings of soup, helpings of broth, helpings of foods served in soup bowls (椀 *wan*), see also 杯 (*hai*)

1 serving of soup	一碗・椀	ひとわん	*hito-wan*
2 servings of soup	二碗・椀	ふたわん	*futa-wan*
3 servings of soup	三碗・椀	さんわん	*sam-wan*
4 servings of soup	四碗・椀	よんわん	*yom-wan*
5 servings of soup	五碗・椀	ごわん	*go-wan*
6 servings of soup	六碗・椀	ろくわん	*roku-wan*
7 servings of soup	七碗・椀	ななわん	*nana-wan*
8 servings of soup	八碗・椀	はちわん	*hachi-wan*
9 servings of soup	九碗・椀	きゅうわん	*kyuu-wan*
10 servings of soup	十碗・椀	じゅうわん	*juu-wan*

Irregularities or Special beyond Ten: none
Notes: none

Index of English Meanings

# (number sign)	221
% (*per cent* sign)	68, 568
¢ (cents sign)	410
£ (Pounds Sterling sign)	681
¥ (yen sign)	24
฿ (*Baht* sign)	569
° (degrees sign)	512, 537, 540
1 quindecillion	234
1 septillion	283, 338
1 trillion	467
1 undecillion	121
1/1,000th of an equally divided whole, later 1/10,000th	708
1/10th of an equally divided whole	773
1/10th of an equally divided whole, later 1/100th	630
10 duodecillion	379
10 octillion	352
10 quadrillion	187
10 sexdecillion	225
10 thousand	694
100 million	30
100 nonillion	220
100 quintillion	54
100 septendecillion	5
100 tredecillion	253
10^1 (ten)	325
10^{-10}	2
10^{12}	467
10^{16}	187
10^2 (hundred)	616
10^{20}	54
10^{24}	283, 338
10^{28}	352
10^3 (thousand)	395
10^{32}	220
10^{36}	121
10^{-4}	284
10^4 (ten thousand)	694
10^{40}	379
10^{44}	253
10^{48}	234
10^{-5}	284
10^{52}	225
10^{56}	5
10^{-6}	607
10^{-7}	403
10^{-8}	310
10^8 (hundred million)	30
10^{-9}	362
16-page, 32-page units in printing, bookbinding	435
24-hour clock	288
30-year periods	378
A (amperes sign)	9
a (ares sign)	1
a rest	635
A. D. (*anno Domini*)	382, 557
A. M. (*ante meridiem*)	288, 289
abilities	563
accounts	173
acres	21
act (law, an act of Congress)	419
actions	733
actions that are out-of-the-ordinary	170
acts of a play	567, 687
affairs	132, 196
afternoon	82
age (how old something or someone is)	538
agriculture	432
Air Force	128
aircraft	128
air-raids	565
alcohol	512, 537, 540
alcohol concentration	512, 537, 540
ammunition	446
amount of a liquid or powder	370
amount of water that one can scoop up in two hands	134
amperes	9
ampoules	523
amps	9
anchored fishnets	524
angle	512, 537, 540
angles	60
animals	525, 610, 611
announcements	675
answer to a poll question	619
apartments in an apartment building	520
April	90
areas	164
ares	1
armies	183, 433
armrests	140, 404
arrow lengths	640
arrowheads	371
arrows loosed	584
articles	76, 115, 345, 419
articles of a law	217
artistic works	509
arts	189
ashes	431, 581
ata (ancient measurement unit)	6
atoms	205
auditoriums	528
August	90
axes	468, 494
B (bytes sign)	574
B. C. (*before Christ*)	382, 557
B. C. E. (*before common era*)	382, 557
Babylonians	363
bag of cement	432
bag of wheat	432
bagfuls	432, 637
bags	432, 637
bags of rice, grain, cereal	618

bags of straw	102
Baht (monetary unit)	569
ballots	619
balls	446
balls of udon, soba	446
bamboo blinds	449
bamboo hats	55, 740
bamboo poles	114
bamboo stalks	114
banks	213
banners	544
bar	133
barrels	448, 590
barriers	387
baseball	427, 441
baseball bases	656, 750
baseball bat swings	645
baseball safe hits	680
baskets	70, 231, 464
bath basins	369
bathtubs	32, 369, 414
battles	399
bbl (barrels sign)	590
bean shells	270
beats	622
bedding	424
beds	341, 535
beiju	252
bells	212
bevies	184
bicycle speeds	421
bills	196, 267
binoculars	707
birds	281, 313, 731, 767
bites	173
bites of food	579
biwa	707
block of fish prepared for sashimi	258
blocks	164
bloopers	507
blunders	507
boat oars	443
boats	110, 321
bodhisattva	426
bolts	123
bonds	267
bonsai trees	583
book chapters	342
bookmarks	729
books	266, 632
books of a single work	113
bottles	627, 653, 680
boundaries	164
bouquets	702
bowlfuls	570
bowling lanes	758
bowls	174, 212, 583
bowls of rice	405, 596
bowls of soup	327
bows	469

bows (violin, archery)	589
bows at a shrine	755
boxes	578
boxfuls	578
boys	547
branches	23
breaths	420
brews of tea	400
British	357
bronze statues	160
brothers	547
brutish persons	610
bu (former monetary unit)	630
bu (former monetary unti)	630
bu (former unit of area)	631
bu (former unit of length)	630
bu (former unit of weight)	630
buckets	32, 43
Buddhas	160, 536
Buddhist household alters	17
Buddhist mortuary tablets	581
Buddhist staues	431
Buddhist temples	287
building stories	53, 412
buildings	198, 700
buildings with roofs	17
bullets	446, 455
bunches	444, 766
bunches of flowers	444
bunches of fruit, flowers	638
bundles	444, 766
bundles of bank notes	444
bundles of crab legs	83
bundles of grain sheaves	417
bundles of papers	167
burdens	43
bus routes	765
bus stops	22
buses	180
butsudan	17
c (cycles sign)	255
C. E. (*common era*)	382, 557
cable television	58
cake	96
cakes of tofu	464
cal (calories sign)	108
Cal (Calories, or kilocalories, sign)	108
Calorie (kilocalorie)	108
calories	108
camera lens power	512, 537, 540
candles	464, 468, 494
canned goods	111
cans	111
capacities	563
Cape Cod	215
capes	215
car gears	421
carats	107
carpenters' tools	464
carriage horses	443

776

cars	180, 308, 742
cartons	48
cartoon frames	241
cases	196
casks	448
castles	348
catered boxed lunches	33, 578
cauldrons	101
caves	527
caviar	587
cc (cubic centimeters sign)	294
CD (carats (gemstones) sign)	107
cellars	539
centigrams	408
centiliters	409
centimeters	407
cents	410
centuries	383
ceremonial dress	423
cg (centigrams sign)	408
chain links	168
chains	762
chairs	140
chaju	252
championship wins	112
chapters	45, 667
characters	286, 710
chemistry	137
chests	256
chests of drawers	256
children	285, 436
Chinese	201, 723
Chinese poems	282, 316, 326, 393, 667, 762
chords	202
chou (former unit of area)	465
chou (former unit of length)	464, 465
chunks of raw fish	243
churches	528
cigarettes	48, 371
circuits	322
circumference of a rotation, revolution, the	693
circumstances	132
circuts	58
cisterns	414
cities	274
city districts	157
cL (centiliters sign)	409
class	143, 176, 192, 522
class periods	204
classes	177, 241
clauses	229
clauses of a sentence	217
cleavers	19
cliques	526
cloth	20, 123, 136, 686
clothing pieces	608
cloves of garlic	66
clumps	184
clusters	184

cm (centimeters sign)	407
coats of paint	577
coins	724
collars	67
college	204
colors	13, 106, 250, 354
columns	759
combinations	533
commodities	509, 625
commodities sealed in plastic packs	585
companies	307, 404
compartments	164
competitions	293
competitive races	757
computer monitor screen size	84
computer viruses	610
concentration	512, 537, 540
condominiums	520
connection points in a series	639
consecutive defeats	442
consecutive events	512, 537, 540
containers	105
containersful	570
contests	353
continuous years	331
copies	266, 268
copper coins	530
corpses	431
corrections	498
correspondence	634
counting system	363, 365
counting-base	363, 365
countries	233
couples	475, 479
court	359
coverings draped, stretched over a frame	589
cows	497
CPUs	126
creases	371
credits	456, 509, 673
cries	230, 380
crowds	184, 702
cubic ○s	738
cubic centimeters	294
cup	97
cupboards	256
cupfuls	370, 570
cups	97
cups of rice	222
curtains	449, 469
cutlery	468, 494
cuts	96
cuttlefish	418, 570
cycles	255
cylinders	483
cylindrical objects	483
D (denier sign)	602
daa/dka (decares/dekares signs)	499
dag/dkg (decagrams/dekagrams signs)	500
daggers	604

daL/dkL (decaliters/dekaliters signs) 502
dam/dkm (decameters/dekameters signs) . 501
dams 126
dances 263
Danish 181
dashes of salt, spices, bonito flakes 490
daughters 337
days of the month 37
dead bodies 431
death anniversaries 56, 330, 545
decagon 95
decagrams/dekagrams 500
decaliters/dekaliters 502
decameters/dekameters 501
decares/dekares 499
December 90
decigrams 504
deciKelvins 491
deciliters 506
decimeters 505
deer 497
defeats 571
degrees 649
degrees (angle) 512, 537, 540
degrees (latitude) 512, 537, 540
degrees (longitude) 512, 537, 540
degrees (temperature) 512, 537, 540
degrees of separation in a familial relationship
 364
denier 602
departments 45
desks 140
destination 180
Deutsche Mark (former monetary unit) 692
dg (decigrams sign) 504
difference in a horse's size 582
digits 192
digon 95
dimensional 302
dimensions 201, 302
dining tables 440
diodes 384
dirt 729
discoveries 438
dishes 158
dishes of food 249
districts 460
divisions 45, 164
divisions into equal parts 531
dK (deciKelvins sign) 491
dL (deciliters sign) 506
dm (decimeters sign) 505
DM (*Deutsche Mark* sign) 692
documents 267, 299, 614
dogs 195
dokufuku 636
dollars 542
dollops of mortar 18
dolls 431
donations 173

doors 398
doses 254, 604, 635
doses of ointment 50, 572
doses of powdered medicine 485
dots 366, 509
downward swings, chops with a sword or
 bamboo practice sword 645, 647
dozen 182, 430
drawers 256
dress size 221
dresses 463
dressing table 126
drinking parties 385
drinks 173, 570
drops 487, 503
drops of liquid 303
drum solo 472
drums 707
dumplings 169
dust 729
duties 731
earth 488
earth-carrying baskets 130
editions 594
Edo period 85, 119, 120, 151, 197, 371, 417,
 481
egg-laying, a single instance of a bird's or
 reptile's 587
eight-hand mirror 6
ejaculations 584
election terms 402
electric lights 513
elevators 126
employees 14
enclosures 62
enemy helmets 586
engagements 222
engine cylinders 138
envelopes 766
errors 76
evenings 597, 717
events 333
events occurring in waves 565
expensive fabrics 488
experiences 512, 537, 540
explosions 584
eye drops 264
facemasks 707
faces 77
factions 526
failures 507, 571
fairytales 768
families 81
fathoms 361, 624
fathoms, Japanese 361, 624
February 90
feet 633
fencing matches 222
field glasses 707
fields 707

films	259, 443
finance	267
fingers	277
finishing position	463
firelight	636, 672
firewood	444
fireworks	381
fireworks explosions	584
fish	244, 313, 610, 749
fish tanks	414
fish-belly's worth of codfish roe	587
flags	256, 544, 739
flakes	665
flakes of *katsuobushi*	639
flares	381
flash lights	513
flights	626
flocks	184, 416, 703
floors	53
flower petals	100, 623, 665, 668
flower pots	653
flowers	23, 263, 748
fluctuation in percentage points	673
fold	20
folding fans	27, 475
folding screens	41, 346, 398
folds	328
folktales	768
font size	673
food and drink orders	684
food portions	554
food rations	131
food served on spits	169
food trays	404
footsteps	669
forests	247
forks	464
forms	533
fountains	397
fraction denominators	650
fragments	665
framed pictures	41
frames	41, 388, 771
francs (former monetary unit)	644
freight train cars	308
French	644
fruits	44, 46, 70, 207
ft (feet sign)	633
fuda	267
Fumizuki	91
fur (furlongs sign)	591
furlongs	591
furniture	299
g (grams sign)	178
gal (gallons sign)	109
galleys	435
gallons	109
games	49, 191, 353
games of mahjongg	11
garments	20
gates	387
gatherings of people	433
gemstones	107
gen (monetary unit)	201
general articles	207
generations	378, 390, 439
girls	337
glassfuls	570
glyphs	286
Go board intersections	709
Go boards	707
Go stones	275
goals	231
god-bodies	581
godowns	539
gods	160, 247, 536, 581
gogo	See P. M.
goods	207
gou (former unit of area)	222
gou (former unit of volume)	222
gozen	See A. M.
grade	143, 522
grade levels	94
grains	487, 741
grams	178
gravestones	126
graveyards	488
great men	581
gross	182
ground pools	707
group	566
groups	179, 184, 416, 703
groups (social)	702
groups of people	174, 433
groves	702
groves of flowers	702
guitar solo	472
guitars	468, 494, 680
gun caliber	598
guns	105, 329
ha (hectares sign)	657
haiku	159
hairs on one's head	708
hakama	235, 261, 725, 730
hakuju	252
halberds	19, 276, 645
half a fish	258
halls	528
hand	548
handfuls	4, 134
handled objects	464
hanging pictures, scrolls	636
hanging scrolls	495
hanko	46
hares	767
harvests in a year	708
hats	52, 207
Hazuki	91
head count	367
headgear worn by nobles in court dress	77

heads of lettuce	446	inches	16, 84
health resorts	521, 722	individual grains of millet	422
hearings	359	industries	432
heaters	513	injections	523
heavy machinery	128	inkstones	707
hectare	1	innings	12, 49
hectares	473, 657	inns	118
Hectogon	95	insects	610
hectograms	658	instruments with flat surfaces	707
hectoliters	660	intelligence reports	675
hectometers	659	islands	517
height of a horse	122	issue	221
helmets	77	items	3, 6, 42, 76, 207, 229, 509, 625, 709
helpings	271	items of business	333, 628
helpings of foods served in soup bowls	774	items wound on a frame	78
heptagon	95	*izayoi*	717
herds	184, 416	January	90
hertz	255	Japanese books	515
Hertz	664	Japanese books wrapped in a shroud	515
hexagon	60, 95	Japanese swords	200
hg (hectograms sign)	658	jars, jugs	103, 210, 489, 587, 653
high-class people	581	jewels	46, 447
highway lanes	758	*jin* (Japanese fathoms)	361
hiki (former monetary unit)	611	*Jizou* statues	426
hiro (Japanese fathoms)	624	*jou* (former unit of area)	349
hits	427	*jou* (former unit of length)	344
hL (hectoliters sign)	660	judgements	359
hm (hectometers sign)	659	judgments received	592
ho (former unit of area)	670	jugs	103, 587, 653
holes	193	July	90
hollowed-out gourds	620	June	90
honored persons	536	junior	439
hooves	497	Kabuki	689
horse lengths in horse racing	582	*kaiken*	604
horse saddles	376	*Kaminazuki*	91
horseloads	429	*kamme* (former monetary unit)	120
horsemen	129	*kamme* (former unit of weight)	120
horses	129, 497	*kan* (former monetary unit)	119
horseshoes	140	*kan* (former unit of weight)	119
hospitals	15	*kana*	61, 286
hot springs	521, 722	*kanji*	61, 286
hours of the day	288	*Kannazuki*	91
households	206, 389	*kanreki*	252
households on a block	520	karat	107, 156
houses	198, 206, 700	*katana*	158, 200, 516
hues	250	*katsu*	89
hulls	270	kegs	448
human beings	549	*kei* (former unit of volume)	188
hundred	616	*ken* (former unit of length)	197
hunting hawks	711, 762	kettles	101, 158, 212
hyakume (former unit of weight)	617	keys	199
ikebana	475	kg (kilograms sign)	152
Ikebana	263	*ki* (former unit of height)	122
image pixels	80	*kiju*	252
images of gods	581	kilograms	152
images of the Buddha in a temple	426	kiloliters	154, 737
imperial regalia	6	kilometers	153
in (inches sign)	16	*kimono obi*	371
incense containers	222, 223	*kin* (former unit of weigh)	155
incense sticks	315	kindergartens	25, 175

kinds	13, 319, 334, 751
kinds of newspaper	278
Kinusaragi	91
Kisaragi	91
kitchen knives	19
kL (kiloliters sign)	154
km (kilometers sign)	153
kn (knots sign)	564
knit, stacked objects	762
knots	564, 629
koki	252
koku	232
koma	388
kopek (monetary unit)	239
koto	707
koto (Chinese, seven-stringed zither)	589
kouju	252
krones (monetary unit)	181
Ksitigarbha	426
kt (karat (gold purity) sign)	107, 156
kyuubi	606
L (liters sign)	737
lakes	26, 209
lamps	513
land registrations	614
landscapes	186
land-surveying unit	141
languages	72, 211
laps	322
large animals	525
large birds	525
large ships	313, 386
large-screen televisions	707
lateness of the night	214
latitude	512, 537, 540
laundary wash basins	414
layered, sticky rice-cakes	374
layers	328, 412
layers of clothing	74
lb (pounds sign)	682
leather	488
leaves	623, 729
lectures	219
legends	768
legged furniture	140
length of a bow	141
length of cloth	312, 375, 450, 452
lengths of cloth	611
lens refraction	512, 537, 540
lessons	45
letter	61
letter size	143
letters	246, 267, 286, 634, 680, 710
level	57, 457
levels	412
libraries	118
lidded utensils	222
lid-shaped objects	55
light bulbs	513
lights	513

light-wave communications	58
lightyears	228
lily bulbs	66
limestone caves	527
lines	759
linked objects	762
Lira (monetary unit)	746
literary language	15, 26, 27, 51, 118, 142, 146, 171, 186, 195, 209, 215, 329, 347, 387, 397, 517, 518, 519, 527, 528, 529, 595, 620, 641, 668, 671, 708, 731
literary works	509
loads	43
loaves of bread	155
locations	580
long and narrow objects	185
long, cylindrical objects	680
long, oblong chests for clothing	428
long, slender weapons	105
long, thin objects with an ill-defined shape	371
longitude	512, 537, 540
loops of 100 銭 (*sen*) strung together equal to one 文 (*mon*)	371
lot number	601
Louis XIV	439
luggage	207, 242
lumped objects	88
lux (unit of of illuminance)	753
lx (lux sign)	753
m (meters sign)	706
machines	126, 435
magazines	266, 632
magic circles (stars used by occultists or in fantasy for summoning or other rituals)	360
mahjong tables	440
man-hours	551, 552
man-months	553
mannequins	431
manners	533, 677
manuscript drafts	216, 218
maps	671
March	90
marks	366, 509, 673
marks obtained	673
marks on a map	509
married couples	475
martial arts	454
mash	770
masks	77
masu (former unit of volume)	690
matches	49, 293, 353, 399
mats	684
matters	132, 196
mausoleums	17
May	90
mbar/mb (millibars sign)	697
meal courses	305, 625
meals	355, 405, 596
meals per day	85

781

means	533, 677
measure of the concentration of a solution	137
measures	196, 455
mechanical devices	435
medicine	254, 604
medicine doses	712
melodies	639
members	14
metal planks	488
meters	706
methods	533, 677
mg (milligrams sign)	696
mi (miles sign)	685
miles	685
military forces	360, 433
military units	207, 433
milk	48
millibars	697
milligrams	696
milliliters	699
millimeters	698
Minazuki	91
minutes	180, 649
mirrors	707
mistakes	507
mL (milliliters sign)	699
mm	698
mobs	702
mochi	74, 207
mon (former monetary unit)	713
monarchical reigns	378
monetary unit	119, 120, 181, 201, 239, 317, 357, 401, 569, 611, 630, 644, 661, 681, 692, 708, 713, 716, 723, 742, 746, 747, 752, 754
money	724
monme (former monetary unit)	716
monme (former unit of weight)	716
month	323
months	194, 480
months of the year	90
morae	575
morning	82
mosquito nets	449, 469, 589
mou (former monetary unit)	708
mou (former unit of length)	708
mou (former unit of weight)	708
mountain ridges	743, 756
mountains	721
mountains of fruit	721
mounted	*See* horsemen
mouthfuls	173
mouthfuls of food	579
movements	733
movie scenes	241
movies	680
M-person group	550
multiples of N	573
multitudes	702
museums	118
musical beats	575
musical parts	472
musical passages	64
musical piece or tune	598
musical step	512, 537, 540
Mutsuki	91
myths	768
N (Normality sign)	137
N o'clock	288
N times as much/many	573
N years old	251
N's place	176
Nagatsuki	91
naginata	645
N-agon	95
name stamps	46
natural springs	397
nautical miles	59, 564
naval fleets	406
needles	358
net meshes	588
nets	469
newspaper pages	707
newspaper subscriptions	278
newspapers	632
N-fold	573
night	82
night's stay	332
night's stays	576
nights	597, 717, 727
night-shifts	214
NM (nautical miles sign)	59
no (unit of area for cloth)	562
No. (number)	221
nodes	639
Noh	263
Noh masks	707
nonagon	95
noon	82
Norwegian	181
notes	267
notices	675
novels	651
November	90
N-sided figure	95
N-some odd...	728
N^{th} act	688, 689
N^{th} block	466
N^{th} day	39
N^{th} generation	434
N^{th} grade	457
N^{th} hour	301
N^{th} in line	599
N^{th} period	301
N^{th} place	599
Nty years old	252
number	221
number of appliances, fixtures that a house has	369
number of arrow feathers obtained from a single bird's tail	356

number of arrows.. 313
number of available shots in a roll of film . 541
number of bags, suitcases one person is
  carrying... 451
number of brush strokes, pen-strokes without
  taking one's pen, brush off the page,
  canvas... 642
number of burning incense sticks 315
number of climbs... 63
number of days...................................... 40, 605
number of foldings 33
number of hours 290
number of hours someone works 551, 552
number of items 673
number of knobs in a stalk of bamboo 639
number of living subjects of a scientific study
  236
number of months 92
number of months someone works 553
number of people involved in an activity... 309
number of roles an actor or actress plays in a
  movie or play 719
number of runners, batters in a baseball
  inning... 309
number of *sake* bottles................................. 262
number of seconds 621
number of shots, shells, bullets, cannon balls
  514
number of soldiers guarding a castle 602
number of steps on a staircase 454
number of strokes 61, 614
number of suitcase bags hanging on one's
  shoulder... 69
number of things piled up........................... 454
number of times... 49, 291, 297, 413, 445, 512,
  532, 537, 540, 666
number of times around a course 693
number of times one casts one's fishing line
  into the water... 514
number of times one jumps with both feet 418
number of times one kicks the ball in the
  game kickball 418
number of times one may use a telephone
  card 537, 540
number of times one soaks fabrics in dyes to
  dye them... 297
number of times one strikes, stabs, or jabs
  one's opponent with a spear, lance, or
  javelin.. 413
number of times paper is passed through a
  printing press.. 532
number of trips one makes carrying loads, the
  86
number of weeks... 324
number of years... 98
numbers 192, 347
numerals... 710
numerical order 291, 437, 598
N-year-long period....................................... 561
oars 468, 494

obire o tsukeru... 606
objects attached to the waist....................... 235
objects grasped in the hand 548
oceans... 51
octagon.. 95
octaves.. 31
October... 90
octopi.. 570
offering tables.. 8
ohms 29
oil, petroleum.. 590
once 49
one's seat... 385
one's job.. 731
one's tidyings 87
onsen 521, 722
opera glasses 707
order..457, 522
order in which things occur 437, 598, 602
order of horses out the gate in a horse race,
  the.. 771
order of stops to a destination.................... 360
order of weeks 323
ordering.. 143
ordinal days... 104
orgasms 584
ounces 35
oz (ounces sign)... 35
P. M. (*post meridiem*) 288, 289
packets of powdered medicine 470
packets of powdered medicine, tea 674
paddy fields.. 707
page number, pages 655
pages.. 729
pagoda 519
pails.. 32
pair of skis... 435
paired things 475
pairs of animals 479
pairs of chopsticks 405, 424
pairs of clothing items 742
pairs of rabbits.. 292
pairs of shoes.. 418
pairs of things 411
pairs of things that form a left-right set...... 418
palanquins 162, 468, 494
panels... 241
paper bundles 306
paper lanterns 589
paper reams 306
paper-covered sliding doors........................ 346
papers 267, 486, 614, 675
parades 565
paragraphs 459, 652
paragraphs of a document........................... 391
parks 25
part... 731
particular parts, sections, places 673
parties 385
parts 650, 719

parts of a book	667
parts *per* million	609
patrols	335
pats of butter	66
patterns	533
pencils	680
pentagon	95
people	82, 549, 705
people's heads	367
per cent	568
performances	372, 687
personal experiences	512, 537, 540
persons	367, 549
peseta (former monetary unit)	661
Peso	662
photographs	488
photosetting	143
phrases	652
physics	36
piano keys	199
pieces	148, 151, 316, 608
pieces of information	675
pieces of *kasane-mochi*	374
pieces of lumber	678
pieces of *nigiri-zushi*	119
pills	351, 487, 674
pinches	490
pinches, dashes of salt, spices, bonito flakes	490
pistols	464
place	10
place at the table	385
placed things	126
placement in a race	522
places	42, 75, 201, 536, 580
planes	128, 684
plants	99, 318, 711
plates	174, 212, 271
play	688, 689
play blocks	648
player's overall wins	112
pleated pants	235
plies	328
plot number	601
ply, fold	20
pods	270
points	143, 509, 673
points earned	509
points made	673
points on a map	462
points won	231, 509
poles	256
polite	63, 250, 315, 321, 538, 563, 614, 636, 672, 705, 711, 729, 749
political factions	566
political parties	526
political party	566
polynomial classes	217
portion of raw material for shochu mash, the	770

portions	650
position	684, 731
post	731
post stations	481
postal letters	766
postcards	729
pots	101, 158, 212, 489, 546, 587
potted plants	583
pounds (weight)	682
powers	347
ppm	609
prayer beads	162, 555
precedence	522
printing corrections	216
printing plates	488
printings	373
prints	268
prior offenses	592
private homes	198
problems	438
professional sports	183
professional/technical jargon	128, 236, 280, 381, 417, 432, 450, 524, 525
proofs	216
provisions	217, 419
provisions of a law	137
provisions, articles, sections of a constitution, act, treaty, etc	419
public works	488
publications	614, 632
puffs of a cigarette	635
punctuated, cut off, or divided things	164
puzzle solutions	533
Q (typesetting letter size sign)	143
questions	438, 715
queues	759
quilts	745
quires of paper	346
quiver	235
rabbits	767
race	463
rafts	535
railway cars	742, 744
rain drops	303
rain events	646
rainfall	7
raised hands in a show-of-hands vote	619
Rakugo performances	438
Rakugo shows	385
rank	454, 522, 598
rank awarded in the martial arts, *Go*, or *Shougi*	454
ranking	10, 684
ranks	759
rate or percentage of a transaction price	68
rattan blinds	449
raw silk	242
rays of light	371, 529
razors	158
reactors	126

real estate	196
reams of paper	417, 762
receptacles	222
reels of a film	113
remains	431
remains of the deceased	581
reports	675
research project	236
restaurants	198
revisions	373, 498
revolutions of revolving objects or rotating objects	693
ri (former unit of length)	736
rice fields	614
rickshaws	468, 494
rin (former monetary unit)	747
rin (former unit of length)	747
rin (former unit of weight)	747
ripples	565
rivers	47, 79, 345, 371, 396, 544, 680
road lanes	758
roads	371, 680
robots	610
role	731
roles	719
rolling stock cars	744
rolls of cloth	764
rolls of fabric	701
rolls of paper	764
rolls of silk	686
rooms	304, 663, 683
roomsize	349
rosaries	762
rosary beads	555
round objects	446
round trips	28
rounds	322, 335, 735
rounds or points of a competition (karate)	680
route	731
row-boats	415
rowboats used in rowing competitions	496
rows	759
rubles (monetary unit)	752
runs	231, 509, 673
Rupees (monetary unit)	754
Russian	239
ryou (former monetary unit)	742
ryou (former unit of weight)	742
S. I. (*Système Internationale d'Unités*)	1, 9, 29, 152, 153, 154, 178, 255, 294, 407, 408, 409, 458, 473, 491, 499, 500, 501, 502, 504, 505, 506, 543, 602, 657, 658, 659, 660, 664, 696, 697, 698, 699, 706, 737, 753
sackfuls	618
sacred books	686
saddles	376
sai (former unit of volume)	248
saints	82
sake cups in sets of three	174
sake decanters	262

sake glasses	272
sake offerings	245
sampuku-tsui	636
Samurai topknots	417
Sanaetsuki	91
sanctuaries	528
sand	4, 488
sanju	252
sashimi	271
satsu (former unit of volume)	269
Satsuki	91
saucepans	546
saws	464
scenery	186
scenes	186, 567
scenes in a ballad, drama	639
scenic spots	63
school	65, 94, 127, 177
school years	65
schools	184, 216, 739
schools of thought	566
scissors	464
scoops	370
score	673
scores	231, 509
screens	126, 469
scriptures	686
scrolls	300, 452, 686
se (former unit of area)	377
sea voyages	224
sealed documents	634
seals	46
seams	588
seas	51
seasons	124
seasons of a serialized television show	163
seat number in a classroom	385
seated statues	247
seats	296, 385
second of the minute	621
sect	566
Section (Air Force)	128
section of a sequence	168
sections	45, 64, 157, 164, 345, 460
sections between two points	165
sections of a constitution	419
sections of a dictionary	632
sections of a novel, musical score	391
sections of a play	186, 687
sectors	460
sembazuru	444
semesters	93
sen (monetary unit)	401
senior	439
senju	252
senryuu	159
sentences	651
September	90
series	484
series, parts of a	484

785

servings	464
servings of broth	774
servings of food and drink	732
servings of soup	774
sets	174
sets of articles	162
sets of books	632
sets of clothing	172, 394, 684
sets of gathered supplies	734
sets of Japanese clothing	73, 745
sets of things	299, 424
sex acts	584
shadows, forms moving in firelight	636, 672
shakes of salt	298
shaku	257
shaku (former unit of area)	311
shaku (former unit of length)	312
shaku (former unit of volume)	311
shamisen	256
shards	66
shares	99, 173
sharp, pointed mountains	676
sheaves	766
sheet steel, steel wire, or cellophane thickness	598
sheets	296
sheets bound Japanese-style	464
sheets of paper	623, 684, 729
shillings (former monetary unit)	357
Shimotsuki	91
Shinto	8
Shinto shrines	17, 247, 307, 720
ships	570
Shiwasu	91
shoe size	630
shops	198, 510
shorts	241
shots	455
shots fired	584
shou (former unit of volume)	340, 343
Shougi boards	707
shouts	230, 380
shower, a	7
shows	241, 372, 687
shrimp	606
shrines	404
shrubs	99
shu (former monetary unit)	317
sides of a folding screen	313
sign curtain hung over restaurant doors	449
sips of tea	635
sisters	337
sites	462
size	136
skewers	169
slender objects	276
slices	684
slices of bread	66
slices of fish	639
slides	771

sliding ponds	435
slips	507
small artifacts	207
small boats	415, 729
small boxes of food	33
small dining tables	405
small fish	606
small round things	46
small shrines	404
smallest unit of the Air Force	128
smoke	371
snowflakes	623
socks	418
soda can	111
solos	472
some . . . more than N	728
songs	639
sons	547
sorts	319, 334
sotsuju	252
soufuku	636
sounds	34
Sounds Sterling	681
space heaters	513
Spanish	661
spas	521, 722
spears	105
speculative-built houses on a block	520
spindles	368
spinning tools	368
spires	676
spirits of the dead	10
spirits of the war dead	581
splendid mansions	493
spoonfuls	265, 370, 570
spoons	265
sporting events	293
sports events	319
sports matches	399
sports seasons	295
sports wins	339
spots	366, 509
spots, animal	595
springs	397
squads	433
square	60, 95
square ○s	654
squid	570
stacks of Japanese books	515
stages	359, 455
stamps	665
standard	10
standard paper sizes	593
standards	544
stanzas	761
stars	184
station	731
stations	149, 165
statues	160
statues of Buddha	426

statues of gods	581
statues of Shinto gods	431
statues of the Buddha	641
steals in baseball	518
steeples	519
steps	454, 455, 669
sticks of ink	468, 494
stitches	588, 629
stockings	418
stocks	99
stone buddhist images	426
stone monuments	126
store houses	539
stores	510
stories	768
storms	360
stormy weather patterns	360
story arcs	667
strands of hair	638
straw mats	346, 623
streamers	544
streams	47, 79, 544
street lights	513
strikes in decisive games	584
string	368
string of characters	544
stringed instruments	469, 589
strings	67, 202, 638
strings (guitar)	589
strings of paper cranes	444
strings of pearls	762
strip-like, slender objects	345
stumbles	507
styles	533
subjects	438
subsections	115
successive matches in *Go*, *Shougi*, or *Sumo*	598
suits	174, 463
suits of armor	162, 745
summits	676
sun (former unit of length)	375
surgical stitches	588
surplice, stole	423
surplices	745
swarms	184
swords	105, 158, 200, 212, 235, 645
syllables in a word	575
syllables in Japanese words	622
symbol	1, 9, 16, 29, 35, 59, 68, 97, 107, 108, 109, 133, 137, 143, 152, 153, 154, 178, 255, 294, 407, 408, 409, 410, 458, 473, 491, 499, 500, 501, 502, 504, 505, 506, 512, 537, 540, 543, 564, 568, 569, 574, 590, 591, 602, 609, 633, 657, 658, 659, 660, 664, 679, 682, 685, 692, 696, 697, 698, 699, 706, 718, 737, 753, 772
symbols	710
systems	190
t (tonnes sign)	543
tabi (socks)	418
tables	140, 404, 440
tablets	351, 674
talents	189, 563
tales	768
tall mountains	247
tall peaks	743, 756
tan (former unit of area)	450
tanka poems	316
tasks	438
tatami	346, 349
tattoos	488
tax levied on Edo merchants	240
tea (canned)	111
tea utensils	424
teacups	212
tear streaks	371
technical skills	563
techniques	533, 677
teeth	280
telegraph	58
telephone	58
telephone calls	680
telescope lens power	512, 537, 540
television	84
temperature	512, 537, 540
temple buildings	17
temples	273, 528
ten-day periods	336
tennis courts	707
tennis racket swings	645
tens	325
tenths	773
tents	589
terms	93, 127
tex (tex sign)	602
Thai	569
the century	382
the grounds within the surrounding walls	62
theaters	118
themes	438
theories	392
thickets	702
thin, flat objects	684
things	474
things broken in half	136
thousands	395
thread	242, 368
thread count	602
thread, wire, or needle thickness	598
threads	208
threads wound on skeins	78
three piece suit	424
three-piece set	636
three-piece suit	636
thrice	49
throngs	702
Tibetan Buddhist monasteries	17
tickets	665
tidal waves	565
tiered boxes	74, 174, 328

ties (railroad) 680
tints 250
tiny particles 487, 741
titles 438
to (former unit of volume) 511
ton (tons sign) 543
tonnes (metric) 543
tons (imperial) 543
torii 126
tournaments 112
towers 519
town blocks 464, 465
toy blocks 648
track number 600
traditions 768
traffic lanes 314
train car numbers 226
train or bus routes 680
train routes 765
train stations 22
train tracks 680
trains 760
transistors 384
transports 626
travel-time 180
treaty 419
trees 99, 318, 320, 428
triad 636
triangle 60, 95
trips 626
troops 360
trousers 463
tsubo (former unit of area) 488
tsuifuku 636
tsuijiku 636
tsunami 565
tubs 43
tunes 639
turn at bat 441
twelve-year periods 125
twice 49
two hour periods in ancient times 534
types 751
types of equipment 135
typesetting 143
umbrellas 55, 589
uniform sets of clothing and supplies 732
unit of area 1, 21, 222, 311, 349, 377, 450, 465, 488, 499, 631, 657, 670
unit of area for cloth 562
unit of arrow length 417, 478
unit of capacity 523
unit of caught fish 417
unit of commodities being sold 585
unit of currency 662
unit of farm area 136
unit of footware size 713
unit of height 122
unit of illuminance and luminous emittance
        753

unit of length 6, 16, 141, 153, 197, 312, 344, 361, 375, 464, 465, 501, 505, 564, 591, 624, 630, 633, 659, 685, 698, 706, 708, 718, 736, 747
unit of mass 152, 500, 504, 543, 658, 696
unit of purity 107, 156
unit of silk packaging 89
unit of spinning mill, spinning wheel
        production output 368
unit of volume 83, 97, 109, 151, 154, 188, 222, 232, 248, 269, 311, 340, 343, 422, 432, 488, 502, 506, 511, 590, 660, 690, 699, 737
unit of weight 35, 107, 119, 120, 155, 451, 543, 613, 617, 630, 682, 704, 708, 716, 742, 747
unit of weight of rice 478
unit of width 602
units 173, 456, 726
units of paulownia wood 446
units of time 42
university 204
urns 103, 587, 653
utensils, teacup, and saucer set for receiving
        guests 139
Uzuki 91
V (Volts sign) 679
valence 36
varieties 319
varieties of food 625
vases 103, 587, 627
vats 103, 587, 653
vegetation 711
vegitables 444
vehicles 347, 435, 744
verses 761
verses of a poem, scripture 632
vials 653
villages 425
violins 468, 494
voices 230, 380
volumes 113, 266
volumes of Japanese books 346
votes in an election 619
W (Watts sign) 772
waka poems 316
wards 157
warehouses 539
wars 399
warships 117, 313, 386
watch jewels 384
watch size 84
watches of the night 214
water flows 544
water hardness 512, 537, 540
water tanks 414
waves 565, 763
ways 533, 677
ways of doing something 677
weeks 545
wheels 748
wind instruments 116

windings	686
windows	398
winning teams	183
wood	83
words	203, 211, 238, 246, 769
work hours	227
works	259, 260
works of art	259, 260
works of literature	259, 260
worship halls	528
wrapped cash, gifts, offereings	634
wreaths	126
wrinkles	371
writing brushes	166, 185
written reports	675
yachts	496
yards	718
yarn	368
yarn count	602
yarn, thread width	602
yata no kagami	6
Yayoi	91
yd (yards sign)	718
year numbers	201
year, the	557
years	538, 559
years after an event	331
years in a row	331
years of exam preparation	763
yen (monetary unit)	24
younger siblings	436
yuan (monetary unit)	723
zoku (former unit of volume)	422
Ω (ohms sign)	29

Bibliography

http://hiramatu-hifuka.com/onyak/onyak2/josuindx.html - many of the counters come from this site. I translated and put into my own words their deifintions

http://www.shurey.com/countdic/index.html

http://www.trussel.com/jcountc.htm - many of the units come from here

http://www.postmeta.com/ - JquickTrans, a freeware software dictionary (though I recommend that you purchase it as I did)

http://cweb.canon.jp/wordtank/lineup/wordtank/english/g55/index.html - my trusty Canon wordtank G55, a Japanese↔English electronic dictionary

http://www.google.com - for their built in measurement converter, which gave me all those nice, long decimal conversions.

Printed in Great Britain
by Amazon